MW01483927

CHOOSE YOU THIS DAY WHOM YOU WILL SERVE

Choose You This Day Whom You Will Serve

A Daily Bible Study to Empower Our Spiritual Battle

Sonja H. Winburn

Edited by Stephen Cooke.
Cover design by Barry Wallace.

Printed in the United States of America.

ISBN: 978-1-947929-35-7

PREFACE

This collection was initially written as social media posts over the past several years to help crystalize, in my mind, a way to think about this "life under the sun." As the Preacher writes in Ecclesiastes, nothing is new, but we must determine how to live our lives on earth in our present day and age. So many influences are at play in the world that confound people and tempt them to serve themselves rather than the living God. Each day we must focus on God and our response to Him and His Word, overcoming the negative influences in the world. Our goal is to consider God's role in our salvation and our personal decision to choose His defined path to justification.

We must understand that all spiritual wisdom, wherever we encounter it, comes from God, not men. It is otherworldly. Each of these devotionals references either a well-known person or, in some cases, comes from an unlikely or unknown source. Each quotation is paired with a single verse or multiple scriptures and/or biblical context that makes the same practical point from God's Word, showing where any true enlightenment comes from. My use of these quotes is not meant to elevate people or express whole-hearted agreement with everything they say or think. Instead, sentiments that agree with scripture are being raised for consideration.

This collection assumes that the Bible is the inspired Word of God and that it is His method of teaching people how to attain the peace His Son provides. It also assumes God created mankind, and we live in a fallen world. We are all on a lifelong journey to find peace with a loving God, with whom we will live in a place prepared for His children in heaven when this life is over. We all falter in our attempts at perfect obedience, so God Himself provided the only acceptable sacrifice to move His obedient children to a justified state. Thus, we are justified by grace. No other method can do this for a person except what God has provided through the death of His Son.

At the same time, God's intent from the beginning has been that anyone, at any time, can be justified by faith and have a personal desire to be obedient to him. We all have free will, and because we can control our choices, anyone can choose to have peace with God, even under the worst circumstances. We all choose to obey or not obey with each decision we make. All rationally thinking people make spiritual choices all day, every day, no matter their circumstances, and thereby choose whether to live a God-directed and spiritually peaceful life.

The world, in these devotionals, represents all things that oppose God. Scripture defines the things of the world as the lust of the flesh, the lust of the eyes, and the pride of life. Those of the world are prideful and seek their good over that of others. These people are self-serving rather than God-serving. The same evil one who tempted Adam and Eve in the garden still influences the fallen world today. God expelled Adam and Eve from the garden because He, as a Holy God, could no longer walk among them due to their sin. And sin still separates men and women from God today.

But those who follow God's Word through obedient faith actively participate with Him as His children and restore the relationship lost in the garden. Everyone is acting like either a child of Satan or a child of God. Everyone is either a slave to Satan or a bondservant to Christ. And we must choose service to God along with all that it entails! But when we do, it is God and every believer against the world.

We can find the proper use of all created things in God's inspired Word. Suffering is not always a bad thing. Neither is discipline. Our work is to learn to see things the way God sees them and to recognize the meaning of things, both seen and unseen, as His Word reveals. But learning, seeing, and hearing the will of God requires a willing heart and mind set on knowing God's truth before we can find it. Each of us must die with Christ through baptism to take advantage of the righteousness God provides. Just as Noah entered the ark by God's command to be saved through water, we must allow God to save us through water by baptism. We all choose whether to enter the metaphorical ark, just like those in the days of Noah—one of many powerful illustrations in the Bible.

Each of these devotionals is intended to stand alone and can be used for daily meditation, five days a week for fifty-two weeks. It may be helpful to write down your own thoughts or experiences that illustrate each point. You are always welcome to compare the thoughts contained here against

Scripture. God is the teacher. His Word alone is inspired. These devotionals are simply my attempt, despite my many flaws, to share the seeds of truth found in His Word. I sincerely pray that they will help you understand Scripture more fully, as they have helped me while I have pondered these concepts over the years.

There are so many people I could specifically thank for helping this book come to fruition, so this is not an exhausted list of contributors. First, I acknowledge God Almighty for this effort and all the blessings He provides, without His wisdom there would be nothing worthy of writing. I also want to mention a few individuals that gave me direct assistance in the writing of this book, along with some of my mentors and encouragers.

Martin Broadwell helped me understand the importance of retaining all my writings in an organized way. Mike Thomley gave me the final push to decide to make these articles into a book. Stephen Cooke edited each article so they could become a daily devotional. Without his help the book would not have ever been published. Ken Craig and Kenneth Chumbley were invaluable resources for advice and the final touches needed to make the book ready for publication. I also want to thank Nathan Ward and DeWard Publishing for their decision to publish *Choose You This Day*. I am beyond appreciative for all these people and their help.

My husband Jefty is always my main encourager along with my children, Janelle and Shane. But I also want to mention Pat DeLong, Patti McClelland, Jeni Roberts, Janna Shannon, and Dana Short, all of whom made me feel capable enough to accomplish this task.

Lastly, I want to dedicate the book to all my grandchildren. My desire for them to make the choice to serve the Lord drove me to write all the articles in the first place. Hopefully I will be able to say in the last day "as for me and my house we chose to serve the LORD."

Sonja Winburn
Summer, 2024

WEEK ONE

DAY 1

Acknowledgments

In friendship ... we think we have chosen our peers. In reality a few years' difference in the dates of our births, a few more miles between certain houses, the choice of one university instead of another ... the accident of a topic being raised or not raised at a first meeting—any of these chances might have kept us apart. But, for a Christian, there are, strictly speaking no chances. A secret master of ceremonies has been at work. Christ, who said to the disciples, "Ye have not chosen me, but I have chosen you," can truly say to every group of Christian friends. "Ye have not chosen one another but I have chosen you for one another." The friendship is not a reward for our discriminating and good taste in finding one another out. It is the instrument by which God reveals to each of us the beauties of others. (C. S. Lewis)

Two are better than one, because they have a good reward for their toil. For if they fall, one will lift up his fellow. But woe to him who is alone when he falls and has not another to lift him up! Again, if two lie together, they keep warm, but how can one keep warm alone? And though a man might prevail against one who is alone, two will withstand him—a threefold cord is not quickly broken. (Ecc 4.9–12)

The family and friends I have had throughout my life are all priceless. Each has contributed to my grand journey, and I pray I have contributed to theirs. This great blessing of beautiful people from God has filled my life's travels with wonder and excitement.

In all the places I have lived or worked or worshiped, I have been blessed to associate with people who have been edifying to me in some way or another. Every day I am thankful to everyone throughout my life who has taught me, lifted me up, and corrected me when I was out of line. And my family truly leaves me speechless as to how to express my appreciation. You are all there in times of great joy and in times of great need.

To all of you, near and far, may the Lord bless you and keep you! I dedicate this effort to you because, in some way or another, you have all had a part in my learning!

DAY 2

View of Self Compared to God

Always believe in God because there are some questions even Google can't answer. (Author Unknown)

For by him all things were created, in heaven and on earth, visible and invisible, whether thrones or dominions or rulers or authorities—all things were created through him and for him. And he is before all things, and in him all things hold together. (Col 1.16–17)

I wonder how often people fail to see the infinitely large gap between God's power and creation versus mankind's ingenuity and inventions. It can be easy to elevate our view of self so high in our minds that we do not feel a need for God. However, all our abilities have been provided by God and are insignificant compared to all that He is and what He has done.

People may have such an elevated view of science, for example, that they deny the power of God, who originally designed and created what science attempts to explain. Some may even start to believe they can control the climate and weather. This is something the Lord claims to control every single day (Ps 148.8). The Lord declares that through Him and His Son everything exists. Christians believe this. Others mock those who genuinely believe that He holds the world together. They also deny His Kingship and His Lordship.

Unfortunately, as long as a person elevates themselves in his own mind, they will not see God nor search for Him. Ultimately, that means they won't find Him. When there is an effort to cling to our selfish, worldly desires, we will not search for or see anything grander. We must be careful not to let the false prophets of our time make inroads into our view of self with respect to who God truly is. Society will always serve the idols of our time. If we are not careful, we may become unknowingly complicit with the worldviews around us without even realizing it's happening. We are constantly bombarded with false messaging, and we must continually learn about God in a way that counters that messaging!

I love to sing the song "My God Is So Big" with my grandkids. It goes something like: *My God is so big, so strong, and so mighty there's nothing my God cannot do! For you!* Like children, we who are older can also benefit from meditating on our insignificant smallness compared to God Almighty's vast grandness. Is our view of God too small and our view of self too large? May our God help us see Him and His truth found only in scripture. Is there anything in our lives that keeps us from seeing and depending on our all-powerful God? Let's set them aside so we can seek and find Him. It's really not that hard to have faith in a God who is so mighty. There's nothing our God cannot do!

DAY 3

Undivided Loyalty

If you miss heaven, you have missed it all. (Dee Bowman, Florida College Lectures, 1979)

Do not lay up for yourselves treasures on earth, where moth and rust destroy and where thieves break in and steal, but lay up for yourselves treasures in heaven, where neither moth nor rust destroys and where thieves do not break in and steal. For where your treasure is, there your heart will be also...

No one can serve two masters, for either he will hate the one and love the other, or he will be devoted to the one and despise the other. You cannot serve God and money. (Matt 6.19–21, 24)

Everyone then who hears these words of mine and does them will be like a wise man who built his house on the rock. And the rain fell, and the floods came, and the winds blew and beat on that house, but it did not fall, because it had been founded on the rock. And everyone who hears these words of mine and does not do them will be like a foolish man who built his house on the sand. And the rain fell, and the floods came, and the winds blew and beat against that house, and it fell, and great was the fall of it. (Matt 7.24–27)

Jesus uses everyday analogies when He explains the gospel of the kingdom. Our country does not have the structure of a kingdom with a royal family, so we do not think of those concepts often. But heaven is our destination, and to go there, we must be part of the heavenly kingdom that Jesus came to earth to establish. So, it helps to have pictures in our mind of what the kingdom of heaven is all about.

In England, the idea of the United Kingdom and a Royal Family is still very much a part of the national mindset. Suppose part of the family wants to leave the kingdom's protection to devote their time and loyalties to other priorities. In that case, it may enable people to better make the connections in their minds about serving two masters. Of course, Christians are part of a kingdom and royal family, not of this world!

The point is that these earthly stories about our current-day sovereigns should contrast the reality of God's kingdom and allow us to contemplate the undivided loyalty our King requires. Christians are always to put God first, never divide their loyalties for personal gain, get credit for charity causes, or split their focus between their personal desires and the furtherance of the heavenly kingdom.

May God's Will be done on earth as it is in heaven. And may no Christian trade the stability of their home with God for another house that cannot stand against the winds of change, the tides of time, or the bombardment of the opposing forces and schemes of enemies. Let us remain in the house that is built upon the rock of His Word!

DAY 4

Starting Where You Are

At first glance it may appear too hard. Look again. Always look again. (Mary Anne Radmacher)

If we let ourselves, we shall always be waiting for some distraction or other to end before we can really get down to our work. The only people who achieve much are those who want knowledge so badly that they seek it while the conditions are still unfavorable. Favorable conditions never come. (C.S. Lewis)

Even though I walk through the valley of the shadow of death,
*   I will fear no evil,*
for you are with me;
*   your rod and your staff,*
*   they comfort me.* (Psa 23.4)

I think some of the most successful devices of evil are those that cause distraction and the fear of failure. Some people believe they will always have more time later to dig in and learn whatever is required to do to accomplish what they want to do. Until then, they just go with the flow, waiting until they feel better or have more energy, time, money, etc.

It is only when a person does their best with whatever opportunities he or she has that they gain the ability and stamina to obtain more of anything—more knowledge, experience, compassion, energy, and even more opportunities. The changes come when each person decides to start where they are and learn and take full advantage of what is available to them at any given moment. And if one does not do their best with what they have and their know how, they would not do better if given more.

Everything is hard until you learn how to do it. But nothing is so hard that you cannot try to understand it. Whatever is in front of you right now is just the first step towards the next something. You can eat an elephant if you do it one bite at a time. Even if a step seems like a giant leap at the moment, take it!

Move forward one step at a time and never give up on yourself or the process! Always remember that everyone must start at their own starting line. Do not compare yourself to others. Start where you are, focus, and run towards your goal! Do not let distractions or fear stop you!

DAY 5

Trust the Process

The secret is Christ in me, not me in a different set of circumstances. (Elisabeth Elliott)

"Do not lay your hand on the boy or do anything to him, for now I know that you fear God, seeing you have not withheld your son, your only son, from me." (Gen 22.12)

Financial, emotional, and spiritual problems will always test us. While we all make choices that impact our circumstances, it is essential to realize that the driving factor cannot be an attempt to run from a problem that needs to be solved. Christ promotes confrontation when armed with His Word and a pure heart.

It has become popular, acceptable even, to put ourselves first. The underlying motive for our choices cannot be fear or an attempt to protect ourselves at the expense of others. This rationale is in direct opposition to the mind of Christ. A Christian should always contemplate how each decision will impact others with God's purpose in mind. When someone runs away from problems instead of using God's wisdom to solve them, they promote the world's wisdom, not God's.

To be Christlike is to do all that one can do to the glory of God. We must exhaust all of God's remedies and use God's wisdom in difficult situations to expose God's wisdom to the world. The failure to do so indicates a lack of faith!

Because of various difficulties, the solutions will also be hard to find and implement. They will require study, wisdom, and prayer. If we can sift through all the *me first* messaging coming from society, use God's wisdom, and watch it work, the process and results prove each person's faith to themselves, to others, and to God.

We see this in God's test to Abraham after he chose not to withhold Isaac. God said, *For now I know that you fear God.* When a person runs from the hard things, they may just be removing their God-given tests and find themselves in a more complicated place, with a more vivid and difficult test to pass!

So let us all work out our own salvation with fear and trembling! Restated, work out your personal redemption with an intense reverence towards God and with a healthy dose of astonishment of God's awesome power to actively work in your heart and the hearts of all people! Trust the process. Your faith in God's ways, along with the His grace, will save you!

WEEK TWO

DAY 1

Ruling the Spirit

We either make ourselves miserable, or we make ourselves strong. The amount of work is the same. (Carlos Castaneda)

Whoever is slow to anger is better than the mighty,
and he who rules his spirit than he who takes a city. (Prov 16.32)

We all have free will to choose how to respond to our circumstances. The circumstances may not be under our control, but our response to them is. And so, the point is well taken by Mr. Castaneda that *we make ourselves* through our choices.

Society has deemed someone else at fault for addictions, for someone's lack of knowledge, or for their station in life. It tells us that our ancestors, pasts, genes, socioeconomic status, or our parents' poor choices control our lives today. We now must change our very climate or else we will all perish! Fear is society's motivator, and it is all rubbish!

Self-control is replaced by several variations of a blame-game mentality. In this thought process, someone must control the actions of others to right their lives rather than taking responsibility and working things out using God-given resources. When one sees themselves as a victim or entitled, they lack wisdom. When one chooses to use God's wisdom in making choices and responding to life's situations, they understand they need a spiritual guide for living this life.

Real strength resides in those who rule their spirit to do what God's Spirit directs. People can become strong when they know they can control and improve each thought, action, and reaction. They can prevail over their present circumstances. Prosperous are those who know they need help! Because after a person admits flaws, they can begin the business of correcting themselves.

DAY 2

Having Hearts Prepared

A person hears only what they understand. (Johann Wolfgang von Goethe)

"To you has been given the secret of the kingdom of God, but for those outside everything is in parables, so that 'They may indeed see but not perceive, and my indeed hear but not understand, lest they should turn and be forgiven.'" (Mark 4.11–12)

Learning truth is a willing, active, and organized process of the mind. Jesus taught in parables so that only thoughtful, willing learners using their conscious free will would understand and obey him. The process is the same today. The Bible says that *Wisdom* shouts in the streets, but who is listening?

The seeds of teaching are everywhere, but they always fall into hearts that are already saturated with each person's prevalent thinking, their current understanding, and the active feelings of each listener. So, what's taught is not always heard or understood unless someone has prepared their mind to capture it.

If a person is not careful, they will choose only to hear what they want to understand. The heart and mind must be open and prepared to come to each learning opportunity with a willingness to slow down, calm down, listen, learn, and apply what they know and the lessons they glean. For any good, open-minded listener, there will always be the humble realization that there are things that they do not yet understand.

But understanding any truth can be entirely lost by one's unwillingness to see or hear it. Suppose anyone blinds themselves to their own ignorance or fails to realize their personal inadequacies. In that case, teaching does not typically translate into learning and has no real impact on their understanding or necessary lifestyle transformations. These hearts remain hardened when exposed to the truth, the seed of God's word can develop no root in them, and therefore it yields no fruit from their lack of development and growth. Ultimately, it adds no value to them.

Let all pray for soft, open, and honest hearts in ourselves and others during difficult times! The apostle Paul prayed in Ephesians:

> I do not cease to give thanks for you, remembering you in my prayers, that the God of our Lord Jesus Christ, the Father of glory, may give you the Spirit of wisdom and of revelation in the knowledge of him, having the eyes of your hearts enlightened, that you may know what is the hope to which he has called you, what are the riches of his glorious inheritance in the saints, and what is the immeasurable greatness of his power toward us who believe, according to the working of his great might that he worked in Christ when he raised him from the dead and seated him at his right hand in the heavenly places, far above all rule and authority and power and dominion, and above every name that is named, not only in this age but also in the one to come. (Eph 1.16–21)

Imagine Paul praying this for all of us today! The more fruit of the Spirit produced by the faithful, the more love and kindness will result, and the more it will manifest itself in today's culture. All soft-hearted hearers will be blanketed with a peace that surpasses understanding. But if hardened hearts prevail, the works of the flesh will carry the day, and there will be nothing but chaos.

The Christian's warfare isn't a physical battle but rather a war in the mind against the unfruitful works of darkness. Each of us must do our part in listening, hearing, and internalizing scripture as God works to implant His Word, which carries wisdom and knowledge from His Spirit to ours. This process is how God creates in us something beautiful, useful, and intended to manifest His glory! No other method operates like this to develop and mature Spirit-filled believers, one person at a time.

The culmination of God's desired result is described by Paul in his letter to Philemon. He says,

> I have derived much joy and comfort from your love, my brother, because the hearts of the saints have been refreshed through you. (Phlm 7)

Philemon heard, listened, understood, learned, and ultimately allowed God's Spirit to prevail in his life to such an extent that his very being could be of use to refresh others! May we all go and do likewise!

DAY 3

God's Brand of Love

But when the Bible speaks of love, it measures it primarily not by how much you want to receive it but by how much you are willing to give yourself to someone else. (Author Unknown)

For God so loved the world, that he gave his only Son, that whoever believes in him should not perish but have eternal life. (John 3.16)

I was recently reading a historical novel about a Roman family. A Christian slave was working among them, but they were unaware that she was a Christian and thought her to be a Jew. The slave's mistress, when explaining what she believed "love" to be, said that in the Roman culture, if you loved someone, you just gave them everything they wanted. This sounds a lot like some people's view of love today!

The brand of love expressed by God through His sacrifice is alien to this world. When a person shows this kind of sacrificial love, they are expressing a sentiment that God means to be His brand. The Greeks had multiple words for different types of love to minimize the confusion. By contrast, Americans only use one word to talk about everything from loving their ice cream, inanimate objects, and animals to their families, boyfriends, husbands, or God! Most of the time, it seems the current definitions have lost all connection to service or sacrifice. The world has such a different message about love and everyone in our time is totally saturated with it.

When God says to love your enemies, the confusion about the meaning of this command becomes evident in light of this world's definition of *love*. People today are confused by the statement and cannot understand how to obey the command. What God means is that a person is to sacrifice their wants and needs for those of others. You can do that for anyone by simply deciding to do so. It takes no squishy feeling to go with it. Whenever a need presents itself, a person who loves like Christ is expected to put His brand of love into the response equation.

When we deploy God's love, it manifests itself as an out-of-this-world concept and gives glory to God, drawing honest hearts to the truth. This process works in our time as convincingly as the miracles that authenticated

God's prophets and truth in times past. It was employed by God Himself with the sacrifice of His Son. Let us all decide to put His brand of love into action, loving others as He has first loved us!

DAY 4

Residuals of Wisdom

A clever person solves a problem. A wise person avoids it. (Albert Einstein)

For the LORD gives wisdom;
  from his mouth come knowledge and understanding;
he stores up sound wisdom for the upright;
  he is a shield to those who walk in integrity,
guarding the paths of justice
  and watching over the way of his saints. (Prov 2.6–8)

A lack of godly wisdom in any situation always shows itself. Both worldly and godly wisdom always leave residual effects behind. A person well-exercised in applying God's wisdom can recognize each for what they are and even use their understanding to impact situations early on before foolishness takes hold. This dynamic is on display in families, churches, cities, and on a large scale. We can see it play out in our country and other nations. The more egregious the departure from God's wisdom, the more chaos exists, and sometimes it is left to reign. We must remember that the end of foolishness is always destruction!

A worldly-thinking mind cannot just stumble onto God's truth without it being sought and revealed to them. This explains why the Bible says, *foolishness is bound up in the heart of a child* (Prov. 22.15). Children have yet to be taught! People must systematically ingest God's wisdom for anyone to spiritually *grow up* and put it to good use. Unfortunately, those without a knowledge of God typically laugh at His wisdom or cannot see any value in using it. In contrast, the influence of godly wisdom prevents the effects of foolishness while enabling good outcomes.

A worldly-minded person sees this, calls it luck or fate, and never recognizes it as something they can employ intentionally. But anyone with God's revealed knowledge can recognize when others use His wisdom. Sometimes it comes from unexpected places, and when God's wisdom negatively impacts evil agendas, the wise are typically persecuted or otherwise silenced. Jesus is the ultimate embodiment of God's wisdom and the suffering that can result. He came to show and teach anyone willing to see and hear God's directed paths. Without Him and the inspired teaching of God's Word, we would never understand God's original intent for everything He created.

Romans 10 explains the process. It says:

> How then will they call on him in whom they have not believed? And how are they to believe in him of whom they have never heard? And how are they to hear without someone preaching?… So, faith comes from hearing, and hearing through the word of Christ. But I ask, have they not heard? Indeed, they have, for 'Their voice has gone out to all the earth, and their words to the ends of the world. (Rom. 10.14, 17–18)

God wants to change your heart; yours is the only one you can control. The more hearts impacted with truth, and the more of God's wisdom we choose to employ, the more rational and peaceful the world will begin to be. So let us all pray for wisdom and for the justice and safety it can bring. Let us learn from God and follow His wisdom rather than our own in all our personal choices. And let us share it with others. This process is how godly wisdom shows up in our lives. His wisdom is what can change families, churches, schools, communities, and, ultimately, our nation!

DAY 5

Dispelling Anger

Anger is nothing more than an outward expression of hurt, fear, and frustration. (Dr. Phil McGraw)

Be angry and do not sin; do not let the sun go down on your anger, and give no opportunity to the devil. (Eph 4.26–27)

In his letter to the Ephesians, Paul tells the Christians to be angry and sin not. We must always be controlled and find righteous ways to dispel our strong emotions. Anger is a strong indicator of what is happening inside a person's heart. People are especially at risk of experiencing anger in frustrating circumstances, in times of unfairness or injustice, and in times of great loss.

God is the author of all emotion, and His word seems to tie anger's proper use to injustice and unfairness. An example is when Jesus was angry with the money changers at the temple. They had perverted God's system of sacrifice and instead used it to cheat the people. Jesus reacted appropriately by turning over their tables and openly rebuking the people.

Unrighteous anger is usually a reaction to the realization that things are outside our control. God tells us that we should relinquish the idea that we can control our circumstances. Instead, we must focus on what we can control: the thinking in our hearts. We all need to learn to trust God, who has promised to bless his children in whatever situation they find themselves in.

The systemic anger and distrust in our society are often a by-product of rapid change and corruption. These include advancements in technology and modes of communication, societal pressures, changing social norms, a charged political landscape with blatant corruption, and health concerns. With all of this added to the daily struggles a person experiences, it is easy to feel out of control. And, to put it bluntly, we are! God is in control and, ultimately, He will take care of you!

God can use all the changes and uncertainty to help people realize their need to lean on Him and cling to His invariable truth. God never changes. He is faithful, He will not leave His children, and His steadfast love will never disappoint. If someone is not close to God, it is because they are the ones who have moved. God is always there, pleading for a relationship with totally undeserving people.

We must spend our time and energy maintaining our relationship with God because we cannot control the actions or hearts of anyone else. We can only contribute to the learning of others from things God has taught us in His Word. And any real impact we have will come because we have been able to control ourselves under times of great stress!

So let us conscientiously dispel worldly fear with God-directed faith and love toward others. In times of prosperity, be reflective; in times of trouble, be very careful; and at all times, be grateful for all of God's blessings. All sin and fall short of God's glory, and no person deserves any grace. If someone knows God and has learned to control themselves, it has been by the grace of God above, and all glory belongs to Him.

Let us pray that we can learn to control our hearts and not let Satan win the day! When anger arises, and it most certainly will, stay in control because it is then that you are at grave risk of sin. Even if the anger is righteous due to some injustice, turn it over to God. It is written, "Vengeance is mine; I will repay" (Heb 10.30). Everything will come with total justice in His time.

WEEK THREE

DAY 1

Considering Ravens

Don't ask God why He is allowing something to happen. Ask Him what He wants you to do and learn in the midst of it. (Author Unknown)

And I will say to my soul, "Soul, you have ample goods laid up for many years; relax, eat, drink, be merry."' But God said to him, Fool! This night your soul is required of you, and the things you have prepared, whose will they be?' So is the one who lays up treasure for himself and is not rich toward God." And he said to his disciples, "Therefore I tell you, do not be anxious about your life, what you will eat, nor about your body, what you will put on. For life is more than food, and the body more than clothing. Consider the ravens: they neither sow nor reap, they have neither storehouse nor barn, and yet God feeds them. Of how much more value are you than the birds! And which of you by being anxious can add a single hour to his span of life? If then you are not able to do as small a thing as that, why are you anxious about the rest? Consider the lilies, how they grow: they neither toil nor spin, yet I tell you, even Solomon in all his glory was not arrayed like one of these." (Luke 12.19–23)

The rich man in Jesus' parable thought he was controlling his destiny, but this was a foolish basis for decision-making. Instead, Jesus instructs His disciples to consider the ravens and the lilies. God feeds and dresses both abundantly, and neither need to worry! Jesus expects his followers to likewise trust in God to provide for all their needs.

The stark comparison between the reckless thought process in a mind where God is absent or insignificant and the absolute peace of trusting God's role in our lives is so impactful that it should move us not to be anxious. We all must realize that God works in our circumstances to grow and feed us spiritually. This faith helps us trust in Him and be patient when times are difficult.

God is our Heavenly Father with our best interest at heart. The fact that He knows so much more about it than we do should cause any fear in us to dissipate. Our eyes need to be on who God is and how lowly we are in comparison to show those around us what faith can do. The question should be how I can get on the same page and use these circumstances to God's glory.

Which mindset will we choose as we reside within our various circumstances? Do we have the faith of Joseph to endure unfairness or the self-interest and elevation found in King Saul? The choice we make will be as evident as it was in the lives of these men, leading us to either usefulness or insanity!

DAY 2

Habitual Growth

You'll never change your life until you change something you do daily. The secret of your success is found in your daily routine. (John Maxwell)

Now therefore, listen to me, my children,
  For blessed are those who keep my ways.
Hear instruction and be wise,
  And do not disdain it. (Prov 8.32–33)

God has always emphasized ongoing study and obedience as His method for daily growth. The process is not a secret. Everyone knows that no growth or productivity will occur when they do not expend any effort. This continual process is how people form habits. People become who they desire to be through these small, repetitive actions.

Self-improvement requires a person to be repetitiously exposed to new teaching and consciously choose to make the necessary lifestyle changes, and then habitually practice them. Of course, this also requires having the ability to make the change and a desire to accomplish it.

Whenever we decide to institute a change or improvement in our home, work, or church environments, we must consciously prioritize it and habitually repeat it. Research shows that it takes approximately ninety days to develop any new habit and make it part of your lifestyle. And it takes about the same amount of time to get out of a habit.

Everyone who desires to improve must practice these principles all the time and not just at the beginning of each calendar year. And success will depend on how willing a person is to make their resolutions a habitual part of their lifestyle. The type of change does not matter. We can always change habits relating to our work, eating, exercise, character improvements, and the list goes on.

The pandemic of 2020 interrupted the daily habits of many people. Some habits may not have been consciously integrated into our behavior and, therefore, would not be considered valuable. A parent, spouse, or employer may have directed our former habits. Trying to reestablish these may take a lot of conscious effort.

On the other hand, disruptive events like these provide great opportunities for people to reevaluate old habits and establish new ones. We know that we cannot form new habits or reinstate old ones without conscious effort. A massive change in norms has occurred over the past few years, and returning to former habits may no longer be an option.

Importantly, all of our newly established "norms" will require alignment with relevant Biblical principles to be advantageous to our spiritual growth. Let's all pray that we all can recognize the disconnects that spring up within our own realms, and that all God's children understand God's direction and truth well enough to apply sound Biblical principles in the context of our culture to become better, more spiritually productive people.

DAY 3

Choosing Moral Courage

Fear is a reaction. Courage is a decision. (Winston S. Churchill)

Then David said to Solomon his son, "Be strong and courageous and do it. Do not be afraid and do not be dismayed, for the LORD God, even my God, is with you. He will not leave you or forsake you, until all the work for the service of the house of the LORD is finished." (1 Chron 28.20)

We see a faith versus fear concept that is prevalent throughout scripture. In his statement above, Churchill was most likely talking about physical courage—a willingness to sacrifice self for one's country or others. But there is also, as spoken of by David, a type of moral courage that is a willingness to sacrifice one's selfish desire to do what is right and just.

We find that courage from knowing God and having fellowship with Him. Adam and Eve had no fear until they sinned. When death entered the world, so did fear. Fear is the natural reaction to losing security, livelihood, or a physical calamity.

Courage is a response to a deep trust or love in something greater than we and our current circumstances. A person must choose to employ it. It comes from somewhere inside a person with a heart looking past the present to what is unseen. In the case of moral courage, it requires a connection to God and His wisdom. It is an obedient response to His direction.

You can have physical courage without possessing any moral courage at all. People with moral courage stand up for God's directives and principles, fight for the little guy, and speak the truth when it is unpopular. We must all show such courage to stand in difficult times. It may come at a great cost! We are always at war with fear, evil, and lies. God's people can fight it with faith, goodness, and truth!

DAY 4

Free-Will Consequences

Evil comes from the abuse of free will. (C.S. Lewis)

But now having been freed from sin and enslaved to God, you derive your benefit, resulting in sanctification, and the outcome, eternal life. For the wages of sin is death, but the free gift of God is eternal life in Christ Jesus our Lord. (Rom 6.22–23)

John to the seven churches that are in Asia: Grace to you and peace from him who is and who was and who is to come, and from the seven spirits who are before his throne, and from Jesus Christ the faithful witness, the firstborn of the dead, and the ruler of kings on earth. To him who loves us and has freed us from our sins by his blood and made us a kingdom, priests to his God and Father, to him be glory and dominion forever and ever. Amen. (Rev 1.4–6)

The first quote above is one of my favorites from C. S. Lewis because it answers the question many people want to know: *If there is a God, why do bad things happen?*

Everything God created was very good before He gave mankind the free will to interact with it. If anyone disobeys God by using His creation in ways other than its originally intended purpose, they have chosen to make themselves their own god. When they do, evil and violence are born, and the consequences and ramifications of their decision will extend to others. This disobedience causes God and even His creation to mourn.

Satan aims to make people resent God's love and care. The evil one is at work in the world just as God is, and his work is to deceive people into thinking God's proper intentions somehow limit them. He convinces people that doing things their way is better than God's. Sometimes these choices are made for personal gratification. In others, they are made from ignorance or inexperience. Either way, evil is set in motion by our selfish choices.

Satan's deception perpetually convinces some people. They improperly use God's direction, His institutions, and discipline. The results are the works of the flesh, which include "sexual immorality, impurity, sensuality, idolatry, sorcery, enmity, strife, jealousy, fits of anger, rivalries, dissensions, divisions, envy, drunkenness, orgies, and things like these" (Gal 5.19–21).

If a person chooses to steal, they hurt another. If someone disregards God's holy teaching and wisdom, they make foolish decisions that negatively impact themselves and others. If one is disobedient to parents, or parents are derelict in their responsibilities, children will make poor choices. The societal and generational cascade can destroy people, families, and nations.

The good news is that God's original plans include a path back to reconciliation that He put in motion following the sin of Adam and Eve. God knew that giving mankind free will with exposure to Satan would bring temptation. He understood that sin and ruin would result from mankind's individual choices. God has ensured that everyone can be redeemed from their state of sin and have a restored relationship with Him.

People can choose to die to their old ways and then unite with Christ's death to be born again and reconciled with God. Even though a person still suffers the consequences of evil in this life from the consequences of free will, they can ultimately find spiritual peace and prosperity (3 John 2).

Because of this, we can look forward to a kingdom not made with hands, eternal in the heavens. There is no need to fear because we now have a home where the soul never dies. Those who are dead to sin cannot be separated from God against their will, even at physical death. The calm that takes hold with this realization is a superpower—the peace of God that surpasses all understanding (Phil. 4.7). Praise be to God for this marvelous blessing of grace by faith!

DAY 5

Unexpected Truth

Besides being complicated, reality, in my experience, is usually odd. It is not neat, not obvious, not what you expect. (C.S. Lewis)

So Jesus said to the Jews who had believed him, "If you abide in my word, you are truly my disciples, and you will know the truth, and the truth will set you free." They answered him, "We are offspring of Abraham and have never been enslaved to anyone. How is it that you say, 'You will become free'?" Jesus answered them, "Truly, truly, I say to you, everyone who practices sin is a slave to sin. The slave does not remain in the house forever; the son remains forever. So if the Son sets you free, you will be free indeed. (John 8.31–36)

Whenever I watch a television show, I can sometimes figure out the plot and how it will end within five minutes of starting the program. Most shows deliver a happy ending. But the ending is much harder to predict when a movie or program is based on a true story. People who have done something extraordinary in real life sometimes fare poorly. Life never really operates like fairy tales.

God's truth is not always what one would expect. Jesus came to earth to show God's intent for mankind in the example of His life. And His followers, through the Holy Spirit, have written it down for everyone who has lived since then. It is wisdom from above that is revealed in scripture. It becomes implanted in our hearts and bears spiritual fruit as people display it through their actions.

The words "truth" and "reality" are sometimes used interchangeably in English, but there is a distinction between the two. In John 8, Jesus uses the word truth in a way that conveys its Biblical meaning. His Word and anything that is done according to His divine authority is truth, and this truth sets people free from sin. From a biblical standpoint, truth is the standard by which God desires His people to live. People who accept it display actions consistent with the direction He has provided through His Word. A person employing His truth hits the mark rather than misses it.

In our secular vocabulary, the word truth has become conflated with reality—that is, an unbiased retelling of factual events, as far as possible. It can mean the reality of what an individual or group has done in the past. The problem these days, I fear, is that many are making up their own reality.

In today's world, objective truth and reality seem to have become utterly obscured by the systemic lack of knowledge of God and His direction for mankind in our society. Some may know the truth or reality concerning a matter, but they either obscure or deny it because of malicious intent or as a mechanism to get their own way. Some, like the Pharisees, do not believe God's Word and refuse to be intellectually honest enough even to consider the evidence when presented with it directly.

Establishing the divine authority of God in our lives is ridiculed and downplayed even among those who should know its value. Paul wrote, *If anyone among you thinks that he is wise in this age, let him become a fool that he may become wise* (1 Cor 3.18). Without the frequent study of His Word, anyone can be at risk of being unable to recognize it.

But those who come to learn it and embody the character of the Lord are spreading God's truth. It carries the message of good news that sets people free from the entanglement of their sins. Everyone who finds it can be released from the bondage of sin so that they can freely walk into eternity. There is undoubtedly a home prepared for all those who find and obey the truth that Jesus came to impart!

WEEK FOUR

DAY 1

The Perfect Mirror

Of all the awkward people in your house or job there is only one whom you can improve very much. (C. S. Lewis)

Do not be deceived, my beloved brothers. Every good gift and every perfect gift is from above, coming down from the Father of lights, with whom there is no variation or shadow due to change. Of his own will he brought us forth by the word of truth, that we should be a kind of first fruits of his creatures. Know this, my beloved brothers: let every person be quick to hear, slow to speak, slow to anger; for the anger of man does not produce the righteousness of God. Therefore, put away all filthiness and rampant wickedness and receive with meekness the implanted word, which is able to save your souls. But be doers of the word, and not hearers only, deceiving yourselves. For if anyone is a hearer of the word and not a doer, he is like a man who looks intently at his natural face in a mirror. For he looks at himself and goes away and at once forgets what he was like. But the one who looks into the perfect law, the law of liberty, and perseveres, being no hearer who forgets but a doer who acts, he will be blessed in his doing. (Jas 1.16–25)

There are many facets to the *life change* process that God expects from His people. Christians must respond to living in a world saturated with sin while not wanting to be a part of it. They have been transformed into new creatures, making them members of an unseen, heavenly realm. While we live in this world, God holds each Christian accountable for their motives, attitudes, and behaviors when confronted with the trials and temptations of this life.

Taking responsibility for having godly attitudes and responses is a full-time job. If we take it seriously, there will be little time for much else. We cannot control others, nor should we try to manipulate them. We can encourage, plead, and even discipline if it is our responsibility to do so. However, simply working on ourselves has all sorts of byproducts that will benefit others in our personal vector.

Each can have a godly influence by yielding spiritual fruit in our lives that promotes good responses in others. It is up to each one to work according to the Will of the *Father of lights* and not for their personal agenda. The choices that must be made by each person become evident when looking into *the perfect law of liberty*. God's Word is the mirror that shows us our imperfections. Some will look into it and make the changes, while others will fail to do so. Either way, the choices can only be made by each person.

God's perfect law is always the same, but each one looks from their own specific vantage point. Everyone's journey takes place at a particular time in history, from a unique set of circumstances, with differing limits of ability, a different chosen heart condition, and varying degrees of scriptural understanding. Everyone's resources and influences are also different, sometimes even for people within the same family. Understanding the personal nature of our growth should help limit all Christians from comparing themselves with others and making unrighteous judgments.

No one can walk the road for another. At the same time, no one walks alone, either. We stride with fellow Christians along the way, and the Lord always walks beside us. God will always provide, and He does so abundantly. We are continually growing. May we each rely on the mirror of the perfect law to show us the way forward from wherever we are.

DAY 2

Hungering for Truth

The birth of Christ is the central event in the history of earth—the very thing the whole story has been about. (C.S. Lewis)

… making known to us the mystery of his will, according to his purpose, which he set forth in Christ as a plan for the fullness of time to unite all things in him, things in heaven and things on earth. (Eph 1.9–10)

Those of this world are confused. Satan's work is to lie about God, His purpose, and His love. And he does a pretty good job of it too. He effectively keeps people from seeing the truth.

The ungodly can look at things like a sunrise, a newborn baby, and the beauty of creation and believe there is no designer or orchestration. They have been fed an alternate theory that allows them to live as they desire rather than in a way that a holy, praise-worthy Creator has prescribed and ordained. Any thought process that leaves God out of the picture has no validity. And when put to the test, it fails.

Because God does not immediately destroy ungodliness, people think He is not active or does not see all the evil happening. Peter tells us, *The Lord is not slow to fulfill his promise as some count slowness, but is patient toward you, not wishing that any should perish, but that all should reach repentance* (2 Pet 3.9). His inaction is evidence of his love and patience.

There have always been those who seek out the one true God and His purpose, and God draws these to repentance. His Son, Jesus Christ, is what life is all about. His entrance into a fallen world to provide a propitiating sacrifice for sinners tells the whole story of the human dilemma.

Christ has been introduced to the world and made known through divine revelation. *In Him we have redemption through his blood, the forgiveness of our trespasses, according to the riches of his grace* (Eph 1.7). His servant life, sacrifice, and teaching all identify God's character to a lost and dying world. Jesus Christ helps open honest hearts see God and find eternal life. He gives this life meaning and direction. Without Him, all is vanity.

But if a person chooses to believe there is no God, judgment, or any absolute truth, then this fallible reasoning leads them to hopelessness and a lack of purpose or meaning in their life. No good or evil can be identified in this reasoning because there is no acknowledged standard. The only result is a prolonged separation from God.

Anyone looking intently at their surroundings can see, at the very least, that there is evil in the world. And if evil exists, it points to the fact that there must also be good. God created, God inserted wisdom in the world, God sent his Son, God provides hope and reconciliation. This is the story God tells in scripture.

Do not be deceived. The truth is active and available. But each person must search to find it. It will not be found by chance! It is sought out of a hunger and thirst for God!

DAY 3

The Only Path to Home

And gradually, though no one remembers exactly how it happened, the unthinkable becomes tolerable. And then acceptable. And then legal. And then applaudable. (Joni Eareckson Tada)

The LORD possessed me at the beginning of his work,
    the first of his acts of old.
Ages ago I was set up,
    at the first, before the beginning of the earth.
When there were no depths I was brought forth,
    when there were no springs abounding with water.
Before the mountains had been shaped,
    before the hills, I was brought forth,
before he had made the earth with its fields,
    or the first of the dust of the world.
When he established the heavens, I was there;
    when he drew a circle on the face of the deep,
when he made firm the skies above,
    when he established the fountains of the deep,
when he assigned to the sea its limit,
    so that the waters might not transgress his command,
when he marked out the foundations of the earth,
    then I was beside him, like a master workman,
and I was daily his delight,
    rejoicing before him always,
rejoicing in his inhabited world
    and delighting in the children of man.

And now, O sons, listen to me:
    blessed are those who keep my ways.
Hear instruction and be wise,
    and do not neglect it.

Blessed is the one who listens to me,
    watching daily at my gates,
    waiting beside my doors.

For whoever finds me finds life
    and obtains favor from the LORD,

but he who fails to find me injures himself;
   all who hate me love death. (Prov 8.22–36)

In the verses above, "Wisdom" is speaking. The passage shows how highly regarded it should be in people's minds and how people come to ruin without it. The quote by Joni Eareckson Tada addresses how people can gradually rationalize foolishness and evil as the world pushes the acceptance of their choices onto others. This process shows how the masses come to deny true wisdom.

Any person who reaches adulthood has seen society accept the unthinkable in some form or another. And those who have lived for multiple generations have seen it happen repeatedly. Its ultimate end is in the vilification of true wisdom under a reign of foolishness. Society becomes filled with people "who call evil good and good evil, who put darkness for light and light for darkness, who put bitter for sweet and sweet for bitter" (Isa 5.20). People want to be their own god and do what is right in their own eyes, so they reject God's wisdom and the truth.

C.S. Lewis made the opposite journey. He went from a total rejection of God to a stance accepting and magnifying godly wisdom. He said, "I think all Christians would agree with me if I said that though Christianity seems at first to be all about morality, all about duties and rules and guilt and virtue, yet it leads you on, out of all that, into something beyond." Lewis understood the value and purpose of God's truth and wisdom. Each person learns from our Heavenly Father what is good and wise, and that training leads us to a victory over death and onto eternal life.

God's plea is that each person seeks wisdom and understanding because, my friends, this is the only way to find any kind of life, eternal or otherwise. It is the only path to home, the only path to real abiding peace and love. And it is revealed in scripture. You find truth and wisdom there! We can even perceive wisdom in the way God originally made the world. His eternal power and divine nature are there for all to see (Rom 1.20)!

Folly also calls. *The woman Folly is loud; she is seductive and knows nothing* (Prov 9.13). The options are available to each person, and both seek preeminence in our choices. Do not fall for all the devices that detract m͞ ⸺ᵏⁱnd from what is sound, reasonable, and God-directed! Choose to seek g
listen to Wisdom when she speaks. It can be much louder than the
the foolish! But it does require listening!

W

DAY 4

The Good Standard

Goodness is, so to speak, itself; badness is only spoiled goodness. (C.S. Lewis)

The Lord God said to the serpent,

"Because you have done this,
cursed are you above all livestock
and above all beasts of the field;
on your belly you shall go,
and dust you shall eat
all the days of your life.
I will put enmity between you and the woman,
and between your offspring and her offspring;
he shall bruise your head,
and you shall bruise his heel." (Gen 3.14–15)

God created with a purpose and intention for His creation, and He has an expectation for our view of Him, others, and everything He has made. All that God created He called "good" (Gen 1), and it is good when we act according to His direction as prescribed in His Word. "Badness" is merely a result of failing to hit the mark of God's prescription. Scripture more commonly describes it as sin.

There is a God-directed answer for anything and everything. When people measure themselves by a self-defined view of what they deem good, they set themselves up as the standard. People can only begin denying themselves and seeking what is truly good when they seek and accept God's Way. Unfortunately, the world does not want to acknowledge a divine standard at all, which results in the mocking and persecution of Christians who have devoted their lives to following it.

People in the world attempt to redefine God's directives and deny that there is a right way of doing things. They oppose the concept of sin and attempt to redefine godly institutions, like marriage and family. This redefinition is done even with common words God uses in the beginning, like "man" and "woman." In essence, worldliness has become a religion in itself, even a government-sanctioned one. People who follow the lies are "disciples" and must attempt to conform to all the conflicting societal norms!

When the world tries to dictate the standards that oppose God, there will be resistance and opposition from Christians who choose a God-directed mindset. When the two sides conflict, it results in chaos, division, and persecution. Everyone makes decisions with a mind and spirit directed by God or the world, and each represents a choice to believe in God or not!

We can see the conflict in nations, organizations, schools, families, marriages, and in each person's mind. Let us all recognize it for what it is and stop expecting that we can compromise on matters that are clearly in opposition to the truth. The only option for peace is to extract sin from the equation. Repentance, forgiveness, and reconciliation become the only path forward; Christians must be the example!

DAY 5

Genuine Communication

Say what you mean—but don't say it mean! (Author Unknown)

*There is one whose rash words are like sword thrusts,
   but the tongue of the wise brings healing.* (Prov 12.18)

Long ago, I was taught that words alone transfer only about 7 percent of a speaker's intended message; 55 percent comes from their body language, and their tone of voice transmits the rest. When a person speaks, the heart is innately involved and conveys one's true intentions, along with the words spoken. And when the speaker is intent on communicating, what is said has a higher probability of being understood and positively impacting the hearer.

The goal of any Bible teacher must be to contribute to the good of the student. And the student (the hearer) must see and hear good intentions through the speaker's words, body language, and tone of voice. Words become a healing medicine from the wise only when all these moving parts are present and aligned in the dynamic.

Both participants must realize their purposes when conveyin͜ derstanding Biblical truths. Listeners must look for the truth very least, be open to receiving it. And the speaker must have a and realize they are mere carriers of the message they are trying to impart. They must always credit our heavenly Father as the author and originator of the Biblical message.

Communication is an art that can be used for good or for evil. A genuine exchange of ideas must involve both parties having an intense desire to communicate in the best possible way. This results in the building of trust and relationships. When someone no longer desires to communicate, relationships become broken and are not repaired again until communication resumes.

Words can become like a spear that can stab people or hammers that pound the words in like nails when used by evil people that desire to be intentionally hurtful to the hearer. People may intend to harm with strong or lying words when provoked, use them as defensive moves when attacked, or use them to accomplish other selfish or traitorous actions. Harm can also happen when people attempt to hide their true intentions or want to be believed by unsuspecting pawns they intend to use to further their deceptions.

Watch and guard your hearts and words! Good motives go a long way toward receiving goodwill from your audience. At the same time, look for signals of wrong motives and consider them before you take words to heart. And remember, there are times when silence transmits just as loudly and should be employed.

Considering these things, we will receive much more information from our interactions with others. In some circumstances, you can discount improper motives and still get good advice from an enemy! You will be able to understand and be understood more often. Effective communication can improve all areas of your life!

Remember to use all avenues and modes of communication properly, with appropriate attitudes for reaching those willing to understand. So, speak and listen with all your heart and mind! It is an act of sincere and steadfast love!

WEEK FIVE

DAY 1

Resilient Strongholds

If the grass is greener on the other side, maybe that's because you're not taking good care of your own grass. (Author Unknown)

Everyone then who hears these words of mine and does them will be like a wise man who built his house on the rock. (Matt 7.24)

According to the grace of God given to me, like a skilled master builder I laid a foundation, and someone else is building upon it. Let each one take care how he builds upon it. For no one can lay a foundation other than that which is laid, which is Jesus Christ. Now if anyone builds on the foundation with gold, silver, precious stones, wood, hay, straw— each one's work will become manifest, for the Day will disclose it, because it will be revealed by fire, and the fire will test what sort of work each one has done. If the work that anyone has built on the foundation survives, he will receive a reward. If anyone's work is burned up, he will suffer loss, though he himself will be saved, but only as through fire. (1 Cor 3.10–15)

Life comes with choices and trials. When a person chooses to build on the only viable foundation, which is Christ, his efforts manifest themselves in how the *building* holds up under pressure. Some endeavors may seem to hold up until a storm comes. But the foundation always has a way of revealing itself when subjected to the various trials life offers.

God and His wisdom always produce resilient strongholds. Bec͏ ͏ the foundation of Christ is always sound, its function and usefulness d when storms rage around the house. Each effort builds on the f͏ with various teachings and life choices that manifest themselves i of fruit produced by the person or the group over the long term.

Sometimes a person's dissatisfaction with his current circumstances can indicate that are building with weak materials. People can misdiagnose their situation and seek what they believe they need from the wrong place in the wrong way. In other words, they use their own proposals and methods to attain their desires rather than having spiritual, God-directed goals.

Removing yourself from difficult circumstances does not change the state of your building methods. It just moves you to a place to start the process of building and growing all over again. And typically, you will end up with the same issues from which you have previously removed yourself. The same heart produces the same results!

In keeping with the quote by the unknown author above, we must not run to places where the grass looks greener and seems easier to manage. The green grass down the street indicates someone else's good work. Our green grass is simply an indicator of our inward health or how we deal with the circumstances we find ourselves in.

All of our lawns must be managed, cut, trimmed, and cared for while considering the current climate of our circumstances. Each person is responsible for maintaining his heart and soul. There are no shortcuts to proper maintenance, and growth only comes with wisdom and assistance from God. He gives the growth!

When people learn to seek God's help, they cease to manipulate their circumstances, attitudes, and behaviors for relief. They stop whitewashing their actions to make themselves look like they are motivated by spiritual truth when their actions are born out of their desires or even fear. They become new with a new heart and make choices that build on the Rock!

Building on the foundation of Christ indicates spiritual maturity. It is a learned process that helps a person trust God more every day. Over time, people learn to make more God-centered choices. They learn to deny themselves and choose to trust and wait on God no matter the climate or circumstance.

Emotional and spiritual growth happens as we build on the only solid foundation with God-directed planning and choices, with His materials and tools. This effort produces the grass people admire as they drive by, and it motivates others to fix their own yards! Not only will these efforts withstand the storm, but they will also improve the neighborhood.

DAY 2

Powerful Seeds

Don't judge each day by the harvest you reap but by the seeds that you plant.
(Robert Louis Stevenson)

And he said, "The kingdom of God is as if a man should scatter seed on the ground. He sleeps and rises night and day, and the seed sprouts and grows; he knows not how. The earth produces by itself, first the blade, then the ear, then the full grain in the ear. But when the grain is ripe, at once he puts in the sickle, because the harvest has come." And he said, "With what can we compare the kingdom of God, or what parable shall we use for it? It is like a grain of mustard seed, which, when sown on the ground, is the smallest of all the seeds on earth, yet when it is sown it grows up and becomes larger than all the garden plants and puts out large branches, so that the birds of the air can make nests in its shade." (Mark 4.26–32)

Jesus' parables explain how God's Word will work in the hearts of men. Good seed enters the soil of the heart, and its goodness can, if allowed by the hearer, produce a root system that totally encompasses the whole heart. The growth of His Word in our hearts is like that of a healthy, well-kept plant. The way the plant grows and the healthier the plant becomes corresponds with the seed's interaction with the rocks and weeds in the heart's soil. Seeds of truth may be newly planted or decades old and still produce.

Jesus will later task the apostles with spreading the gospel of the kingdom and "watering" the seeds planted with God's Word! Of course, the seed illustration helps explain the process of God spreading truth in terms we can understand. Hearts need to be worked just like soil. The apostles would be concerned with planting and watering while God does the rest.

Jesus wants the men listening to understand how His truth works in people's hearts. Truth in a heart grows and produces in small ways until its fruits are recognizable. Growth can occur even if there is still some stony ground to work on or some stubborn weeds to pull. As time goes on, the process produces a person that is firmly planted in God's word and valuable to others as a waterer himself.

But each heart is responsible for the soil into which God's seed is planted. A good, unadulterated seed of truth can yield fruit and grow no matter when planted, if both the seed and soil are good. And the truth—the good seed—can further refine the heart.

Each person grows individually while at the same time producing fruit and offering shelter to others. Each new plant or even old tree still has to contend with weather conditions, so they must be maintained and kept free from weeds. All grow through unseen help and produce seeds that can be planted again to yield a significant increase. The power is in the seed and its Creator!

It is fascinating to study the various plants, their seeds, and how they spread. Think about a tumbleweed. It dies, breaks loose, and then rolls and spreads seed along the prairie. The palm tree drops its seed in the ocean, and it may float to faraway places and land on distant beaches only to sprout new palm trees. When grown, they will produce coconuts ready to be eaten, which can send out even more seeds. Even certain kinds of pine trees have cones that only open with the onset of a fire, which can then replenish a forest.

There is much to be learned and understood in the parables about seeds and God's Word. The quote above helps us remember that we are responsible for doing our part in the process: spreading God's truth and watering the seeds already planted. How each sown seed grows is the business of the Him who created it. And how well the soil of the heart accommodates the growth is really up to each individual person. In many ways, much of the process is still a miraculous mystery. At the same time, we can remain confident that the power is in His Word!

DAY 3

Unrecognized Warriors

If one does not know to which port one is sailing, no wind is favorable.
(Lucius Annaeus Seneca)

A man without self-control
    is like a city broken into and left without walls. (Prov 25.28)

Individuals can live without direction; and families, businesses, churches, cultures, and entire nations can also lose their way. We live in a time when some wish this for our country. There are cities where the voices of a few call for little or no law enforcement. This loud minority ridicules those who try to restore order and safety. The voices of reason are overrun by angry mobs who are allowed to exercise a complete lack of self-control!

People applaud the shameful state of affairs and seem to desire to leave our country exposed and scared. They intentionally abandon sound reason and manipulate circumstances to obtain power and control. The onlookers are attacked using the same age-old tactics and well-worn formula: tear down the agreed-upon walls, boundaries, and tenets of belief, then spread fear and confusion. Take away and destroy all hope.

In this great "war game," those with nefarious motives use mobs formed of the untaught. They enlist soldiers without direction and self-control and use them to oppose those who look to God for direction. This dynamic happens in any realm, large or small, where people seek power. However, godly people know God has already won the ultimate war against any who oppose Him. Now each person just has to choose a side!

Everyone must work out their side in the battle. Each person learns and accepts the truth and wins or serves as a pawn for the other side. Those on the winning side already see the result of the endgame. Fear does not work on them, and they never lose hope because it follows them into eternity. They have God on their side.

Christians have the ultimate sovereign ruler working things out so they can continue overcoming them no matter the circumstances. God uses unrecognized warriors and unsung heroes to thwart the enemy's attempts. He develops them through His Word and the battles themselves.

The real work in this world is to help all men choose the side that has already won! Then when the next battle begins in their life, they too can read the direction of the wind and keep the city walls sound. They can operate safely within them without being deceived!

DAY 4

Dressing for Success

You need to learn how to select your thoughts just the same way you select your clothes every day. This is a power you can cultivate. (Elizabeth Gilbert)

The night is far gone; the day is at hand. So then let us cast off the works of darkness and put on the armor of light. Let us walk properly as in the daytime, not in orgies and drunkenness, not in sexual immorality and sensuality, not in quarreling and jealousy. But put on the Lord Jesus Christ, and make no provision for the flesh, to gratify its desires. (Rom 13.12–14)

The first step toward conscience healing is to realize that we have control of our thoughts and mind as opposed to being a victim of circumstance. We all must choose to have a mind set on the flesh (ourselves) or the Spirit (God). This choice will determine if our lives will be filled with the works of the flesh or the fruit of the Spirit. It all starts with where we allow our minds to wander and where we allow our feet to travel.

Christians should spend all this life learning how to trust and obey or actually trusting and obeying! When someone is young, they may feel they have time on their hands and currency to spend. They think they know how to operate and will learn how to do things themselves. But as people age and grow wiser, they become more aware and accustomed to how this life really works. It becomes readily apparent that we humans are nothing without the grace of God and the love of Jesus. Each one is no more than a little child needing a faithful, Heavenly Father.

Your mindset is *put on* every day, just like your clothes. And what thoughts a person chooses to wear can be easily seen. They may be well fitting and appropriate or gaudy. They may be traditional or reflect a rebellious heart. They may be spiritually motivated or fleshly. They may be age, time, and place appropriate or not. They may reflect modesty or an invitation to immorality. They may help someone blend in or stand out. They will be intended to cure or intended to hurt. And they may be either self-righteous or God directed!

Everyone chooses all day, every day, what they will think about and do. Only some people realize it! Let us be ever mindful. If one does not see themselves as a learner looking up to a caring savior for direction, they will be lost. And they will never find their way to true faith because they will be too wrapped up in themselves *to dress for success*.

DAY 5

Our Unguarded Selves

Surely what a man does when he is taken off his guard is the best evidence for what sort of man he is. (C.S. Lewis)

You brood of vipers! How can you speak good, when you are evil? For out of the abundance of the heart the mouth speaks. The good person out of his good treasure brings forth good, and the evil person out of his evil treasure brings forth evil. I tell you, on the day of judgment people will give account for every careless word they speak, for by your words you will be justified, and by your words you will be condemned. (Matt 12.34–37)

When speaking to the Pharisees, Jesus tried to get them to understand the same concept that C.S. Lewis emphasizes above. He desired much more than to control their behavior. He wanted a true inward change. On the outside, they were dressed in religious garb; on the inside they were proud, malicious, cunning, and insincere!

Jesus desires the kind of change people can only accomplish with a whole-hearted desire to be like Him. It results in people saturating their hearts and minds with His Word. It is a change that originates from the inside out and shines in their actions and words.

Jesus was harsh with the Pharisees because they represented the most dangerous kind of error. They believed and represented themselves to be righteous when they were not! He explains how they were to check their unguarded words to see who they were. Christians should perform the same test.

How do we react to things when they are challenging or unexpected? Is our speech God-directed? Do careless words or actions emerge when we are under stress? What comes out of our mouths when we leave ourselves unguarded? Do we use an accusing or haughty tone when speaking to others? Whose welfare do we consider first? What makes us sad, mad, or happy? What makes us laugh? How we respond when caught off guard reveals our hearts!

Jesus says we will all be judged and justified by our unguarded and careless words, because these words reveal what is actually inside us. The words that overflow unintentionally from a heart not focused toward God represent who we are and what is really inside us! Let us all be aware and allow God to change our hearts. Let our words and actions be from a heart filled with godly love and not with the unrighteous thinking of the world!

WEEK SIX

DAY 1

Wait on the Lord

The chief cause of failure and unhappiness is trading what you want most for what you want right now. (Zig Ziglar)

Wait for the LORD;
*   be strong, and let your heart take courage;*
*   wait for the LORD!* (Ps 27.14)

We all hate to wait, and we no longer need wait for much of anything. If you have Amazon Prime and live near a distribution center, you can order something from your home and have it arrive that day. You think of what you want, and with a few clicks, it is on your doorstep. So much for saving up for a favored gift over time. Money is spent on the trivial before taking time to think or dream of something more significant.

We no longer must wait until the following week to find out what happens on our favorite TV show. Now people binge-watch. Finding a show that is fit to watch is nearly impossible now. Maybe it always has been. I recently watched some of the old "classic" shows and found that they were more propaganda-like than I was aware of at the time. Try watching something like *The Real McCoys* with Walter Brennan. The political overtones will shock you!

Young children need to realize the value of learning to wait. One of my grandchildren was complaining because their younger brother did not have to wait as long as he did to do something he thought was fun. He does not know it yet, but that lesson of waiting will be very valuable for him long after the joy of whatever he waited for fades.

We are impatient because few societal norms today teach us to wait for the right things, let alone wait on the Lord or reach forward to a spiritual house in eternity. We must look beyond this world to the Lord's teaching to learn these lessons. If we use God's Word to balance the fast pace of our time with a hefty dose of self-sacrifice, thanksgiving, and patience, we may learn how to choose what is good over what is immediately available. Then glory goes to God as His wisdom is seen in our character, which should always mirror the nature of Christ.

Parents must be inventive in teaching these lessons without appearing too petty and arbitrary. One way is to match up long-earned accomplishments with age-appropriate rewards. We can provide opportunities to earn money for something desirable and profitable, then make a big deal when the child saves the money and buys the item for himself. But if your efforts to teach the lesson seem unfair or without value when they reach a milestone, they may not see your actions as being for their good.

I heard an older man tell a story from his youth. He wanted some old-fashioned knickers one Christmas and cowboy boots the next. So, for the third Christmas, he got both, and his parents made him wear them together on his first day of high school. After all, he asked for them, hadn't he? How could he be so ungrateful now and not want to wear them? The experience made him resent his parents many years after the incident.

Parenting is extremely hard; even when someone gives it their best shot, it may not work out as they intend. Make sure you are not pushing on a child what you think they should want. Making them wait for something in which they have no interest accomplishes nothing! And giving the gift past the time for its proper use may even be worse than not giving it at all!

Always remember what you are attempting to teach! A quote by Mary Shelley says, "No man chooses evil because it is evil; he only mistakes it for happiness." You want your child to learn to sacrifice the fleeting physical pleasures of the here and now for a greater spiritual reward in the future! Keeping that goal in mind will influence how we teach godly patience to our children. And, as always, modeling it yourself works wonders for their development. We must continually discipline ourselves to learn to wait!

DAY 2

Seeing Ourselves Third

It never hurts to think too highly of a person; often they become ennobled and act better because of it. (Nelson Mandela)

For when dreams increase and words grow many, there is vanity; but God is the one you must fear. If you see in a province the oppression of the poor and the violation of justice and righteousness, do not be amazed at the matter, for the high official is watched by a higher, and there are yet higher ones over them. (Ecc 5.7–8)

I heard a story, credited to Homer Hailey, once told about a high school graduation speech. The speaker spoke of his college roommate, who put a plaque on his wall that read, "I am third." In their last semester, the speaker finally decided to ask his roommate about the quote's meaning. He had recognized the exceptional character of his friend with the plaque throughout their college years. The young man's answer was simple, "It means God is first, everyone else is second, and I am third." This was how this young man saw himself!

When people understand their place in relation to others and treat them accordingly, it glorifies God and encourages others to be more noble in their responses. If, in our minds, we put God first, we will not be fearful of the chaos around us, no matter its origin. When we understand that love never fails, we will be able to act as 1 Corinthians 13.4–7 directs:

> Love is patient and kind; love does not envy or boast; it is not arrogant or rude. It does not insist on its own way; it is not irritable or resentful; it does not rejoice at wrongdoing, but rejoices with the truth. Love bears all things, believes all things, hopes all things, endures all things.

And when we cannot see someone's proper motivation, the way to deal with them is to assume the best, as the quote from Nelson Mandela advocates. Anyone can show love by choosing to treat others properly. By doing so, we can promote civility or expose those with selfish motivations.

When someone lovingly assumes the best of another, it encourages the person to act on their expectations. That sure could help in our time. And actually, God expects us to see ourselves as "third." It would help all of us to have a plaque that reminds us of this every day.

DAY 3

For His Good Purpose

For you will certainly carry out God's purpose, however you act, but it makes a difference to you whether you serve like Judas or like John. (C.S. Lewis)

So Judas, having procured a band of soldiers and some officers from the chief priests and the Pharisees, went there with lanterns and torches and weapons. (John 18.3)

God, in His infinite wisdom, allows everyone to have free will. And he can always use each person's choices to work His purpose. In my mind, God's omnipotent orchestration in the affairs of man has always been the greatest evidence of His power and faithfulness. It anchors my faith. It allows me to attempt hard things knowing God can use even my failures!

Even though God does not control people like robots, He can still work His purpose using their own choices. He used an unfaithful Israelite nation to bring Christ into the world. He used the corrupt Jewish leadership and a weak Roman governor to have Jesus put to death. Throughout history, God has used all kinds of people to accomplish His predetermined scheme of redemption. He used good hearts, dishonest hearts, hardened hearts, Jews and Gentiles, the faithful and faithless, good nations and evil nations, all to work his Will!

Oh, what power and wisdom! God still employs His providence today to accomplish His purposes and ensure all have an opportunity to learn and repent. And He does these things, asking His people to trust Him, even while His unrevealed work remains a mystery.

Judas is an excellent example of how God uses a person who makes poor choices. Jesus must have chosen Judas while knowing he had a heart that could betray Him. His weaknesses were likely already evident in his character. Jesus did not lose any of the others He chose. Each apostle did flee and forsake Him, but all of them repented—all but Judas. Judas gave up in his self-pity and lost hope.

In contrast, John seemed to have had the Lord's servant-heart from the beginning. And the more he learned, the more like Christ he became. God can use each of us to work His good, but we will determine our eternal destiny by our own heart's choices and our willingness to repent, align with the truth, and take on the character of God.

People do not know how God is working unless He has revealed it. But if you look back on your life, it is not hard to see how God has used your choices in inexplicable ways. Everyone can marvel at what they see with their spiritual eyes as they look back on history, in their own lives, and in the lives of others.

DAY 4

Choosing Habits

Active habits are strengthened by repetition but passive ones are weakened. The more often he feels without acting, the less he will be able ever to act, and, in the long run, the less he will be able to feel. (C.S. Lewis)

They have healed the wound of my people lightly,
  saying, "Peace, peace,"
  when there is no peace.
Were they ashamed when they committed abomination?
  No, they were not at all ashamed;
  they did not know how to blush.
Therefore they shall fall among the fallen;
  when I punish them, they shall be overthrown,
says the LORD. (Jer 8.11–12)

Habits can either give one strength or lead to their downfall. When someone practices something repeatedly, with choice and intent, like attending worship, it strengthens their faithfulness. But if they go to services for any other reason, their action may stifle something deep inside with simmering resentment. Such a process can lead people to a state of being lukewarm. C.S. Lewis explained the process poignantly above.

Habits someone cherishes are tough to give up, but those formed with no concrete conviction can also lead to compromise and complacency. They may lead to a lack of fervor, or worse, a lack of being able to blush! That is why we must praise good habits, and bad ones take so much effort to expunge. They both reflect attitudes of the heart.

Good habits show conviction, faith, and effort. Bad ones show weakness and an inability to act out of conviction. Many habits can form without a strong underlying belief. Examining ourselves means examining our habits and their origin, purpose, and intent. We need to employ good habits by choice to further our faith. And a person only takes on new spiritual habits by an act of their will.

If someone does not practice habits by their own choice, their actions may not ever come to reflect their true motivations. Considering this in the context of worship service attendance, it may not be so shocking that some teenagers fall away, and it becomes easier to explain lackadaisical attendance. The true work of parents is to help children make habits of service by their own choice!

Christians should view all teachings in this light. Everyone wants to ensure their choices are their own and not predicated on incentives or punishments. Both have a place in discipline to create good personal and work habits in the short term when someone is first introduced to something new. But they do not work in the long term to develop individual stability.

C.S. Lewis warned that acting without forethought will lead to a lack of ability to feel or the inability to be inwardly touched. At that point, a conscience will sear and cease to be a weapon in a person's arsenal to guide them toward reconciliation with God. One either has to use it or lose it! They are not allowed to abuse it. So as Joshua said to the Israelites, choose you this day whom you will serve, and choose to develop habits to enforce the right choice!

DAY 5

Know Enough to Know

By steadfast love and faithfulness iniquity is atoned for,
and by the fear of the Lord one turns away from evil. (Prov 16.6)

Because they hated knowledge
and did not choose the fear of the LORD,
would have none of my counsel
and despised all my reproof,

therefore they shall eat the fruit of their way,
  and have their fill of their own devices.
For the simple are killed by their turning away,
  and the complacency of fools destroys them;
but whoever listens to me will dwell secure
  and will be at ease, without dread of disaster. (Prov 1.29–33)

The wisdom in Proverbs helps everyone live this daily life, and we should devote time to meditate on and digest the truisms within. The point is that those who choose God's wisdom will be guided more safely in their decisions, especially in their emotional and spiritual wellbeing. They will navigate difficulties wisely while avoiding major disasters of their own making.

On the other hand, those who want to make their way without direction or counsel from God will fall into the traps laid by Satan. Proverbs addresses many pitfalls like wine, poor choices in friends, materialism, and carnal pleasure. After making such decisions, some may turn to God for help while also enduring some of the consequences of their former choices.

These individuals can still find redemption from the eternal consequences of poor choices through mercy and truth, but sometimes the earthly ramifications of youthful foolishness can last a lifetime. That is why, before a person fully understands the truth in their early years, it is vital to have good direction and be wise enough to follow it. Godly choices help protect anyone at any age, but youth are the most vulnerable, primarily because their understanding is so limited.

The good news is that anyone can choose wisdom and take advantage of Christ's sacrifice at any point in their lives. They can also be willing to share that same mercy and truth with others while not taking one step that does not consider the fear and reverence of the Lord! They know enough to know they do not have all the answers, but trust God's Word and the godly parents and teachers attempting to direct them.

But there is one thing that even a wise person cannot do—they cannot always make others choose wisely! They can teach, plead, and discipline, but the teacher must eventually allow others to make their own choices. Otherwise, the learner may never understand the truth or appreciate God's mercy so that they "fear the Lord" and seek His safety and quiet rest in their own lives!

Let us always remember that the avenue of prayer is afforded to all to beseech God for help in such matters! He can provide opportunities for learning and repentance without interfering with a person's free will! And when people are not asking for help, God may highlight opportunities for repentance with judgments that have the ultimate end of providing everyone the hope of salvation. And even in times of judgment, the righteous will be comforted by their faith, trust, and fear of the Lord.

WEEK SEVEN

DAY 1

Seeds of Learning

Sometimes you will never know the value of a moment, until it becomes a memory. (Dr. Seuss)

You shall therefore lay up these words of mine in your heart and in your soul, and you shall bind them as a sign on your hand, and they shall be as frontlets between your eyes. You shall teach them to your children, talking of them when you are sitting in your house, and when you are walking by the way, and when you lie down, and when you rise. You shall write them on the doorposts of your house and on your gates, that your days and the days of your children may be multiplied in the land that the LORD swore to your fathers to give them, as long as the heavens are above the earth. (Deut 11.18–21)

The quote by Dr. Seuss reminds me of something I learned from one of my mentors years ago about training in the work environment. She said you must find ways to capture your training efforts so they can be pulled out and revisited later, like making small cheat sheets that people can use to recall information or remember how to perform a new task. These simple techniques help the learner remember long after the teaching is over.

To extend that training to teach others, a person has to develop ways to push them forward so others can use them over and over again. This way, the principles continue their usefulness long past the efforts you initially put forth in a class. And others can use them again later or even add to them.

My mentor's point was that you need to think about future use as you prepare your material, instead of leaving it up to chance that the information will be remembered and shared. Some teachers or famous people are quoted long past their time in this life. But because what they said was written down, it is still relevant because somebody captured it in a way that would touch others on subjects that are always relevant. Someone else can now use it as an illustration and share the knowledge it contains.

We can capture our work in organized ways so that others can find and use it again. Put main points on refrigerator magnets, use social media to share information others may be interested in, share appropriate websites, or put your originals in church library files. You get the idea.

Teachers in the church environment, along with trainers for the work and school setting, spend hours creating their learning activities. These valuable servants should all find ways to push these efforts forward for others to use and access. They can be seeds of learning at some other time, located in many places by multiple people. We must move these valuable activities into the future for continued use!

Whoever develops material, writes something, decides to make handouts, or puts an article in their local church bulletin does not always see how it would be possible for someone to find and share it again. It may be helpful to an untold number of people, even in another century. I remember seeing old church bulletins with helpful information belonging to my husband's grandmother!

The verse in Deuteronomy explains something else about how people learn. God directs the Israelites to keep all His teaching before everyone's eyes. He directs them to expose themselves and their children repeatedly and consistently to His statutes. Whenever one is repetitiously using a skill or a habit, they remember how to do it. They forget and lose their ability when they stop doing anything correctly.

Hopefully, these training tips can help someone today! And maybe, if shared, they can help someone tomorrow. My mentor's advice has remained with me whenever I train or teach. And God's directive to the Israelites is still sound and relevant today!

DAY 2

Not of This World

The more objects you set your heart upon, the more thorns there are to tear your peace of mind to shreds. (Charles Spurgeon)

Ahaz was twenty years old when he began to reign, and he reigned sixteen years in Jerusalem. And he did not do what was right in the eyes of the LORD, as his father David had done, but he walked in the ways of the kings of Israel. He even made metal images for the Baals, and he made offerings in the Valley of the Son of Hinnom and burned his sons as an offering, according to the abominations of the nations whom the LORD drove out before the people of Israel. And he sacrificed and made offerings on the high places and on the hills and under every green tree ...

So Tiglath-pileser king of Assyria came against him and afflicted him instead of strengthening him. For Ahaz took a portion from the house of the LORD and the house of the king and of the princes, and gave tribute to the king of Assyria, but it did not help him.

In the time of his distress he became yet more faithless to the LORD—this same King Ahaz. For he sacrificed to the gods of Damascus that had defeated him and said, "Because the gods of the kings of Syria helped them, I will sacrifice to them that they may help me." But they were the ruin of him and of all Israel. And Ahaz gathered together the vessels of the house of God and cut in pieces the vessels of the house of God, and he shut up the doors of the house of the LORD, and he made himself altars in every corner of Jerusalem. In every city of Judah he made high places to make offerings to other gods, provoking to anger the LORD, the God of his fathers. (2 Chron 28.1–4, 20–25)

Ahaz was one of the most wicked kings of Judah. It was not that he did not have access to the truth because he did. But he chose to worship anything and everything other than God. He even sacrificed his children on the altar of foreign gods and worshiped the gods of his enemies! People have a hard time understanding idolatry today. It may be because the concept of worship is so misunderstood. But there are still idols today, and all men "worship" something.

Anything can become an idol to anyone when they take things out of their proper use and rightful place as designated by the God of heaven and earth. When people elevate themselves, their work, relationships, sports, hobbies, or anything else so that it becomes more important to them than God, these become the idols they worship. And they know it has become their idol when they allow it to have preeminence.

When a person refuses to defer to God because of pride, youthful ignorance, or stubbornness, the actions that follow always cause havoc and destruction to themselves and anyone in their path. We all watch this play out on the stage of life every day. Do not give in to it! Instead, choose to be like King David, who filled his heart with a great desire to do what was right. He sometimes failed to do so, but he always held fast to the fact that God was always the only One to follow. When he did fall, David got up and got right with God every time.

Suppose all would arm themselves for this battle for their mind with God's truth, forsaking all other idols and returning to the proper use of things for their God-directed purpose. It would solve the personal, family, community, and social problems of our day! Everyone has power over themselves and, sometimes, over others. And when we use it properly, God is glorified. Though we watch the opposite play out in front of our eyes every day, let each of us choose to be "not of this world!"

DAY 3

The Same Choice

One small positive thought in the morning can change your whole day. (Author Unknown)

Take care, brothers, lest there be in any of you an evil, unbelieving heart, leading you to fall away from the living God. But exhort one another every day, as long as it is called "today," that none of you may be hardened by the deceitfulness of sin. For we have come to share in Christ, if indeed we hold our original confidence firm to the end. As it is said,

"Today, if you hear his voice,
  do not harden your hearts as in the rebellion." (Heb 3.10–15)

These verses in Hebrew lay out the daily battle of the Christian. Every day, we must see ourselves faced with the same choice given to the Israelites when God sent spies into the promised land. The spies decided to advise on whether to enter and take possession of the land, while the Israelites determined whether to believe in the faithful promises of God.

We can decide to believe God or allow deceitfulness dressed up like impossibility, difficulty, and discouragement to defeat us before we start. Will we be faithless, fearful, complaining, ungrateful, and self-motivated, exposing hard hearts like the ten spies and the complaining people after that? Or will we be like Joshua and Caleb, who chose to be faithful, fearless, encouraging, and grateful, giving glory to our Lord?

We must have the hearts of Joshua and Caleb! Let us all choose each day whom we will serve and show it in how we interact with the circumstances and opportunities in our daily lives! Let us encourage and help all those in our God-given spheres of influence!

DAY 4

Lifelong Learners

Until I learned to trust, I never learned to pray.
And I did not learn to fully trust till sorrows came my way.

Until I felt my weakness, His strength I never knew;
Nor dreamed till I was stricken, that He could see me through.

Who deepest drinks of sorrow, drinks deepest too of grace;
He sends the storm so He Himself can be our hiding place.

His heart, that seeks our highest good, knows well when things annoy;
We would not long for heaven, if earth held only joy. (Hayden Kisamore Terri)

Finally, brothers, whatever is true, whatever is honorable, whatever is just, whatever is pure, whatever is lovely, whatever is commendable, if there is any excellence, if there is anything worthy of praise, think about these things. What you have learned and received and heard and seen in me—practice these things, and the God of peace will be with you. (Phil 4.8–9)

There are so many learning opportunities that God has put in our lives. I always tell people that I did not understand faith until I had to let my children drive alone. I say it in jest, but I did not understand the concept of letting go and letting God take care of something before my children drove! I think it's because I did not comprehend what having or allowing free will meant.

The presence of sin dictates there will be dangers. And God must allow mankind to be exposed to the dangers if one is to learn. If people are ever to understand anything about faith and trust, they will need to engage in the risky business of striving to overcome evil. And if one's choice to obey is to have any real advantage for them, they must realize the consequences of disobedience and obedience!

We all have our own stories corresponding to each of the elements in the poem by Ms. Kisamore. The magnitude of the stresses of life may differ, and the opportunities for learning them may vary, but the lessons we must learn are the same. Some people take discipline early and learn quickly, while others oppose God's discipline and learn the hard way. Unfortunately, some will oppose God throughout their lives and never learn.

Let us all learn to value God's training and discipline. Let the quality of our learning be stellar! Let us all use this day and every day that follows to be lifelong learners of truth.

DAY 5

It Is Possible

The most courageous decision that you can make each day is to be in a good mood! (Voltaire)

The heart of the wise makes his speech judicious
*   and adds persuasiveness to his lips.*
Gracious words are like a honeycomb,
*   sweetness to the soul and health to the body.* (Prov 16.23–24)

Every day, every person chooses how they will respond to life. How will they react to the issues of the day, approach difficulties and setbacks, and present themselves to others? Will they be surly or encouraging? Will they be victims or victors? Will they control their emotions or react with irritation and frustration to every little thing that goes against their preferred path?

Everyone's actions and words display the state of their mind and heart! God expects His children to not only control their emotions but also learn to manufacture and direct them. He commands His people to love their brethren *and* their enemies. And if God demands these things from His children, it follows that they can obey!

If you want to help yourself and others grow emotionally, teach people that it is possible to control themselves—their actions and emotions. It is hard work, but this knowledge helps people realize they are free to respond to life as they choose. We are not merely pawns in the game of life.

We can create proper emotions by practicing the thoughts and actions that produce them. You may first have to "fake it till you make it." But anyone can do it with the proper desire and effort. People can choose their mood in the same way.

We can all deal with life one day at a time. And if need be, we can break it up into hours or minutes when necessary. When pain, loss, or persecution come, and emotions are heightened, we may have to focus our minds on the smaller measurements. Control your mind and heart as life comes to you and make of it something good no matter the immediate circumstance!

So let us all choose this day to speak truth, be wise, and spread sweetness and healing as we go through the day! Tomorrow will have its own trouble. And when tomorrow becomes today, then you will deal with it then!

WEEK EIGHT

DAY 1

Hear His Whispers

God whispers to us in our pleasures, speaks in our conscience, but shouts in our pains: it is his megaphone to rouse a deaf world. (C.S. Lewis)

The nations rage, the kingdoms totter;
*   he utters his voice, the earth melts.*
The LORD of hosts is with us;
*   the God of Jacob is our fortress. Selah*

Come, behold the works of the LORD,
*   how he has brought desolations on the earth.*
He makes wars cease to the end of the earth;
*   he breaks the bow and shatters the spear;*
*   he burns the chariots with fire.*

"Be still, and know that I am God.
*   I will be exalted among the nations,*
*   I will be exalted in the earth!"*
The LORD of hosts is with us;
*   the God of Jacob is our fortress. Selah (Psa 46.6–11)*

A phrase found repeatedly in the Old Law is, "Then they will know that I am the Lord." God reveals the motives for His works and judgments—to know Him! As we recognize God's power at work around us, in our lives or in the world, He presents us with a choice to attribute what we see to a grand designer or chance.

When we experience pleasure where God has placed it, we can "hear" His whispers in the blessings. When life gets us down, it should cause us to seek Him in our pain. These are opportunities to learn to know God. As C.S. Lewis says, this is how God speaks to us in whispers and shouts.

God has put Himself in little things. He is in a beautiful sunset, a loving spouse, a forgiving heart, lilies and roses, in mountain vistas and the rolling hills. He is in industrious ants, the stars, cool breezes on a hot day, smiling children, the feelings for our pets, or the fondness for bird watching. Anything that is wholesome and brings pleasure should cause us to consider the existence of the Giver of all good things.

God also supplies each person with an innate understanding of right and wrong on some level. We can feel it when we work against what we know is right. The conscience can help people see God or cause anger and resentment and even produce a victim mentality that blames all manner of things for the innate feelings they wish to deny. These manifest in hostility towards a parent or anyone who disagrees with the choice to satisfy some fleshly desire. The innocent targets will likely get a regular tongue-lashing by those playing the age-old blame game.

It seems God speaks to us the loudest when we are emotionally hurt because of injustice, sin, or just the way the world works. But when we are consumed with loss, we also have a chance to look to God. When we come face to face with injury, hate, jealousy, or are persecuted for no good reason, we can respond as God would direct or react as all others of this world do. Even when we suffer life-long consequences from the missteps of ourselves and others due to simple ignorance or inadequacies, we can wallow in our bitterness and pain or live for God.

Sometimes debilitating or painful instances can wear us down, but we need to learn to get back up. Or when we see others suffer and it screams that there must be something better than all this chaos, we can believe there is, or we can lose hope. Surely there is more to life than what we experience in a world filled with lust, greed, and sin. And those who know that God is know there is something better. All others are still searching for God in the wrong places or have just plain given up. Where are you?

Have you listened to God's voice, soft or loud, that hints of something greater to strive for? Do you stand for truth and principle or cave to pressure? Do you submit to evil or rebel against it? Do you choose to see or stay blinded?

God wants so much for all men everywhere to see Him and to seek His will, to learn His purpose, and to experience His great love. He has revealed Himself in His Son. And His character and teaching reveal it all! Jesus is His Name.

DAY 2

The Battles Within

There is a battle going on. Keep your eyes open and the sword sharp! (Author Unknown)

For we do not wrestle against flesh and blood, but against the rulers, against the authorities, against the cosmic powers over this present darkness, against the spiritual forces of evil in the heavenly places. (Eph 6.12)

We all fight within our minds against the forces that Satan brings to bear while we travel through his territory in the world. Simply understanding what we fight every day is much of the battle. We oppose the unfruitful world of darkness! We fight frustration, irritation, false religion, evil desires, governmental persecution, financial pressure, family difficulties, and the list goes on.

John reminds us that "all that is in the world—the desires of the flesh and the desires of the eyes and pride of life—is not from the Father but is from the world" (1 John 2.16). But if we use the written Word and the life of Jesus as our guide, we can enter a heavenly, spiritual realm where there is safety. We then can reflect Christ to the world. We are always willing and able to explain to anyone who asks where our hope and purpose reside.

We do not wage war with personal attacks against others. Instead, our positive impact on the world is a byproduct of winning personal battles within ourselves. They are fought one false idea at a time. We can identify threats, see the fallacy in worldly wisdom, and control ourselves and our thinking. We do not march against the people in Satan's army; rather, we fight to ensure Satan cannot use us for his cause. And by doing so, we become soldiers in the army of the Lord, ready for Him to use us as He sees fit!

•

DAY 3

Authorized Changes

If the plan doesn't work, change the plan, but never the goal.
(Author Unknown)

Has a nation changed its gods,
even though they are no gods?
But my people have changed their glory
for that which does not profit.
Be appalled, O heavens, at this;
be shocked, be utterly desolate,
declares the Lord,
for my people have committed two evils:
they have forsaken me,
the fountain of living waters,
and hewed out cisterns for themselves,
broken cisterns that can hold no water. (Jer 2.11–13)

Throughout history, there have always been monumental changes due to technological advancement. People from all different places and times make decisions about, evaluate the viability of, and place a value on the changes they experience in their lifetime. But what standards do we use to make those decisions?

William Draves and Julie Coats book *Nine Shift: Work, Life and Education in the 21ˢᵗ century* compares the invention of the car at the beginning of the 20ᵗʰ century to the techonolical changes with computers and the internet in this century. The book says the invention of the car transformed how we transported everything from people to goods. But it also necessitated all sorts of new regulations for traffic laws. Driving altered how far apart cities were because the buggy could only go so far so towns were closer together. The car made it possible for towns to be farther apart. This is demonstrated by all the abandoned Opera Houses in the Midwest. It also created a need for gas stations, repair shops, and mechanics, and even gave rise to the auto racing industry. A massive change happened again at the turn of the twenty-first century with the invention of the computer, cell phones, and smart watches!

Think about all that change for a minute. The more radical a change is, the more impactful it is on other elements of the preexisting systems. It may add or eliminate services. Some people hold on too long to the old ways, necessitating services for those operating in the old and new paradigms.

People refuse to embrace technological changes for various reasons. A big one is that it makes them feel uninformed or irrelevant. There are always unintended or unforeseen consequences whenever a society makes a change. And there are always those lobbying for their own preferences. Change is usually a mess, for a while at least.

But overall, man's personal, societal, and all-important spiritual needs have not changed. Consider the points from the verses above about the unlawful changes in ancient times. Though not technological, we see the Israelite society digress by adopting evil practices. God establishes the principles we must remember to live by as we encounter times of societal change. We never want to lose our underlying purpose of serving Him in the adoption of new things. We are never to leave God's purpose behind.

Technological change is not bad in itself but can become so if used for greed, to disenfranchise people, or to elevate man and his supposed genius. People can begin to believe too highly in themselves. We must examine each potential change in technology for the way it services the underlying needs of the people and the values it represents. The same is true as new businesses take shape or change their underlying practices. First and foremost, we must use anything we adopt with the godly principles that He has directed man to maintain from the very beginning.

The goal must always be glorifying God in everything we say and do. Anything we adopt must work to help us accomplish that plan. We must be able to distinguish the difference between changes designed for progress and changes intended to deny God.

And we cannot ever make things holy that have been unauthorized by God in the first place. They cannot be set apart for His use in any way! At the same time, altering some of our behaviors to accommodate changes in the surrounding environment is not unholy. You just must figure out how the changes you are experiencing can be utilized to God's glory!

DAY 4

Remembers

We become like what we focus upon. Fix your eyes upon Christ and be conformed into His image. (Steven J. Larson)

This is now the second letter that I am writing to you, beloved. In both of them I am stirring up your sincere mind by way of reminder, that you should remember the predictions of the holy prophets and the commandment of the Lord and Savior through your apostles, knowing this first of all, that scoffers will come in the last days with scoffing, following their own sinful desires. They will say, "Where is the promise of his coming? For ever since the fathers fell asleep, all things are continuing as they were from the beginning of creation." For they deliberately overlook this fact, that the heavens existed long ago, and the earth was formed out of water and through water by the word of God, and that by means of these the world that then existed was deluged with water and perished. But by the same word the heavens and earth that now exist are stored up for fire, being kept until the day of judgment and destruction of the ungodly. (2 Pet 3.1–7)

Anyone with access to a Bible can learn God's plan of salvation. But without the repetitive reminders from His Word, those who scoff about the truth can get a foothold with weak Christians. These mockers intentionally reject any truth presented to them and deliberately overlook anything about the truth they previously knew. The world draws away those who do not stay grounded and causes them to forget. Each person is either going towards God or moving away from Him.

Peter stirs up Christians about things they already know but need to keep at the forefront of their minds. The repetition of truth is life-altering and transformative to a person with an honest heart. It keeps them focused on the truthful things that really matter!

This "reminding" process insulates God's children from the scoffers and mockers. Remembering is vital. Christians are to remember each first day of the week and the blood sacrifice of Jesus that saves them and restores their life. Peter tells his readers to remember what the prophets taught, those mouthpieces of God Almighty during the Old Testament period. They were also to remember the commandments of the Lord made by the apostles sent to teach and explain the gospel message!

I first heard this concept expressed as, "Whatever you are repetitiously exposed to, you are transformed by." The thing is, we all choose what we are repetitiously exposed to. Knowing how this works, how careful are we about what we allow into our minds? And then, do we determine what is right based on how we see it through lenses conditioned by the world?

The reason why focusing on Christ works is because He is the embodiment of godly living. Most of what we expose ourselves to in the world is orchestrated by the great enemy of God. Let us not be tricked into following along. We must remember that an end is coming:

> Since all these things are thus to be dissolved, what sort of people ought you to be in lives of holiness and godliness, waiting for and hastening the coming of the day of God, because of which the heavens will be set on fire and dissolved, and the heavenly bodies will melt as they burn! But according to his promise we are waiting for new heavens and a new earth in which righteousness dwells. Therefore, beloved, since you are waiting for these, be diligent to be found by him without spot or blemish, and at peace. (2 Pet 3.11–14)

Those who remember eagerly await the coming of the Lord. The "re-memberers" always try their very best to be holy and at peace no matter the circumstances. How do you think the church of our Lord, established centuries ago, is doing today? If you think there could be improvements, let us start with ourselves, and remember!

DAY 5

While We Wait

Sometimes, it is not about the answer to prayer. It is what you learn while you are waiting for the answer. (Author Unknown)

Be still before the LORD and wait patiently for him;
fret not yourself over the one who prospers in his way,
over the man who carries out evil devices!
Refrain from anger, and forsake wrath!
Fret not yourself; it tends only to evil.

For the evildoers shall be cut off,
but those who wait for the LORD shall inherit the land. (Psa 37.7–9)

When I was younger, I remember feeling the need for instant gratification for whatever I wanted help with. I wanted it to be taken care of right then! But complicated things like church issues, family problems, and the enduring consequences of life choices cannot have rushed solutions, no matter how uncomfortable the waiting process is.

One of the hardest lessons to learn or teach is how to wait. We look at situations and feel as if consequences for all the actions of ourselves and others will come swiftly, and then they do not. While we wait for the Lord to answer our prayers, He works out what is spiritually best for everyone involved.

Through this process of waiting on the Lord, we learn not to worry about whatever we give Him. Sometimes, maybe even years later, we look back and see what He accomplished in so many lives, and we marvel at how little we knew even about what we were asking. We learn not to try to control people or situations but to let them play out and deal righteously with whatever consequences come to bear.

Looking back, I cannot help but thank God for making me wait. At the moment, it seems it takes time we do not have. But in all the waiting, we learn to trust and are enlightened about how to view discipline, difficulties, blessings, and so much more. Let us all be strong, take courage, and wait daily on the Lord!

WEEK NINE

DAY 1

Recognizing the Tramplers

You can never win an argument with a negative person. They only hear what suits them and listen only to respond. (Michael P. Watson)

Do not give dogs what is holy, and do not throw your pearls before pigs, lest they trample them underfoot and turn to attack you. (Matt 7.6)

In my lifetime, I cannot remember when intellectual dishonesty and hypocrisy were more on display in the public square than they are today. God expects Christians to try their best to inform, encourage, and exhibit godly living to those they encounter. But in His first sermon Jesus warns His audience that there will be people who do not want to hear the Word.

His language may take us aback because there is so little tolerance for plain talk these days. Jesus is not calling people dogs or pigs. He describes worldly people who do not want to know the truth. These people do not appreciate its value. They have hearts that are so negative and turned off by the truth that it becomes a waste of energy and even a danger to try to reach them.

Sometimes, the most negative people we deal with like to see themselves as righteous, while they are deceivers. They have already made up their minds. They want to protect themselves instead of helping others and strive to get what they want at all costs. Jesus warns that they can be very dangerous.

Of course, we should be willing to help anyone, but those who trample the truth will not be receptive to it. A Christian is better off leaving them alone than risking getting their hand bit off! We should be able to recognize these tramplers and not present that which is holy to them. Let us spend our valuable time teaching those who want the truth and salvation!

DAY 2

A Spiritual Perspective

May you approach this season with gratitude and a deeply rooted hope that every day will teach you something that is an integral part of your growth. (Morgan Harper Nichols)

Blessed be the LORD, my rock,
  who trains my hands for war,
  and my fingers for battle;
he is my steadfast love and my fortress,
  my stronghold and my deliverer,
my shield and he in whom I take refuge,
  who subdues peoples under me.

O LORD, what is man that you regard him,
  or the son of man that you think of him?
Man is like a breath;
  his days are like a passing shadow.

Bow your heavens, O LORD, and come down!
  Touch the mountains so that they smoke!
Flash forth the lightning and scatter them;
  send out your arrows and rout them!
Stretch out your hand from on high;
  rescue me and deliver me from the many waters,
  from the hand of foreigners,
whose mouths speak lies
  and whose right hand is a right hand of falsehood.

I will sing a new song to you, O God;
  upon a ten-stringed harp I will play to you,
who gives victory to kings,
  who rescues David his servant from the cruel sword. (Psa 144.1–10)

David's life was scattered with conflict, just as ours is today. So may we cry out in trust to God, just as he did! God is our trainer and our stronghold. He is faithful, in control, and our only hope for true rescue. God provides redemption from the lies of our enemies and the wisdom to train our children. He gives us daily bread, so we need not be anxious.

He is the stronghold that stabilizes us in times of trouble. If we seek Him habitually when problems come, we automatically turn to Him, knowing where our true safety lies. We are in His pasture and under His protection. He moves around us in times of trouble.

We don't always know how this all works, just that it does. At almost any age, one can look back and see God's handiwork. His Word provides the lens that allows us to see all things from a spiritual perspective. If we have a good grasp of the gospel message and the history of God's people, we can understand that He can use almost anything to continue our learning in any given time or circumstance. His children can hear wisdom shout in the streets when the world only sees mayhem!

God can work with the kind of humble heart that is grateful and gives Him the glory for all that is good and profitable in their lives. A heart that trusts and is not self-serving! We are learning to overcome when we can begin to recognize Satan's devices as he attempts to draw us away from real safety. And we are learning how to live and walk as God directs us.

We are constantly learning to be holy and set apart from this world's view. We may even be helping others learn from God as we strive to follow Jesus. Whether we choose to walk the straight or crooked path, learning is happening with someone. If we can't see it ourselves, our lives may be an example for someone else.

God can help us all to see when we ask Him! He is the light! Let us be disciplined to study enough to know God and His wisdom. Let us ask God to help us use His Word rightly so that we can learn throughout our days as we walk in His light!

DAY 3

Only in Him

[F]or Jesus peace seems to have meant not the absence of struggle, but the presence of love. (Frederick Buechner)

And we also thank God constantly for this, that when you received the word of God, which you heard from us, you accepted it not as the word of men but

as what it really is, the word of God, which is at work in you believers. For
you, brothers, became imitators of the churches of God in Christ Jesus that
are in Judea. For you suffered the same things from your own countrymen as
they did from the Jews, who killed both the Lord Jesus and the prophets, and
drove us out, and displease God and oppose all mankind by hindering us from
speaking to the Gentiles that they might be saved—so as always to fill up the
measure of their sins. But wrath has come upon them at last!

…For what is our hope or joy or crown of boasting before our Lord Je-
sus at his coming? Is it not you? For you are our glory and joy. (1 Thess
2.13–16, 19–20)

The terms peace and love are so often misused and misunderstood in light
of their intended spiritual meanings. God provides teaching for His children through Christ, the apostles, and the help of the Holy Spirit so they
can enjoy the peace found only in Him and His kingdom. Anyone who acknowledges and obeys the gospel message has peace, even in difficult times!

In his letter to the Thessalonians, Paul explains how Satan, through
persecution, has hindered him and his companions from coming to them.
We see his love and concern. Their common understanding of the truth
makes their connection possible. They had peace in Christ and fellowship
with each other.

God calls His children with the written Word. The Spirit directed all the
apostles' teaching. When Jesus completed His work, He made redemption
and peace with God possible. And when anyone reading the Bible comprehends that it is the mind of God, it elevates its value in the reader's mind and
leads one to a relationship with God.

This relationship brings peace with God, glory, and joy. All these emotions are so very deep, and we can only discern them with a spiritual mindset. Peace and love are emotions that the Spirit of God provides through
His Word. They become morphed when the world attempts to understand
them from a fleshly mindset. The world defines them in ways that ignore a
fundamental understanding of God: His plan, His purposes, and His marvelous blessings in Christ Jesus.

Let us all strive for the spiritual knowledge and understanding provided
through the Bible, which is the Word of God. Let us comprehend the wisdom from above in the things God has made and where it is made manifest.
Let us partake in the peace and learn His kind of love in the same way the
early Christians did.

DAY 4

Like the Teacher

To be right with God has often meant to be in trouble with men. (A.W. Tozer)

It is enough for the disciple to be like his teacher, and the servant like his master. If they have called the master of the house Beelzebul, how much more will they malign those of his household. (Matt 10.25)

Sometimes, the disciples of Jesus were persecuted for doing what was right. We shouldn't expect things to be much different in our fallen world with its "woke" or "postmodern" philosophy. Because of sin, God put enmity between good and evil. If we live like Christ, God's children will be the targets of evil. We all suffer the consequences of our wrong actions and attitudes, but even when we act in God-directed ways, those who disparage God will target Christians for persecution.

Godly wisdom and absolute truth always affect people. For some, it produces joy. For others, it results in hate and retaliation. Those in opposition to God often feel threatened or convicted by righteousness and lash out at what they see as their enemy. They must feel as if they are right.

God expects us to do what He dictates as righteous, even if it brings conflict. Jesus said He did not come to bring peace but a sword. His sword is truth—the sword of the Spirit. We should not run from using it properly nor run towards intentional controversy. Instead, when confrontations come, we pray we will stand, use the sword of truth effectively, and not faint or grow weary.

Sometimes, mistreatment can indicate whether we are standing firm and stable in God's word. This is especially true if the mistreatment is done by those who directly oppose God. Christians are endeavoring to present the truth to a fallen world that may not want to hear it. And when dealing with hearts that are in rebellion with God, the very nature of His followers may be perceived as a threat to the godless.

If you have never experienced this, consider evaluating your interactions with others. Your godliness may not be showing. And remember, the more godless a group of people or a nation becomes, the more persecution will exist. In the worst of times, evil people and nations will tolerate and encourage it!

DAY 5

The Proper Standard

What we do see depends mainly on what we look for. (John Lubbock)

Not that we dare to classify or compare ourselves with some of those who are commending themselves. But when they measure themselves by one another and compare themselves with one another, they are without understanding.

But we will not boast beyond limits, but will boast only with regard to the area of influence God assigned to us, to reach even to you. For we are not overextending ourselves, as though we did not reach you. For we were the first to come all the way to you with the gospel of Christ. We do not boast beyond limit in the labors of others. But our hope is that as your faith increases, our area of influence among you may be greatly enlarged, so that we may preach the gospel in lands beyond you, without boasting of work already done in another's area of influence. "Let the one who boasts, boast in the Lord." For it is not the one who commends himself who is approved, but the one whom the Lord commends. (2 Cor 10.12–18)

The apostle Paul reasoned differently than the common man. Worldly men are without understanding as they compare themselves to what other men do or have done before them. Instead, Paul made judgments within the limits of God's commands and direction.

Most people compare things to their current understanding or point of view. Just listen to how most people respond to almost anything that is said. The first reaction to a story is usually about when the same thing happened or did not happen to them. When someone hears a statement with new information, they usually seek verification, not because they want to know, but rather to defend their position. It is easy to do!

Using ourselves or others as a measuring stick is not a profitable way to see the world around us. Instead of comparing other's experiences to our own, we must compare information to the proper standard. People must do their research before dismissing new things out of hand. Just because you do not know something does not make it less true!

Sometimes, we are so sure of our preconceived notions that we totally miss what is happening in a situation. And because people do not know they have misinterpreted something, they don't realize they are wrong.

C. S. Lewis said, "What we learn from experience depends on the kind of philosophy we bring to experience."

Chaos results when people do not agree on a standard to judge a situation. This concept is true when discussing the Bible, the Constitution, local laws, or even an architectural plan. One of the reasons we have lawyers and judges in our justice system is to disentangle erroneous perceptions among parties and apply the appropriate standard to the issue. They try to determine the underlying intent of the author on what is the accepted standard and come up with a fair application. Or at least this is the way it is suppose to work.

The Bible is used when determining God's mind on a subject, the Constitution is used when determining the founders original intent, an archtects vision and plans and specifications when a construction project is under consideration. These are all examples of accepted standards. The original intent, the context and the purpose are examined against a current application under consideration.

But when people believe that everything is relative and no standard exists, there can be no basis for agreement, unity, or progress toward a common goal. If everyone is right in their own eyes and no one is wrong, there can be no consistency of thought or unified action. No one feels that justice is served.

Even if we believe there is a standard from God revealed in His Word, are we using it in our dealings? Are Christians really using it to soberly discern the things we are seeing and hearing? Is there peace in our homes, marriages, and families as we agree on a common standard?

We must always strive to find out what God's Word says about any matter to conduct ourselves properly. We are all influenced by our environment in all facets of life. All too often, it seems that the current worldview or social norms influence our view of authority rather than a humble view of ourselves in relation to God.

God is the standard. His revealed Word provides a right and wrong way to operate in this world. He directs the life of each follower, and His followers make up a kingdom of people who adopt the same God-directed standard! The people in this kingdom can have peace with God and each other. They all elevate God, not themselves. There is unity and calm when people revere God as the one who is trusted.

But there will not be peace when a fleshly mindset exists in any dynamic, whether a business venture, city council meeting, church, or family. There will never be unity. Only conflict will result. We cannot expect anything different. And this is a good thing because it helps us to recognize His peace, His people, and His Kingdom when we see them!

WEEK TEN

DAY 1

His Faithfulness

Only a real risk tests the reality of a belief. (C. S. Lewis)

Jesus said to him, "Have you believed because you have seen me? Blessed are those who have not seen and yet have believed." (John 20.29)

By faith Abraham obeyed when he was called to go out to a place that he was to receive as an inheritance. And he went out, not knowing where he was going. (Heb 11.8)

Thomas demanded sight before he would believe in the resurrection. Jesus said, "Blessed are those" who believe and have not seen Christ with their physical eyes. Everyone has the potential to develop eyes of faith that make the unseen visible. And God demands faith, which requires the ability to see truth apart from visual evidence using spiritually minded eyes.

The old Kevin Costner movie *Field of Dreams* presents the idea of this type of faith. A voice says, "Build it, and they will come." The main character's faith that building a baseball field had an elevated purpose that he did not understand prompted his efforts. Everyone thought he was nuts. The people of Noah's day would have viewed him the same way when he built the ark. And Abraham certainly had this kind of faith when he left the home of his fathers, not knowing where he was going. He shows this faith again when he journeys to sacrifice his son Isaac.

While the faith of a Christian does begin with some firm evidence of Jesus' life, burial, and resurrection, there is always an aspect of the unseen at its core that serves as the essential motivator. People are saved by grace through faith. God provides grace, but everyone must respond in faith for the scheme of redemption to work. All have grace extended to them, but only those who choose faith are chosen by God.

How often do we reveal our faith in action to ourselves and others? How often do we obey when there are real negative consequences at stake? Do we sacrifice our time when we do not know how long something will take? Do we help people we know God wants us to help when it may cost us our livelihood to do so?

Do we trust God to take care of us, or do we think we have to do everything ourselves? Do we stand for truth and say the right things when it is unpopular? Do we stay calm, knowing God is in control when societal pressure mounts? Do we really believe God will provide for us?

Let us build our lives upon the word of God just as Noah built the ark. Let us strive to go out at His command, even when we do not know where we are going. When we act in faith, and He delivers, it builds our faith all the more. May we all show faithfulness to God so that we and others will see His faithfulness as well!

DAY 2

Apprentice Learners

Learn everything you can, anytime you can, from anyone you can, there will always come a time when you will be grateful you did. (Sarah Caldwell)

For it was fitting that he, for whom and by whom all things exist, in bringing many sons to glory, should make the founder of their salvation perfect through suffering. (Heb 2.10)

Learning is considered a lifelong endeavor in many areas of study. *Lifelong learning* is an architect's motto. It is usually called continuing education or professional development in the corporate world. In the New Testament, the word for learner is disciple, translated from the Greek word *mathētēs*. The Biblical usage indicates an apprentice-like learner who takes on the attributes of their teacher or mentor.

Its original meaning is much broader than that of a pupil in a modern-day classroom. In the Greek training system, young men were taught one-on-one with an assigned mentor throughout their learning years. And Jesus expects His followers to continue the discipleship process. He told His apostles to "Go and make disciples." He meant that you now go to all nationalities of people and repeat the discipleship process via the gospel.

This learning originates in a reverence for God and a love for Him as our Master. God, through His manifestation in Christ, is the ultimate mentor. Jesus mentored His apostles and the disciples of that day. It was so important to Jesus that after He left earth, He sent the Holy Spirit to remind the apostles of *all* of His instructions. Early disciples continued the process and wrote our Bible so they could push the process forward throughout all time. Today, His followers plant seeds of truth in people's hearts, and God still provides the growth!

Christians are to become so like Jesus that people know who their Master is. And if one knows Jesus, they know the Father. All are to learn not only His words but also His attitudes and behaviors that result from them. A disciple emulates what they learn from Christ to be like Christ.

The Greek text says even Christ was made perfect through suffering. This statement may be startling because our culture avoids any kind of suffering at all costs. But suffering is a primary component in salvation on multiple levels. Christians, too, are made perfect through Christ's suffering. And by suffering various trials, they are made perfect and complete, lacking nothing (Jas 1.2–4).

Faith and belief mean more than just a mental assessment or acknowledgment of something. They facilitate change and transformation. His disciples are changed into a likeness of Christ and His character because Christ's suffering completes its purpose in His sacrificial offering. It provides the choice and opportunity to unite with His death, burial, and resurrection. They are born again into a new person who becomes more like Him daily.

Our learning matters. It must be intentional and sustained. We are ever learning and moving towards a knowledge of truth and transformation that we see in ourselves and others. Our reaction to suffering in the form of persecution will reveal the depths of our faith.

Let us remain steadfast under trial. Let us use it as an indicator of learning and motivation to strive to be more like Christ, our example and teacher, so that we can grow in faith. Christians must be living sacrifices! And they wait on the Lord! They are steadfast, immovable, and always abounding in the work of the Lord. They are lifetime learners of the Master of the universe!

DAY 3

Continual Correction

We must allow the Word of God to correct us the same way we allow it to encourage us. (A.W. Tozer)

My son, do not despise the LORD's discipline
*   or be weary of his reproof,*
for the LORD reproves him whom he loves,
*   as a father the son in whom he delights.* (Prov 3.11–12)

There is no shame in not knowing something you have not yet been taught. And people should try to realize they sometimes have become dull of hearing and need to relearn things they should have already known. Asking questions and discovering truths should be sought after and applauded. A prevalent attitude today expressed in people of all ages when they are corrected sometimes comes across more like resentment, fear, or maybe even anger, rather than appreciation.

Some people have an unreasonable sense of failure when they are corrected. They perceive it as embarrassing. It is as if they expect that they should know things without being taught. It starts when we are young.

Children especially want to act as if they already know things. They will say, "I know," when they have just shown by their actions that they do not! Some of the earliest phrases spoken by most little children are, "Me do it" or "I can do it myself." As many continue into their teenage years, their behavior continues to say, "No need to direct me; I can figure it out myself."

Let us be willing at all ages to elevate the teaching, learning, and correction process in our own lives. We must show this as a practice that should be appreciated and sought after. This process of continual correction is the way God teaches His children. Only fools despise instruction!

Do not let your children have unrealistic expectations of their competence at a time when societal norms are trying to be all too careful with the feelings of our younger generation. This is an evil time when adults are discouraged from even telling children they are a boy or a girl. Oswald Chambers once said, "It takes God a long time to get us to stop thinking that unless everyone sees things exactly as we do, they must be wrong."

We really need to make sure we see things like God sees them. He is continually working with us, and we may sometimes be in different learning places from those around us. Learning God's Will and character is a "growing up" process. And we never start with a mature, godly, spiritual mindset. We should moderate our expectations and create environments where people can feel comfortable without knowing all the answers.

All our steps toward God develop us towards His mind and away from our own way of thinking. And any understanding we obtain is more a gift than an accomplishment. As Christians, we actually give up our thinking altogether. Paul writes, "Have this mind among yourselves" (Phil. 2.5). If we make everything about our knowledge, ability, and way of thinking, then we have entirely missed the point!

DAY 4

Promise-Keeping/ Faithfulness

Promises may get thee friends, but non-performance will turn them into enemies. (Benjamin Franklin)

Know therefore that the LORD your God is God, the faithful God who keeps covenant and steadfast love with those who love him and keep his commandments, to a thousand generations, and repays to their face those who hate him, by destroying them. He will not be slack with one who hates him. He will repay him to his face. You shall therefore be careful to do the commandment and the statutes and the rules that I command you today. (Deut 7.9–11)

[B]y which he has granted to us his precious and very great promises, so that through them you may become partakers of the divine nature, having escaped from the corruption that is in the world because of sinful desire. (2 Pet 1.4)

Everyone wants to be around people they can trust. Employers expect conscientiousness and diligence from employees. Marriage partners expect faithfulness from their mates. Children expect their parents to come through on their promises. People appreciate it when someone is faithful to their word. On the other hand, people typically scorn those they cannot depend upon.

Promise-keeping is powerful! And by keeping all His promises throughout time, God shows us His faithfulness. If He has done what He has said in the past, we can trust that He will continue to do so today. The Christian sees the goodness and severity of God and is rational enough to put their faith in Him and follow His commands. It allows them the strength to step up and step out, knowing what He directs is best, even if they do not yet understand why.

All people fail even when they try their hardest, but God never does! The perfect, promise-keeping faithfulness of God identifies Him as being worthy of praise. And there is a correlation between faithfulness and fairness. The desire for faithfulness propels one to seek fairness and justice where they can find God! He is the ultimate epitome of faithfulness. It contrasts the sovereign power and majesty of God to the lowliness of men.

As humans, we inherently know that when someone doesn't follow through on their promises, we cannot depend on them. While we can feel comfort from the faithful actions of others, a lack of trust in others leads people to cynicism and drives them in the wrong direction. This decline in trust gradually happens as one learns they have been let down.

Nowadays, some may have very few, if any, faithful people in their realm. This fact may help them see and appreciate the faithfulness of God, or it could lead them to be so disgusted with people that they become difficult to reach. Their only hope is the sustained evidence that God is faithful.

Christians should elevate the concept of promise-keeping so others can trust them. Unlike most people, they should always be reliable concerning what they say they will do. They should show up when they say and let people know when they cannot participate. They should be able to manage commitments so that others never fear they will be left hanging when they depend on them.

Do we see the things we say we will do as promises we should keep? Are we careful not to overcommit ourselves to the point where we let people down? In our society, people are often disappointed. Let us choose to be faithful to our word. God's people must be the ones who model His promise-keeping faithfulness and trustworthiness to the world!

DAY 5

Unworldly Jetsons

I am just mad. I waited my whole life for 2020. Not a single George Jetson car in sight. (Author Unknown)

For the protection of wisdom is like the protection of money,
*   and the advantage of knowledge is that wisdom preserves the life of him*
*   who has it.*
Consider the work of God:
*   who can make straight what he has made crooked?*

In the day of prosperity be joyful, and in the day of adversity consider: God has made the one as well as the other, so that man may not find out anything that will be after him. (Ecc 7.12–14)

I saw the Jetsons quote on a picture of George Jetson flying around the sky in his car and just loved it. As a kid, I only liked *The Jetsons* and *Underdog* and have always been fascinated by futuristic technologies. Years ago, in the workplace, I would always ask our IT people when it would be like the Jetsons. They were so young, and I was always surprised if they knew what I meant.

Back then, I was not necessarily talking about flying cars but rather, about how we communicate. This was before Zoom or any virtual meeting format; before smartphones even. Most of these talented young people would tell me somebody had already developed the technology, but it was not on the market yet.

Most of us have witnessed or participated in a technological revolution that has brought us closer to *The Jetsons*. Even the technology for flying cars is already here. Our government regulators are still learning how to develop a system for people to use them.

We do not have a problem perceiving advanced concepts. Our minds are fascinating. We can imagine, work towards, and achieve marvelous things. We can fly to the moon, send robots to Mars, and send all kinds of things to space. Change is always possible, even if not always desired, manageable, or practical.

Our Maker gave us minds that can see an unseen world and that can think freely and imagine. We can perceive all things with minds created by a Being outside this world! Our Maker loves us and wants us to use His standards and continually apply them to our time and situations. He grafts unworldly wisdom into our minds using His Word to make us truly His.

Our new technologies have not necessarily improved or by themselves corrupted the hearts of mankind. They are just like any other previous advancement. Each can still be used for right and good or abused to be a detriment to oneself and others.

All must remember that from the formation of any thought that leads to advancement, everything is possible using things that God provides. We must give credit where credit is due! After advancements of any kind come to fruition, each person must evaluate them properly and align their use in ways that can advance the cause of Christ.

No one should ever use new advancements for nefarious intents. And no one should use them to advance personal greed or selfishness. Instead, people should utilize them to further the purposes God has designed for mankind. In all times of adversity, people should consider how they want to use their assets, resources, and time to accomplish good. Let no one get caught up in the mere trappings of new things as we move closer to *The Jetsons*!

WEEK ELEVEN

DAY 1

Withstanding Earthly Fears

Half our fears arise from neglect of the Bible. (Charles Spurgeon)

When I saw him, I fell at his feet as though dead. But he laid his right hand on me, saying, "Fear not, I am the first and the last, and the living one. I died, and behold I am alive forevermore, and I have the keys of Death and Hades." (Rev 1.17–18)

When Christ speaks in Revelation, He directs His followers to "fear not" or "do not fear." These phrases are used throughout scripture when God speaks to His people. Knowing God and the sacrifice of Jesus Christ can produce an abiding faith in those who choose to follow Jesus. The antithesis of obedient faith is fear.

Consider the kinds of situations God's people are facing and the odds they are going up against when this phrase is said. Some may be surrounded by an army besieging their city. Some could be facing imminent death. They could be going before kings at their peril. Or they may even be being asked to surrender to an ungodly besieging force.

Today, most people get out of comfortable beds and get in comfortable cars. People today have a little traffic or some irritable people to deal with throughout their day, but this generation is not familiar with the level of threat we see in scripture. We do not yet see the kinds of trouble we read about that would produce an intense fear that needs to be overcome. It may, however, be on our horizon.

I do not want to ignore nor minimize the threats found in our society that can impact mental and spiritual well-being. Still, I want to highlight the contrast of our physical fears to consider the quote above. When people face their "giants" today, are they looking to see how their faith should be calming them?

Examine the difficult situations people are facing these days. Are saints today like David facing Goliath? Or do the Lord's followers run away like fearful soldiers? I remember watching as US tanks drove into Iraq, merely to find uniforms abandoned on the ground. There were no actual fighters.

Is this how Satan wins? When God's people are too fearful to stand and fight against their enemies or if they are caught off guard without their armor on, isn't this just conceding the win to evil? Even if God's followers are not facing imminent peril from the same kinds of enemies, Christians are still required to live their lives in faith and not in fear. None can wait until they are about to be fed to the lions to develop an abiding faith. It must happen now in the present by using what you do know to fight against the real enemy which is Satan using the tools God prescribes.

Faith comes by hearing, and hearing through the Word of Christ. Let us not leave our Bibles unopened and discarded! A person must read what God says, in context, from beginning to end, over and over again, if they ever want to have a chance at developing a faith that will withstand their earthly fears!

And there is no substitute for reading the text for yourself. The power is in the Word because it is the inspired direction given to people by God to learn how to live in this fallen world. So, let us continually study to find ourselves approved, stable, calm, and faithful!

DAY 2

Difficult Improvements

If you want to be good at something, you first must be willing to be bad at it.
(Author Unknown)

For to everyone who has will more be given, and he will have an abundance. But from the one who has not, even what he has will be taken away.
(Matt 25.29)

My most vivid memory of feeling inadequate at something was learning to play golf. I used to say that it was the best way to practice patience in a socially acceptable way. You must be patient with yourself and overcome the embarrassment when you swing and miss or when you swing incorrectly and hit the ball out of bounds. Golf is a complicated sport! And you must be willing first to be bad before you can be good.

Using our God-given ability to learn and be good at something requires a myriad of things, but the most important is humility. Anything we can accomplish as children of God comes from the abilities and opportunities God supplies us. The parable of the talents addresses the idea of using what God provides in preparing for the final judgment. However, its concept is also generally true in life. We must be willing to use the abilities we have if we are to grow in them!

Being skilled at any sport, instrument, or level of intellectual knowledge requires you to first recognize the blessing of having a mind and body fit to accomplish it. Then, you can use those talents to practice any skill over and over to develop the competence level you desire. Or you can be lazy or arrogant and bury any aptitude you may possess.

Jesus points out that failing to use what we have to improve ourselves and further the kingdom of heaven is spiritually catastrophic. If you don't use a talent, you will lose it! Eternally! Parents must teach their children this principle at a young age as they learn new things and try to improve in any area. As they grow, they must learn to be willing to apply their talents on a spiritual level as they labor in the kingdom. Most times, this involves being bad at something first!

There will always be a time when a child needs to improve at new skills and perform awkwardly. This juncture is the most important moment in the teaching process. As parents or teachers, do we allow children to be overly embarrassed and quit? Do we do this ourselves, thus modeling it as a valid reaction? Or are you boldly willing to look foolish when learning something new and encourage children to keep doing what is difficult while helping them understand they will improve with practice?

Anyone must start as a novice as they learn to master anything! This concept is true whether it be a school subject, sport, or spiritual competence. And whenever someone magnifies embarrassment at the beginning of the learning process, it puts a major stumbling block in the path of progress.

We can begin to understand the process the Lord uses to prepare us for emotional and spiritual maturity when we realize it occurs through difficult improvements. It also helps us encourage others when we see even a bit of advancement in any area as they work toward competence. Rocky starts and gradual improvements apply to learning any new subject or skill. After that, you practice, practice, practice. If you want to improve at something, don't stop doing it!

Let us use our current talents and continually learn new things to encourage others. You never know who is watching! Those who never learn how to learn may have their growth stunted for life, and we can show others how to do it by modeling the process ourselves. God commands competence in several areas, such as study, communication, and showing love to others. And the more humility a person possesses, the easier it is to start on the path towards learning God's will. And as we do, we diligently practice His directives that move us towards holiness and godliness.

DAY 3

Death to Life

I have come to the conclusion that none of us in our generation feels as guilty about sin as we should or as our forefathers did. (Francis Schaeffer)

We know that our old self was crucified with him in order that the body of sin might be brought to nothing, so that we would no longer be enslaved to sin. (Rom 6.6)

Romans tells us that the price for sin is paid by uniting with the death of Christ. When our sins are removed by the blood of Christ, the penalty of sin (separation from God) is removed. To sin means to transgress the Will of our Creator and the sovereign God. All men sin and break God's law, but somehow, this is normalized in our society. The world does not see it as really all that bad.

The perception of sin by the world over time has never changed. It is the job of the evil one to deceive people about their true condition as a rebel against the God of heaven. However, God's people see sin differently and call it out for the ugly thing it really is.

The Christian sees that sin separates them from God, the source of eternal life. And they know Christ is the healer of their condition because He is the Great Physician. In Romans 6, Paul discusses how Christians should not pervert God's grace to tolerate sin. It requires Christ's death and our uniting with His death in baptism to remedy the condition so that redemption can occur. But baptism (our immersion in a watery grave) has fallen out of favor in modern-day religious circles. It has evidently become too difficult!

Some want to make the conversion process easier to save large stadiums of people. They convince people they have no part to play in the conversion process and that changing their lives for Christ is not really hard. Instead, preachers have devised a new method for people to follow. They prescribe that people just need to ask Jesus to come into their hearts. You aren't required to die like He did, suffer persecution like He did, or help others find the truth.

The fact is that God has direct instruction as to how to accomplish deliverance. When there is a disconnect in the minds of people about what it means to break God's law, there is no understanding that they have put themselves in opposition to the sovereign God of heaven and have separated themselves from Him (Isa 59.2). Sometimes, there is no awareness that there is a God or that he has any law at all. And so, people ignore His right to govern mankind. On top of it all, "religious" people attempt to rewrite the gospel message (Gal 1) to altogether remove the freewill obedience of man, denying the very basis of God's truth.

Sadly, people with this mindset do not realize they are in opposition to God and are essentially rebels, fighting for something that they cannot win. They have trusted in themselves and consciously decided to do things their own way. They are lost and need a savior and are blind to that reality. If only they would know to look to the gospel message for the proper remedy for sin!

The job of teaching the truth has always been to make people aware of their need for redemption. They must learn of their true condition and accept God's remedy that works. Each man has been given the free will choice to decide. Teachers of truth want to ensure everyone is exposed to God's Word so their decision is informed.

God has provided His message in written form. He has provided a sacrifice that is qualified to pay for sin. But each person must decide to accept or reject it. Faithful obedience through baptism moves one from death in sin to life in Christ and accepts the gift of His salvation (Rom 3.23).

DAY 4

Good, Good News

If you see yourself as a "little sinner" you will inevitably see Jesus as a "little savior." (Martin Luther)

Then he turned toward the woman and said to Simon, "Do you see this woman? I came into your house. You did not give me any water for my feet, but she wet my feet with her tears and wiped them with her hair. You did not give me a kiss, but this woman, from the time I entered, has not stopped kissing my feet. You did not put oil on my head, but she has poured perfume on my feet. Therefore, I tell you, her many sins have been forgiven—as her great love has shown. But whoever has been forgiven little loves little."
Then Jesus said to her, "Your sins are forgiven." (Luke 7.44–48)

How do we view ourselves with respect to God? How black do we paint our sins in our minds? Do we realize the abundant blessings we have from God by providing us a way to righteousness? The answers to these questions determine our reverence and humility and the degree to which we can love and show mercy to others.

In his interaction with the sinful woman, Jesus shows that our sense of sin equates to the level of love, praise, and appreciation we either offer or fail to show God. The Pharisee's sins were no less egregious than the woman's. However, his behavior shows that he did not truly appreciate his sinful state or how Christ could reconcile it!

There is a relationship between the view of our sins and our appreciation of God. When we appreciate what God supplies, it changes how we see Him, view ourselves, and how we treat others. And our willingness and eagerness to help others find God is an indicator of how valuable we see Him ourselves.

Let all realize there is none "good" but One, and that any righteousness we have was bought and paid for by someone else. We are undeserving of His grace, but God has offered it anyway. We deserve death, but God shows us mercy.

Paint every failed attempt to follow the will of God as black as it is so we can better realize how in need of a Savior we are. It helps us recognize how lowly and humble we should show ourselves to be. As a gift, God has given mankind an opportunity for redemption by having an obedient faith.

The gospel is good news! Such good, good news! And it needs to be understood, appreciated, and shared. Let those who have died with Christ live by their humble and grateful example so we can be lights in a world dominated by darkness.

DAY 5

Close and Attainable

Great moves of God are usually preceded by simple acts of obedience. (Steven Furtick)

Manasseh led Judah and the inhabitants of Jerusalem astray, to do more evil than the nations whom the LORD destroyed before the people of Israel.

The LORD spoke to Manasseh and to his people, but they paid no attention. Therefore the LORD brought upon them the commanders of the army of the king of Assyria, who captured Manasseh with hooks and bound him with chains of bronze and brought him to Babylon. And when he was in distress, he entreated the favor of the LORD his God and humbled himself greatly before the God of his fathers. He prayed to him, and God was moved by his entreaty and heard his plea and brought him again to Jerusalem into his kingdom. Then Manasseh knew that the LORD was God.

Afterward he built an outer wall for the city of David west of Gihon, in the valley, and for the entrance into the Fish Gate, and carried it around Ophel, and raised it to a very great height. He also put commanders of the army in all the fortified cities in Judah. And he took away the foreign gods and the idol from the house of the LORD, and all the altars that he had built on the mountain of the house of the LORD and in Jerusalem, and he threw them outside of the city. He also restored the altar of the LORD and offered on it sacrifices of peace offerings and of thanksgiving, and he commanded Judah to serve the LORD, the God of Israel. (2 Chron 33:9–16)

And by that will we have been sanctified through the offering of the body of Jesus Christ once for all. (Heb 10:10)

You know God is somehow involved whenever there is a recognizable and drastic change in behavior towards goodness. Manasseh's obedience was unexpected because he was one of the most evil kings in Israel. Unfortunately, he was old when the Assyrians took him captive and had already influenced an entire generation of Israelites to do evil! Even so, the Chronicles' narrative highlights God and his steadfast love that responds to anyone who is obedient and humbles themselves.

He was the son of Hezekiah, a good king, so Manasseh must have known about God from his early life, but he decided to do what was evil in God's sight anyway. He had no faith. But after the Assyrians took him captive, his attitude changed when he sought and received God's deliverance. Now, he knew God in a way that impacted his decisions and behaviors. He had an obedient faith and displayed it before all the people.

God never intended His ultimate deliverance for men to come through perfect adherence to the rules of Mosaic Law. The sacrificial system involving bulls and goats depended on the sacrifice of Christ that God planned before the foundation of the world. Christ completed the Old Law and brought salvation to all people in all times. Leviticus 16.30 tells us the sins of those under the Old Law were forgiven. Redemption for all occurs because of Christ's sacrifice that paid the price for sin, making salvation available to all who have obedient faith. People are saved when the steadfast love of God gifts it to those who by faithful obedience have cleansed their garments with the blood of Christ. By this they show that they want a relationship with God just as badly as He wants one with them. Before the Old Law, Abraham by faith was accounted righteous. Christ's sacrifice also made possible his salvation. God authors salvation, it is not based on works but requires faith. It always has!

Everything that has been created, every story ever told in scripture, and every Spirit-filled action from the beginning of time until now should be seen in this light and perspective. His complete Word will produce believers, even among those who have previously chosen a path of evil. Reconciliation is based on the heart of each person, along with the spiritual gifts that God provides through His Son.

Let our eyes be opened to the truth through faith in Christ and obedience to the gospel message! May we teach it properly and pray for wisdom and understanding while humbling ourselves in the sight of the Lord! May we not lose hope and continue to teach those who, like Manasseh, were taught but have not yet obeyed. Everyone can turn towards God while they live. He is always close and attainable to anyone who has the desire to come to Him!

WEEK TWELVE

DAY 1

A Literate People

The illiterate of the twenty-first century will not be those who cannot read and write, but those who cannot learn, unlearn, and relearn. (Alvin Toffler)

Brothers, I do not consider that I have made it my own. But one thing I do: forgetting what lies behind and straining forward to what lies ahead, I press on toward the goal for the prize of the upward call of God in Christ Jesus. Let those of us who are mature think this way, and if in anything you think otherwise, God will reveal that also to you. Only let us hold true to what we have attained. (Phil 3.13–16)

There is little illiteracy today from the standpoint of people being unable to read or write. However, some people refuse to learn or use new technologies when they are first introduced into culture. Most of the time, it is not because they are physically or mentally incapable of doing so but because they have decided they will not learn something new. Sometimes, people just flat resist change! They like the old way or need help understanding the new system, so they refuse to acknowledge, learn, or change to accommodate new advancements.

If we are honest with ourselves, most can admit to having this attitude when learning how to do things in new ways, like setting up a new phone or learning how to use WiFi. One must resist their own anger and impatience. We can be mad and irritable about having to change. We feel that someone has taken something in which they were fully competent and altered it just to hinder us. It takes a willingness to work through the frustration!

Considering this type of "illiteracy," we may be able to better understand the concepts of being "stiff-necked" or "uncircumcised in heart" when it comes to adopting God's Word. In Philippians, Paul is talking specifically about Christians moving from being under the direction of the Old Law to the New Law. This struggle was significant for the first-century Jews, but all Christians must grow through a spiritual transformation. It requires a malleable heart, a boatload of patience, emotional maturity, and a new way to look at things.

Today, Christians must become citizens of a heavenly kingdom even while living in a fleshly body. The Spirit of God is transforming them to house a resurrected self who wants to learn and understand every plan and direction God has for His people under the New Law of Christ. Christians must remember that God directs us to embrace any righteous change and to hunger and thirst for it. We cannot view it as trivial or unimportant.

Unfortunately, God's principles of morality have become attacked as old-fashioned. But some things do not change with the times. His Word contains the underlying principles that should determine our response to any change, technological or otherwise! We must always maintain the integrity of godly directives. Even as we adapt to external, systematic, technological change in different time periods, we must always preserve our holiness under God's direction.

DAY 2

False Prophets

Telling someone to live like Jesus while living like the devil is like striking a wet match and expecting to start a fire. (Author Unknown)

Thus says the LORD of hosts: "Do not listen to the words of the prophets who prophesy to you, filling you with vain hopes. They speak visions of their own minds, not from the mouth of the Lord. They say continually to those who despise the word of the Lord, 'It shall be well with you'; and to everyone who stubbornly follows his own heart, they say, 'No disaster shall come upon you.'"

For who among them has stood in the council of the Lord
    to see and to hear his word,
    or who has paid attention to his word and listened?
Behold, the storm of the LORD!
    Wrath has gone forth,

a whirling tempest;
  it will burst upon the head of the wicked.
The anger of the LORD will not turn back
  until he has executed and accomplished
  the intents of his heart.
In the latter days you will understand it clearly.

"I did not send the prophets,
  yet they ran;
I did not speak to them,
  yet they prophesied.
But if they had stood in my council,
  then they would have proclaimed my words to my people,
and they would have turned them from their evil way,
  and from the evil of their deeds.

"Am I a God at hand, declares the LORD, and not a God far away? (Jer 23.16–23)

He made Him who knew no sin to be sin on our behalf, so that we might become the righteousness of God in Him. (2 Cor 5.21)

False religion is one of Satan's most potent weapons. He especially likes to use it on those who want to do things their way. These people are stubborn, unwilling to humble themselves. They hold onto what they perceive as controlling the situations and people around them. Like the false prophets of old, they want to maintain their positions and make the appearance of righteousness. They see it as an advantage.

It took me a long time to figure out how to explain righteousness. It is an unfamiliar word not frequently used very much in secular vernacular. Ultimately, righteousness is provided to men from God along with their justification when they obey the gospel. They are put back in alignment with God into a holy relationship that is mended and restored.

To explain righteousness, one must understand sin and what it does. Sin separates people from God. Righteousness reinstates this loss. Sin is doing something against the will of God, and righteousness involves mending the relationship to make it right. Ultimately, God provided access to reconciliation to everyone for all time by providing His Son as a sacrifice for sin. Christ was righteous because He never sinned. This qualified Him to be the innocent sacrifice for sin thus paying the price for sin in our behalf. By uniting with His death, we become righteous (without sin too) and begin a new life on a different footing!

Righteousness is always accomplished within God's design and with His direction and approval. Noah was a preacher of righteousness when he preached to those on earth at that time of God's plan to save people by entering the ark, so as to be lifted up by water during the worldwide flood. The Israelites passed through the water of the Red Sea. And we are baptized in Christ's death and raised up out of the water to a new life.

False teachers are not practicing righteousness. They are idolaters, and they worship themselves. They are not trying to put people in alignment with God but rather have self-serving agendas. They make up their own rules and expect others to follow their will rather than that of the Holy God. Sometimes they even fool themselves! They are confused when their efforts do not produce the fruits of a godly character in others. They do not see that they have missed the mark and failed to speak the truth. Ultimately, God's truth when accepted by honest hearts brings about spiritual peace; not always physical peace, because truth brings a sword when we teach the truth to those who desire to remain unrighteous. Jesus tells us that.

Today, in our political realm, people want someone to bring about stability. I am sorry, folks, but this is impossible if injustice and sin reigns. All candidates will cause a ruckus with some faction. And if a person enters the fray to work righteousness, they will be crucified. Only a penitent population can accomplish any semblance of calm, and I do not see any signs of that happening soon. However, it may be constructive to see the true colors of unrighteousness shine!

Proponents of compromised religious alternatives make it all worse because they enable people to feel comfortable in their sin. The culmination and acceptance of false prophets are what brought on the judgments of God in times past. It was the last straw for Him. God steps in when the lies saturate environments. He shows up with judgments as a last-ditch effort to expose the truth so that any interested person can see the warning, repent, and allow God to justify them again.

DAY 3

Moving Mountains

Faith is like WIFI. It's invisible but has the power to connect you to what you need. (Author Unknown)

Then the disciples came to Jesus privately and said, "Why could we not cast it out?" He said to them, "Because of your little faith. For truly, I say to you, if you have faith like a grain of mustard seed, you will say to this mountain, 'Move from here to there, and it will move, and nothing will be impossible for you." (Matt 17.19–20)

The teachings from God throughout scripture give us a knowledge of the "unseen" realm that provides the spiritual sight to overcome the "seen" world. We are all saved by faith in the unseen power of God and the realm of His Kingdom. Christians know the resources are there, and they connect to them using faith to capture and utilize the power of the gospel message.

Christians can access the information and apply the strategies that will make life work as God always intended. As Abraham believed in God's promises, we are all saved by the same faith in His Word. His followers understand that there is something unseen out there and in operation; we only need to connect to His Word and obey it! With faith, we must listen and go where the Bible says to go in our thinking and lifestyle. Then, the same power that created the world recreates the landscape of our lives and becomes active in them.

Jesus tells us that with faith in God, we can "move mountains" (Mark 11.23). With God's help and grace, anyone can overcome sin and their ability to be productive and fruitful in His spiritual kingdom. And it is attainable to anyone with a solid and sound faithful connection in Him who is always faithful to His Word. There is immense power in the Word and the blood of Christ. Connect now and often!

DAY 4

The Right Words

Today will never come again. Be a blessing. Be a friend. Encourage someone. Take time to care. Let your words heal and not wound. (Author Unknown)

And they were bringing children to him that he might touch them, and the disciples rebuked them. But when Jesus saw it, he was indignant and said to them, "Let the children come to me; do not hinder them, for to such belongs the kingdom of God. Truly, I say to you, whoever does not receive the kingdom of God like a child shall not enter it." And he took them in his arms and blessed them, laying his hands on them.

And as he was setting out on his journey, a man ran up and knelt before him and asked him, "Good Teacher, what must I do to inherit eternal life?" And Jesus said to him, "Why do you call me good? No one is good except God alone. You know the commandments: 'Do not murder, Do not commit adultery, Do not steal, Do not bear false witness, Do not defraud, Honor your father and mother.'" And he said to him, "Teacher, all these I have kept from my youth." And Jesus, looking at him, loved him, and said to him, "You lack one thing: go, sell all that you have and give to the poor, and you will have treasure in heaven; and come, follow me." Disheartened by the saying, he went away sorrowful, for he had great possessions ...

...And the disciples were amazed at his words. But Jesus said to them again, "Children, how difficult it is to enter the kingdom of God! It is easier for a camel to go through the eye of a needle than for a rich person to enter the kingdom of God." And they were exceedingly astonished, and said to him, "Then who can be saved?" Jesus looked at them and said, "With man it is impossible, but not with God. For all things are possible with God."

And they were on the road, going up to Jerusalem, and Jesus was walking ahead of them. And they were amazed, and those who followed were afraid. (Mark 10.13–22, 24–27, 32)

Mark shows us the methods and illustrations Jesus uses to accomplish growth in the hearers. He gives us a glimpse of how the people emotionally interacted with the message. All the while, He highlights the truths in what Jesus is teaching about the gospel of the kingdom.

In Mark 10, Jesus teaches the truth concerning who can enter the coming kingdom. He uses the disciple's action of sending children away as an opportunity to teach. What is there about the children coming to Him that can be compared to entering the coming kingdom of God? He gives us a hint while answering the rich man's inquiry. Children have attributes that we seem to lose as adults.

All things are possible in the minds of children. They have faith in things they cannot see. Children run to those they trust and are excited about the very presence of their caregivers. They show their real emotions and recover quickly when hurt. Children do not hold grudges and are generally encouragers. And these are just a few. So many of these traits are required of people who choose to accept the gospel of the kingdom.

Using children as an example, Jesus exposes adult perspectives and behaviors while accomplishing His purpose in the midst of ignorance, persecution, confusion, fear, amazement, and dishonesty. He can even address the Pharisees with nefarious motives who try to trick Him. As He deals with them, He instructs His apostles about the things that are about to take place and He teaches the gospel of the kingdom, simultaneously! Oh, that we all could learn this ability to teach so effectively!

With an attitude of love, Jesus provides both truth and discipline to each sector of His audience using the exact, chosen method most needed for repentance to take place in the lives of His hearers. Lord, teach us to use our time as wisely as you have modeled. And help us find the right words to say the things that will accomplish Your purpose in the moment they are needed. And in doing so, may You glorify Your marvelous name!

DAY 5

Simplicity of God's Word

If you cannot explain it simply then you do not know it well enough. (Albert Einstein)

Then the disciples came and said to him, "Why do you speak to them in parables?" And he answered them, "To you it has been given to know the secrets of the kingdom of heaven, but to them it has not been given. For to the one who has, more will be given, and he will have an abundance, but from the one who has not, even what he has will be taken away. This is why I speak to them in parables, because seeing they do not see, and hearing they do not hear, nor do they understand." (Matt 13.10–13)

Communication is hard. Learning is hard. But paradoxically, the better we understand a concept, the more simply we should be able to teach it to others. I like to consider the numerous ways God and Jesus taught people in the Bible. Multiple methods were used in the Old and New Testaments, but the spiritual lessons were always presented in ways that could be understood by the audience receiving instruction. What's more is that the spiritual lessons preserved in God's Word are timeless, such that we still read and apply them to our lives today.

Nathan used an allegory with David that he knew would help him see his sin with Bathsheba. God used the illustration of the potter and clay to explain to Israel about His power, intent, and ability to shape both nations and people for their own good, even if that meant tearing them down to build them back up again. Parables were used so honest hearts could see spiritual lessons in simple day-to-day illustrations that led to a deeper understanding of the Kingdom of God. As Jesus explained in the parable of the sower, God's truth is a powerful seed that can lead to an accurate spiritual understanding in a properly cultivated heart. It can also land on "soil" in a heart not adequately prepared by the hearer, so the truth of God never takes root and grows.

God ultimately provides the seed in His Word while also providing for its growth and increase in honest hearts that desire to know Him. We must keep our hearts with all diligence while also being mindful of the intentional and unintentional roadblocks in hearts continually under construction. We are all a work in progress! Let us all learn and communicate in ways that give God all the glory and model the simplicity found in His word.

WEEK THIRTEEN

DAY 1

Forsaking this World for the Next

If you live for the next world, you get this one in the deal; but if you live for only this one you lose them both. (C. S. Lewis)

Blessed are those who are persecuted for righteousness' sake, for theirs is the kingdom of heaven. (Matt 5.10)

God has prepared a heavenly home for those who choose to walk with Him and forsake this life, even to the point of physical death if necessary. But Satan deters most people from taking advantage of this blessing by simply offering them more sleep on Sunday morning or tempting them with the trivial things that those in the world call fun. He does not need to threaten their life, just their comfort. Most do not realize that anything we forgo or give up in service to God is "light" in comparison to the eternal "weight" of glory in the world to come (2 Cor 4.17).

A popular hymn contains the words, "there is a place of quiet rest near to the heart of God." In the ongoing conflict between goodness and wickedness, those who belong to God can find a peaceful relationship with the Creator of the universe. They find peace because they are protected and safe from being separated from God. They will be spiritually prosperous in this life and the next, as they have a realm in heaven prepared by God for those who choose to love Him (John 14.3).

Persecution for righteousness' sake happens because God put enmity between good and evil (Gen 3.15). The more evil the world becomes, the more direct and severe the persecution is against those who live a God directed life. The unrighteous rage against the righteous. Evil hates good. You can see it in their faces. In contrast, a peaceful, quiet rest can be seen on the face of the godly by those that are looking. This difference is what draws honest hearts to God!

Do not be overly concerned with the social dynamic between the righteous and unrighteous. It results from what God has intentionally placed into spiritually conflicting interactions. Instead, let's understand what it is and use it for God's glory. Do not react in kind to others' rage and overreactions to things. Be at peace with all men and learn to find a way to softy touch those close to you when disagreements arise. Avoid disputes that are not yours to fight and enter a calming word into conflicts when you have a God-given responsibility to do so (Prov 15.1). Remember also that our retaliation is sometimes veiled in passive-aggressive behaviors. Reside in your heart in that place of quiet rest, and when any conflict arises, help others see the contrast to any unrighteous anger or rage that is present. This will make a huge difference in all your personal interactions!

DAY 2

Freewill

Why then did God give them freewill? Because freewill, though it makes evil possible, is the Only thing that makes possible any love or joy worth having. (C.S. Lewis)

Now therefore fear the LORD and serve him in sincerity and in faithfulness. Put away the gods that your fathers served beyond the River and in Egypt, and serve the LORD. And if it is evil in your eyes to serve the LORD, choose this day whom you will serve, whether the gods your fathers served in the region beyond the River, or the gods of the Amorites in whose land you dwell. But as for me and my house, we will serve the LORD. (Josh 24.14–15)

Joshua understood it was a personal choice to serve the Lord. Before his passing, he encouraged everyone to follow his example in choosing to serve the one true God. Freewill is a beautiful thing. If not for freewill, we would be nothing more than mechanical robots. There would be no glory to God for our choices, nor any conviction in ourselves.

But there is a price for having freewill in that we live with the consequences of our own and other people's choices. Sometimes these are choices made by those around us without our knowledge. The choices may have been made by people we never knew who lived before us. We may be so far removed from the decision of another that we don't understand the reason for their choice, yet we still must live with the consequences. This offers insight into the question we all have, "Why do bad things happen to good people?" If we all can choose, then we all live with our choices and the choices of others.

If we choose faithfulness with our freewill it can be a wonderful thing. It allows us the opportunity to change circumstances with our good, conscious choices. Good choices also pass to others. It also helps us realize that we should not try to overtly control others. Freewill allows us to show God's love to others and offer them godly choices so they too can understand the implications of freewill. We can worship God as creator even when bad things happen.

When parents attempt to train their children without a proper understanding of freewill, all manner of problems can arise. If a parent is too controlling and doesn't allow a child to see value in their own good choices, they can break mentally, just like mechanical toys. If a parent is too lax too soon before a child understands the consequences of his choices, it could leave them in precarious situations.

The good news is God can "repair" us, and we are not at the mercy of our upbringing. Thanks be to God that He models the proper father figure role for everyone in Himself. And he shows us His wisdom and character through the scriptures and His Son. This makes it possible for anyone to find true spiritual joy and love even when we experience difficulties caused by the poor choices of others. Understanding this makes us free so we can choose to be independently dependent on God, and it helps us develop self-control. So let us all choose with Joshua, this day and every day to serve the Lord!

DAY 3

Immanent in Creation

God dwells in His creation and is everywhere indivisibly present in all His works ... He is transcendent above all His works even while He is immanent within them. (A.W. Tozer)

The earth was without form and void, and darkness was over the face of the deep. And the Spirit of God was hovering over the face of the waters ... And God said, "Let the waters under the heavens be gathered together into one place, and let the dry land appear." And it was so. God called the dry land Earth, and the waters that were gathered together he called Seas. And God saw that it was good. (Gen 1.2, 9–10)

We can learn so much from the creation story. One of the things God accomplished on the third day of creation was to make the sea and dry land. Some nearly inexplicable concepts about God are innately understood when you are by the sea—the vast ocean, the open sky, the pounding waves, and the innumerable grains of sand. In the quote above, Tozer uses the word "immanent," which is infrequently used in our present vernacular. Immanent means existing or operating within; inherent. We are told in Romans that we can see God's invisible attributes in His creation, which are His eternal power and divine nature (Rom 1.20). He spoke it into existence, and He is part of it. He made everything from nothing, and is in it all, He reveals something about Himself. The culmination of all He made is called "good," or we might say, "just right."

God created man in His Image. Man served the purpose of providing someone with whom God could fellowship. God wants a relationship with His people. We understand the ability to fellowship with another through the creation story. To illustrate this, God brought all the animals before Adam to name so he could realize there was a need in him to have someone fit, or suitable, for fellowship with him. God then provided the woman to man, who was the suitable helper. So, God created man in His image, and then made the woman out of man. Both are ideally created for fellowship with Him!

He created, and then, knowing we would fall, had plans in place to recreate us again when we became broken with sin. This plan of God was in place before the very foundation of the world (Eph 1.4)! God's creation shouts to us to seek Him. If we too desire fellowship, we are assured that we will find Him (Matt 7.7).

DAY 4

Conflict of the Mind

Our mind is like a beach: Sometimes it's sunny, sometimes wavy, sometimes crowded, sometimes empty and lonely; at times stormy, at nights cold and windy; in the morning, very clear; at twilight, foggy! Our mind is like a beach from one moment to another. (Mehmet Murat Ildan)

So, I find it to be a law that when I want to do right, evil lies close at hand. For I delight in the law of God, in my inner being, but I see in my members another law waging war against the law of my mind and making me captive to the law of sin that dwells in my members. Wretched man that I am! Who will deliver me from this body of death? Thanks be to God through Jesus Christ our Lord! So then, I myself serve the law of God with my mind, but with my flesh I serve the law of sin. (Rom 7.21–25)

There is an actual internal conflict waging within all of us. Paul expresses how a Spirit-directed mind works in a physical body mingled with all the fleshly thinking a person has been exposed to. Our freewill choice allows us the ability to control our minds by allowing the Spirit of God to direct our thoughts through His word. Our faith or lack thereof determines whether the spiritual war for our mind is won or lost to a fleshly mindset.

The idea of overcoming our weakness in the "flesh" is so often misunderstood. Some believe our physical bodies are innately sinful. People are not born sinful, nor do they inherit sin. Rather, sin or oppositional thought and actions opposed to those God intended are now in our world. There is a war within each mind between our will versus God's will. It results in an internal decision to do either what God intends or whatever one may want to do through the lusts of their eyes, flesh, and selfish pride. It results in personal choices made all day long, day after day. We must bend our will to align with God's as directed by His word and repent and realign again when we fail to do so in order to be, as the Bible discusses, in the Spirit.

This battle changes every hour because of what may be within someone's mind at any given time. And the state of our mind is perpetually changing, as the quote by Mr. Ildan describes. A person does better when their mind is in good shape. When one allows their attitude to deteriorate, they do much worse. We do well when rested and happy and much less so when we are sick or tired. And even when our mind is in the best condition, it is impossible to win the battle without divine direction from the Spirit's work.

We all need help, and that help is provided in a multitude of ways. The blood of Christ and a Spirit-filled mind works with one's inner self to make them pure and whole. Jesus Christ also takes up the slack with His grace and mercy throughout one's life while one is learning. Inner strength is inexplicably provided to those who know God. He has given them everything they need to overcome whether they are strong or weak, rich or poor, old or young, happy or sad. He sent Christ first to show us the way and teach us how it is done, both through His words and by living example.

Thanks be to God for this wonderful blessing! Let us each draw closer to God and depend on His word. Let us draw strength from Christ and His example as we engage in the spiritual war for our minds.

DAY 5

Bless Your Heart

Bless your heart! (A phrase common in the southern United States)

Keep your heart with all vigilance,
* for from it flow the springs of life.* (Prov 4.23)

As a child, I heard the expression *Bless your heart!* a lot. It was usually said to me when I was hurt in some way, whether physically, emotionally, or spiritually. The hurt could have been caused by a slight physical ailment, such as a cut or a skinned knee, or even a monumental, life-changing loss. The common sentiment was used for anything that might have hurt me enough that I could choose a reaction that was not advantageous to my spiritual health.

As a general rule, this kind of vocabulary, its meaning, and the thinking behind it have been nearly forgotten by today's norms. Our society seems to have lost all concern for the spiritual health of anyone. There is an obsession with physical health. Physical doctors abound while we overlook the mental and spiritual aspects of health, and these last two are unavoidably related. We may even ignore our mental health because dealing with it will lead to discussions with a deeper scriptural component.

My spiritually minded role models of yesteryear realized that difficult circumstances could put my heart at spiritual risk. They were concerned that I might want to retaliate in a way that would dishonor God. They knew that if God was left entirely out of the situation, I could give into negative thinking, such as that I was somehow a victim. They recognized that I needed help from the Lord above with how I would choose to respond to whatever I was experiencing. They wanted good thoughts to enter my heart at just the right time.

So, *Bless your heart!* was really a prayer for me. My caregivers knew to be concerned about the spiritual well-being of my heart, and they expressed compassion toward me at just the right moments. They knew that my next thought or action could either promote trust in God or cause me to move away from Him. When thinking is formed by wisdom from above, it extends to others' healing and provides a balm for all kinds of pain. Jesus is called the Great Physician for a good reason. So, during trying times, I pray that God will bless all our hearts! Let's respond to our difficulties in ways that honor God while also being mindful of the condition of the tender young hearts around us.

WEEK FOURTEEN

DAY 1

Choose to Be Chosen

Keep Calm and Carry On. (A motivational slogan created by the British government prior to World War II)

"But I say to you, love your enemies and pray for those who persecute you..." (Matt 5.44)

The focus of our Lord when He started His ministry was on proclaiming the good news about His kingdom. Matthew explains, "And he went throughout all Galilee, teaching in their synagogues and proclaiming the gospel of the kingdom and healing every disease and every affliction among the people" (Matt. 4.23). There were many differences between what many thought (and taught) His mission would be and what His mission really entailed. When we understand the context in which Christ's teachings were originally written, it becomes easier to know how to apply Christ's teachings today.

I encourage you to reread the first recorded sermon found in Matthew 5–7. In it, Jesus made efforts to expose the false teachings promoted by the Jewish leaders of His day so that His message could be properly understood. The verse above represents one of these misconceptions. Evidently, praying for your enemies was not commonly done as one of the religious activities of the day. The difference between what the Jewish leaders taught and what they practiced was epic (Matt. 23). Even beyond that, there was a great deal of disconnect between what they taught and what Christianity was meant to look like and accomplish.

God planned the primary goal and outcome of Christ's sojourn here on earth to reconcile our relationship with Him that is lost by sin beginning in the garden. It was to provide each person the opportunity to be made clean, holy, and without spiritual blemish, so that they could be made righteous, holy, and useful to Him. The scheme of renewal has been completed and supplied by God through Christ to those willing to take on His purpose and nature. Those who accept the offer of grace through Jesus Christ, using their own free will, are the "predestined" spoken of in scripture (Rom. 8.29–30). Any can choose to be chosen and be among those predestined by God if they follow Christ's teaching.

Christians will always see things differently than those with a mindset learned from the world. When people respond with a kind heart to the evil surrounding them, they manifest a holy God to a blind and dying world. Christians are peculiar because they stand out and do not reflect the times. They reflect Jesus instead. In difficult times, find the opportunities to practice what you've learned from Christ in scripture. Show your faith in action. Those that do this shine a light on the proper path forward.

So, stay calm and carry on, folks! Be about the Lord's work. Be steadfast, immovable, and always abounding in the work of the Lord. Do not get sidetracked by the world and its lusts.

DAY 2

God's Use of Pain/Our Response to Pain

I am not a theologian or a scholar, but I am very aware of the fact that pain is necessary to all of us. In my own life, I think I can honestly say that out of the deepest pain has come the strongest conviction of the presence of God and the love of God. (Elizabeth Elliott)

He went a little farther and fell on his face, and prayed saying, "O my father, if it be possible, let this cup pass from me; nevertheless, not as I will but you will." (Matt 26.39)

There are various kinds of pain: physical, emotional, and spiritual. We all realize that the purpose of physical pain is to alert us to something broken in our bodies, and without the pain, we would not be aware of our problems. A few years ago, I suffered from a ruptured disk in my back that was extremely painful. It hindered all my movements and required a lot of attention. There was not a quick fix. The approach used for treatment included medication and steroid shots, while the general strategy was to allow my body gradually to heal itself. We quickly understand these concepts regarding physical pain, but what about when we experience emotional and spiritual pain?

Pain in these areas also alerts us that something must be corrected to make us whole again. It causes us to understand our need for help. The healing in these areas rarely has a quick fix. As with our physical ailments, sometimes the pain is so severe it hinders our movement in life and requires immediate attention. It takes time, effort, and (in some cases) diligent change to regain our emotional and spiritual health.

There is a point where we can, if we choose to, realize our relationship with God and His Son is broken and let it prompt us to seek the only remedy. It is no wonder that the price paid for a broken relationship with God required all types of pain. When we go to Christ as the Great Physician, we find healing for our spiritual and emotional pain. God Himself provides the medication for our emotional pain in the form of comfort. He also provides all the directions for healing in interpersonal relationships.

Sometimes our pain is ignored, misdiagnosed, or denied. In these cases, we, the patients, are at real risk. If we are prideful and deny our needs, we remain unaware of the spiritual illnesses that need correcting. If we refuse to look in the mirror or compare ourselves to the correct standard, then we can never choose to make the proper adjustments toward recovery, leaving us unprepared for judgment.

Let us all see spiritual pain as the alert that it is and respond with the intended growth. Let it move us in the direction of wellness and wholeness. Jesus, the great healer, speaks to our spirit on this point when He says, "Come to me, all who labor and are heavy laden, and I will give you rest. Take my yoke upon you, and learn from me, for I am gentle and lowly in heart, and you will find rest for your souls" (Matt 11.28–29). What a blessing!

DAY 3

The Ultimate Lawgiver

Sin, even if legalized by man, is still sin in the sight of God. His doctrine is not ours to change. (Russell M. Nelson)

"But in order that it may spread no further among the people, let us warn them to speak no more to anyone in this name." So they called them and charged them not to speak or teach at all in the name of Jesus. But Peter and John answered them, "Whether it is right in the sight of God to listen to you rather than to God, you must judge, for we cannot but speak of what we have seen and heard." (Acts 4.17–20)

Therefore, just as sin came into the world through one man, and death through sin, and so death spread to all men because all sinned— for sin indeed was in the world before the law was given, but sin is not counted where there is no law. (Rom 5.12–13)

Everyone who makes a practice of sinning also practices lawlessness; sin is lawlessness. (1 John 3.4)

Throughout time, the earthly kings of all nations have always ruled their kingdoms by imposing a law. Our democratic government has local, state, and federal laws. However, when leaders misunderstand the concept of God's law, all manner of abuse ensues. Some modern-day legislators, for example, may impose their will for personal gain or to further an agenda. Some will impose laws they believe to be for the good of all. We hope the government's legislative laws are always for the public interest, but they can sometimes be enacted for nefarious, self-serving reasons.

Any entity creates a law when it has the responsibility and right to dictate, enforce, and impose its will on those under its jurisdiction. But sin still happens when the Will and intent of God, the ultimate lawgiver, is violated. Sometimes it seems that this concept is lost on people. God is sovereign over all, and His Will always takes precedence over any other.

God has commanded his people to remain subject to the governing authorities (Rom 13.1). Even so, man cannot make a law that supersedes that which God ordained because God has absolute power and control over mankind, whether people choose to believe it or not. Sometimes we must make determinations about the rightness of our contrived legislative laws, and God's instruction must always take priority when a contradiction arises.

God not only has the right to legislate, but His direction is always intended to make one righteous. He intends for us to enter a relationship with Him and gain eternal life. And He has passed His authority to His Son. Following Jesus' baptism, the heavens were opened, and God said, "This is my beloved Son, with whom I am well pleased." Further, when Elijah (the prophet), Moses (the lawgiver), and Jesus were together on the mountain, Jesus was transfigured before them, and God said, *Listen to Him* (Luke 9.35). Jesus was then made the ultimate lawgiver, replacing Moses and the prophets, far above all rule and authority (Eph 1.21). Today, God directs His children through Jesus. He revealed God's will for mankind through His life and the written word, using His apostles as the writers.

God had a purpose and Will for mankind before time began; He had law from the beginning. When speaking on the subject of divorce to the Jews, Jesus refers to it in Matthew 19.8 when He says, "from the beginning it was not so." We can know some of God's laws instinctively or by observing His invisible attributes in the creation (Rom 1.20). Moses revealed a written law for Israel that served as a shadow of His plan to impart righteousness to all through His Son (Heb 10.1). God later sent His Son to reveal His Will through the gospel message. By sending Jesus, God fulfilled the Mosaic law, and He ratified a New Covenant by Christ's death.

When people disregard God's law, enmity, conflict, and confusion result. But all mankind has been subject to some God-imposed law, all have sinned and fallen short of the God-directed law of their time, and all need redemption! But all are saved by our one and only Lord and Savior's death on the cross, once for all and for all time (Heb 10.10, 12). May God help us to trust and obey His Will, and may His Will be done in all things! That is where true peace originates and resides.

DAY 4

Gleaning the Unseen

The sweetest thing in all my life has been the longing to find the place where all beauty came from. (C.S. Lewis)

One thing I have desired of the LORD,
    That will I seek:
That I may dwell in the house of the LORD
    All the days of my life,
To behold the beauty of the LORD,
    And to inquire in His temple.

For in the time of trouble
    He shall hide me in His pavilion;
In the secret place of His tabernacle
    He shall hide me;

He shall set me high upon a rock.
    And now my head shall be lifted up above my enemies all around me;
Therefore, I will offer sacrifices of joy in His tabernacle;
    I will sing, yes, I will sing praises to the LORD. (Psa 27.4–6)

So many people love the beach. Why do you think that is? Think about it awhile.

The salty air soothes wounds, physical and spiritual. The blowing wind reminds you how God's Spirit moves. The sound of the waves coming in and out provides hope that you can start over and over and over again. You can look out at a sky so expansive above a sea without end, accommodating all the birds God provides for. And the sand at your feet, as far as the eye can see, reminds you how all-powerful God really is, knowing He can count all those innumerable grains of sand.

The wonders of creation scream to you at the beach. Could it be that the beach provides hope for anyone paying attention? That the beach is a place where you can viscerally connect with the unseen? Some may not have been blessed with the experience of sitting on a beach for an extended period, but other places offer the same kind of rest for some. It can be experienced in the mountains while hiking or skiing, or perhaps on a lake while fishing, in the woods or farmland, or riding horseback through scenic countryside.

It's in any magnificent place where you can relax and ponder, where God's beauty explodes before you and in you.

This kind of hope and calm can be felt in marriages or other relationships too. It can be seen in Christian people who have been blessed with it. And it will be in heaven. If you can experience it in earthly places, God can provide it when and where He promises to do so. They often serve as reminders that there is a spiritual place above the fray, a place of quiet rest near the heart of God that can heal the soul.

These moments help us realize that quiet rest and fulfillment are within God's power to supply. And this makes you want to look for it. Those who seek it will find it (Luke 11.9). Let us all keep our eyes and hearts looking for true peace, gleaning it from creation, and finding it in His Word. And may all those manifesting God's quiet rest in a lost world be blessed with the peace that surpasses understanding.

DAY 5

Freewill and Freedom

It is the duty of all nations to acknowledge the providence of the Almighty God, to obey his Will, to be grateful for his benefits, and humbly to implore his protection and favor. (George Washington)

But the LORD of hosts, him you shall honor as holy. Let him be your fear, and let him be your dread. (Isa 8.13)

Anyone who understands American history can see that godly principles reside in its founding documents. Even though the people recognized as our nation's founders were flawed, and some extensively so, the principle of a Creator, the idea of personal responsibility, and individual freedom are all found within the American founding principles. The founders' personal lives have caused many to discount their contributions to the concepts of freedom and personal responsibility that are fundamental to the American idea. However, the rights of free will and freedom were initially presented to all people by God (Gen 1.18–20), and these concepts only come under assault when God is not revered in our culture.

In the absence of godly teachings, all manner of falsehoods takes hold. Without God, no nation can prosper for long. Freedom rings when the American dream does not elevate men or government over God. People do not need to depend on governments, dictators, themselves, or any entity other than God for protection. By relying on God, each person gains control over their destiny. Those who realize this know they are responsible for their soul and its eternal resting place. These insights go a long way in pointing people toward an abiding trust in the God of heaven and earth, and these spiritual principles will remain even if the America we know is lost.

Christians must fight for the American dream in ways that reflect the precepts and Will of our Father above! Let prayerful hearts always be "the power of the people" in difficult times. Let us ask the true ruler of heaven and earth for protection. He has always protected a remnant of His people throughout time to accomplish His work. Remember that He uses all people, both the evil and the good, in times of turmoil or peace, to either establish or pronounce judgments on all countries and peoples according to His Will (Dan 4.35).

WEEK FIFTEEN

DAY 1

Breaking the Cycle

If you never heal from what hurt you, you will bleed on people who didn't cut you. (Author Unknown)

To you, O Lord, belongs righteousness, but to us open shame, as at this day, to the men of Judah, to the inhabitants of Jerusalem, and to all Israel, those who are near and those who are far away, in all the lands to which you have driven them, because of the treachery that they have committed against you. To us, O Lord, belongs open shame, to our kings, to our princes, and to our fathers, because we have sinned against you. To the Lord our God belong mercy and forgiveness, for we have rebelled against him and have not obeyed the voice of the Lord our God by walking in his laws, which he set before us by his servants the prophets … As it is written in the Law of Moses, all this calamity has come upon us; yet we have not entreated the favor of the Lord our God, turning from our iniquities and gaining insight by your truth. Therefore the Lord has kept ready the calamity and has brought it upon us, for the Lord our God is righteous in all the works that he has done, and we have not obeyed his voice …O Lord, according to all your righteous acts, let your anger and your wrath turn away from your city Jerusalem, your holy hill, because for our sins, and for the iniquities of our fathers, Jerusalem and your people have become a byword among all who are around us … While I was speaking and praying, confessing my sin and the sin of my people Israel, and presenting my plea before the Lord my God for the holy hill of my God, while I was speaking in prayer, the man Gabriel, whom I had seen in the vision at the first, came to me in swift flight at the time of the evening sacrifice. He made me understand, speaking with me and saying, "O Daniel, I have now come out to give you insight and understanding. At the beginning of your pleas for mercy a word went out, and I have come to tell it to you, for you are greatly loved." (Dan 9.7–23)

The Bible uses the nation of Israel to teach us how God, the Creator, our loving Father, and our Lord and Master, operates within the world to provide redemption. He uses whatever means necessary to help people see that they need to forsake sin and repent. God provides guidance and direction, but He also steps back and allows nations to go their own way and do what is right in their own eyes and afterward experience the consequences of their decisions. We see this in the book of Judges where, over and over, we watch the calamity ensue, and later the nation cries out to God and repents. We see it during their captivity. Sometimes we can see the consequences of our sins unfold, just as we do the sins of our country or any group of people. The cycle is so repetitive that it is predictable.

When people forsake God, they hurt themselves and others. This process makes it difficult for some to see God's goodness. But an honest heart can be drawn to God by comprehending that things have gone too far. People may seek God when the scales have been tipped so far that evil is made blatantly manifest. God responds to all looking to seek His ways and His thoughts, just as He sent the angel who came to Daniel while he was praying.

But unless people demonstrate a genuine restorative attitude, there will be continual repercussions for each calamity. Everyone must repent, stop their bleeding, seek the truth, and stand up for it. We do not have to wait for others to be sorry for hurting us—we can choose to love the unlovable and forgive those who have allowed Satan to use them. We don't decide the personal fate of others by choosing to forgive them personally. Their own heart does that. Instead, we are manifesting God's love to a dying world and saving ourselves from all that is worthless. The cycle needs to stop.

We all need to be like little children as Jesus taught us. I'm reminded of what Judge Kavanaugh's ten-year-old daughter said when he was brutally harassed during his Supreme Court confirmation hearing. She said, "Daddy, maybe we need to pray for the woman." There are always good examples coming from the most unexpected places. God's plan is complete, and all is ready for anyone to choose faith, hope, mercy, and love. And we know, the greatest of these is love!

DAY 2

God's Gift

[H]e saved us, not because of works done by us in righteousness, but according to his own mercy, by the washing of regeneration and renewal of the Holy Spirit. (Titus 3.5)

But now that you have been set free from sin and have become slaves of God, the fruit you get leads to sanctification and its end, eternal life. (Rom 6.22)

The saying is trustworthy, and I want you to insist on these things, so that those who have believed in God may be careful to devote themselves to good works. These things are excellent and profitable for people. (Titus 3.8)

The penalty for sin is separation from God—spiritual death. And all sin and fall short of the will of God. But grace be to God that Jesus paid the price for sin—death—at one time, for all men. In his encouragement to Titus, Paul reminds him of the underlying point that must be understood by those who would give their lives to Christ. It is not of ourselves but rather a gift of God (Rom 6.23). It is provided because of His grace, giving us what we do not deserve—life and His mercy (the complement of grace), relenting on what we do deserve, namely, death. Through God's grace (and mercy), the price of death is paid by a sacrifice that removes our sins. This removes separation from God caused by sin and reconciles us to a holy God.

Keeping all of God's direction would work to save a person if they could actually do it, but since none can, the price has been paid by God Himself through the innocent sacrifice of His Son. Jesus became a man and lived a sinless life to qualify Himself to be a sacrifice for this very purpose. Christ's perfect sacrifice provided a way for God to make a man righteous, while His justice was still served because the price for sin—death (Heb 9.32)—was carried out by His Son to pay the price for our sins. This payment is something only a true and honest heart can access by faith when they choose to unite with Christ's death in baptism.

To take advantage of God's gift, each person must repent of their sins, give their broken heart over to Christ, be baptized into Christ and His death, and be born again to a new life. This new faithful life is then justified and brought back into alignment and into a relationship with the God of heaven, not because infractions are no longer committed, but because there is now a sacrificial payment for them. The passage from death to life joins each person to an eternal kingdom made without hands in the heavens. All the people in God's kingdom are His chosen people. They are called out of this world to participate together to bring the good news of His kingdom to others that need the same spiritual healing.

The knowledge of this one-time sacrifice (Heb 10.10, 12) should make each person forever grateful and aware that their actions have not saved them, but rather that the humiliating sacrifice of another has paid the price for their sins. Christ is their lamb without spot or wrinkle, and He takes away the sins of those in this world if they choose to accept this gift in faith.

This knowledge and our acceptance of it should dictate how a person spends their time after renewal. We are not to be involved in the conflicts or controversies of the world but rather in preparations for our final destination. Although conflicts and persecution may arise in response to a person's godly obedience, God's followers should be the instigators of neither. Jesus said these would happen when a person chooses to follow in His steps (John 15.20). Instead, we must live as a people who have received a most wonderful gift and be grateful enough to glorify God in the changed body each now inhabits. May we all determine to remember the Lord's sacrifice today and every day!

DAY 3

Justice and Righteousness

My argument against God was that the universe seemed so cruel and unjust. But how had I got this idea of just and unjust? A man does not call a line crooked unless he has some idea of a straight line. What was I comparing this universe with when I called it unjust? (C.S. Lewis)

Hear the word of the LORD, O king of Judah, who sits on the throne of David, you, and your servants, and your people who enter these gates. Thus says the LORD: Do justice and righteousness, and deliver from the hand of the oppressor him who has been robbed. And do no wrong or violence to the resident alien, the fatherless, and the widow, nor shed innocent blood in this place. For if you will indeed obey this word, then there shall enter the gates of this house kings who sit on the throne of David, riding in chariots and on horses, they and their servants and their people. But if you will not obey these words, I swear by myself, declares the LORD, that this house shall become a desolation. (Jer 22.2–5)

When a soul sees justice, it can partake of God's righteousness. Similarly, when justice is forsaken, a soul sees the absence of God and His goodness. God's people should carry out all of their dealings in a fair and just manner. When anyone is unjust in their decisions concerning others—whether in families, businesses, governments, etc.—they dishonor God.

In the book of Jeremiah, God elevates justice and righteousness as the identifiers of His people. He pleads with the people to return to Him, forsake their idols, and be aware of their responsibilities to the downtrodden. The language and symbolism used in the text are also Messianic, and the concepts are just as applicable today. God blesses those who promote justice, and he makes desolate those things that do not.

Interestingly, the absence of justice provides the very evidence needed to know that true justice does exist. It's like the way the absence of light defines darkness. A lack of justice, or suffering an injustice, declares to us that there is a just alternative. C. S. Lewis expresses this as one of his main arguments for belief in God rather than nonbelief. Ironically, God's wisdom works so that people can be brought to the truth from both sides of the experience and are presented with optimum opportunities to trust and obey.

When a man shows himself to be merely ritualistic in their service to God, it contrasts the very nature of who God is and the effect of what the person does is lost. Service to God and others should be built on a foundation of justice, mercy, kindness, and love. This is the fundamental concept upon which our belief, service, and obedience are to be properly carried out. May we all choose honesty of heart and the worship of God over pride and the worship of the idols of man and self. This daily choice has consequences in the here and now and into eternity.

DAY 4

Abiding Peace

Simple truths to repeat when you are in a spiritual battle:
> *God's got this*
> *The Lord fights for me*
> *Jesus loves me*
> *Not today, Satan*
> *I am a child of God*
> *He is able*
> *It is finished*
> *His grace is sufficient*
> *Joy comes in the morning*
> *I am not alone*
> *I am fearfully and wonderfully made*
> *Fear has no grip on me*
> *Christ is enough for me*
> *He had overcome the world*
> *I am a new creation in Christ*
> *Jesus conquered the grave*
> *Sin doesn't' define me Christ does*
> *Be still and know*
> *God is Good* (Author Unknown)

Answer me when I call, O God of my righteousness!
> *You have given me relief when I was in distress.*
> *Be gracious to me and hear my prayer!*

O men, how long shall my honor be turned into shame?
> *How long will you love vain words and seek after lies?*   Selah.
But know that the LORD *has set apart the godly for himself;*
> *the* LORD *hears when I call to him.*

Be angry, and do not sin;
> *ponder in your own hearts on your beds, and be silent.*   Selah.
Offer right sacrifices,
> *and put your trust in the* LORD.

There are many who say, "Who will show us some good?
> *Lift up the light of your face upon us, O* LORD!*"*
You have put more joy in my heart
> *than they have when their grain and wine abound.*

In peace I will both lie down and sleep;
  for you alone, O Lord, make me dwell in safety.
Hear me when I call, O God of my righteousness! (Psa 4.1–8)

The list of coping strategies above has been compiled from what God has revealed to His children throughout all of scripture. To take advantage of their power, we must have learned them from God's Word or seen them used by someone who understands and practices the spiritual concepts. Ultimately, we must put them into practice ourselves.

The Psalms speak of the tenuous fragility of our physical needs compared to having our spiritual and emotional needs satisfied by God's steadfast love. God provides safety in conflict and distress. His people are perpetually kept safe in the eye of any storm. They sleep soundly because they have learned the secret to real abiding peace. Their focus has changed from trusting in themselves and others to trusting and having faith in their creator. The only one who is truly faithful is God.

Psalm 4 is attributed to David as he pleads with his son Absalom and those who followed him. Really, all of us need to understand that the way of unrighteousness has no value when compared to the joy found from repentance. May we all listen and take advantage of these strategies. God still provides for His family so that we, too, can dwell in peace and safety!

DAY 5

God's Power and Might

God is our only comfort. He is also the supreme terror: the thing we most need and the thing we most want to hide from. He is our only possible ally, and we have made ourselves His enemy. (C.S. Lewis)

And people shall enter the caves of the rocks
  and the holes of the ground,
from before the terror of the Lord,
  and from the splendor of his majesty,
  when he rises to terrify the earth. (Isa 2.19)

When God's power and might are manifest in some form around us, it should remind us of His ever-presence and our accountability for sin. At the same time, we must remember that his steadfast love provided for our desperate plight through the sacrifice of His Son. The world wants us to re-define destructive weather events in a way that is devoid of any reference to a mighty God. Instead, they attribute it to a fabricated problem with the climate, as if it's something we can fix if we just stop driving our cars so much.

Even though we realize the need to be environmentally conscious and respectful of our God-given role over creation, we must not take it so far as to deny God's part as the creator and the sustainer of life in the world. Nor should we deny that God reminds people of the important things in life by using His power. He is always reaching out to a lost world.

Let us heed God's warnings and instructions in whatever form they take. When we see His power displayed around us, let's take time to establish fellowship with our Heavenly Father, who loves us all and wants none to be separated from Him!

WEEK SIXTEEN

DAY 1

Learning to Learn

Everything is hard before it is easy. (Johann Wolfgang von Goethe)

What you have learned and received and heard and seen in me—practice these things, and the God of peace will be with you. (Phil 4.9)

There are multiple quotes I repeat over and over to my children and grand-children. I am not sure they appreciate them, but I do it with the hope that they will hear the words in their minds at the right moment when they might be helpful. One I use frequently is a variation of the quote above: "Everything is hard if you do not know how to do it, and everything is easy if you do." I use this one when I see they are learning how to learn. That's when the information might help them the most if they only take it to heart.

Learning is ultimately in the hands of the learner because it is a choice and something everyone has total control over. The role of a parent, a teacher, or a coach is to provide love, help, and assistance, but if progress is ever made, it will be because the learner decided to learn. Most of the credit should go to the learner because no meaningful advancement is made without his or her gumption.

Each person must decide to acquire whatever skill is under consideration. Then they must choose to put forth the effort to practice and push through to the end of learning and not quit when it gets hard or inconvenient. To do something well, a person must repeat it over and over again. I believe this process is a gift from God and ties into a person's ability to find hope, trust, and stability. But the dynamic of true learning seems to be a lost practice. In some schools, the goals and achievements are so minimized that a learner's actual progress cannot really be recognized, even by them. The lack of incentive for children to overcome and do hard things is one of the tragedies of our time!

Schools require children to try and "learn" the curriculum, but everyone still decides whether they will or not. You really cannot make them. School should be about learning to learn. And the progress cannot be ascribed or manufactured. Conscious thought and habitual effort are required to learn or accomplish anything. And mastery of anything from basketball, to golf, to playing the violin, to knowing how to use the Bible takes spaced repetition of the activity. As for the latter, a love of Biblical learning and putting God's teaching into practice is paramount. As Paul told the Philippians, we must be practicing spiritual things!

There are multiple roadblocks to learning, but two come to mind. First, each person must accept that they may look foolish doing something new; and second, they must realize that failure always precedes success. Pride and the fear of failure can keep people from learning anything very well. A person can consciously choose not to learn something, but the reason should not involve pride or fear.

To overcome these roadblocks, we must replace pride with humility and the fear of failure with a trust that learning is possible with God's help. A learner's thinking starts to change when they experience incremental achievements within their heart. An active willingness to try, along with practiced effort, must be repetitiously expended over time before progress toward any life-altering learning or achievement is made.

Working with others on the learning process can go a long way in helping them be successful. But it will not affect a heart unwilling to try or practice. Remembering this will help us learn how to use our time and efforts. Teach the willing and desirous. And let the others alone while they learn through experience not to be so unwilling! Above all, Christians must be putting God's Word into practice. We cannot be like the unjust steward who hid his talent in the ground. We must overcome our fear of learning and doing new things for God. Let us boldly put His teachings into practice!

DAY 2

Planting Ourselves

When you can't control what is happening, challenge yourself to control the way to respond to what's happening. That's where the power is. (Author Unknown)

And Jesus said, "Father, forgive them, for they know not what they do." And they cast lots to divide his garments. And the people stood by, watching, but the rulers scoffed at him, saying, "He saved others; let him save himself, if he is the Christ of God, his Chosen One!" The soldiers also mocked him, coming up and offering him sour wine and saying, "If you are the King of the Jews, save yourself!" There was also an inscription over him, "This is the King of the Jews."

One of the criminals who were hanged railed at him, saying, "Are you not the Christ? Save yourself and us!" But the other rebuked him, saying, "Do you not fear God, since you are under the same sentence of condemnation? And we indeed justly, for we are receiving the due reward of our deeds; but this man has done nothing wrong." And he said, "Jesus, remember me when you come into your kingdom." And he said to him, "Truly, I say to you, today you will be with me in paradise."

It was now about the sixth hour, and there was darkness over the whole land until the ninth hour, while the sun's light failed. And the curtain of the temple was torn in two. Then Jesus, calling out with a loud voice, said, "Father, into your hands I commit my spirit!" And having said this he breathed his last. Now when the centurion saw what had taken place, he praised God, saying, "Certainly this man was innocent!" (Luke 23.34–47)

Even on the cross, Jesus exhibited the power to touch people's hearts in ways the world cannot comprehend. The criminal offering insults on one side of Jesus expresses the thoughts held by those using human wisdom. On the other side, the robber expressed a divine understanding. The centurion, as he witnessed the entire spectacle, began to understand the nature of the kingdom preaching that Jesus demonstrated with His life and His death.

Christians are to die with Christ all day long. Their free will choices to deny the flesh and its lusts, along with all their responses to life's challenges, are different from the people of this world. Their actions identify them as partakers of the out-of-this-world kingdom message. Their obedience glorifies God, not themselves, and elevates the message to a status that can be understood by honest, onlooking hearts. All those seeing the culmination of heaven-directed choices will either see love and sacrifice or mock their efforts. The scene on the cross epitomized this dynamic.

If Christians want to see the same results Jesus had in His life, they must operate like Him. No one can see a message of power or hope when a person thinks like a victim, retaliates with anger, or lives in fear of persecution! This Christ-like example may impact only a few people watching. Nevertheless, onlookers will have the opportunity to see the evidence of God's influence as the seeds of spiritual truth are planted. They may even sprout in the future, just as in the case of the centurion.

Sometimes it seems as if the screaming mob gets their way in the short term. To those who are perishing, godly actions will seem foolish as the godless choose to do what is right in their own eyes. But those seeking Christ will be taught and instructed in righteousness by the hand of our almighty God. God's children must submit to God and gratefully follow His direction! They realize God is in control and are so thankful that He is! Even more, people watching are able to learn about Him by His exemplified Word.

Let us all be mindful of the God-directed teaching process, then take each thought captive as we do the Will of the Father. Watch and wait as the mighty hand of God works in the lives of the people around you! The process works wherever your conduct is "planted" to make a difference! You don't have to travel the world to teach the gospel message, just make sure your actions reflect God's desires and not your own.

DAY 3

Being Refreshed

Some people could be given an entire field of roses and only see the thorns in it. Others could be given a single weed and see the wildflower in it. Perception is a key component to gratitude. And gratitude is a key component of joy! (Amy Weatherly)

Oh give thanks to the LORD, for he is good,
for his steadfast love endures forever!

Let the redeemed of the Lord *say so,*
whom he has redeemed from trouble
and gathered in from the lands,
from the east and from the west,
from the north and from the south.

Some wandered in desert wastes,
finding no way to a city to dwell in;
hungry and thirsty,
their soul fainted within them.
Then they cried to the Lord *in their trouble,*
and he delivered them from their distress.
He led them by a straight way
till they reached a city to dwell in.
Let them thank the Lord *for his steadfast love,*
for his wondrous works to the children of man! (Psa 107.1–6)

Praise, thanksgiving, and gratitude are meant to keep us all refreshed! From the smallest examples of a cool, fresh glass of water on a hot day to an edifying worship service, a Christian will respond to the refreshing experience with a sense of peace. A bit of heaven. And that inner rejoicing manifests itself in an intense desire to share it.

Thanksgiving, peace, and joy come with the realization that the Lord is always there with us, which is especially comforting in times of trouble. Sunday is the day each week when Christians look up with thankfulness and realize God is there and that He is worthy of their praise. They have taken advantage of the great sacrifice He offered for all people, for all time. The first day of the week is His time when He asks us to "remember," and we love to give it to Him! Have a joyful Lord's Day!

DAY 4

Standing on our Knees

It is men, not God, who have produced racks, whips, prison, slavery, guns, bayonets, bombs; it is by human avarice or human stupidity, not by churlishness of nature, that we have poverty and overwork. But there remains, nonetheless, much suffering which cannot thus be traced to ourselves. (C.S. Lewis, *The Problem of Pain*)

The LORD your God will raise up for you a prophet like me from among you, from your brothers—it is to him you shall listen—just as you desired of the LORD your God at Horeb on the day of the assembly, when you said, «Let me not hear again the voice of the LORD my God or see this great fire any more, lest I die." And the LORD said to me, "They are right in what they have spoken." (Deut 18.16–17)

The world sometimes portrays God as a kind of Santa Claus who gives out goodies to children on His lap. However, this picture of God blinds people to the truth about who He is. Moses explained that a prophet like him would be raised up from among the people to speak God's word to them. God sent human mouthpieces with His voice, but the hearers were not to forget to esteem God as they did when they experienced His descent on Mt. Horeb. Although a man would do the talking, God reminds the people that to fear and stand in awe of Him was the correct mindset to maintain. Likewise, we need to behold "the goodness and the severity of God" in order to have the right picture of God in our minds (Rom 11.22).

God's abilities, His power, and might are manifested in the worst of times when the feebleness of mankind is exposed! Suffering and pain can come as the consequences of the free will choices made by ourselves or others. They also result from things that happen seemingly by chance that cannot be explained. God oversees and controls it all. In difficult times, we can "stand in awe" of God and realize the need to fall on our knees. Although the spirit desires to serve in hard times, the frailness of mankind is revealed in the presence and revelation of His awesome power.

Worthy of glory and honor is the God and Father of our Lord Jesus Christ, who has provided all the spiritual blessings found in Christ (Eph 1.3). Jesus came and revealed how Christians are to respond in times of great distress. While on earth during difficult times, He maintained a spirit of calm and profound gratefulness for everything God provides. Jesus explained to his parents as a lad of twelve that he was here on earth to do the Will and work of God, His Father. He explained to all His followers that they were to leave the world behind, repent, and be born again to follow Him and desire to enter a heavenly kingdom with a ruler who is not of this world. And so are all His followers today that choose to be His disciples!

DAY 5

Trying Jesus

Many people say, "Try Jesus;" you don't try Jesus. He is not there to be experimented with. Christ is not on trial. You are. (A.W. Tozer)

And they came to Jesus and saw the demon-possessed man, the one who had had the legion, sitting there, clothed and in his right mind, and they were afraid. And those who had seen it described to them what had happened to the demon-possessed man and to the pigs. And they began to beg Jesus to depart from their region. As he was getting into the boat, the man who had been possessed with demons begged him that he might be with him. And he did not permit him but said to him, "Go home to your friends and tell them how much the Lord has done for you, and how he has had mercy on you." (Mark 5.15–19)

The motive from which we approach any matter is relevant to the outcome. And in the case of spiritual things, it is paramount. You do not "try" Jesus. You either reject Him or come to Him after you have allowed yourself to be exposed to His power and preeminence. In the passage above, the people understood that Jesus had cast out demons from a man into beasts and it scared them. Most wanted to send Jesus away. Only the man who had been healed desired to follow and obey Jesus.

Christians are often like that demon-possessed man whom Jesus made whole. But sometimes, even when Jesus heals the hearts of His people today, it may scare some so much that they ask Him to leave. For them, the personal cost of repentance may be too great, and the life changes that have been made and that still need to take place are too significant for the faithless to comprehend or be willing to pay. Indeed, like the healed man, a Christian's reformed spiritual behavior should be so dramatic that it reveals a godly source as its only possible origin.

Christians must follow and obey, realizing Jesus has made them all part of His company of healers! Their purpose is to help lead others to Christ. Each must stay in their lives and engage with those who can see the transformation to show them what real redemption looks like. And a Christian always gives credit to his Savior for a transformed spirit by following Him even during extreme difficulties. That is when our efforts can have the most revealing and overwhelming effect!

WEEK SEVENTEEN

DAY 1

White Fields

For if you keep silent at this time, relief and deliverance will rise for the Jews from another place, but you and your father's house will perish. And who knows whether you have not come to the kingdom for such a time as this? (Est 4.14)

Ask, and it will be given to you; seek, and you will find; knock, and it will be opened to you. For everyone who asks receives, and the one who seeks finds, and to the one who knocks it will be opened. (Matt 7.7–8)

There is always someone just around the corner who is seeking answers. And anyone seeking God will find Him. All disciples need to be aware of these opportunities to try and help an interested person learn about God. Christians usually do not have to look very far away to find these seekers. Though the times are different, the fields are still "white for harvest" (Jn. 4.35).

It is not our will at stake but rather that of our Father above. God will assure all honest hearts find the opportunity to learn. His people are simply tools to accomplish that purpose. And God has always taught using the few to reach the many. Jesus taught relatively few people while on earth, but those then spread the gospel throughout the world, and their writings still impact the world today!

Christians should be focused on people who will appreciate the God-directed teaching. God's mind and words are precious and holy, but some people do not want to hear it. This stubbornness is their personal heart problem, and only they can heal it. You may be able to circle back to someone like this if they learn to desire and seek the living water. And never worry that you are someone's only hope. Someone far more powerful than you has that covered.

Let all follow and zealously participate in the model shown to us in scripture. Christians teach who they know what they know, and then those will be able to go on and do likewise. The important thing to remember is that each Christian must make a righteous determination as to when to teach and when to walk away. Let's be ready and take every opportunity provided. Start with yourself, your family, your workplace, and your congregation!

DAY 2

Freewill Parenting

Sometimes the best way to help our kids is not to help them. (Kristen Walsh)

Or do you presume on the riches of his kindness and forbearance and patience, not knowing that God's kindness is meant to lead you to repentance? But because of your hard and impenitent heart you are storing up wrath for yourself on the day of wrath when God's righteous judgment will be revealed.

He will render to each one according to his works: to those who by patience in well-doing seek for glory and honor and immortality, he will give eternal life; but for those who are self-seeking and do not obey the truth, but obey unrighteousness, there will be wrath and fury. There will be tribulation and distress for every human being who does evil, the Jew first and also the Greek, but glory and honor and peace for everyone who does good, the Jew first and also the Greek. (Rom 2.4–10)

As a parent of any child, no matter the age, we must always emulate how God works with His children and use it as a model for discipline. While parents are their children's teachers and instructors, they must never be manipulative or controlling much past his or her infancy. The way a parent works with their children should reveal to the child how God works with His people, and so the concept of free will must necessarily be passed on and communicated.

Parents are looking to develop what I once heard explained as independent dependence. At about age twelve, children should be given enough independence to make some of their own decisions. The parent should empower the children to make decisions under their guidance and supervision and learn from the consequences of their own choices. And they do not necessarily need to create all their children's consequences. God intentionally designed many consequences that are naturally inherent to everyone's good or bad decisions. These are built into how things work in the world, where His wisdom and providence are constantly at play.

This concept is under discussion within the first few chapters of Romans. Both peace and discipline come from God and apply to both Jews and Gentiles. Each soul sins and needs to be reconciled to God, but free will is still intact and justice is still served. If a parent always dictates their child's good behavior, then the child does not give himself credit for making a good decision, and the peace of God does not result. If parents water down or eliminate the natural consequences of bad behavior, children may feel emboldened to repeat it!

Parents, do not be afraid to allow your children to suffer the consequences of their actions! Resist the urge to step in before they have learned the life lesson. If your child chooses well, they will understand what it feels like to own a good decision. If they choose poorly, they will experience the grief that results. Child rearing is both challenging and time-consuming, and there are so few years to pass the truth on to your children. It must be done with much thought and prayer! Taking the time when children are young to teach and exemplify how God treats His children will pay significant dividends when they are older, both for them and for you, the parents!

DAY 3

Faithful Poise

If you wake up feeling fragile, remember that God is not, and then trust him to be everything you need today! (C. S. Lewis)

And Daniel went in and requested the king to appoint him a time, that he might show the interpretation to the king. Then Daniel went to his house and made the matter known to Hananiah, Mishael, and Azariah, his companions, and told them to seek mercy from the God of heaven concerning this mystery, so that Daniel and his companions might not be destroyed with the rest of the wise men of Babylon. Then the mystery was revealed to Daniel in a vision of the night. Then Daniel blessed the God of heaven. Daniel answered and said:

"Blessed be the name of God forever and ever,
*   to whom belong wisdom and might.*
He changes times and seasons;
*   he removes kings and sets up kings;*
he gives wisdom to the wise
*   and knowledge to those who have understanding;*
he reveals deep and hidden things;
*   he knows what is in the darkness,*
*   and the light dwells with him.*
To you, O God of my fathers,
*   I give thanks and praise,*
for you have given me wisdom and might,
*   and have now made known to me what we asked of you,*
*   for you have made known to us the king's matter."* (Dan 2.16–23)

Although there is no indication that Daniel felt fragile in the way C. S. Lewis refers to above, he was in a fragile position. He was about to be killed because the king could not trust his "magicians" (i.e., advisors). Nebuchadnezzar had asked for a feat from them that only God could provide. So Daniel trusted that God would deliver and help them through their dilemma.

Daniel requested time to pray and asked his friends to join in the petition. God responds to reveal both the dream and the interpretation Nebuchadnezzar demanded, and His answer provides a way of deliverance for Daniel, his friends, and even the magicians. Daniel, before any continued action, prays to God to praise and recognize His sovereignty over everything.

Note that there seems to be no fear or frantic responses by Daniel or his friends, and he demonstrates faithful poise even though, at the time, he was a young man. The same quality of faith is evident throughout all of Daniel's life. It is expressed in his friends' lives as well. They were all subjected to difficult circumstances, and their faith became a shining light to future generations. We are the beneficiaries of his example as it demonstrates how to deal with challenging situations by responding with great faith.

Daniel's example should encourage us to strengthen our faith and hope in God. May we all resolve to operate the way he did in response to king Nebuchadnezzar. While we will not be given the ability to interpret dreams or visions the same way as Daniel, we all have access to the words and wisdom given us by God! We must learn to trust God in our present times. We, too, can glorify God through faith and properly using His Word in the time we all live!

DAY 4

Trusting God's Will

We will never fully appreciate God's grace if we have never understood His justice. (Ken Craig)

And when they prevailed over them, the Hagrites and all who were with them were given into their hands, for they cried out to God in the battle, and he granted their urgent plea because they trusted in him. (1 Chron 5.20)

The Israelite tribes won many battles when they put their trust in the one true God, and He proved faithful to answer their pleas. Today, as a spiritual Israel, Christians are called to do the same. When Christians are in the battles of life, they can see God as faithful as they seek His assistance and follow His directives, knowing He has their best interests at heart.

The physical Israelites knew they were on a mission for God and doing His work. Likewise, spiritual Israel understands that fellowship with God changes them and obligates them to His service, and it comes with God's protection and care. This lasts as long as they align themselves with His Will. Let us not allow the world's view to mold what we think is good or measure goodness against some self-defined standard. God's Will is the true standard, and His people have always overcome by trusting in it.

God still responds to petitions from those who acknowledge His rule today. We must be assured that God is faithful and just. He knows how to protect us and help us grow as we learn to be more like Christ. He can use whatever circumstances exist to accomplish His purpose and help His people. Hold on to this hope, for God cares for you! He is in control, and He has power over all things! Whatever you do in word or deed, do all using His Word and emulating the character of His Son (Col 3.17).

DAY 5

Shake off the Dust

In life, it is important to know when to stop arguing with people and simply let them be wrong! (Author Unknown)

Do not give dogs what is holy, and do not throw your pearls before pigs, lest they trample them underfoot and turn to attack you. (Matt 7.6)

And he could do no mighty work there, except that he laid his hands on a few sick people and healed them. And he marveled because of their unbelief.
    And he went about among the villages teaching.
    And he called the twelve and began to send them out two by two, and gave them authority over the unclean spirits …
    And he said to them, "Whenever you enter a house, stay there until you depart from there. And if any place will not receive you and they will not listen to you, when you leave, shake off the dust that is on your feet as a testimony against them."
    …When he went ashore, he saw a great crowd, and he had compassion on them, because they were like sheep without a shepherd. And he began to teach them many things. (Mark 6.5–11, 34)

When Jesus came into the world, He had compassion for all the common people with whom He came in contact. Especially the ones without leadership. Frequently, He not only helped them to improve their circumstances, He also taught them how to transform their lives, how to be reborn, how to gain spiritual sight, and how to live their lives.

Like today, all were interested in being physically healed or fed, but people did not always appreciate the spiritual teaching. When Jesus indicated that there might be some self-reflection, principled choices, or lifestyle changes that may need improvement, many said thanks but no thanks. Some were even enraged that Jesus would dare indicate there may be some personal responsibility attached to improving their attitude (Matt 3.7–10).

In the verses above, Jesus addresses this issue and gives direction on when to stop and teach or walk away and refuse to argue. He indicates by His first sermon, referred to by some as the Sermon on the Mount found in Matthew 5–7, that the word is holy and divinely dedicated. In the Mark passage, He warns the twelve about the possibility of being rejected. Jesus gave them directions on how to deal with this phenomenon, telling them to "shake off the dust" from their feet. And in the latter part of Mark 6, Jesus modeled compassion when He approached those needing teaching.

In some cases, His words sound harsh to us. However, Jesus simply states that when people are unappreciative of the teaching, it's time to move on to the next person. Go and find someone who sees the value of the message. Patiently seek people who show interest because they are always out there. Time is limited, and those spreading God's truth need to spend whatever time they have judiciously.

Being judicious doesn't mean we have any less compassion or make fewer attempts to teach. It just means we need to realize there are situations in which the Word is not well received. In fact, in a society that preaches that everyone can do and have everything just like they want, you will be hard-pressed not to face rejection regularly. All you need to do is listen to how coffee is ordered at Starbucks to realize that most people like things to be "just right" for them. A message that requires life changes is often declined.

Let all Christians learn to follow this direction from our Lord. Let's be hearers and teachers. Each must make a personal decision to stop and listen to the truth, and anyone trying to teach truth can walk away when it irritates the hearers. God will provide the lost with another opportunity to learn when their hearts become receptive. Each Christian must do what they can, wherever they are, whenever an opportunity presents itself. Each needs to be able to explain the truth. And each needs to know when it is more prudent to just walk away.

WEEK EIGHTEEN

DAY 1

Roadmap for Overcoming

No pain, no gain! (Author Unknown)

For it was fitting that he, for whom and by whom all things exist, in bringing many sons to glory, should make the founder of their salvation perfect through suffering. ... For because he himself has suffered when tempted, he is able to help those who are being tempted. (Heb 2.10, 18)

And being made perfect, he became the source of eternal salvation to all who obey him... (Heb 5.9)

The illustration of the caterpillar's transformation into a butterfly shows a process that involves a necessary struggle. As the butterfly labors to escape from the cocoon, it gains the strength and ability to fly. The butterfly's life is negatively impacted if the struggle is thwarted through intervention from an outside source. It is said that they will never be able to learn to fly if the cocoon is cut by someone trying to make it easier for the butterfly to extract itself. It will then likely die.

The struggle of the emerging butterfly demonstrates an essential spiritual concept that is truly life-altering when we comprehend it. Value, learning, and stability come from enduring the struggles that come from a dramatic change. Jesus showed us that even He needed to endure suffering to complete His ultimate fullness, or using the Biblical terms, perfection, or completeness. The fact that Jesus had to become a man, suffer, and sacrifice himself to come to the aid of mankind helps us accept the fact that suffering is necessary and valuable, especially in the Christian life.

Jesus' death on the cross as payment for man's sins was imperative to pay our price for sin resulting in our justification. And the suffering itself gave

Jesus the fullest understanding of our human struggles. It enabled Christ to achieve His purpose and become perfectly fit for His dual roles as our King and High Priest. By living the life of a suffering servant, Jesus paved the way for everyone to learn how to overcome this world and its temptations. In other words, the Lord provided mankind with the roadmap for overcoming.

Once sin had entered the world, no mentally competent person would be able to avoid its impact. And that meant all would spiritually die when they chose to participate in sin. In the process of each person's maturing, all will eventually fall, and we all must learn how to get back up again. Suffering, then, must necessarily be something God can use as a positive, such that it can contribute in some worthy manner to our spiritual welfare (2 Pet 2.9). We all need to learn how to deal with the consequences of sin because we will encounter them throughout our life.

Through suffering, Jesus provides the way for all of mankind to escape death. It becomes necessary for each disciple to learn, understand, and appreciate life's struggles as being instructive. Each disciple must learn how to suffer with grace. When we understand the benefit of suffering, we will stop trying to remove all forms of difficulty from our environment. We must recognize it as a tool that God Himself uses to help us mature spiritually. We will not remove it from our children's paths. Instead, we must learn how to use suffering effectively. If we do not, the lack of it will stunt our growth as we unintentionally hinder ourselves and others from ever being able to fly!

DAY 2

True Worship

Worship will get you through the roughest times of your life because it shifts your focus from the problem to the problem solver. (Author Unknown)

How precious is your steadfast love, O God!
The children of mankind take refuge in the shadow of your wings.
They feast on the abundance of your house,
and you give them drink from the river of your delights.

For with you is the fountain of life;
in your light do we see light. (Psa 36.7–9)

I once visited the Church of the Nativity in Bethlehem, one of the oldest church structures in existence. It is purported to be built over the site where Jesus was born. The original building is thought to have been erected by the Roman Emperor Constantine and his mother Helena in AD 326. During that time, people were trying to pinpoint the exact locations referenced in the Biblical text. Bethlehem is located in Israel's West Bank, and many church groups use it regularly for their services.

Although the structure has been used for many years and boasts of great historical significance, worship can take place wherever any of the true worshipers of God gather together. It's not required to take place on "this mountain" or in Jerusalem. True worshippers worship in spirit and truth, and God desires such people to worship Him (John 4.21–23). When Christians attend worship services and learn from scripture, they can see God and what is good. Of course, good is that which precedes from God.

The activity of worship can allow each worshipper to see their imperfections. That is because when a person is faced with the character of our Lord, they can see the discrepancies within their own lives and then make corrections, not just being listeners but doers of the His word. They are strengthened in the activity of worship as they use the time to remember what their deliverance cost, which was the cruel death of the Lord. All who have received grace can do it—those who have chosen to repent and drink freely of the living water provided by God and His Son. Oh, how marvelous and wonderful that this activity has been given to us so we can learn about God and remember His great works! He truly is our great problem solver!

DAY 3

Becoming a Radiance

Bloom where you are planted. (A popular saying in religious circles)

Bind up the testimony, seal the law among my disciples. (Isa 8.16 KJV)

The integrity of the upright guides them,
  but the crookedness of the treacherous destroys them.
Riches do not profit in the day of wrath,
  but righteousness delivers from death.
The righteousness of the blameless keeps his way straight,
  but the wicked falls by his own wickedness. (Prov 11.3–5)

It is truly astounding how God works with his people. His righteousness is a light that shines anytime it is manifested in the lives of godly people. The absence of light indicates the lack of godly influence.

When people do little things that reveal a heart and spirit filled with love, hope, and mercy, they transmit spiritual signals that indicate they are obedient to God's truth. While explaining the coming destruction of Israel, God said in Isaiah 8.16, "Bind up the testimony, seal the law among my disciples." God's true disciples, who have been remade into his image, without manipulation, equipped only with the intent to glorify and praise God with their actions, can influence the world.

God's disciples are equipped with proper teaching and renewed by His Holy Spirit. They are dispersed around the world to spread God's word when His love and His nature are seen in them. These learners reflect God in their actions because they decided on a purpose to glorify God rather than themselves.

Every minute of every day, the true disciples emit a spirit filled with the knowledge of God. Each one impacts others, one person at a time. It is not contrived. It is not systemized. It is not manipulated. Instead, it occurs because of the character of God's followers. They do it without knowing who is looking because it results from a pure and transformed heart. The inner change directly impacts the day-to-day character of those who are made good.

And, my friend, this is how God uses His Word and His disciples to change the world, shine light in it, and give hope to others. God's people, as they interact with God's Word and change in spirit, become a radiance to all the persons in their sphere of influence. They need not worry so much about how they are placed for their work, but rather be willing to work wherever they are and where God has seen fit to place them.

We must spread seeds of truth with our lives and bloom where we are planted! Our placement may be as a parent, a husband, a wife, an employee, a leader, a follower, a student, or a teacher. No matter where God's people are, once they have been made whole and holy, they affect their environments in ways they may never realize!

DAY 4

Watch and Pray

We will never appreciate Jesus' agonizing prayer in Gethsemane, we will never appreciate his sweating, as it were, great drops of blood, until we grasp in the depths of our being that Jesus was staring at the wrath of God we deserve. (Jerry Bridges)

Then he said to them, "My soul is very sorrowful, even to death; remain here, and watch with me." And going a little farther he fell on his face and prayed, saying, "My Father, if it be possible, let this cup pass from me; nevertheless, not as I will, but as you will." And he came to the disciples and found them sleeping. And he said to Peter, "So, could you not watch with me one hour? Watch and pray that you may not enter into temptation. The spirit indeed is willing, but the flesh is weak." (Matt 26.38–41)

This passage in Matthew has always confounded me. It is hard for me to believe that Jesus was asking God to choose some means for our redemption other than the one He originally purposed. Over time I have heard many explanations for the words spoken by Jesus, such as that He may have been asking for the crucifixion to go quickly (which it did). He could have been saying something like *let's go on with this*. The quote by Mr. Bridges offers another possible explanation. If people attempt to grasp the idea of Jesus as both God and the Son of man, we can then realize that only Jesus could genuinely understand the cost our sins deserve. The true depth of His words may even be beyond our understanding from a mere human perspective.

Jesus knew God would have to look away when He took on our sins. Jesus was not looking forward to this happening. But we know it did happen because when Jesus was on the cross He said to God, *My God, My God, why hast thou forsaken me!* That is what was excruciating for Jesus.

But what really stands out is the frailty of those that could not even stay awake to pray with Jesus. He had told them of His deep distress and explained what was going to happen, but they did not comprehend the magnitude of the situation and just went to sleep. The contrast is stark.

Do we do that? Are we presented with a supercharged grandness that we meet with superficial semi-acknowledgment? There are times when I worry that I have not risen to the importance of such occasions. I know, in retrospect, that I must have treated some things casually that were deserving of awe or respect. Or maybe we see this played out in reverse. We recognize the grandness or danger in a thing, while all those around us are, well, "sleeping." Either way, we all need to be aware of this human frailty in ourselves so we can warn others to "watch and pray!" as Jesus did.

Our sin was not overlooked. Jesus stood in for us and took our punishment. In this one short period of time, justice was made available to each one by God through Him. He willingly chose to stand in and take our punishment with the only possible acceptable sacrifice—His own sinless body. He loved us all so! And as His people, we are also to love one another.

DAY 5

God's Way

If you want God to close and open doors, let go of the doorknob. (Author Unknown)

All the men and women, the people of Israel, whose heart moved them to bring anything for the work that the LORD had commanded by Moses to be done brought it as a freewill offering to the LORD.
Then Moses said to the people of Israel, "See, the LORD has called by name Bezalel the son of Uri, son of Hur, of the tribe of Judah; and he has filled him

with the Spirit of God, with skill, with intelligence, with knowledge, and with all craftsmanship. … He has filled them with skill to do every sort of work done by an engraver or by a designer or by an embroiderer in blue and purple and scarlet yarns and fine twined linen, or by a weaver—by any sort of workman or skilled designer." (Exod 35.29–35)

I can't explain how God works in the hearts of people. We know He has done so in the past and that He still does today. At the same time, we understand that in no way does God interrupt a person's free will. All His children are willing participants in allowing Him to do His work in their lives.

God reveals Himself through His written Word, and so personal study is a significant component in understanding the mind of God. A person seeking God must present themselves with a desire to accomplish His purposes and offer themselves freely to Him for His use. They willingly alter their resolve to match God's, forsaking their desires when the two are in conflict. As in the parable of the talents, they use what they have to glorify God, whether little or much.

As God's children, we should look for and take advantage of the growth opportunities God provides us rather than attempting to control circumstances to fulfill our plans. In no way does God require us to be manipulative for His Will to be accomplished. Remember the story of Sarah and Hagar and so many others, where a lack of faith prompted individuals to carry out plans in ways that were not God-directed. At the time, they convinced themselves their motives were righteous.

It is so popular today to adopt the mantra of the old song by Frank Sinatra entitled, "I Did It My Way." If you think about it, God molded anyone He ever used to accomplish a profound purpose by using extraordinarily difficult circumstances. Examples include Joseph in prison before ruling Egypt, Moses in Midian before leading the Israelite nation, Daniel in Babylonian captivity before prophesying to the remnant, and so on. We see the pattern through the entirety of scripture. All learned trust from great tribulation and difficulty. Not one did things "their way."

In stark contrast, our society doesn't want to suffer at all to achieve excellence. It seems people today take themselves out of any circumstance that may not be to their liking. Everyone wants their "trophy" regardless of their skill level or how hard they work. The worst byproduct of a culture that gives everyone a trophy is that it tends to vilify those who run each race with profound practice and dedication. It creates a crowd of emotionally stunted and ill-prepared adults unable to mature properly. Each one actively retreats from what God could use as their training ground.

The world must not fool us! God will find another avenue to help people grow, which may be far less pleasant. Let all God's children be prudent to let "God take the wheel" in their lives. Let Him open and close all the doors! Let us all learn to deal with difficulties with godly wisdom, grace, and humility. For God to be glorified through those He influences, others must be able to see Him acting in their lives! Life may indeed be more difficult from a worldly standpoint, but we can "consider it all joy" knowing that we are choosing to allow God to make us "perfect and complete, lacking nothing" (Jas 1.2–4).

WEEK NINETEEN

DAY 1

He Holds All Things Together

And when the Lord smelled the pleasing aroma, the LORD said in his heart, "I will never again curse the ground because of man, for the intention of man's heart is evil from his youth. Neither will I ever again strike down every living creature as I have done. While the earth remains, seedtime and harvest, cold and heat, summer and winter, day and night, shall not cease." (Gen 8.21–22)

He is the radiance of the glory of God and the exact imprint of his nature, and he upholds the universe by the word of his power. After making purification for sins, he sat down at the right hand of the Majesty on high. (Heb 1.3)

God's promise following the flood assures us that the climate cannot be controlled or destroyed by men. He established the seasonal changes and will ensure that they never cease. However, today there is not even a consensus that God exists. There is a void of Biblical teaching and ideals in our country and worldwide. And even when some recognize that there is a God, little is known about Him or how He works. This ignorance is why so many are fooled by the godless and erroneous arguments of the day.

Jesus came down to earth to show mankind the Father. The Bible tells us that He holds the universe together, and it will not be destroyed again by flooding or any other weather event until the final judgment comes. Following the great flood, God gave a sign in the rainbow to remember His covenant, and it is as relevant today as it was to Noah and those early generations. While His promise doesn't negate our responsibility to manage the natural resources God has provided, it does mean that it is close to blasphemy to suggest that we humans can thwart the plans and promises God has made.

I once heard a quote by Kenneth Wuest that struck me. It was not necessarily his main point, but the illustration caught my attention. He said:

> When the Lord was seated at the well of Sychar, completely exhausted in His humanity, He in His deity was spinning the earth on its axis, rotating it around the sun, holding the stars in their courses, and hurling the entire universe with incomprehensible speed through space. The dual nature of our Lord, that of God and that of man, is seen here in one of its most glorious manifestations.

We all need to see how far above mankind God really is. Jesus tried so hard to show God to His followers, but most of the time it just went over the heads of His audience. And it will go over our heads, too, if we do not learn about Jesus, study His Word, and accept the gospel of His kingdom. Let God's people remember the sentiment expressed by Mr. Wuest as we are being bombarded with errors and ridiculed by those that want to use these issues for political gain. Some with a Christian knowledge of such things could assert that non God infused scientic arguments go against true sound scientific thought and rational reasoning. Even more importantly, they go against the promises of the Lord God Almighty!

DAY 2

Touching His Hem

When you are hanging on by a thread make sure it is the hem of his garment. (Author Unknown)

> *So, Jesus went with him, and a great multitude followed Him and thronged Him.*
> *Now a certain woman had a flow of blood for twelve years, and had suffered many things from many physicians. She had spent all that she had and was no better, but rather grew worse. When she heard about Jesus, she came behind Him in the crowd and touched His garment. For she said, "If only I may touch His clothes, I shall be made well."*
> *Immediately the fountain of her blood was dried up, and she felt in her body that she was healed of the affliction. And Jesus, immediately knowing*

in Himself that power had gone out of Him, turned around in the crowd and said, "Who touched My clothes?"

But His disciples said to Him, "You see the multitude thronging You, and You say, 'Who touched Me?'" And He looked around to see her who had done this thing. But the woman, fearing and trembling, knowing what had happened to her, came and fell down before Him and told Him the whole truth. And He said to her, "Daughter, your faith has made you well. Go in peace, and be healed of your affliction." (Mark 5.24–34)

Have you ever given much thought to the mindset of this woman? How tired, overwhelmed, spent, and physically weak she must have been? But she wholeheartedly believed that Jesus could heal her of something she had been fighting for years with no success. She had been taken advantage of by doctors who did not know how to heal her. She thought if she could just get close enough to Jesus to merely touch the hem of his garment, she would be healed.

Jesus had previously cast out the demons in Decapolis. He had left there and was on his way to heal the daughter of Jairus when this incident happened. During this time in Palestine, Jesus was extremely popular. People were talking about His teaching and healing. The news was spreading, and many people desired to see Jesus.

Can you see the woman maybe squeezing and elbowing her way to Him through the throng of people? And when she does make it, she touches the lower portion of the garment and is immediately healed. Jesus wants to see her. He wants her to know that her faith was the element that had extracted the power from Him. And He wanted audiences both then and now to understand how Jesus-led healing occurs, whether physical or spiritual. She was healed because Jesus as God is holy.

The demon-possessed man Jesus healed was now somewhere teaching his friends and family. This woman would go home to people who would see her revived and ask her what happened. And then Jesus goes on to raise Jairus's twelve-year-old child from the dead as well. Even so, few people who saw and heard about these events believed in Jesus and responded to the message and miracles the same way as the woman.

May all see and hear the teaching of Jesus so each may believe and seize the opportunity to be spiritually healed! Let us be like the woman, doggedly doing whatever it takes to approach Jesus for healing. And once healed, let us tell others about Him, for He says, "Come to me, all who labor and are heavy laden, and I will give you rest. Take my yoke upon you, and learn from me, for I am gentle and lowly in heart, *you will find rest for your souls*" (Matt 1.27–28).

DAY 3

Seeing God in Suffering

May I never forget, on my best day, that I need God as desperately as I did on my worst day. (Author Unknown)

When we experience trials, we may not know for sure if it is from God disciplining us to grow our faith, or Satan trying to destroy our faith, but our reaction should be the same—to strengthen our faith. (Ken Craig)

I know that you can do all things,
*   and that no purpose of yours can be thwarted…*
I had heard of you by the hearing of the ear,
*   but now my eye sees you;*
therefore I despise myself,
*   and repent in dust and ashes.* (Job answering God, Job 42.2, 5–6)

Through suffering, a person can see God. Through His creation and in the righteousness of others God is manifested. Job, after questioning God about the purpose of his suffering, in his final statement reveals a level of understanding that could have only been realized through his own personal suffering and subsequent interaction with God. In the darkest of times, and even in the absence of this world's justice, God makes His presence known. With suffering comes the potential for God's wisdom to dawn in the hearts of men to shine brightly in His people.

Suffering can cause the contrast between good and evil to become further evident to a God-influenced mind. Anything that originates from God is good, while evil is anything in which God has no part. A person's days may be declared evil if God is absent and no justice is found in them (Deut. 31.29). But when God is intentionally left out of a person's thinking for self-serving reasons, sin will eventually result. Something could be done with the absence of God's supplied direction and not necessarily result in a transgression of law. But no good or God-produced spiritual fruit will ever come from it. Sin is defined as transgression of law. Good comes when one follows God's direction. Evil is the absence of God's direction. Suffering can come from serving God or from Satan's attempts to harm or tempt a person. God uses both for His purpose. Job was attacked by Satan, and God used it to increase his faith. Jesus only did good and suffering was the way forward in God's plan from the beginning to accomplish good for all men.

Our suffering helps us to remember that God, our faithful Father, is still revealing Himself to a lost and fallen world! We must not forget this even when what some call their "good" days come. Those "good" days—free from immediate suffering, when one is walking firmly in step with God—should be appreciated. But we also need to remember that in actuality suffering can be "good' too. God has always helped people understand themselves and how He works using suffering. He really had to use all things for good because after sin entered our world His children would always have to deal with it. Both through suffering and the absence of it good can be accomplished. The Lord proved that.

God is always protecting His children, but no one can reasonably expect God's protection to exclude suffering. Christ's sacrifice required intense suffering. Those that follow Him will experience suffering too, especially in times of persecution. This should not be a fearful or unexpected thing because God made suffering useful.

Through suffering, our faith is strengthened and peace of mind results! Through suffering comes multiple opportunities to grow and to see God manifested in the both the presence and absence of justice. Through suffering, hearts can be led to repentance when we start to grasp the proper view of self in relation to who God is. And through suffering, a penitent heart can see and know God, then trust God, and then one can obtain a faith and willingness to obey God without question!

DAY 4

Hearing Wisdom

Wisdom is the ability to view life as God perceives it. (Charles R. Swindoll)

For the LORD gives wisdom;
    from his mouth come knowledge and understanding;
he stores up sound wisdom for the upright;
    he is a shield to those who walk in integrity,
guarding the paths of justice
    and watching over the way of his saints.
Then you will understand righteousness and justice
    and equity, every good path;
for wisdom will come into your heart,
    and knowledge will be pleasant to your soul;
discretion will watch over you,
    understanding will guard you,
delivering you from the way of evil,
    from men of perverted speech,
who forsake the paths of uprightness
    to walk in the ways of darkness,
who rejoice in doing evil
    and delight in the perverseness of evil,
men whose paths are crooked,
    and who are devious in their ways.

So, you will be delivered from the forbidden woman,
    from the adulteress with her smooth words,
who forsakes the companion of her youth
    and forgets the covenant of her God;
for her house sinks down to death,
    and her paths to the departed;
none who go to her come back,
    nor do they regain the paths of life. (Prov 2.6–19)

The Proverbs personify wisdom. It is woven throughout all nature, throughout all interactions, throughout the written word, and seen in all justice and righteousness. God put it in the world at creation and gifts it to those who seek to understand Him. The fear of the Lord is the beginning of wisdom (Prov 1.7).

Wisdom becomes apparent only with an appreciation for God. It equips the wise to walk circumspectly. It is a precious gift, and those who have it are aware of dangers and can discern the right paths to follow. Unfortunately, it is also seen as foolishness to someone who sets their mind on themselves and worldliness. And when wisdom is absent, evil is present. The natural enmity that God has placed between good and evil manifests itself such that the distinction is easily recognized by those who can "see" (Gen 3.15). At the same time, it helps us identify where God's wisdom is completely lacking.

When conflict and confusion are all around, let's be wise and look hard for God's mind in all matters. Wisdom is loudly proclaimed and readily apparent to those who diligently seek her. She cries aloud in the streets and raises her voice in the markets (Prov 1.20), but she will entirely escape those who have decided to deny God and go their own way. They refuse to listen! May we all seek and find wisdom daily. Let us listen to her council!

DAY 5

The Heart's Response

When you come out of a storm you won't be the same person that walked in. That's what the storm is all about. (Haruki Murakami)

Then the LORD said to Moses and Aaron, "When Pharaoh says to you, 'Prove yourselves by working a miracle,' then you shall say to Aaron, 'Take your staff and cast it down before Pharaoh, that it may become a serpent.'" So, Moses and Aaron went to Pharaoh and did just as the LORD commanded. Aaron cast down his staff before Pharaoh and his servants, and it became a serpent. Then Pharaoh summoned the wise men and the sorcerers, and they, the magicians of Egypt, also did the same by their secret arts. For each man cast down his staff, and they became serpents. But Aaron's staff swallowed up their staffs. Still Pharaoh's heart was hardened, and he would not listen to them, as the LORD had said.

Then the LORD said to Moses, "Pharaoh's heart is hardened; he refuses to let the people go. (Exod 7.8–14)

Before He sent Moses to stand before Pharoah, God said, "I will harden Pharaoh's heart," which is interpreted by some to indicate that God took away Pharaoh's choice. But the passage above comes closer to the point that Pharoah hardened his heart in response to God's miracles and direction. Through Moses and Aaron, God introduces Himself to Pharaoh and directs him in righteousness. He offers Pharaoh the option to obey because his current state of mind opposes God.

Pharaoh thought himself a god, one of many served by the Egyptian people. And the one and only Lord God Almighty, through the entire plague story, showed Pharoah His majesty and power over all the Egyptians and their so-called gods. In scripture, we see that when a person faces the impending consequences that stem from disobedience, God offers another path and calls for a response. Whether that person decides to believe and obey or stubbornly refuses to see the truth, the catalyst for each heart's choice originates with God. Pharaoh had no intentions of letting the children of Israel leave Egypt. He was unwilling to consider any other action no matter the evidence.

Our current American culture is saturated with the erroneous teaching that there is no free will and thus no accountability for our choices. Those with addictions are considered unable to change, and those in difficult circumstances are excused when they make poor choices. Our culture believes that people are merely victims and should not be held accountable—it assumes that they cannot exercise good judgment in difficult situations. Society concludes that people must be manipulated and coddled because they cannot help themselves.

Each person chooses how to respond to their introduction to God through the creation and His teaching in scripture. The stimulus for that response comes from each person's heart as it interacts with God's direction. A person's dire circumstances may result from free will choices made by others in the past or by their personal decisions. But the next move is always theirs. As with Cain, God presents the option to do "well" (Gen. 4.7).

The truth is that, even in the worst of conditions, a person can still choose a right reaction to difficult circumstances. People can choose godly and positive alternatives when given God's direction. Every mature person is capable of making responsible freewill choices. Of course, babies and the mentally incompetent are excluded from culpability, but competent adults are not. When someone is exposed to the truth, they actively choose whether to believe or reject it.

Without God's revelation to mankind regarding good and evil, no man could know God's mind on any matter. Nor could anyone take advantage of it! No person can obey without being taught by Him. God, in His infinite mercy, gives each person the wisdom and understanding to choose the righteous way in response to all circumstances. Everyone can choose the path that leads to life and godliness.

As such, the more an honest heart studies and learns scripture, the easier God-directed decisions will become! Of course, we must first desire to do the will of God and be willing to forsake our own! When people make the right choices, growth will result as they are changed from the inside out. They become new creatures begotten of God.

WEEK TWENTY

DAY 1

Hope in Suffering

When someone is broken do not try to fix them.
  You can't.
When someone is hurting, don't attempt to take away their pain.
  You can't.
Instead, stand beside them in the hurt.
  You can.
Because sometimes the only thing people need is to know they are not alone.
(Author Unknown)

Behold, my eye has seen all this,
  my ear has heard and understood it.
What you know, I also know;
  I am not inferior to you.
But I would speak to the Almighty,
  and I desire to argue my case with God.
As for you, you whitewash with lies;
  worthless physicians are you all.
Oh that you would keep silent,
  and it would be your wisdom!
Hear now my argument
  and listen to the pleadings of my lips.
Will you speak falsely for God
  and speak deceitfully for him?
Will you show partiality toward him?
  Will you plead the case for God?
Will it be well with you when he searches you out?
  Or can you deceive him, as one deceives a man?

He will surely rebuke you
    if in secret you show partiality.
Will not his majesty terrify you,
    and the dread of him fall upon you?
Your maxims are proverbs of ashes;
    your defenses are defenses of clay.

Let me have silence, and I will speak,
    and let come on me what may.
Why should I take my flesh in my teeth
    and put my life in my hand?
Though he slay me, I will hope in him;
    yet I will argue my ways to his face. (Job 13.1–15)

The basis of Job's response to his friends is that God is God and people are not. The main problem with the arguments of Job's friends is that they fail to recognize that they have no idea what God is doing. They only think they know. They take it upon themselves to pronounce judgment on Job based on their view of the situation. On the other hand, Job understood from the outset that only God knew why he was suffering. The same is true for people today. God alone holds the answers.

Job's friends thought they knew why all the suffering was happening without God's council. Meanwhile, Job did not assume or presume to know anything about God's side of the equation without sound teaching. He felt assured of his innocence in his own heart but still wanted God to reveal his iniquity if he had failed. And Job also knew that being allowed to plead his case before the only Sovereign with the answers would still mean God's acceptance. Being allowed in His presence would show that God had extended the royal scepter, allowing Job an appointment with the King. Job still hoped in God!

Life on earth is truly about God and each person against the world. Of course, the "world" is the realm in which the father of lies works, where lust and pride flourish. God's answer to Job should help us avoid trying to figure out what is happening behind the scenes. The Bible is full of bad things happening to good people. It is also full of people who are not immediately punished for their bad behaviors. Satan's attempts to confound God's people can ultimately be used by God for their good!

No one ever knows what God is doing or how He works unless He's told us in His Word. Through Job, God allows us to see that suffering can have a purpose attached to it. Only God knows the work He is accomplishing in each person. Let's try hard not to be like Job's judgmental friends in trying times. Instead, let us wait on the Lord to work his purposes in the world.

DAY 2

Allow God to Show Himself Faithful

Give God room to show Himself faithful! (Author Unknown)

And if you say, «What shall we eat in the seventh year, if we may not sow or gather in our crop?" I will command my blessing on you in the sixth year, so that it will produce a crop sufficient for three years. When you sow in the eighth year, you will be eating some of the old crop; you shall eat the old until the ninth year, when its crop arrives. (Lev 25.20–22)

The physical children of Israel had continuous opportunities to see God working directly in their lives when they kept His commandments. In Leviticus, God told them not to plant or gather crops in the seventh year. They were to trust Him to keep them fed for that year and then the eighth year until the ninth-year crops arrived. Do you think they all trusted Him enough to keep this command?

Faithful action was not just for those who saw the cloud by day and fire by night that God provided after His people left Egypt. At that time, He led them openly and daily, and His presence was directly in front of them in a way that is hard for people today to comprehend. However, seeing God feed them and provide for their physical needs was intended to be an ongoing process, even after they reached the promised land.

Future generations were to keep a "Sabbath" rest every seventh year. They were to have faith that God would provide for them in that year to serve as a reminder that He was providing in the previous years also. The fiftieth year was also a Sabbath. So they could not plant in the forty-ninth year or the fiftieth year until the planting season of the fifty-first year. But God made the land produce three years' worth of food in that last planting year before the Jubilee.

This concept shows how God expects His people to trust and realize that He does supply ongoing sustenance in His role as our provider. But some may not see this if they do not allow Him to show Himself. We will not readily see God's blessings if trust, obedience, and waiting do not come first.

Are people today depending on themselves or God? When a hardship presents itself, do we rush to fix everything ourself? Keep the commandments relevant to your life and trust in God to provide. Hang back and watch Him work. There is so little trust today. We must exemplify God's prescribed faithfulness to those under our charge. When we experience His faithfulness, our faith increases, and so does the faith of those watching.

Our faithful Heavenly Father is still working! His work may not always be easily understood or comprehended, but He still works. And those following His commands can usually see it. If not when looking forward, then more assuredly when looking back. Let's all be faithful towards others and allow God to show Himself faithful in our lives.

DAY 3

The Soul's Mirror

Blessed is the man who remains steadfast under trial, for when he has stood the test he will receive the crown of life, which God has promised to those who love him. (Jas 1.12)

Therefore, put away all filthiness and rampant wickedness and receive with meekness the implanted word, which is able to save your souls.

But be doers of the word, and not hearers only, deceiving yourselves. For if anyone is a hearer of the word and not a doer, he is like a man who looks intently at his natural face in a mirror. For he looks at himself and goes away and at once forgets what he was like. But the one who looks into the perfect law, the law of liberty, and perseveres, being no hearer who forgets but a doer who acts, he will be blessed in his doing.

If anyone thinks he is religious and does not bridle his tongue but deceives his heart, this person's religion is worthless. Religion that is pure and undefiled before God the Father is this: to visit orphans and widows in their affliction, and to keep oneself unstained from the world. (Jas 1.21–27)

I remember this passage from my youth, but I do not think I fully grasped its meaning until much later. That happens so much. Without regular study and meditation, readers can fail to see what the Holy Spirit is revealing through the inspired writers.

The first chapter of James distinguishes between the terms *test* and *temptation* so learners can recognize the difference. A test can come from God but the temptation to sin does not. This distinction is crucial because it helps us see how Satan works in the world. The context also shows us that our Almighty God implants His word into our hearts through intentional study.

We see that learning the truth is not simply a superficial matter of what someone looks like from a heart and knowledge standpoint. Its effectiveness is determined by how someone uses their newly acquired understanding of God's Word. The Word must translate into personal changes a disciple makes to their actions and reactions over time.

Jesus taught that the spiritually prosperous are disciplined in their faith. They are the people that act in love and trust that God is always right. They obey what they hear and incorporate change into their lives as soon as they know what God wants them to do. They do not have to worry about death or when Jesus will come again because they are always ready. And when the end does come, they will be doing His will because they are doers of the Word.

They do not become embroiled in the things of the world because they see themselves as citizens of a heavenly kingdom. They are patient and endure whatever comes their way. They practice self-control. They recognize the orphans and widows are without a support system and help fill the gaps left by the absence of a caregiver anytime they see it. They are the firmly planted trees that weather the storms of life. Worldliness does not sway them, nor does it have any appeal to them.

Let us all use the perfect law of liberty as a spiritual mirror for our souls to check for flaws and start the needed transformations today! We cannot walk away from the wisdom of God without taking the steps required to implement the lessons we learn. Let's remember that not all Christians are always at the same juncture in this continual learning and testing process. Let's all use the mirror to look at ourselves and not others. The real questions are how you are doing with the information you have, and what are you doing to gather more?

DAY 4

Walking with God

Imagine yourself as a living house. God comes in to rebuild that house. At first, perhaps, you can understand what He is doing. He is getting the drains right and stopping the leaks in the roof and so on; you knew that those jobs needed doing and so you are not surprised. But presently He starts knocking the house about in a way that hurts abominably and does not seem to make any sense. What on earth is He up to? The explanation is that He is building quite a different house from the one you thought of—throwing out a new wing here, putting on an extra floor there, running up towers, making court-yards. You thought you were being made into a decent little cottage, but He is building a palace. He intends to come and live in it Himself. (C.S. Lewis)

But you were washed, you were sanctified, you were justified in the name of the Lord Jesus Christ and by the Spirit of our God...

Do you not know that your bodies are members of Christ? Shall I then take the members of Christ and make them members of a prostitute? Never! Or do you not know that he who is joined to a prostitute becomes one body with her? For, as it is written, "The two will become one flesh." But he who is joined to the Lord becomes one spirit with him. Flee from sexual immorality. Every other sin a person commits is outside the body, but the sexually immoral person sins against his own body. Or do you not know that your body is a temple of the Holy Spirit within you, whom you have from God? You are not your own, for you were bought with a price. So glorify God in your body. (1 Cor 6.11b, 15–20)

Before their conversion, the Corinthians struggled with many sins that involved joining themselves to idols in worship. The people Paul is speaking to had escaped from those elements of their former sins. While warning them to flee the idolatry around them, Paul uses the opportunity to explain a truth about the relationship between God and His followers that can be hard to comprehend.

Paul uses the illustration of joining ourselves to a marriage partner to compare how we must subject our minds, spirits, and bodies to the Spirit of God. We become one with God in a way that resembles the relationship formed in holy matrimony. Idolatry is evidence of the exact opposite. It is a joining of ourselves with something other than God. In contrast, His people must become holy as God is holy for Him to join with them in their walk-through life.

We must become fit for the divine association so God can dwell in his children. We become one with His spirit as He resides within our hearts so that our minds and bodies operate with His direction. God does all the heavy lifting as He works to change us. He uses teaching and discipline to help each disciple become fit for His ongoing fellowship. God rebuilds those who are His from the inside out. He changes them into white garments, and they are thoroughly and continuously cleansed as they walk with Him.

C.S. Lewis adds to this concept by using the analogy of a building project. People sometimes think they know the plan God has for their lives. But as he works with his children, they change and become a suitable dwelling place for His Holy Spirit. God makes His glory manifest in what they become. And it is always evident that the work is accomplished with outside, divine help.

Try to visualize all those who have joined with Christ all walking together, each with God walking alongside them. All are going in the same direction, walking down a road while in deep conversation with the Lord, holding hands with God. All have a sense of peace beyond worldly understanding. At the same time, there is still chaos and bedlam just out of sight. People who are not walking with them do not understand the picture. They are out there throwing rocks at those on the road or wondering how to get onto it too!

As each of us faces our perceived difficulties, let us do so with the confidence that God knows what He is doing even if we do not! He is changing us so that He can dwell more fully with us. And through those changes, we will better glorify Him. Not only is it fitting for those on the road, but for those wishing to be.

DAY 5

Our Holy Editor

God is the producer. The Holy Spirit is the director. And I am the horrible actor. I am so thankful Jesus is the editor. Thank God for Grace. (Author Unknown)

But now the righteousness of God has been manifested apart from the law, although the Law and the Prophets bear witness to it—the righteousness of God through faith in Jesus Christ for all who believe. For there is no distinction: for all have sinned and fall short of the glory of God, and are justified by his grace as a gift, through the redemption that is in Christ Jesus, whom God put forward as a propitiation by his blood, to be received by faith. This was to show God's righteousness, because in his divine forbearance he had passed over former sins. It was to show his righteousness at the present time, so that he might be just and the justifier of the one who has faith in Jesus. (Rom 3.21–26)

Paul tells us that no person, except the Lord himself, has ever been able to keep all of God's will without error and sin. Everyone needs help—lots of help—to find salvation. When anyone becomes aware of just how poor a servant, a follower, or an actor they are on the stage of life, then they are ready with open eyes to learn of their need for redemption.

Every Christian must understand that the need for mercy and grace is ongoing. Someone has to edit all the imperfections out of the script because each actor is so inept. Jesus is always willing and able to do this for people. But each person must approach him with complete faith, ask Him for help, and subscribe to the prescribed path to holiness that He put in place for those working towards redemption.

Some choose not to participate with God in this endeavor but are still on a stage. They have an evil producer, a selfish director, and, most significantly, they do not have a viable editor! Ultimately, acting in such a situation can only result in dissatisfaction, depression, confusion, chaos, and loss.

Praise be to God for the sacrifice He made so we can switch stages! Each actor must work diligently on their skills as they participate in their new life purpose. Even when directed by God, we all have inadequacies that require continual grace and mercy. Let each of us make sure we have made it onto the stage where Jesus works with each horrible actor!

WEEK TWENTY-ONE

DAY 1

Trusting the Creator

Blessed are they who see beautiful things in humble places where other people see nothing. (Camille Pissarro)

Is it by your understanding that the hawk soars
*   and spreads his wings toward the south?*
Is it at your command that the eagle mounts up
*   and makes his nest on high?*
On the rock he dwells and makes his home,
*   on the rocky crag and stronghold.*
From there he spies out the prey;
*   his eyes behold it from far away.*
His young ones suck up blood,
*   and where the slain are, there is he.* (Job 39.26–30)

Suffering can benefit the spiritually prosperous because it directs them on a journey to find the truth. The realization that we must trust in our unseen creator is designed to be hopeful. It leads people to understand that someone is undoubtedly in control and that it is not them! They are blessed with a humbled heart, looking for direction from an almighty creator.

God responds to Job's questions concerning suffering in the latter part of Job. Job's eyes looked up and outside of himself for the answers. God, through multiple glimpses of His work in creation, invokes Job to have even greater trust in His all-knowing, all-seeing, all-powerful nature. When anyone contemplates the grandness of creation, they also see how lowly they are in comparison.

Suffering and trusting create a dynamic that prompts a continual seeking for answers to life's questions from God. And it is in God's realm to reveal them. Unfortunately, while one person contemplates the high and holy evidence of the existence of an Almighty God, another may see the same sights and realize nothing. They set their minds on the things of this world and look inward for their answers. They elevate themselves and are self-serving.

But this generation has all the revealed words of God to facilitate complete learning of the mystery of the gospel—His plan of salvation and scheme of redemption. These things angels have longed to learn all through time (1 Pet 1.12). They cause the devils to believe and make them tremble (Jas 2.19). God's words are available to all in the world but are so often denied and neglected! What a pity!

Let all who are suffering look to God for their answers! In doing so, let's stop and contemplate the wonders of creation. It was calming to Job when used by God to teach him something he needed to understand in his time of great suffering. All the evidence is still there, and those words of God are recorded for any one of us to gain the same understanding. His wisdom is the only avenue of true comfort in a world where Satan dwells!

DAY 2

Trusting Like Job

When the root is deep there is no reason to fear the wind. (Author Unknown)

Wisdom is with the aged,
*   and understanding in length of days.*

With God are wisdom and might;
*   he has counsel and understanding.*
If he tears down, none can rebuild;
*   if he shuts a man in, none can open.*
If he withholds the waters, they dry up;
*   if he sends them out, they overwhelm the land.*
With him are strength and sound wisdom;
*   the deceived and the deceiver are his.*
He leads counselors away stripped,
*   and judges he makes fools.*

He looses the bonds of kings
  and binds a waistcloth on their hips.
He leads priests away stripped
  and overthrows the mighty.
He deprives of speech those who are trusted
  and takes away the discernment of the elders.
He pours contempt on princes
  and loosens the belt of the strong.
He uncovers the deeps out of darkness
  and brings deep darkness to light.
He makes nations great, and he destroys them;
  he enlarges nations, and leads them away.
He takes away understanding from the chiefs of the people of the earth
  and makes them wander in a trackless waste.
They grope in the dark without light,
  and he makes them stagger like a drunken man. (Job 12.12–25)

When anyone understands the character of God, they can also see themselves better. During his suffering, Job describes to his friends whom he understands God to be. This understanding leads him to trust that God is in control over all things on the earth. As people see God, they become more aware of their inadequacies and can more readily leave the problems they encounter in God's capable hands. Their fear of the unknown dissipates into a trust in God that will increase over time.

Understanding why things happen is less important than learning God's expectations for a person's proper response. One of the primary points a person should learn from Job is not to wrangle and haggle about God's dealings, purposes, and judgments. Instead, a person should meditate on what a trusting, righteous response to the realities of each situation might look like and then react properly.

Those who fear outcomes try to exercise control of their circumstances. However, those who deeply trust God obey His direction and seek the truth. They do their best to do justice, love mercy, and walk humbly in whatever circumstances they find themselves (Mic 6.8). They do not attempt to manipulate people or circumstances and their motives are open and transparent.

Remember that later in Job, God declares him correct in his assessments of Him. He says to Job's three friends, "And my servant Job shall pray for you, for I will accept his prayer not to deal with you according to your folly. For you have not spoken of me what is right, as my servant

Job has" (Job 42.8). Let us all meditate on what Job says about God. His declarations can motivate us to trust in God as we react to this day's trials, whatever they may be!

DAY 3

Waiting on the Lord

Some people's idea of [free speech] is that they are free to say what they like, but if anyone says anything back, that is an outrage. (Sir Winston Churchill)

Where is the one who is wise? Where is the scribe? Where is the debater of this age? Has not God made foolish the wisdom of the world? For since, in the wisdom of God, the world did not know God through wisdom, it pleased God through the folly of what we preach to save those who believe. (1 Cor 1.20–21)

God and the way He operates is foreign to those who do not know God's wisdom. They cannot see it. God says in Habakkuk 1.5, "Look among the nations, and see; wonder and be astounded. For I am doing a work in your days that you would not believe if told." Of course, in this context, God is talking about the impending judgment that would occur through Babylon. But He also explains to the remnant that He has a plan to save and protect them.

We must never forget that our Lord and Savior is our protector. We may not always be able to understand or identify how God works in our time, but we can see glimmers of His wisdom played out in the world when we consider how He has worked in times past. All people, including ourselves, are mere men used by the creator of the universe. And He can use us however He finds us, whether good or evil, for His purposes.

We cannot assume to understand God's plans or how He is working around us. We do not know what we do not know! One of the things God hates is a proud and haughty spirit. Let us always remember whom we serve and that He is the only one worthy of praise. Let us be humble and remember to wait on the Lord! He always comes through, in His time, to save and protect in the micro and macro levels of our lives.

DAY 4

Continual Healing

No amount of falls will really undo us if we keep on picking ourselves up each time… It is when we notice the dirt that God is most present to us: it is the very sign of His presence. (C.S. Lewis)

I know you are enduring patiently and bearing up for my name's sake, and you have not grown weary. But I have this against you, that you have abandoned the love you had at first. Remember therefore from where you have fallen; repent, and do the works you did at first. If not, I will come to you and remove your lampstand from its place, unless you repent. (Rev 2.3–5)

As a young person, I remember there were people who believed that if you attended worship services and had not mastered your faith to the point of sinlessness, then it followed that you were being hypocritical. The very opposite is true. The assembly of the saints is a hospital for sinners who need healing and want to repent.

The Lord's church contains people who desire to be spiritually disciplined. People who want to remove sin from their life. People who have a conscience that is operating correctly. And finally, people who understand that true sinlessness is only made possible by God sacrificing His Son. We can be justified only through Jesus.

The reality is that people need to be washed and continually treated with preventive measures to remain holy. Hopefully, we can all correctly understand the concept of spiritual healing. Let us constantly watch ourselves and repent when we have missed God's commands for our attitudes and behaviors. Let us all properly understand the processes God has put in place. Then, our expectations and validation of ourselves and others will allow us to be as loving and merciful as God is towards us!

DAY 5

Faithful Steps

What saves a man is to take a step. Then another step. (C.S. Lewis)

Is not calamity for the unrighteous,
*   and disaster for the workers of iniquity?*
Does not he see my ways
*   and number all my steps?*

"If I have walked with falsehood
*   and my foot has hastened to deceit;*
(Let me be weighed in a just balance,
*   and let God know my integrity!)*
if my step has turned aside from the way
*   and my heart has gone after my eyes,*
*   and if any spot has stuck to my hands,*
then let me sow, and another eat,
*   and let what grows for me be rooted out.* (Job 31.3–8)

Everyone is either directed by their own will or God's will, and each step a person takes indicates whose will they choose to follow. In these verses, Job wonders why evil has come upon him when he has done as God directed. Isn't this what everyone wants to know? Job is confused and wants to understand. He is not aware of the agreement God has made with Satan. There are forces at work in the unseen realm to which he has not been made aware.

Job learns that God's power is continually at work in many ways. After a person initially submits to God, they then learn to keep obeying even when they do not understand and even when it costs them. They choose trust over and over again at increasingly deeper levels. As they do so, their faith deepens as well!

How do we know God intends our ultimate good? Do we truly believe God has no part in evil? Do we believe He can use even the intended evil of Satan and His followers and make it work for good? Remember Joseph and His brothers when Joseph, at his revealing, told them, "As for you, you meant evil against me, but God meant it for good."

God is faithful, even if we are at a loss as to why something has been allowed to happen that seems inexplicable to our lowly human minds. We can keep walking in trust even while not knowing God's purpose simply because we know that He is sovereign. God is the creator, and He has the right to allow or not allow what happens in the world, even when Satan may have some restrained power.

May we all keep on walking in the light, even amid suffering. We are walking in a dying world when the times are evil. We are continually taking steps towards a heavenly home where there will be no more sorrow and pain! And this will be so because there will no longer be those who follow their own way. Faith will be finally realized by those with total and complete trust in God! Their faithful walk will ultimately lead them to the dwelling place of God, where all will see Him as He is.

WEEK TWENTY-TWO

Day 1

Ever after Joy

The art of being happy lies in the power of extracting happiness from common things. (Henry Ward Beecher)

Behold, what I have seen to be good and fitting is to eat and drink and find enjoyment in all the toil with which one toils under the sun the few days of his life that God has given him, for this is his lot. Everyone also to whom God has given wealth and possessions and power to enjoy them, and to accept his lot and rejoice in his toil—this is the gift of God. For he will not much remember the days of his life because God keeps him occupied with joy in his heart. (Ecc 5.18–20)

One of my preachers used to say that the primary joys of this life on earth are good friends and good food. It seemed too simplistic when I first heard it, but the older I get, the more I see its wisdom. Ecclesiastes also tells us that we find joy in contentment in a job well done.

Mr. Beecher would call this the power to extract happiness from common things—things like a good marriage, good familial relationships with children, and faithful friends. When these relationships operate in the ways God intended, joy is inherited. When people take the time out of their busy lives to spend time with these people, bits of joy result. These are God-given and make one grateful for His blessings.

Sometimes life is hard because we live in a fallen world where the results of sin coexist with us. Our expectations at times are so high and unrealistic that we cannot find happiness. And sometimes, in the pursuit of it, some miss it altogether because they do not know where to find it.

People believe happiness is something that comes and lasts forever after. They believe the world's lies that they would be happy if they just had more money or the right house. They think that if they could lose weight or find the perfect mate or the perfect job, then happiness would result. Then, when they attain some of these things, they realize happiness does not come with them and disappointment follows. If we try to find joy and happiness in things without God's instruction, they will always fail to satisfy us.

We must realize that the "ever after" joy is not a fairy tale here on Earth; it is only ultimately attained in the life after. People on earth must prepare for that now, but it only begins when we come to know God. When one does not realize this, the disappointments of this life will destroy their false ideas of hope, faith, and happiness. Joy results from a real relationship with the God of heaven and Earth. We must seek it in all the places He has placed it and nowhere else!

We must realize that happiness in this life happens in small capsules of time. It comes when your soul is at peace, and loved ones are all around, or when you see the wonders of creation and realize how blessed you are to have a loving God who never leaves you. It comes when you survive hard times or after a good day's work. It comes when you see old friends or in the memories of former times. Look for it in these places where God has designed it to be, and you will find it, even in our fallen world!

Day 2

Prepared to Receive

A beautiful garden is a work of the heart. (Author Unknown)

And he told them many things in parables, saying: "A sower went out to sow. And as he sowed, some seeds fell along the path, and the birds came and devoured them. Other seeds fell on rocky ground, where they did not have much soil, and immediately they sprang up, since they had no depth of soil, but when the sun rose they were scorched. And since they had no root, they withered away. Other seeds fell among thorns, and the thorns grew up and choked them. Other seeds fell on good soil and produced grain, some a hundredfold, some sixty, some thirty. He who has ears, let him hear." (Matt 13.3–9)

Years ago, I watched a film with my children about how seeds are spread. I remember marveling at the many ways they are scattered. When we think of spreading seeds, our minds typically think of the modern-day vegetable garden. Here, you find straight rows, and you space the seeds in a row according to the way that is most appropriate for each kind of seed. A gardener designs the layout and decides where he will plant everything.

Spiritual seeds are spread and planted very differently. The process is more like how the earth's natural processes move seeds around. A child may pick and blow on a dandy lion, and the seeds scatter. A tumbleweed rolls along, dropping its seeds along the path the wind directs. Certain kinds of pinecones only open when there is a fire, and a coconut seed can travel from ocean to ocean to plant a seed on a distant shore that will then grow a new palm tree.

Just as natural seeds spread in various ways and fall in different places, the Word is also spread. But it will only take root under the right conditions, at the right time, and in the right weather—when the heart has been prepared to receive it! God directs this process, demonstrating His role in transforming hearts through His Word.

God is the ultimate gardener, and He gives the increase even when others plant and water (1 Cor 3.6–8). Spiritual growth happens in the way the Lord plans. The Word, or spiritual seed, is delivered through God's Son. He is the One through whom God has chosen to speak to us in these "last days" (Heb 1.2). He is the heir of all things, the radiance of God's glory, and upholds all things by His powerful Word.

Christ sent the Holy Spirit to the apostles and the writers of His Word to continually provide His seed to multiple generations. It spreads all over, and when conditions are right, it is possible for His Word to recreate our hearts. When we are obedient to it, His blood cleanses us from all sin. The Word brings us to a land that is fairer than day, a place where the soul never dies. May His Word accomplish the spiritual increase for which it was designed.

Day 3

Receiving the Word

The serpent did not tempt Adam and Eve to steal, to kill, to commit adultery; he simply tempted them to question God's Word. (Author Unknown)

As you come to him, a living stone rejected by men but in the sight of God chosen and precious, you yourselves like living stones are being built up as a spiritual house, to be a holy priesthood, to offer spiritual sacrifices acceptable to God through Jesus Christ. For it stands in Scripture: "Behold, I am laying in Zion a stone, a cornerstone chosen and precious, and whoever believes in him will not be put to shame."

So the honor is for you who believe, but for those who do not believe, "The stone that the builders rejected has become the cornerstone," and "A stone of stumbling, and a rock of offense." They stumble because they disobey the word, as they were destined to do. (1 Pet 2.4–8)

The departure from God we are witnessing in our present-day society is no different from what it looked like at the beginning. Satan is using the same methods he used then to undermine all that God directs his children to do. In some circles, people ridicule the entire Biblical message. They question God and all He has ever done and revealed. Creation, God's design for things, and recognizing His control of nations are replaced with idolatrous hearts unwilling to follow God.

Some believe there is no such thing as law or sin and that everyone can do what is right in their own eyes. Godless societies deny all things that God has defined, as they always have. No absolute truth is acknowledged, so laws cannot be understood or broken. You cannot define crime, so you do not need to stop it. Everyone has their own rules, and their actions are justifiable, whether or not God approves them. These kinds of environments in some sectors of society today like certain cities, courts, and groups are lawless, just like the old Western movies! Some authorites are metaphorically allowing the bad guys to ride through town shooting up the place.

The Old Testament explains God's plan in a veiled mystery. He has always been working His message and plan into historical events that culminate over time. That message is that there is a God. He has a will for man,

He has revealed that will, and He provides a means by which each person can be redeemed from sin. This message is not difficult to understand with a heart that seeks to draw near to Him and understand His Word.

Those with honest and repentant hearts are receptive to God's Word. However, seeing His revealed truths can become very difficult when people encounter stumbling blocks in their path of understanding. This is especially true if means of stumbling are self-imposed as people choose an idolatrous lifestyle, meditate on evil things, or retain bad habits that they should remove.

Each soul who chooses to take on God's attributes must make adjustments. Receiving the Word instructs and convicts a person's spirit and helps them recognize what they need to change in their heart, behavior, and attitude. And when those who profess to know the truth see no progress within themselves, it should concern them. They may be stumbling over something they do not wish to acknowledge.

People change as they learn. A person's true heart is only known by God and themselves as He reveals it to them through His Word. It exposes sin to each believer by comparing the mind of God to the works of those who have previously followed their own counsel. Let all study God's Word to show themselves approved, always looking into their lives for the fruit of God's nature and Spirit!

Day 4

Breathes His Spirit

Be Patient. God's just moving the pieces around. (Author Unknown)

And you shall know that I am the Lord, when I open your graves, and raise you from your graves, O my people. And I will put my Spirit within you, and you shall live, and I will place you in your own land. Then you shall know that I am the Lord; I have spoken, and I will do it, declares the Lord. (Ezek 37.13–14)

Apocalyptic literature can be challenging to understand, but it holds transformative power when one grasps God's redemption story. His Word tells the old story over and over again using picture concepts like land, kingdoms, buildings, and seeds. Throughout the Old Testament, we read about God's relationship with mankind and how to maintain it.

God uses the Israelite nation as a living illustration to reveal His workings with individual people and nations. He blesses the righteous while the rebellious are chastened through prophets, hardships, and judgment. God finally unveils the complete scheme of redemption in the life of Jesus and the complete New Testament.

He also taught those in captivity the message. In Ezekiel's vision of the valley of dry bones, God illustrates the state of a sinful people without Him. God says He will put His Spirit into the resurrected bodies of His saints as the culmination of the redemption process.

Through obedience to the gospel, we come to emulate and understand what is explained in Ezekiel. When we die with Christ in baptism, each person is resurrected to new life. We are placed in the land dedicated to those who trust His promises. Those who come to Him as He directs are given abundant life in an everlasting kingdom.

These make up His holy temple, not made with hands. He makes them a building that He builds up. The God of heaven breathes His Spirit into those as they find spiritual life, analogous to how He gave physical life to Adam in the Garden of Eden at Creation. There is repetition in scripture. God tells the same story in many ways so everyone can understand and obey the gospel!

Day 5

Faith and Love of Jesus

Faith is deliberate confidence in the character of God whose way you may not understand at the time. (Oswald Chambers)

"And you shall love the Lord your God with all your heart and with all your soul and with all your mind and with all your strength.' The second is this: 'You shall love your neighbor as yourself.' There is no other commandment greater than these." (Mark 12.30–31)

Jesus displayed the highest form of love and empathy while suffering the consequences of our sins when He said, "Father, forgive them, for they know not what they do" (Luke 23.34). He displayed great faith in God while being subjected to the harshest of circumstances. Jesus has all authority and is our example. When we compare self-centered societal norms to the love of Christ, we can easily see through the deceptions perpetuated by the world.

The dynamic enmity between good and evil is constant. Social events over the past few years have helped me comprehend how the Jewish leaders incited a mob to crucify Jesus and how his response to it changed the world. We are here to learn how to live with love and peace of mind rather than conform to the hate and chaos around us. God's people have many opportunities every day to express steadfast love to the people around us.

Harboring an uneducated opinion is the lowest form of human knowledge. It requires no accountability and no understanding. In contrast to the chaos, brutality, and fear that exist in the world, we must choose to be servants of an all-knowing, all-powerful God. In so doing we will manifest peace, kindness, and calm, both in ourselves and those around us. We can either behave and act on truth with a peaceful heart in a way that brings glory to God or allow fear-driven opinions to divide and thwart our spiritual progress. How are you doing?

WEEK TWENTY-THREE

DAY 1

A Bigger Yes

You have to decide what your highest priorities are and have the courage— pleasantly, smilingly, non-apologetically, to say "no" to other things. And the way you do that is by having a bigger "yes" burning inside. (Stephen Covey)

There are a dozen views about everything until you know the answer. Then there's never more than one. (C.S. Lewis)

The end of the matter; all has been heard. Fear God and keep his commandments, for this is the whole duty of man. For God will bring every deed into judgment, with every secret thing, whether good or evil. (Ecc 12.13–14)

One of the most urgent problems we all face is how to deal with the mounting level of tasks and decisions we need to make in our lives. We deal with changing rules, times, life circumstances, dynamics, and levels of uncertainty. With everything going on, knowing how to make decisions and spend our time wisely while prioritizing our values and the desired relevant outcomes is daunting!

Several years ago, I read an article in a workplace periodical that helped me with my time management skills. It was entitled, "Manage Your Commitments." I do not remember who wrote it, but the message is summed up in the opening quote by Stephen Covey. Though the advice usually applies to the work environment, it is a universal truth we can use in decision-making.

If anyone wants to be genuinely productive, each person must make a deliberate attempt to manage the scarcity of their time. Each person may have different choices because of differing responsibilities. When this truly profound concept is understood, anyone can use it to master the art of making more relevant and productive decisions.

Sometimes we seem to think we must do everything others ask us to do without considering our limited time, energy, and resources. When the time constraints force us to identify our biggest "yes"—our primary intention and responsibility—it becomes easier to identify priorities and say no. And when we do, we find how much more quickly we can effectively accomplish the important things. All the while, we must remember, as the writer of Ecclesiastes tells us, that the primary purpose and duty of man is to "Fear God and keep His commandments."

The choices are different for every individual. We all have different roles, responsibilities, and abilities with unique time constraints and resources. Each one will need to adjust to their specific set of restraints as they prioritize the essential things in life. No one needs to make judgments on the choices of others. We must learn to be more understanding when others feel the need to decline things they consider to be, at the time, not something they can do.

At some point, our scarcity of time and resources may force us to choose between doing one of two godly activities. At that point, people should look to their primary personal responsibilities at that particular time and place. Identifying these becomes easier when one can make a firm distinction between their responsibilities and personal desires. Learning to make those fine distinctions can help us with our financial allocations as well as time management.

The primary ingredient is to identify our bigger yes. For Christians, it is an unyielding love and profound reverence towards God, while continually cultivating a thankful and grateful heart. A proper concept of self, relative to God, is key, which is easier if each person follows God's two greatest commandments. First, to love and reverence God, then to love others as themselves. This obedience will help us properly fulfill responsibilities that accompany our life situations as spouses, parents, workers, and church members. Of course, these commandments were best modeled by Jesus, and following His example can help us demonstrate a self-sacrificing spirit in all our choices.

Identifying and prioritizing our biggest yes becomes harder to accomplish the more responsibilities we have. Deal with your life in small doses, one day at a time. Allow God to take care of the physical needs while you focus on the God-allocated ones. When it seems most difficult, remember that Jesus said:

Therefore, do not be anxious, saying, 'What shall we eat?' or 'What shall we drink?' or 'What shall we wear?' For the Gentiles seek after all these things, and your heavenly Father knows that you need them all. But seek first the kingdom of God and his righteousness, and all these things will be added to you. Therefore, do not be anxious about tomorrow, for tomorrow will be anxious for itself. Sufficient for the day is its own trouble." (Matt 6.30–34)

DAY 2

Worry Free

One of these days I am going to preach a sermon on present tense Christianity. (Homer Hailey)

Therefore I tell you, do not be anxious about your life, what you will eat or what you will drink, nor about your body, what you will put on. Is not life more than food, and the body more than clothing? Look at the birds of the air: they neither sow nor reap nor gather into barns, and yet your heavenly Father feeds them. Are you not of more value than they? And which of you by being anxious can add a single hour to his span of life? And why are you anxious about clothing? Consider the lilies of the field, how they grow: they neither toil nor spin, yet I tell you, even Solomon in all his glory was not arrayed like one of these. But if God so clothes the grass of the field, which today is alive and tomorrow is thrown into the oven, will he not much more clothe you, O you of little faith? Therefore, do not be anxious, saying, 'What shall we eat?' or 'What shall we drink?' or 'What shall we wear?' For the Gentiles seek after all these things, and your heavenly Father knows that you need them all. But seek first the kingdom of God and his righteousness, and all these things will be added to you.

Therefore, do not be anxious about tomorrow, for tomorrow will be anxious for itself. Sufficient for the day is its own trouble. (Matt 6.25–34)

When Jesus taught His first sermon, He dealt with the *gospel of the kingdom*. Before the opening *therefore* statement in the verses above, Jesus had already discussed various thought processes that the people needed to change their current misunderstandings of the law given by Moses. One of the points that He made was concerning how His disciples should view their daily needs.

Christians do not need to spend their days working as if driven by the same worries as the world. Jesus taught that each disciple should consider their physical needs and use their time without anxiety. To accomplish this, we must live our life as if we only have one day before us. We only need to concern ourselves with the day we are in because it's the only one of which we have assurance.

The true disciples of Jesus must live each day to its full. They expend the resources and energy they possess doing the work of the Lord. Whatever their hands find to do, they do it with all their might. They operate knowing that each day has enough trouble of its own. There is no need to worry about the past or future. We cannot change the past, and no one knows what the future holds

Each disciple's thoughts and actions in each moment should be executed while striving to emulate the character our Lord. He had modeled the proper heart and his children as disciples of Jesus follow His lead. Each day, God gives everyone a new opportunity to work out his salvation by fearing God, not the fearsome circumstances around him. In the meantime, each disciple must ignore the world's attempt to redefine all things spiritual. And the righteous can thwart Satan's attempts to disquiet God's people with fear, a common trait of those of the world. Work for the Lord is accomplished while one is doing whatever prescribed work is being done that day.

Jesus encourages His own never to get so wrapped up in the cares of this world that the righteous work of our Holy God is left undone. Jesus concludes His first sermon by directing His listeners to put God's work first in this life. God defines the purpose, priorities, and roles of everyone in His kingdom. He will provide what we need in this world so that the godly can seek after the things of God. We prioritize these activities, my friends, because they further the gospel of the kingdom that Jesus came to explain openly to us all.

DAY 3

Acknowledging God

When you do something beautiful and nobody notices, do not be sad. For the sun every morning is a beautiful spectacle and yet most of the audience still sleeps. (John Lennon)

*Praise the L*ORD*!*

*I will give thanks to the L*ORD *with my whole heart,*
*   in the company of the upright, in the congregation.*
*Great are the works of the L*ORD*,*
*   studied by all who delight in them.*
Full of splendor and majesty is his work,
*   and his righteousness forever.*
He has caused his wondrous works to be remembered;
*   the L*ORD *is gracious and merciful.*
He provides food for those who fear him endures;
*   he remembers his covenant forever.*
He has shown his people the power of his works,
*   in giving them the inheritance of the nations.* (Psa 111.1–6)

I would not typically look to a rock star for advice about God, but this quote from John Lennon is striking. The implied point is that people want appreciation for giving something to others out of love. He explains the concept by comparing a person's meager attempts at service to God's awe-inspiring creation. John Lennon said that when a beautiful effort goes unnoticed, "do not be sad."

All people are made in God's image with His feelings and emotions. There is always some potential to learn powerful truths from the people around us. Here, the words of Mr. Lennon help us imagine the heartbreak inflicted on God when people fail to acknowledge His efforts to show himself faithful. He lovingly bestows marvelous blessings for all in every moment of life, and some do not appreciate it. They are blinded to the evidence of God's overwhelming blessings every day because they are too busy focusing on themselves and their problems.

We have been guilty of being unthankful and ungrateful, even when we are acutely aware that we need to be. God's blessings are so grand and marvelous that the mortal mind cannot even fully grasp the love and grandness contained in them. John Lennon learned that from seeing God's handiwork. Yet we should do our best to acknowledge what God has done. David said, "Great are the works of the Lord, studied by all who delight in them." God's works are an act of love that should be observed, embraced, and appreciated by us all!

DAY 4

Defined by Faith

Two things define you. Your patience when you have nothing, and your attitude when you have everything. (Author Unknown)

Not that I am speaking of being in need, for I have learned in whatever situation I am to be content. I know how to be brought low, and I know how to abound. In any and every circumstance, I have learned the secret of facing plenty and hunger, abundance and need. I can do all things through him who strengthens me. (Phil 4.11–13)

We learn a lot from Paul in his letter to Philippi, written from prison no less, regarding how a Christian ought to be *defined* when they have nothing and everything. Earlier in Paul's letter, we learn the secret to attaining his level of faith:

"But whatever gain I had, I counted as loss for the sake of Christ. Indeed, I count everything as loss because of the surpassing worth of knowing Christ Jesus my Lord. For his sake I have suffered the loss of all things and count them as rubbish, in order that I may gain Christ" (Phil 3.7–8).

A person's ability to withstand the loss of "all things" pertains directly to how they view themselves relative to this world's value system. The things of this world meant much less to Paul than his spiritual blessings. Paul's loss of status as a Pharisee, along with his material possessions, whether plenty or little, were of no consequence as they related to his work as an apostle and his relationship with the Lord. At least twice, Paul encourages the Philippians to imitate this attitude.

A person's underlying value system is reflected in how they react in various circumstances. It is a priority thing. Their level of faith changes when they devalue their worldly position or material possessions. It propels them forward to more faith in God. Pride is replaced with humility. When someone has much, selfishness is replaced with the willingness to share. And when a person has little, they are not fearful but instead trust that God will supply their needs.

Paul's regard for the spirituality of the Philippian congregation was so high because they had shown their faithfulness in these things. He chose to speak to them about this subject in response to their great concern for His current circumstances. Paul knew these brethren would understand God could use even his time in prison for good.

In Paul's letter, he reminded them that his immediate circumstance was of no account because of the immense value of his relationship with the Lord. He considered it of much greater importance than this world's status or goods. May we all strive to imitate Paul's level of trust as persecution from whatever source on the macro or micro level seems to swell for some with each passing day.

DAY 5

Eyes that Look to God

Our cause is never more in danger than when a human, no longer desiring, but still intending, to do our Enemy's will, looks round upon a universe from which every trace of Him seems to have vanished, and asks why he has been forsaken, and still obeys. (C.S. Lewis)

And without faith it is impossible to please him, for whoever would draw near to God must believe that he exists and that he rewards those who seek him. (Heb 11.6)

The opening quote is from the book *The Screwtape Letters* by C.S. Lewis. The statement is spoken by Screwtape, a senior tempter trained by the devil, who is teaching a more junior tempter the art of seduction. The "Enemy" referred to in the excerpt is God. Screwtape explains to his protégé when their attempts to devour a subject are in danger of failing. The tempters know they are running out of ammunition when their human prey chooses faith, even when everything seems hopeless. It helps us imagine what faith in God might look like from the devil's perspective.

We see the same idea from a godly standpoint in Hebrews 11.6. Faith requires a trust that God is still there and that He is still faithful even when all evidence of such seems obscured by evil. He rewards those who seek him and step forward in faith. This attitude allows a Christian to act with eyes that look to God, the author of all truth. His children act on what He says. They believe in His faithfulness even when they cannot see what lies ahead with their physical eyes or comprehend how God will accomplish it.

When someone has this faith and acts on it, it shows they genuinely believe, like the "heroes of faith" used in Hebrews 11 to exemplify and explain the same concept. Heroes like Abraham, "who went out not knowing where he was going." Abraham learned to be faithful enough to be willing to sacrifice his son, knowing God would still be able to fulfill His promises through Isaac. Heroes like Isaac, who blessed Jacob and Esau, and then Jacob, who blessed the sons of Joseph. They all believed in God's promise that He would bless all the world through their lineage.

Many others afterward in Biblical history demonstrate what faith looks like in practice. People like Moses, who chose to suffer with his people rather than enjoy riches for a season, or the Israelites who left Egypt and crossed the Red Sea. Faith was shown by the next generation when they entered the Promised Land and conquered Jericho by merely following God's directions. As the Hebrew writer tells us, these were people who:

> "[T]hrough faith conquered kingdoms, enforced justice, obtained promises, stopped the mouths of lions, quenched the power of fire, escaped the edge of the sword, were made strong out of weakness, became mighty in war, put foreign armies to flight. Women received back their dead by resurrection. Some were tortured, refusing to accept release, so that they might rise again to a better life. Others suffered mocking and flogging, and even chains and imprisonment. They were stoned, they were sawn in two, they were killed with the sword. They went about in skins of sheep and goats, destitute, afflicted, mistreated—of whom the world was not worthy—wandering about in deserts and mountains, and in dens and caves of the earth.
>
> And all these, though commended through their faith, did not receive what was promised, since God had provided something better for us, that apart from us they should not be made perfect" (Heb. 11.33–40).

But sometimes, in today's world, it seems too much to ask people to make it to church on Sunday morning or show a willingness to suffer anything for their belief in God. Yet God has made promises to take care of His own that are still in effect today. God is eternal, and His home is in the heavens, but He still works here on earth as well. In this place, we are all merely sojourners and pilgrims like the heroes of old. All Christians must further the gospel message by demonstrating our faith to those in the dying world. Like them, we trust and act on the promises of our faithful God every day!

WEEK TWENTY-FOUR

DAY 1

The Great Campaign

Enemy-occupied territory—that is what the world is. Christianity is the story of how the rightful king has landed, you might say landed in disguise, and is calling us all to take part in a great campaign of sabotage. When you go to church you are really listening in to the secret wireless from our friends: that is why the enemy is so anxious to prevent us from going. He does it by playing on our conceit and laziness and intellectual snobbery. (C. S. Lewis)

Woe to those who go down to Egypt for help
   and rely on horses,
who trust in chariots because they are many
   and in horsemen because they are very strong,
but do not look to the Holy One of Israel
   or consult the LORD!
And yet he is wise and brings disaster;
   he does not call back his words,
but will arise against the house of the evildoers
   and against the helpers of those who work iniquity.
The Egyptians are man, and not God,
   and their horses are flesh, and not spirit.
When the LORD stretches out his hand,
   the helper will stumble, and he who is helped will fall,
   and they will all perish together. (Isa 31.1–3)

There was a choice for those who found themselves in the enemy-occupied territories of the evil Nazi regime during WWII. Every man, woman, and child would become a collaborator or a resister. They would either join the fight or actively resist and help the fighters or the oppressed. Lewis's illustration was well understood by its original audience, especially those in the occupied territories and those fighting to free them. In time, each person's choice was revealed, as some part to play in the fight was presented to everyone. For example, when the allied armies came into France on D-Day, the resistance was so entrenched and ready with all types of sabotage that they contributed to the success of the invasion.

Even the slightest resistance by some in the heart of Germany was effective. A movie called *Alone in Berlin* is about one man and his wife who had lost a son and knew what was going on with their government. They wrote small note cards with the truth about the regime and left them all over the city of Berlin. Residents turned in most cards to the local police, but some individuals passed on about 18 of these small notes cards of the some 242 they spread to tell the truth about what was really happening in an attempt to refute the German propaganda. The man and his wife were eventually caught and beheaded, but their efforts so haunted the policeman who read them that he committed suicide. The intellectual snobbery of the German elite was so blinding that they felt justified in committing mass murder. After the war, those who actively collaborated with the Germans were eventually punished, along with the recognized war criminals.

Fear, personal comfort, the elevation of self, or greed drove some people's decisions, but most did not engage in any resistance, not even in their hearts. They simply watched as the Nazis harassed, oppressed, starved, and murdered their Jewish neighbors. It is hard for us to imagine the stress they endured, perhaps until only recently. In our present day, any political opposition has become construed as "evil" in the sight of some of the most influential people in government, who feel the need to oppress and censor entire segments of the population.

These examples are merely illustrations that the real war each Christian fights is against rulers, authorities, the cosmic powers over the present darkness, and the spiritual forces of evil in the heavenly places (Eph 6.12). Sometimes, these worldly forces collide with truth in such a way that the evil is clearly manifested. God can use enmity to bring injustice to light. In that case, people can either work with Christ to sabotage evil or surrender to work as a collaborator with the devil.

DAY 2

Words Fitly Spoken

Tact is the art of making a point without making an enemy. (Howard Newton)

Let your speech always be gracious, seasoned with salt, so that you may know how you ought to answer each person. (Col 4.6)

An acquaintance of mine who is a management consultant used to say, "Words are hammers," and they sure can be. This metaphor can be especially true when there is a conflict of worldviews between those having the conversation. I am finding that in our world, people no longer appreciate the art of tactfulness. Finding and searching for the right and fitly spoken words are difficult. Crafting them takes conscious and intentional care.

We should choose our words to reflect our concern for others, but even when we do this, they may not be received as intended by the hearer. Everyone operates in the world using their own internal mental map. Sometimes people's maps conflict. When this happens, it can make communication difficult, stilted, or even impossible. Sticks and stones hurt physically, but unguarded words can hurt emotionally. The truth is that words can negatively impact or destroy our relationships.

The problem may be that two people have different understandings of a topic or different intentions for communicating. Whatever the conflict, choosing our words with a recognition of the underlying and unseen roadblocks is truly an expression of our love and concern for others. It is an art we need to learn, and we should practice it until we obtain a "master artist" status. That necessarily makes it a lifelong and ongoing endeavor.

Mistakes in communication will be made and should be acknowledged. We should examine these instances for clues on how to implement improvements next time. Sometimes it becomes immediately apparent when reviewing the fallout or damage of some miscommunication when we did not take proper care to consider the impact of a spoken word on a hearer or a group of listeners.

At the same time, Christians must remember God has directed His people to speak, especially when it involves something to which God has given direction. Jesus employs times of silence when responding to accusations, but these times were also intentionally chosen to accomplish the same good purpose as the fitly spoken word. Our ultimate purpose must represent God's mind and direction on all things pertaining to life and godliness, with the underlying intention to get ourselves and others to eternal life.

Even when it is difficult, words fitly spoken should be inserted into the Christian's conversation when they are acting as workers for the Lord. Christians should not choose their words to promote themselves. Our words should always be tactful and appropriate. They must not be used as weapons but rather as acts of love. And being crafted very carefully, they will prove to be more like nails that support the building of a house, not made with hands!

DAY 3

Like Little Children

Someday you will be old enough to start reading fairy tales again (C.S. Lewis)

[B]ut Jesus said, "Let the little children come to me and do not hinder them, for to such belongs the kingdom of heaven." (Matt 19.14)

Some time ago, I was listening to a CD of children's Bible songs with my youngest granddaughter, and "The Wise Man Built His House Upon the Rock" came on. It so describes our times. The storm our world is in is the rain coming down. Those lives or "houses" built on rocks of truth stand firm, while those built on lies or "sand" go "splat!"

Children have minds that see with faith and can understand the Bible narrative without making it all too difficult. As people grow older, they seem to want to complicate everything. Maybe it appears to the adult minds that they are more intelligent that way.

But if you are blessed with the spiritual wisdom and insight found in the revealed word, you may become "old enough" to learn how to think and see this life simply again. You will learn to operate on faith in our loving Father who resides outside this world! When that happens, we can sing joyfully and wholeheartedly with our precious little children about building our lives on the rock that is Christ!

DAY 4

God-Directed Steps

It's not denial. I am just very selective about the reality I accept. (Bill Watterson, in a Calvin and Hobbs cartoon caption)

Why do you not understand what I say? It is because you cannot bear to hear my word. (John 8.43)

I once visited the ruins of an ancient idol temple in Delphi, Greece, where a guide explained that the idol's priests would hide under the floors and use trickery to communicate with the visiting worshipers to give the impression that the "god" had spoken. They used fear and manipulation to control the population and pass on teachings they wanted them to believe. This kind of indoctrination was dominant in ancient cultures, but it is not much different now. Governments throughout time have controlled their people with lies and propaganda. Even our government seems to do the same in difficult, politically charged times.

In His discussion with the Pharisees, Jesus tried to help them see that their unbelief was an act of their choosing. His true words would have set them free from spiritual misunderstandings, but they had already decided not to believe, so they could not hear, appreciate, or comprehend His message. After Jesus exposed the Pharisees' hypocrisy and claims to be the "I AM," they sought to stone Jesus.

The deniers of God today are no different from the ancient Grecian priests or the Pharisees. Neither people teaching false religions nor those choosing to live their lives without God are listening to the truth. No one should be surprised when unbelievers react to God's teachings on truth or justice with violence and hate. They may be instructed either overtly or covertly to do so.

Today, the faithful learn of the true and living God through His written Word. Belief is accomplished by hearing God's truth with an honest heart, and we must choose to listen and understand before repentance and obedience are even an option. Let us always remember that "it is not in man who walks to direct his steps" (Jer 10.23). We must not forget to choose belief daily through an act of our own free will and pray for others to do the same!

DAY 5

In the Way They Should Go

Never ever, ever give up! (My six-year-old son)

Train up a child in the way he should go;
even when he is old, he will not depart from it. (Prov 22.6)

Years ago, when I lived in Nevada, we were trying to get to church services on Sunday morning after a heavy snowstorm. My children were very young, with my son about six years old, or maybe younger. The main roads were passable, but first, we had to get out of our driveway with two feet of snow. We were in a standard car, and my husband was on his fourth or fifth try to back out. I was scared to death and said I thought we should give it up. From the back seat, my son said, "Mom, you never ever, ever give up." On the next try, my husband got out.

Life is that way. We cannot allow our fears to stop us from trying to do the important things. My son instinctively knew, even at an early age, that to continue to try in our situation was necessary. Children are watching, learning, and sometimes, as in my case, teaching. My children are grown now, and my son still never gives up. Throughout his young life, I remember having to push him sometimes to keep trying when things were hard. When I did, the instruction was always understood and appreciated.

But life can be challenging. Pushing my asthmatic child to practice on an 80+ degree day in the humid south in full football gear would probably be viewed by most today as child abuse. But it can be done if you have competent coaches with an inhaler on their whistle. The day's motto for young football players was, "If you can't play hurt, you just can't play." Such things allowed my son to deal with difficult circumstances in a controlled environment.

I have two very strong children who are grown, with children of their own now, who can push through challenging problems, most times without complaint. They see it as part of the process. While you may not want to use football to develop a high level of grit in your children, I would suggest something that involves some level of risk to help them learn hard lessons in a controlled setting. I've always appreciated the sports environment. It helps them learn not to give up when losing, win gracefully, work hard to appreciate their accomplishments, and learn that they must practice regularly to improve their performance. The lessons go on and on, and the parents and coaches are there to help point them out.

Teaching these lessons is important. Our goal is to "instruct them in the way they should go." The lessons are all the more valuable when we can draw spiritual parallels as they relate to their service to God. When our children have gone from our homes and are no longer available to receive direct instruction, we want to make sure they can still hear sound teaching in their heads. They will complain about repeating the same lessons over and over, but it accomplishes the task of proper instruction. Whatever you teach will come to them when they make personal decisions in the small moments that make up their lives.

They will always have the choice of whether to listen to sound advice, but we must make sure they have the wisdom to recognize their options and the associated consequences of wise or foolish decisions. It all takes constant and active thought and involvement throughout the parenting process. Otherwise, children only get bigger and may not learn much of anything. All of their activities and school experiences can be used by active parents as training grounds! They don't stay young for long. We must make the most of our time with them!

WEEK TWENTY-FIVE

DAY 1

Trained by Suffering

We mature with the damage, not with the years. (Author Unknown)

But we see him who for a little while was made lower than the angels, name-ly Jesus, crowned with glory and honor because of the suffering of death, so that by the grace of God he might taste death for everyone. For it was fitting that he, for whom and by whom all things exist, in bringing many sons to glory, should make the founder of their salvation perfect through suffering. (Heb 2.9–10)

The word "perfect" in Hebrews 2.10 also translates in our modern-day English as mature or complete. Jesus left heaven to become a man, suffer as a man, and provide an acceptable sacrifice for sin with His death to allow all people an opportunity to be justified by faith. If Jesus had to suffer as part of God's process to be made perfect and complete, then suffering has real value and is still helpful to God's people today.

Our society does not know how to view suffering or tribulation as valuable life experiences. But all God's children must learn to endure and overcome because we can never eradicate them from this world. Suffering is present because sin is present, and overcoming sin is tied to suffering in multiple ways.

Our ability to trust and overcome is developed by enduring suffering in a God-prescribed manner. Those who are God's children should look to Him for guidance as a loving Father. God desires parents to illustrate this role in the family dynamic. I believe care for orphans and widows is prioritized in scripture partly because they have lost access to their own families where such learning can occur.

However, today most people are constantly trying to control things in all environments to create a status in which there are no difficulties to overcome. These restrictions, in their view, create peace. Everything is so "safe" that children have no opportunity to learn to watch out for hazards. These days, so-called "safe places" are even being provided by institutions of higher learning to protect young minds from hearing any opposing views. This is tragic, and we should view it as psychological abuse!

Instead of removing every hazard, we must teach children early on that they should listen to sound teaching because there are dangers in this sinful world they need to avoid. Each child must learn to trust what all honorable protectors tell them to understand that negative consequences result when they don't heed God-directed instruction. We must help establish the avenue by which they learn to trust God and His commands.

When a parent doesn't understand their primary role of showing God's care to their children, then all manner of difficulties arise in society. Some governments try to take over this role, even with the malicious intent to control people for their own use. Respect for authority decreases, and the ability of people to trust God suffers drastically. The loss of the bond, relationship, and dependence that should be modeled in the parent-child dynamic leaves behind instability and fear in children who are not properly trained by it!

No one will come to God who does not see a need to do so. It is in times of difficulty and suffering that God reveals Himself as the sustainer of everlasting life. He alone is the ultimate problem solver of mankind's primary need to be made whole again. If a person feels they can take care of and control things themselves, they will not reach out for help and find their only real access to spiritual protection!

God provided for mankind's redemption using the suffering of Jesus. Knowing that each person would have to endure suffering in a fallen world, God found a way to use suffering to eradicate it in the world to come. God's children prepare to enter a new world beyond the skies that He has prepared for those who overcome suffering and death. In this place, God, in His mercy, has made it so there will be no more sin, sorrow, or tears. There will be no more darkness or night there. We look to a place where God's glory is the light that shines in the land. There truly is a great day coming! May all join the happy band of those who choose a life in Christ.

DAY 2

Conscience Rejoicing

We have to pray with our eyes on God, not on the difficulties.
(Oswald Chambers)

Though the fig tree should not blossom,
nor fruit be on the vines,
the produce of the olive fail
and the fields yield no food,
the flock be cut off from the fold
and there be no herd in the stalls,
yet I will rejoice in the LORD;
I will take joy in the God of my salvation. (Hab 3.17–18)

Everyone looks at life through a lens that usually takes their circumstances into account, and the level of difficulties each person experiences varies. Habakkuk tells us that even if the condition of his life included an absence of all the necessities needed for his survival, he would still trust in God. He was determined to make a conscious decision to rejoice in the Lord no matter his circumstances.

Where do we focus our thoughts? Are they on troubles, difficulties, economic instability, oppression, irritations, politics, or self-advancement?; or are they focused on God, who is our "all in all" and the great I Am? The lens in which we choose to see and operate in this life demonstates our to the level of our faith through obedience. The absence or presence of biblical teaching is exposed when we use God as the authority and soverign and try to live life His way.

Just as Habakkuk rejoiced in the Lord regardless of his circumstances, so should we. Even when things are difficult, our faith should provide us with real joy, even in the worst times. This spiritual outlook is what sets God's people apart from the world!

DAY 3

Time to Think

The quieter you become the more you can hear. (Ram Daas)

Think over what I say, for the Lord will give you understanding in everything. (2 Tim 2.7)

When you read this, you can perceive my insight into the mystery of Christ. (Eph 3.4)

Paul encourages Timothy to meditate on the inspired revelation in his letters because understanding, growth, and stability reside through them. To meditate on God's Word, an intense desire to learn from God must be the goal. People can study scripture for many purposes, but God's Word will not have the intended result if hearts are unprepared to learn from it.

Learners can benefit in various ways from the teachings found in scripture. They reveal the mind of the creator of the universe. Through Paul, God encourages His people to take the time to "think" on the pure and honorable Word to gain "understanding in everything" and "insight into the mystery of Christ." But to think about God's Word, we need to plan for times of quiet when we extinguish all other noise.

We must cultivate our mindset and behaviors to carve out the necessary time for scriptural learning and the applicable change. Failure to do so will leave us tossed around by the waves of our circumstances with no anchor to grasp for daily stability. There are far more "untaught" in our environments than those who have been enlightened by the wisdom from above. For this reason, believers must champion spiritual stability and the ability to make reasoned decisions that override our superficial emotional responses.

Being spiritually stable is not possible when people abandon the concept of objective truth for the more subjective directives that the world incessantly delivers to us. If too many people decide to abandon their clear-cut moral compass, there will no longer be any agreed-upon, upright societal norms. If there are no standards, then people cannot meet expectations. And when people fail to keep promises, we cannot develop trust. Without trust, there can be no stability or righteous judgment. Ideally, the rule of law should be based on truth originating from scripture.

God asks his people to rely on His Word as the primary standard, God always keeps His promises so His children can trust Him. He also asks that each of his children model the behavior set forth by His Son. He asks them to be faithful and keep their promises so other people see this and glorify God. But His people cannot do these things without constant exposure to the Biblical text and record. The resulting heart changes will put us in direct opposition to a world under the sway of the evil one. The enmity itself is evidence of the conflict between good and evil! Bible study and conscious meditation are how we can remain stable amid a world that lacks principle, understanding, and righteous judgment!

DAY 4

A Better Kingdom

Sometimes I need to focus on the battle God wants to win in me more than the battle I want Him to win for me! (Author Unknown)

Its heads give judgment for a bribe;
*   its priests teach for a price;*
*   its prophets practice divination for money;*
yet they lean on the LORD and say,
*   "Is not the LORD in the midst of us?*
*   No disaster shall come upon us."* (Mic 3.11)

The prophet Micah provides a glimpse of the political climate in his time. Micah speaks to the various kings of Judah, including Hezekiah, explaining that God's judgment will come on Samaria and Jerusalem. God always precedes judgment on a physical city, kingdom, or civilization with a genuine entreaty, a plea for people to turn back towards Him and reenter into their covenant relationship with Him. He also provides promises of a better kingdom that has now been completely established in Christ.

The people in Micah's day were blind to their state as a people and as a nation. People can only discern God's deliverance with eyes and ears that see and hear the truth. They must be more concerned with pleasing God rather than man. It is possible to seek relief from the physical difficulties of this life in ways that forfeit spiritual reliance on God. On the other hand, if someone seeks spiritual peace with God, they may forfeit peace in the world.

Since ancient times the world has been somewhat like it is now, only with varying degrees of peace or conflict. Throughout time, God pleads with all people on an individual level to trust Him, serve Him, and wait on Him. He then separates His people from the world where those who pervert justice cannot spiritually harm them. In this sense, God eternally protects His people. This knowledge allows the godly to avoid complete despair even when they experience all the physical consequences that result from living in a fallen world.

God's own are in a kingdom that cannot be shaken. It operates here and will be in existence for eternity. It does not operate like any other kingdom that has existed throughout time, and it never will. It is established in the hearts of men. The worldly kingdoms of old are vastly different from the kingdom described as one that "shall stand forever" (Dan 2.44). We long to dwell in it long after the world fades in new bodies, "a building from God, a house not made with hands, eternal in the heavens" (2 Cor 5.1).

Most Jewish leaders in Jesus' day were so caught up in their politics and misconceptions that they could not recognize the risen Lord when He was physically in their midst! Throughout time, Satan uses the same stumbling blocks to distract people from taking advantage of the eternal kingdom of God. However, God still pleads with each one to enter! May we cultivate seeing eyes and hearing ears and stand firmly in God's eternal kingdom.

DAY 5

Ongoing Repair

The grand point is not to wear the garb, nor use the brogue of religion, but to process the life of God within, and feel and think as Jesus would have done because of that inner life. Small is the value of extended religion, unless it is the outcome of a life within. (C.S. Lewis)

Practice these things, immerse yourself in them, so that all may see your progress. Keep a close watch on yourself and on the teaching. Persist in this, for by so doing you will save both yourself and your hearers. (1 Tim 4.15–16)

I have visited many historic religious buildings that are dressed up to appear grandiose and beautiful. Many are shrines to more than one world religion with ancient creeds and traditions. But many of the buildings are in shabby shape. If you look closely, slow dilapidation comes from age and neglect. This disrepair can happen to people too. True believers cannot simply be "dressed up" in the trappings of false religion. They must live an obedient life that is Christ led.

The transformation process inside each of God's children is slow and ongoing. Usually, one can recognize God's help and goodness when looking back on their life, even when they cannot immediately see it in the present. With God's help and wisdom, saints can be His authentic, reborn, and transformed children. Their faith shines and provides hope in the midst of despair!

Saints must stay vigilant and involved in their growing up and maturing. We cannot control others and, most times, not even the circumstances in which we operate. But everyone can control how they choose to react to difficulties, mistreatment, or unfairness. We must not grow weary nor fail to show the glory of the one and only awesome God! We are not merely religious actors but are being made holy from the inside out! And it is a result of ongoing repair and care! The difference between God's authentic children and the "actors" is obvious!

WEEK TWENTY-SIX

DAY 1

Working in Our Sphere

Compliment people. Magnify their strengths, not their weaknesses.
(Joyce Meyer)

And if I have prophetic powers, and understand all mysteries and all knowledge, and if I have all faith, so as to remove mountains, but have not love, I am nothing. (1 Cor 13.2)

Someone once said that America is only great when America is good! I believe we would all desire the nation in which we live, more than anything else, to be what God can call "good." The rest will always take care of itself. But it starts with each person. We must show love and respect to others, reject injustice, and fully trust in God and Him alone! His wisdom is not of this world, so we must put all our efforts into recognizing the difference.

Remember to make the most of your time because the days are evil (Eph. 5.16). Let all be very careful not to fall into the world's trap of manipulation and disparagement. Listen to the context, seek to determine the intent and motivation behind the comments of others, and do not get caught up in gossip. Never blindly repeat another's biases, interpretations, or propaganda.

We all know that the truth gets lost amid lies. Try not to fall for it! Have a heart that sees the good in people and recognizes true injustice. Be skeptical of those who seek to solve your problems using anything that does not reflect God's wisdom. Distance yourself from those near or far who are blatantly seeking their personal will or gain.

Be good to all people! Life is hard and very, very hard for some! Most can work only in their own little sphere. Make yours peaceful and lovely! And if you happen to be in a position that influences events on a larger scale, do it using all the God-directed principles and emotions you can muster! Either way, God will use each person doing good where they are to change darkness into light! And this will always impact someone else's world!

DAY 2

Trusting Contentment

When life is sweet, say thank you and celebrate. And when life is bitter, say thank you and grow. (Shauna Niequist)

Not that I am speaking of being in need, for I have learned in whatever situation I am to be content. (Phil 4.11)

While speaking from prison, Paul shows appreciation to the church at Philippi for their help and encouragement, while at the same time taking the opportunity to teach about contentment. Christ was Paul's real reason for being content in all situations. Paul could rejoice, be grateful, and learn in the good times, and in the bad ones too, because he knew God was always there.

It is so easy to talk about how God changes the nature of His children, but how is it done? How did Paul mature into this attitude toward life? Some may answer by God's grace, which is true. There are parts of the transformation process that are surely inexplicable. But what does the Bible teach us about accomplishing our internal regeneration?

At the very outset, any person who can be content must have learned to do so from a source outside our natural, earthly realm. Let's start with grace. Grace is a term that requires its context to always be defined because God has expressed His unmerited favor, or undeserved gifts in many ways. Broadly put, the gift under consideration here is God's divine influence on the heart, which is complex and cumulative. A person must have been intentionally taught by God's Word and be honest enough with the information to accept it.

Of course, Paul had accepted God's Word, but there are more layers to the process by which one learns contentment in all circumstances. I believe the next step is learning to trust or develop faith in all the promises God has given us. This process can be hard to identify because it is ongoing and occurs over time. But it results in contentment that transcends problems with family and church, pandemics, wars, economic downturns, and anything else that might distress us in our lives.

What makes a person trust anyone else? Whoever it is, there must be enough interaction to know they will do what they say they will do. This principle is true whether they are a teacher, an employer, a politician, a husband, a wife, a parent, a child, a sister, or a brother. The repeated interactions over time confirm them as someone trustworthy and faithful. Beyond the blind trust that a small child might give someone in authority, this is the primary process that allows anyone to trust someone else genuinely.

The point is that God must be seen as faithful by any believer before they will act on His directives. He has always kept his promises, whether to bless or curse. History and nature show this. The words God spoke at the beginning of time still stand firm in the created world around us! The more internal and external evidence a person understands over time, the more faithful they will become. The more time spent in God's Word, the more convinced a believer becomes.

Our faith grows as we understand that God defines what it is to be trustworthy! He is always faithful, and our faith will become a habit when we internalize this truth! We will always be let down as long we trust in others or ourselves. As the Hebrew writer says, "Keep your life free from the love of money, and be content with you have, for He has said, 'I will never leave you nor forsake you'" (Heb 13.5). When someone trusts that God will do what He says he will do, they will be content no matter their earthly circumstance!

If we intend to represent God in our lives, we must ensure we are trustworthy in word and deed. Do what you say, or do not say it! Let people know as soon as you can when you will not be able to keep the commitments you have made. And do not ever commit to something you do not intend to keep. Don't sign up for something you cannot do. Don't promise your children things you cannot deliver. As a parent, if you say a certain punishment is coming and then do not follow through, you have undermined your child's trust. You never know how much damage you do to the other person's ability to trust anything.

Whether or not anyone keeps their promises, people will respond with actions that show how much someone is trusted. Paul appreciated the saints in Philippi because they were trustworthy. They also trusted Paul. Can you imagine, with his background, how many promises to them he must have kept for them to trust him? Paul was letting them know he was content in his distressing situation because he wanted them to feel comfortable knowing he could handle it.

We live in a fallen world, and we will all experience heartache, at least for the little while we are here! And true believers, just like Paul, look forward to being present with the Lord, in this body or out of it! They wholeheartedly believe in His promises of redemption and will follow whatever road He directs them to walk in this life right into the next one! They just let God use them how He sees fit without fear of this life's consequences. And if we do this, all our hearts and minds will perpetually focus on learning from Him what He wants us to do next!

DAY 3

A Peculiar People

Life with God is not an immunity from difficulties, but peace in difficulties. (C.S. Lewis)

Behold, I am sending you out as sheep in the midst of wolves, so be wise as serpents and innocent as doves. Beware of men, for they will deliver you over to courts and flog you in their synagogues, and you will be dragged before governors and kings for my sake, to bear witness before them and the Gentiles. (Matt 10.16–18)

When speaking to His apostles before sending them out to teach, Jesus warned them of coming persecution. The Bible records Jesus sending his followers out at least twice before His death, first the twelve and later the seventy. On these first trips, He told them they would be welcomed in many places so that they would need no provisions. However, on the night of His betrayal, he gave different instructions because the conditions had changed. They needed to take provisions because Jesus would be numbered with the transgressors.

By the time of Jesus' mock trial and arrest, the religious leaders had a better understanding of Jesus. He was not in the world to do what they had always imagined. They thought He would be a physical king, heal all their sick, and defeat the Romans so the Jews could rule their physical land again. Instead, those in power felt threatened by Jesus and the people who followed him. From Jesus' death, His followers would be persecuted and denied access to whatever the Jewish leaders controlled. The reproaches of Jesus had begun and will continue until judgment day.

Persecution was more likely when the apostles worked in an environment that directly opposed true heavenly wisdom. They could not always expect favorable treatment or for their message to be comprehended and received by the masses. Their worldview was on an opposing sphere. We experience the same kind of thing in our time. Earlier in my life, people seemed receptive to differences in thinking. But now, only voices in agreement with the prevalent mob are allowed in the public square!

Then and now, Jesus expects a calm and peaceful demeanor to identify His true believers in times of turmoil. They were warned not to fear those who could kill the body but rather Him who could destroy both soul and body in hell (Matt 10.28). That advice still applies today! The apostles were to remember that they were at peace with God, which was the more significant feat. His people need not be identified as belonging to the world of the unregenerate. They are peculiar people, different from the rest.

But the apostles did not immediately understand Jesus when He gave them those instructions. This teaching is new ground, judging by how much time Jesus spends explaining the concept. And He continues to explain it until his death and beyond through his disciples. Indeed, his death demonstrates the point, and His resurrection proves the validity of His promises of deliverance.

Like the apostles, let none be anxious in our time but pray for deliverance from evil. Even if we do not see it physically here and now, Christians know they already have spiritual deliverance when they actively "run the race" and "walk in the light" in the same ways the Lord directed His disciples. Those taught of God are recognizable by their ability to hold up emotionally and spiritually under persecution. They always have been!

Jesus promises, "Whoever finds his life will lose it, and whoever loses his life for my sake will find it" (Matt. 10.23). Seeing the world in this way may bring as much sorrow as it does relief, but it truly is what redemption is all about! The change in perspective will be so dramatic that a person will see the difference in themselves, and so will all the people around them! The apostles eventually learned this lesson. Hopefully, we can today as well!

DAY 4

Willing to Suffer

Let no man pull you low enough to hate him. (Martin Luther King Jr.)

It is he who made the earth by his power,
who established the world by his wisdom,
and by his understanding stretched out the heavens.
When he utters his voice there is a tumult of waters in the heavens,
and he makes the mist rise from the ends of the earth.
He makes lightning for the rain,
and he brings forth the wind from his storehouses.
Every man is stupid and without knowledge;
every goldsmith is put to shame by his idols,
for his images are false,
and there is no breath in them.
They are worthless, a work of delusion;
at the time of their punishment they shall perish.
Not like these is he who is the portion of Jacob,
for he is the one who formed all things,
and Israel is the tribe of his inheritance;
the LORD of hosts is his name.

You are my hammer and weapon of war:
with you I break nations in pieces;
with you I destroy kingdoms;
with you I break in pieces the horse and his rider;
with you I break in pieces the chariot and the charioteer;
with you I break in pieces man and woman;
with you I break in pieces the old man and the youth;
with you I break in pieces the young man and the young woman;
with you I break in pieces the shepherd and his flock;
with you I break in pieces the farmer and his team;
with you I break in pieces governors and commanders.

I will repay Babylon and all the inhabitants of Chaldea before your very eyes
for all the evil that they have done in Zion, declares the LORD. (Jer 51.15–24)

It is at perilous times when verses like the one in Jeremiah are most easily understood. Here we see God working in the affairs of men to fulfill His plans and purposes. God used the nation of Babylon to punish Judah's faithlessness and "break the nations in pieces," but they were also very corrupt and later punished for it. God's control of world events still works in the same way as was prophesied in these verses. Today, God has given Christ authority over the nations, to rule them "with a rod of iron, and dash them to pieces like a potter's vessel" (Psa 2.9, Rev 2.27).

While God is still controlling nations, His purpose is to save sinful man. He provides a kingdom for them that is not of this world. His people live in and among the physical nations, but they are set apart as holy people. The nations are used for God's purposes to ultimately accomplish His plan to offer redemption to men through all the earth.

Our obedience to God will lead to differing reactions depending on the spiritual degradation of the physical nation in which we reside. If you are in a place where God is appreciated, you may find peace on earth. If you live as a Christian in a place where false or no religion is valued, you will find conflict and persecution. It is the way of things on both small and large scales.

The gospel message is such that it matters not where you are in time or circumstance; deliverance is always at hand because Christ is our king and redeemer! Entrance into His spiritual kingdom is available to anyone for the taking. This is true even in devastating circumstances, which will make the gospel more appealing for some.

Christians can live above the fray even when suffering persecution by unlawful governments, unfair employers, business partners, patrons, or any other form of persecution. One may lose their physical life, but the eternal soul is safe when one has been born again into a new spirit. This knowledge brings a level of peace that allows for an eternal calm beyond all understanding.

Paul said it best, "The Lord is at hand; do not be anxious about anything, but in everything by prayer and supplication with thanksgiving let your request be made known to God. And the peace of God, which surpasses all understanding, will guard your hearts and your minds in Christ Jesus" (Phil 4.5b–7).

The purpose of this life is to find Christ. He fights all the necessary battles to provide for our hope. The rest is just noise that distracts and makes God's people less effective, but only if we let it. The problem with persecution for Satan is that it doesn't work to dissuade the plans of God. The more persecution Christians face, the more apparent wickedness becomes and the more the gospel spreads. It provides opportunities to provide light in the darkness when God's love conquers the hate.

Jesus shows everyone how the dynamic works through suffering death on a cross. He even loved all the haters! If one is willing to look, you really cannot miss it. His death allows all those who were once enemies to reconcile with Him. Only remember, when you participate, you may be the one who must suffer loss! And our willingness to do so may be how God saves and dashes the nations to pieces.

DAY 5

Letting God Work

When we have done our best, we also have to learn that we still need to rely on God. Our best—no matter how good—is incomplete if we leave God out of the picture. (Dr. Ben Carson)

For you shall go out in joy
*   and be led forth in peace;*
the mountains and the hills before you
*   shall break forth into singing,*
*   and all the trees of the field shall clap their hands.*
Instead of the thorn shall come up the cypress;
*   instead of the brier shall come up the myrtle;*
and it shall make a name for the LORD,
*   an everlasting sign that shall not be cut off.* (Isa 55.12–13)

There is a monumental difference between man's work and God's work. When people have done everything, they can to live faithfully—operating with good motives and using what they know to be God's directives—they need to let go and allow God to work. The results must be in God's loving hands so He can be glorified.

When God is in the picture, things work out good. If there has been some misstep by you or others, God will still find a way to use it for His purpose. The fruit is good in any activity where people follow His will. We must spiritually discern His ways because they are different from the worldly thinking around us. But remember, whatever happens, His will may not be what we initially think is good. It may not resemble our expectations at all.

But if you leave God out of your efforts, you are at risk of great peril. We may suffer in this life, but let it not be because we excluded God from our efforts. If there is something we need to know or learn, we will find it. If there is an area where growth is necessary, you will have opportunities to learn and grow up in the Lord. Even if we stumble, He is just and forgiving, and all will eventually be all right. We cannot fret or fear to the extent that we try to go our own way!

Sometimes our immediate circumstances may not appear to be working out very well. I'll bet Joseph, while he was in the pit and being sold into slavery by his brothers, did not think things were going too well. However, he later understood that it was all a part of God's plan. He told his brothers in Egypt, "So it was not you who sent me here, but God" (Gen 45.8). On the other hand, it is possible to believe that things in our lives our just fine when they are not. I am sure that the day Pharaoh met Moses, he did not think he would be toppled and lose everything.

Remembering that the workings of God are far greater than those of man, and they can keep us calm and sane. He tells Habakkuk, "Look among the nations, and see; wonder and be astounded. For I am doing a work in your days that you would not believe if told" (Hab 1.5). In this case, God was raising the Chaldean nation to destroy the nation of Judah and provide a place for His remnant to be taken captive and then flourish in captivity. No one knows how God is working when they are in the moment. But we can know He is, even when we do not understand His plans.

We must remember Isaiah 55.9, "For as the heavens are higher than the earth, so are my ways higher than your ways and my thoughts than your thoughts." Have you ever looked back at your own life and marveled over where you started and where you are now? God's work is clearly seen in hindsight by those with hearts and eyes that He has refined.

Let us all follow God's way and patiently watch and wait for the good fruits as He continues to work. Let us do our best while never leaving God out of the picture. But let us also know when to give things entirely over to God. Then, we can step back and watch as God reveals His mighty power!

WEEK TWENTY-SEVEN

DAY 1

Humility

Humility is not thinking less of yourself, but thinking of yourself less. (C.S. Lewis)

Whoever humbles himself like this child is the greatest in the kingdom of heaven. (Matt 18.4)

Jesus provides a clue as to how he wants His followers to view themselves when he compares the humility we should have to that of a child. Just before His statement in Matthew 18, Jesus called a child and put him in the "midst of them." And in Mark, we see parents bringing their children toward Jesus to bless them, seeking attention, love, and direction (Mark 10.13–16).

Our view of Jesus should include that of a loving parent with the right and ability to give us direction and protection, always knowing he or she is available to us. That acknowledgment will allow us to be more willing to take God's guidance and not be overly consumed with ourselves, this life's troubles, or even its advantages. His children will think about how to please and glorify Him as Lord and help others along life's way, much more than what others may think of us.

In times past, people have demonstrated a profound misunderstanding of the true concept of humility. Back in the Middle Ages, some intentionally caused their own physical discomfort, confusing humility with self-punishment. These perversions missed the point being made by Jesus entirely. In the quote above, C.S. Lewis may be trying to clarify this difference for a good reason. It can be easily misunderstood.

God's people should understand that they are children of a King who desires their good. We should all feel a responsibility to serve Him with an understanding that whatever we do in word or deed needs to be done according to His will and authority while also emulating His character. It is a relationship where the child glorifies the parent through respect and obedience. Not because the Father lords His power over them, but rather from appreciating the love, sacrifices, and protection He provides.

It is because of who He is that we love and praise Him. The thought reminds me of the hymn "He's My King" by James Rowe. It goes:

He's my King, and O I dearly love Him;
He's my King, no other is above Him;
All day long, enraptured praise I sing,
He's my Savior, He's my King!

May we all humble ourselves in the sight of our Lord and King today.

DAY 2

Other-Centered Love

Love God and He will enable you to love others even when they disappoint you. (Francine Rivers)

And he said to him, "You shall love the Lord your God with all your heart and with all your soul and with all your mind. This is the great and first commandment. And a second is like it: You shall love your neighbor as yourself." (Matt 22.37–38)

It can be difficult to understand the command to love others just like God loves us. In our modern English, *love* can mean anything from loving ice cream to a spouse. Worldly love is typically self-centered, but God introduced an other-centered love into this world.

God's love has a view and consideration of what is in the best interest of another. We can learn to express God's love to others because He has shown us what sacrificial love is. Learning to love is possible when we understand how undeserving we are to receive God's love in the first place.

Understanding how Jesus sometimes uses the word "hate" in scripture can also help us understand the meaning of love. He said, "If anyone comes to me and does not hate his own father and mother and wife and children and brothers and sisters, yes, and even his own life, he cannot be my disciple" (John 14.26). Here, hate means to prefer something much less than something else. We are to choose God over all other relationships in this life.

God demonstrates His expectation of what it means to love through the sacrifice of His son. It is well defined in how He has manifested it to us: "God shows His love for us in that while we were still sinners, Christ died for us" (Rom 5.8). God's love is not deserved by the recipient or earned by good behavior. It is not motivated by the giver's benefit, nor does it necessarily provide a warm, fuzzy feeling.

Instead, God's love elevates the needs of others in a way that moves a person with a genuine desire to give of himself and sacrifice for others. The focus moves away from a person's needs, wants, and expectations toward those who need them with God's will in mind. People choose to express it to others with the intention that the outcome will glorify God. His love shows a total lack of self-centeredness and is very unlike the *love* of those in our world.

This world typically does not love the unlovable or the unlovely. Those of the world expect something in return for their love. They usually hate their enemies. And since God's people are not to be of the world, none of these traits should typify our attempts at loving others.

Christians are to love and prefer one another, love their enemies, and love when persecuted. God's kind of love does not retaliate. It does not abandon. Yet, it can be tough and loving to discipline a child when need be. First Corinthians 13 provides a complete list of attributes exhibited when someone expresses it properly. The most extraordinary evidence of God in the working world is the presence of His type of love. And we can all love others only because God first loved us.

I expect all of us need improvement. God's love is the hardest to express to those who have hurt us greatly, but it can be the most effective when expressed to those people. God can use each expression of His love to change the thinking of those with a worldly mindset. And everyone who practices God's love will show themselves to be a gift from God, with a peace that can withstand persecution from all the haters.

DAY 3

Dependent on God

If everything seems to come simply by signing checks, you may forget that you are at every moment totally dependent on God. (C.S. Lewis)

Long ago, at many times and in many ways, God spoke to our fathers by the prophets, but in these last days he has spoken to us by his Son, whom he appointed the heir of all things, through whom also he created the world. He is the radiance of the glory of God and the exact imprint of his nature, and he upholds the universe by the word of his power. After making purification for sins, he sat down at the right hand of the Majesty on high, having become as much superior to angels as the name he has inherited is more excellent than theirs. (Heb 1.1–4)

When things happen in our lives to remind us that we are not in control, it always has some effect on our actions and reactions. God's presence brings peace, stability, and rational thinking to a Christian. For those in the world, it can bring paralyzing fear, or the person can embrace attitudes of denial, accusation, and self-preservation. They may even intend to manipulate the crisis to complete their agenda.

We all watch daily as these behaviors play out in the public square. Even people who know better may have to fight panicked responses and stress. We are all indeed at war with forces opposing God and His direction. Wisdom cries out in the street to anyone who will listen. We must hear her cries and pray that others do as well.

Using God's inspired word to counter these forces in our personal realm is essential. Our peace within should show up in our responses. God's wisdom should be on our tongues and in our behavior. Let us all remember Paul's words in 2 Thessalonians 3.16, "Now may the Lord of peace himself give you peace at all times in every way. The Lord be with you all."

God is in control whether any of us realize it or not. He had a plan from before the beginning of time to make sure all of mankind was given a pathway to righteousness, and he accomplished it. Let none of us forget that we are totally dependent on God in every moment. Nothing else can satisfy, not even money. And it is incumbent on His children to represent Him in the spiritual and cultural wars we encounter during our time.

DAY 4

Shining in Darkness

But I may say that the impossibility of conceiving that this grand and won-
drous universe, with our conscious selves, arose through chance, seems to me the
chief argument for the existence of God. (Charles Darwin)

They bend their tongue like a bow;
*   falsehood and not truth has grown strong in the land;*
for they proceed from evil to evil,
*   and they do not know me, declares the* Lord.
Let everyone beware of his neighbor,
*   and put no trust in any brother,*
for every brother is a deceiver,
*   and every neighbor goes about as a slanderer.*
Everyone deceives his neighbor,
*   and no one speaks the truth;*
they have taught their tongue to speak lies;
*   they weary themselves committing iniquity.* (Jer 9.3–5)

In Jeremiah 9, God convicts the people and outlines one of the reasons why
He will send them into captivity. In short, falsehood was rampant among
the people. No one spoke the truth. They proceeded from "evil to evil" and
did not know the Lord.

Yet, even the *father* of the evolutionary theory recognized the evidence of
God. Somehow the work of Charles Darwin has been used by the lovers of
lies to perpetuate one of Satan's most successful tactics—twist the truth and
present it over and over again as fact.

At no other time in my life has this tactic been more obvious to me than
now. Darwin's quote is one example of a disconnect between who a person
truly is versus their reputation created by the masses. This kind of falsehood
happens around us every day on all scales. But truth does shine out of the
darkness. It exposes lies.

Let us not be deceived. Anytime we have open hearts and minds and
look for it, the truth is right there. Creation points to it, and the written
word explains it. And people can escape captivity through Christ. He is the
Way, the Truth, and the Life.

DAY 5

Kind Responses

Love is never wasted for its value does not rest upon reciprocity. (C. S. Lewis)

But I say to you, Love your enemies and pray for those who persecute you, so that you may be sons of your Father who is in heaven. For he makes his sun rise on the evil and on the good, and sends rain on the just and on the unjust. (Matt 5.44–45)

Anyone can be *kind* to someone who is kind to them. One of the first things Jesus made sure his audience knew about the coming kingdom was that attitudes of goodwill and a preference for the good of others are required no matter the circumstances. His instruction includes loving our enemies and praying for those who persecute us.

When I worked outside the home in a formal workplace, I had the most challenging time explaining to others why I chose not to retaliate when people mistreated me. Some may have only perceived the mistreatment, but they thought I should use my position as a human resource director to make decisions that would, as they would say, *get them back.* Some even thought my lack of action was troubling. Many believe retribution is a natural part of the way things work.

In this world, this may be true. But if you are a child of God, there is a difference in how you respond to mistreatment. We must confront our issues directly with those involved and not talk behind someone's back. We avoid and pray for those who may want to hurt us, and we assume the best about the actions of others. These are the kind of loving actions and attitudes that Jesus promoted during His ministry.

By behaving this way in the world, God's word is manifested in our behavior. How our actions contrast the normal way of things allows others to see His divine instruction as wisdom that is *not of this world.* The difference in how the Christian acts and reacts to others allows His light to shine in the darkness.

WEEK TWENTY-EIGHT

DAY 1

Providing the Growth

Gardening is cheaper than therapy and you get tomatoes. (Author Unknown)

I planted, Apollos watered, but God gave the growth. (1 Cor 3.6)

We have always had a garden, and my husband always grows lots of tomatoes. In one of the first years of our marriage, we lived in a cottage on a property along the Hillsborough River in Tampa, Florida. My husband tried to grow a garden in that loose sand. I still remember watching him in astonishment. Anyone can guess how it turned out.

Later, when we lived in Nevada, we had a solar indoor greenhouse. We had the tallest, most beautiful tomato plants with lots of blooms. However, there was no fruit because there were no bees or wind. It took time and practice for my husband's gardens to produce.

My husband's grandfather always had a garden. When he got out on his own, he never really considered not growing one. He started with what he knew, kept trying, and learned as he went. He planted seeds in different types of ground and circumstances with varying results. He lived and learned and never gave up. Now our gardens produce beautifully.

He has also always preached God's word and has spread many spiritual seeds. In these efforts, he does not know the condition of the people's hearts. The soil may not be optimal, and people may not have people of influence around to pollinate or water them. Christians must do as directed and trust God to provide the increase.

Unlike physical gardens, where human know-how, effort, and the laws of nature provide growth, God will cover any deficiencies. He gives all that is needed for any honest heart to be discipled by Christ. The words from the scriptures do the planting, Christians do the watering, and God provides the growth. Praise God for that!

DAY 2

Unadulterated Spiritual Food

Modern Christians hope to save the world by being like it, but it will never work. The church's power over the world springs out of her unlikeness to it, never from her integration into it. (A.W. Tozer)

You are the light of the world. A city set on a hill cannot be hidden. Nor do people light a lamp and put it under a basket, but on a stand, and it gives light to all in the house. In the same way, let your light shine before others, so that they may see your good works and give glory to your Father who is in heaven. Do not think that I have come to abolish the Law or the Prophets; I have not come to abolish them but to fulfill them. For truly, I say to you, until heaven and earth pass away, not an iota, not a dot, will pass from the Law until all is accomplished. Therefore whoever relaxes one of the least of these commandments and teaches others to do the same will be called least in the kingdom of heaven, but whoever does them and teaches them will be called great in the kingdom of heaven. For I tell you, unless your righteousness exceeds that of the scribes and Pharisees, you will never enter the kingdom of heaven. (Matt 5.14–20)

This warning from Jesus can be hard to understand because Pharisees thought they were keeping every aspect of the Law. They believed they were elevating God by promoting the Law given to Moses. But Jesus is pointing out that they were doing none of these things. Instead, they were elevating themselves because they had access to The Law.

The Pharisees were rule-keepers without being God-loving believers. They were using the Law more as a weapon against Jesus rather than seeking its original purpose and intent: to come to know the only true and living God. Because they viewed it incorrectly, they were blind to the fact that the author stood right in their midst. First and foremost, God requires trust in His word, and faith in Him must be a Christian's top priority.

Jesus says there was nothing wrong with the Law itself, but a lot wrong with those who were misusing and abusing it to control others. The proper use of The Mosaic Law was to lead them to the gospel of the kingdom that Christ would establish. Both Laws, when properly applied, always glorify the Father in Heaven. Obedience and faithful service do not elevate the keeper of the Law, but rather God Himself, the giver and supplier of truth.

God's truth and wisdom stand out and draw people to Him. He can use the behavior of the faithful to illuminate His presence in a world full of the stubborn, self-promoting actions of the faithless. We must avoid acting from carnal-mindedness or selfish schemes to draw attention to ourselves. Instead, let us have an appetite for the unadulterated, behavior-transforming, hope-providing, faith-building spiritual food God has provided us. And let our practices come directly from His authorized direction found in the revealed word.

DAY 3

An Independent Dependance

If I was meant to be controlled, I would have come with a remote.
(Author Unknown)

…that according to the riches of his glory he may grant you to be strengthened with power through his Spirit in your inner being.… (Eph 3.16)

Have you ever thought about God offering us a *free will* choice in His plan for man's redemption? He could have made us obey Him like robots or pull our strings like puppets. Instead, He chooses those who want to make Him their Lord by a reasoned choice. He wants those who desire to follow Christ's to die, be buried, and then be raised again through baptism. He chooses those who make a conscious choice to love and serve Him.

In our roles as earthly fathers and mothers, do we use this same method to train our children to be productive members of our families and followers of the Lord? Or are we just using our *remote control* tactics to manipulate their behavior? It is much more challenging to live by example, teach the wisdom of making good decisions, and then allow each child to make their own choices and experience the consequences in small increments.

This method of instruction is more valuable than merely keeping your *thumb on the scale* to try and control their behavior so that it aligns with your desired outcomes.

As a young mother, it was explained to me that independent dependence is the goal of raising godly children. No child or adult can give control of their life over to God if they do not see that they alone are responsible for the good and bad consequences of their choices. They cannot be productive citizens, good employees, loving fathers or mothers, or citizens of the heavenly kingdom without first taking control of themselves and learning to serve, give, and forgive.

Self-control is learned and takes constant practice from each person. Nobody can do this for another, but anyone can show others how it is done. And nobody learns it without examples from the Lord's life and His word. We must learn from Him to get it.

There will always be someone out there who wants to pull your strings. Manipulation is how the worldly work and acquire their power. If you can't operate independently, you will allow others to use and control you.

So let us depend on God's word and study and worship regularly. God knew we needed constant exposure to what is good to grow and learn spiritually. And let us independently seek God, practice self-control, and consider how to build up our brethren. Our free will choices to faithfully serve glorifies God as the revered Father in heaven, the creator of all things.

DAY 4

Looking toward Eternity

There are two days in my calendar: This day and that Day. (Martin Luther)

But whatever gain I had, I counted as loss for the sake of Christ. Indeed, I count everything as loss because of the surpassing worth of knowing Christ Jesus my Lord. For his sake I have suffered the loss of all things and count them as rubbish, in order that I may gain Christ and be found in him, not having a righteousness of my own that comes from the law, but that which comes through faith in Christ, the righteousness from God that depends on

faith—that I may know him and the power of his resurrection, and may
share his sufferings, becoming like him in his death, that by any means pos-
sible I may attain the resurrection from the dead.

Not that I have already obtained this or am already perfect, but I press
on to make it my own, because Christ Jesus has made me his own. Brothers,
I do not consider that I have made it my own. But one thing I do: forgetting
what lies behind and straining forward to what lies ahead, I press on toward
the goal for the prize of the upward call of God in Christ Jesus. (Phil 3.7–14)

Converting from a worldly to a spiritual mindset might appear monumental to a new Christian. Some new and youthful Christians might even insinuate that living a Christian life is next to impossible. In their minds, they do not yet understand it all, so they do not know where to start. However, God helps every new Christian understand a worldview that includes an abiding faith in our loving Holy God.

Bill Widener says, "Do what you can, with what you've got, where you are." In the quote above, Martin Luther also provides insight into the mindset of tackling life one day at a time with a view toward eternity. In talking to a mature group of Christians in Philippi, Paul encourages them to focus on what is before them. They should start each day making sure they are always in a position of spiritual fellowship with God so that they will find the ultimate rest on the day of judgment.

This method of thinking will help Christians decide what to do in each situation, with each decision and activity in every minute of the day. They will contemplate what to do next based on whether the move will take them closer or farther away from God. They will put everything in the proper perspective, considering the value each choice should hold. And they will be careful not to create rocks of stumbling for themselves or others.

Paul is a great example to follow because everything in his value system changed position when he saw Jesus on the Damascus road. His daily routine changed. He forgot all his former dreams and aspirations and adopted what God prescribes as spiritually healthy. Like Paul, Christians must keep moving forward daily as a changed people.

After a person has died with Christ, they decide each day, from then on, to do the best they can with what they have. This statement is true whether they have knowledge, available resources, stamina, or opportunities. They move forward with what they have today while striving to obtain more to work with tomorrow.

Remember that all Christians are responsible for learning God's will through studying His word, to keep striving towards completeness, and to just keep on keeping on. Let all remember the unseen and abundant assistance supplied to them by their loving Father and always use their eyes of faith to see it. At the same time, let us know that even when we have done all we can, we are still not worthy of the sacrifice that paid the price for our inability to keep God's will without mistakes.

All Christians are ultimately justified by faith. Only then can anyone come before Him in judgment with the hope of obtaining justification. No imperfect person can enter God's presence. But God, in His mercy, has made us perfect through Christ. This message is the good news; really good news.

Let us all help others daily, acting from whatever phase of the learning process we are in. We are all on a journey to overcome this world and its lies that cause the unstable and untaught to give up on life. But we know we can count on His steadfast love. Indeed, all can find redemption in Christ.

DAY 5

Confident Hope

Prayer will become effective when we stop using it as a substitute for obedience.
(A. W. Tozer)

We know that everyone who has been born of God does not keep on sinning, but he who was born of God protects him, and the evil one does not touch him.
(1 John 5.18)

Faithful saints do not knowingly stay in a state of rebellion against God. God's people sometimes disobey out of ignorance, weakness of the flesh, or misunderstanding His word. At our very best, we still need access to grace and mercy to cleanse us and make our relationship with God possible. His children always strive to learn and align themselves with the truth, knowing God is the Almighty.

Christians know they have spiritual life and a union with God and know He hears their prayers. They are willing to trust God's answer to their petitions. And they are at peace in a world under the sway of the evil one.

In contrast to the concept of obedience we see in the Bible, seemingly religious people promote misconceptions to the contrary. These untaught people believe that to elevate God's grace, they must deem all behavior acceptable as if our choices or attitudes do not matter. The belief is that you can intentionally spread hate, compromise truth, make unrighteous judgments, avoid suffering, malign, and participate in all manner of activities that God does not authorize and still remain holy. It is the belief that redemption has everything to do with God and nothing to do with our obedience to Him.

And so, when life's events do not align with their expectations of how they want their lives to proceed, they pray and ask God to make all things well. A self-elevation of this kind puts them on the same level as God, allowing them to think they know what is best. And then, when God does not hear, or He responds differently than what they ask, they hold Him accountable for the natural consequences of their own choices.

In the quote above, Tozer is trying to highlight the differences between these two systems of thought. It is important to understand that we must trust and obey God in the manner He has revealed and authorized in His word. If we do not, we will be lost in the weeds, and a lack of faith and knowledge will diminish our hope of redemption.

If we want prayer to be effective, it must come from a knowledge of the truth and an obedient and humble heart. John writes, *And this is the confidence that we have toward him, that if we ask anything according to his will he hears us* (1 John 5.14). What a blessing! Each of us must love and seek the good of others no matter the cost if we are ever going to live with a confident, steadfast hope of heaven. We must strive to be obedient to His will so that our creator will hear us and answer as we live and await our eternal reward.

WEEK TWENTY-NINE

DAY 1

Overcoming Physiology

Perception is awareness shaped by belief.
Beliefs "control" perception.
Rewrite beliefs and you rewrite perception.
Rewrite perception and you rewrite genes and behavior …
I am free to change how I respond to the world, so as I change the way I see the
*   world I change my genetic expression.*
We are not victims of our genes.
We are masters of our genetics. (Bruce Lipton)

Be not wise in your own eyes;
*   fear the LORD, and turn away from evil.*
It will be healing to your flesh
*   and refreshment to your bones.* (Prov 3.7–8)

We all grapple with how to explain how God works with people in the world. I am not saying that it is even entirely explicable, but the quote above portrays an accurate contrast between self-will and the belief that everyone is a product of their physiology. Our beliefs and thinking impact and change how we see the world and ourselves, which affects how we behave.

God warns us that using our own wisdom is dangerous and can cause us to be blind and deaf to His will. We will find light, love, and safety using God's wisdom. As Jesus said, "Everyone then who hears these words of mine and does them will be like a wise man who built his house on the rock" (Matt 7.24).

People can believe that there is no God and that somehow men control the nations and world apart from Him. Or they can choose to consider what the Bible says in Colossians 1.13–17:

He has delivered us from the domain of darkness and transferred us to the kingdom of his beloved Son, in whom we have redemption, the forgiveness of sins. He is the image of the invisible God, the firstborn of all creation. For by him all things were created, in heaven and on earth, visible and invisible, whether thrones or dominions or rulers or authorities—all things were created through him and for him. And he is before all things, and in him all things hold together.

God inserted wisdom into His creation. We know this is one way God works in the world because we can consistently see it play out in ways consistent with the "truisms" we see in Proverbs. We also see it in the dependable natural laws He established at the world's creation. I marvel at how fearfully and wonderfully made mankind is and how we can see God in the creation. Who do people think holds this world together?

An individual's perceptions come down to the free will choices each makes in response to what they see and hear. Even collective thinking reveals how wisdom works in our world. Groupthink can bring peace or chaos depending on whether the people acknowledge God in their decisions. It has never in my lifetime been so apparent.

May we choose to have eyes that see and ears that hear. Everyone can take control of themselves and trust in God our father because He knows best. The alternative is to trust in ourselves and live in utter chaos and fearfulness. The latter leaves mankind with no absolute truth, putting us all at the mercy of our own subjective assumptions and self-serving behaviors.

We all choose a path every day when we decide whom to trust. The choice is either to trust in ourselves or God, and this choice will express itself in our behavior. And if Dr. Lipton is correct, our spiritual understanding leads to personal decisions that can even overcome our physiology. The question is, whom have you chosen to trust today?

DAY 2

Ordained Paths

"There are two kinds of people: those who say to God, 'Thy will be done,' and those to whom God says, 'All right, then, have it your way.'" (C.S. Lewis)

And since they did not see fit to acknowledge God, God gave them up to a debased mind to do what ought not to be done. (Rom 1.28)

God's desire is always to reconcile man to Himself. He has created all things, including mankind, with a plan and a purpose. He made roles for males and females, the institution of marriage, the family unit, roles for young women, older women, young men, older men, and so on. Everyone has instructions for the purpose and function they should play in their daily living as He originally intended.

The verse above acknowledges that some do not see fit to follow the God-directed paths. They do not honor or respect God or their ordained purposes that would lead them toward Him. We now live in a nation with so many people who refuse to have God in their knowledge that we are suffering the consequences of their attempts to pull everyone down.

With love, God works within people's hearts through His holy scripture. But when people refuse to listen or hear, God, in His silence, gives them their last chance to see His value and experience the consequences of sin. The works of the flesh are evil and not at all satisfying. They always end in perpetual confusion, chaos, and fear.

At this point, anyone with an honest heart will see that their thinking is part of the problem and may look for a way back to peace. But it requires a humble heart and a 100-percent turnaround to the mindset of seeking God and saying, *Your will be done.* We must be willing to see the truth, repent, and die to ourselves and with Christ to find the rest and peace that result from following God's original design.

And believers should not lose heart when circumstances are seemingly adverse because they, too, have a purpose. Do not be deceived. God's work will be accomplished. He uses whatever free-will choices people make to draw those toward Him that are willing to follow. This providential care is one of many marvelous blessings God provides. He is still working in this earthy realm even today.

God will individually judge each person. No one has to allow anyone to pull them down. Each person controls his spiritual destiny, even in a culture or circumstances that oppose God and even when the state sanctions lies and persecution. God's word teaches Christians how to respond to these attempts. It shows us how to overcome the world by holding fast to our confession and not loving our physical lives even to death. Overcoming the obstacles, persecutions, and the consequences of sin can help the Christian become stronger.

Everyone must stand for the truth in all circumstances. Praise God that we are not yet threatened with death in our country. Each Christian has to live within their God-ordained ordinance, showing faith and love while fighting "against the principalities, against powers, against the rulers of the darkness of this world, against spiritual wickedness in high places" (Eph 6.12). The fight should not be seen as against our friends, neighbors, or even our human enemies. We are fighting against the evil one who seeks to destroy faith in our Redeemer.

Ecclesiastes sums it all up when, upon much reflection, the Preacher concludes with instruction on how to live this life by saying, "Fear God and keep his commandments, for this is the whole duty of man" (Ecc 12.13). And Jesus says to the sinners, "Come to me, all who labor and are heavy laden, and I will give you rest" (Matt 11.28). All people on the earth make a free-will choice as to how they want to spend eternity. An old hymn asks, "What shall it be? What shall it be? Where will you spend your eternity? What will your answer be?"

DAY 3

Secure for Eternity

Rest is a weapon given to us by God through Jesus' finished work at the cross. The enemy hates it, because he wants you stressed and occupied. (Author Unknown)

Come to me, all who labor and are heavy laden, and I will give you rest. (Matt 11.29)

Some Biblical terminologies are much richer than we sometimes realize. The concept of *rest* is one of these terms. The word in Matthew 11.29 passage means *to take ease*. We first see the idea when God rested on the seventh day because what he had made in creation was *very good*.

Jesus and His once-for-all sacrifice can release souls from the bondage of spiritual death, and this knowledge allows Christians to travel on life's journey with calm. They can always return to where everything is *very good*. This spiritual rest remains true even when physical circumstances appear difficult.

A Christian need not fear or fret during conflict, pain, and turmoil. They know they are secure for eternity, even if their physical lives are threatened. Christians are on earth to share the message of the cross and allow God to use their lives in His service. When usefulness here ends, usefulness begins again in another realm.

The impact of Jesus' gentle and lowly spirit in our hearts should manifest itself in our responses to difficulty and chaos. A Christian's lack of fear should be apparent for all to see. Christians should be seen as different from those without this hope, and their response in times of trouble should be different too.

So stay calm and carry on, folks. Let us be as those who "loved not their lives even unto death" (Rev 12.11). Our Lord came to this earth to conquer death and fear. He passes on this ability to those who choose to be His disciples. So, walk with the Lord. Trust and obey Him. Otherwise, we are no different from the world.

DAY 4

Given the Victory

Every little thing [is] gonna be all right! (Bob Marley, "Three Little Birds")

When you go out to war against your enemies, and see horses and chariots and an army larger than your own, you shall not be afraid of them, for the LORD your God is with you, who brought you up out of the land of Egypt. And when you draw near to the battle, the priest shall come forward and speak to the people and shall say to them, 'Hear, O Israel, today you are drawing near for battle against your enemies: let not your heart faint. Do not fear or panic or be in dread of them, for the LORD your God is he who goes with you to fight for you against your enemies, to give you the victory. (Deut 20.1–4)

Fear not, therefore; you are of more value than many sparrows. (Matt 10.31)

As the Israelites were about to enter the promised land, they had the Law repeated to them to remind them of God's presence and direction. They were going to engage in physical battles for the land. They were encouraged to remember they were not alone. Today, Christians also engage in spiritual battles for the Lord. The enemy is fear and lies. God will fight for Christians today; His help is always there. Remember that!

Joseph directed Jacob to leave Canaan in the midst of famine so God could keep His promise to Abraham. The nation grew in numbers, and His people and all of Egypt experienced the Lord's power through the God-directed plagues they encountered there. After leaving Egypt, they were to learn to trust the Lord in the wilderness.

Once God eradicated the faithless, the next generation had forty years to look to God for their protection and sustenance. And upon entering the land, when Achan did not follow God's direction after they fought at Ai, the consequences that God had forewarned about were realized. His punishment was an illustration for the people of that day.

Over the years, after the Israelites had failed to do as directed after taking the land, it is recorded that most abandoned God in their times of prosperity and turned to worship idols. So, when their blessings vanished, and the worthless idols could not deliver, they could return to dwell in God's safety.

The circumstances we find ourselves in these days also have some purpose that likely should involve repentance and learning. We can use the past to guess these purposes, but none of us really know why events happen or how God is working in our time. What Christians do know is that they need to always trust under all conditions because God does not fail. He never stops trying to help us prepare our souls for eternity.

God takes care of the birds and flowers, and aren't people also of value to the Father in Heaven? The text says *of more value* because each person has a soul that will extend into the next life, an eternal life. And that soul must be spotless and without blemish to enter eternity under God's protection. And that state must be attained during life on earth.

Let us not be short-sighted or fearful as we face the giants of our time. Let us not be unaware of the stakes or blinded to our real purpose of being here in this life under the sun. Remember to *fear not*, for God is with His people even in times like these!

Let all prepare for the divine association by learning to be set apart from the world and ultimately made holy with God's help. God has provided a sacrifice for sin to allow His people to enter life everlasting. Each one must decide to take advantage of the offering God has made for a place in the land of the sweet by and by.

He desires that all choose eternal life over eternal death. But God leaves that choice up to each person by giving them the opportunity to learn and decide whom they will serve. They can serve themselves and find no peace, or they can serve the creator and find peace and safety as a beloved child who receives such from a loving, faithful Father.

All can live without fear of death because it is just a stop on the road leading to eternity, where all will be made new! So let not your heart faint. Do not fear or panic or be in dread of them, for the Lord your God is He who goes with you to fight for you against your enemies, to give you the victory over sin and death.

DAY 5

Infallible Wisdom

It is the peculiar quality of a fool to perceive the faults of others and to forget his own. (Marcus Tullius Cicero)

For with the judgment you pronounce you will be judged, and with the measure you use it will be measured to you. (Matt 7.2)

Wisdom comes when people see themselves clearly, as they really are, compared to what God created them to be. Men cannot improve themselves without knowing their weaknesses. If they refuse to see the disconnect between God's law and their behaviors, they have no hope and cannot help anyone. They are blind to any spiritual light or wisdom.

When people cease to use God as their standard and choose their own will as their guide, they become fools. Then being blind, they tend to judge others using the same faulty reasoning. So, "the blind lead the blind, and both fall into a pit" (Matt 15.14).

But a God-directed man using godly wisdom can encourage and assist others on their path to righteousness. This wise person is appreciated because he presents any advice as coming from an infallible God and not from his fallible self. So let us demonstrate humility by first removing the *log* from our own eyes. Only then can we see clearly to help remove the *speck* in our brother's eye.

Let us not be wise in our own eyes, but rather improve ourselves using God as the standard.

WEEK THIRTY

DAY 1

All Things Possible

God is looking for people through whom He can do the impossible. What a pity that we plan only the things we can do by ourselves. (A.W. Tozer)

But Jesus looked at them and said, "With man this is impossible, but with God all things are possible." (Matt 19.26)

Jesus makes the statement above in Matthew 19 after teaching that it is easier for a camel to go through the eye of a needle than for a rich man to enter heaven. Sometimes we miss the point because we focus on what is impossible rather than what is possible. Of course, with God, all things are possible.

When people think they have riches of any kind, whether they be monetary, a skill, or some knowledge, and then proceed with confidence in that rather than operating by obedient faith in Christ, they have abandoned their faithful service. Faith is elusive to them because they are dependent on self. They are also unwilling to sacrifice or forsake whatever is required. Instead, we must trust God enough to obey what we do not understand or perceive by sight.

Rather than *walking* using God's wisdom, most people are accustomed to walking in their own way. They cannot see that *all things* are possible because they do not trust Him who makes them possible. The word *all* in most biblical texts usually has some very limited meaning. In this context, *all things* pertain to finding the real *treasure* that leads to eternal life.

In Luke 18.8, Jesus asked, "when the Son of Man comes, will he find faith on earth?" Is this level of faith truly understood? Faith is trust in the unseen hand of a loving God. Do Christians today really do that? Usually, people decide on a course of action using their own determination and intellect about how to proceed.

When was the last time you ventured to do something based on an abiding faith without using your own sight and ability? One in which God leads you to areas where you cannot yet see or understand the outcome? This level of trust requires us to allow ourselves to be put at risk or even sacrifice ourselves so that God can be glorified. And those looking on and watching can only point to divine intervention for the resulting outcomes rather than a person's skill or intellect.

Do you remember the last time you allowed God to work, and you, and others also, knew that something extraordinary was happening? Something that could not have been done without some divine assistance? Remember, God is made perfect, complete, and manifest when human weakness or frailty is present. Let God's light shine, not our own. Let us not be the rich people compared to that camel.

DAY 2

Redemptive Love

People, even more than things, must be restored, renewed, revived, reclaimed, and redeemed. Never throw out anyone. (Audrey Hepburn)

And if I have prophetic powers, and understand all mysteries and all knowledge, and if I have all faith, so as to remove mountains, but have not love, I am nothing. (1 Cor 13.2)

We all see great value in repurposing things. It just takes ingenuity and effort. But when dealing with people, your love should be the catalyst to help others revive themselves with the Lord's help. This kind of love uses God's wisdom in the redemptive process.

So often, in essence, we throw people away because we are afraid, self-involved, or simply cannot be bothered. We cannot see a good use for them, so we do not take the time. Or worse, we help others to continue their destructive behaviors in an enabling way.

Most know how the butterfly develops. It changes in many ways through the struggle of its exit from the cocoon. And if anyone interferes with the process to make it easier on them or causes them to escape the cocoon early and without struggle, the butterfly will never recover. It would be stunted. It may be deformed. And it can never fly.

People have to struggle and overcome too. We must learn to use God's gifts, even those involving labor pains and discipline. We must show others the same love and kindness that Jesus offers us. In I Corinthians 13, Paul defines love and explains that love with God's teaching is more adequate in our day than the spiritual gifts were in his.

Using God's word, we can access that same wisdom and love to impact the world one person at a time. Let us not fail to achieve that goal because it identifies God to others. Without Him, there would be no redemption for any of us. The world will know His people when we love others as He has loved us.

DAY 3

Experience in Overcoming

Mountaintops inspire leaders but valleys mature them. (Winston Churchill)

Count it all joy, my brothers, when you meet trials of various kinds, for you know that the testing of your faith produces steadfastness. (Jas 1.2–3)

It is essential to see the value found in difficulty. We should not create it but, when it comes, we need to see it as an opportunity to grow. This mindset is how we learn to overcome the various trials life has to offer.

What happens when we overprotect ourselves and our children so there are few opportunities to deal with hardship, disappointment, and the realities of life we all face? The popular response today is to run when things get hard, from any hint of conflict, and instill unrealistic beliefs in children about their skills and abilities. The result is weakness, an inability to cope, a lack of leadership, and mass immaturity.

Experience in overcoming is necessary to improve when a weakness is exposed so it can be redesigned and corrected. Our actions have natural consequences and so do the actions of others. We live in a fallen world. We must learn how to be strong, endure, and grow in the midst of it.

DAY 4

Honest Hearts

There's always a little truth behind every "Just kidding,"
a little knowledge behind every "I don't know,"
a little emotion behind every "I don't care,"
and a little pain behind every "It's OK." (Author Unknown)

But what comes out of the mouth proceeds from the heart, and this defiles a person. For out of the heart come evil thoughts, murder, adultery, sexual immorality, theft, false witness, slander. These are what defile a person. But to eat with unwashed hands does not defile anyone. (Matt 15.18–20)

When my children were young, I tried to ban the words *just kidding* from their vocabulary because in *child talk*, those words typically followed speech that was not productive at all. While I doubt they understood my point until years later, I felt very strongly that they should not be allowed to talk hurtfully to others and then try to erase it with those two tiny words: *Just kidding*. I was drawn to the above quote with that memory in mind.

But I think the real point is that we never hide our feelings from others with generalized responses like, *just kidding or I don't care*. Even statements like these can expose our hearts and motives. And sometimes when people say these things, they try to hide their true feelings from themselves. Some may want to brush them off and ignore their deviant behavior instead of correcting it.

Heart sickness in a person is always the root cause of evil. Everyone knows this, even if they will not admit it. Our society often tries to normalize, compromise, and relabel all the evil they wish to deny so they can participate in it. Human beings want to vindicate themselves from the culpability of sin.

People do this by denying that there is a God-directed law they are breaking. They reason that if there is no God, then there is no law. If there is no law, then there is no sin. If there is no sin, then there is no judgment. And there you have it! They will not be held accountable, or so they reason.

It is only when a person admits there is a sovereign God who has the right to impose His law for all of mankind (and has done so in various manners throughout time) that a person will realize that they have broken His law. They have sinned against the rightful lawgiver and need redemption to remove the penalty for disregarding His authority. Repentance can only happen once this concept is understood and accepted.

This thought process is similar to our understanding of getting a traffic ticket. The legislature makes a law, we break the law, and therefore a fine is imposed. We are responsible for paying the fine or must somehow plead with the judge to relieve us from the guilt of the infraction. We must pay the penalty or our freedom is lost. More severe traffic violations or motor vehicle accidents may involve other people, who must also pay the consequences of those violating the law. A traffic violation may even take a life, and the penalty is even more severe.

But in the case of God's laws, the penalty for sin is always the same. It is always spiritual death, a separation from God in this life and the next. A man may receive justification when he admits the infraction and takes advantage of the only available avenue for payment to release him from the penalty, which is the death of the Lord Jesus Christ. The sinful person must die with Christ and become a new creature with clean and unstained garments. He can then be allowed into the presence of the only Holy God again.

And this process for redemption remains available as long as the person continues walking in the light and keeps taking advantage of God's sacrifice for sin. But sometimes, the consequences of a person's sin may remain in life. If a person has committed murder, they will still go to jail. The results of sins may linger for a lifetime, even if someone restores what they can and receives forgiveness from others. The point is that if we are never honest with ourselves, the process of spiritual justification can never take place.

We must listen to the advice found in Proverbs 4.19–27:

> The way of the wicked is like deep darkness;
> they do not know over what they stumble.
> My son, be attentive to my words;
> incline your ear to my sayings.

Let them not escape from your sight;
   keep them within your heart.
For they are life to those who find them,
   and healing to all their flesh.
Keep your heart with all vigilance,
   for from it flow the springs of life.
Put away from you crooked speech,
   and put devious talk far from you.
Let your eyes look directly forward,
   and your gaze be straight before you.
Ponder the path of your feet;
   then all your ways will be sure.
Do not swerve to the right or to the left;
   turn your foot away from evil.

Manage your heart, words, and actions according to their God-intended use. Then you will be assured of God-approved behavior. And for the times you fail, remember there is still access to a loving and holy God when you are in Christ. This access provides for forgiveness and a process provided for redemption and justification to regain righteousness, which always requires an obedient, abiding faith and repentant heart.

DAY 5

A Purpose for Everything

The world breaks everyone and afterward many are strong at the broken places. (Ernest Hemingway)

And the LORD said to Satan, "Have you considered my servant Job, that there is none like him on the earth, a blameless and upright man, who fears God and turns away from evil?" Then Satan answered the LORD and said, "Does Job fear God for no reason? Have you not put a hedge around him and his house and all that he has, on every side? You have blessed the work of his hands, and his possessions have increased in the land. But stretch out your hand and touch all that he has, and he will curse you to your face." And the LORD said to Satan, "Behold, all that he has is in your hand. Only against him do not stretch out your hand." So Satan went out from the presence of the LORD. (Job 1.8–12)

The Lord knows more about pain and suffering than Satan. When righteous people suffer, they learn many things that really cannot be learned any other way. In the case of Job, God used what Satan intended for evil to teach him what is good.

Not only did God teach Job about the value of pain and loss, but also his friends, as well as all of us today. He used Job and his exchanges with his friends to teach us by example. The primary lesson is that we do not know what we do not know. And it teaches us that God can use pain and suffering for good purposes.

Suffering is not always a consequence of a person's sin. We should always ask ourselves what there is to learn when we experience pain, ruin, or failure. With Job, God defeats Satan by employing Satan's own tools for Job's benefit. And He does the same for us today if the suffering person will allow it.

The dialogue between Job and his three friends represents human wisdom and reasoning about why bad things happen to good people. And Job learns, to an even greater magnitude, that the answer is that God is in control and has created a purpose for everything. Even though we live in a sinful and polluted world, God can still educate and redeem mankind in the way of righteousness.

So many insightful concepts are found in the book of Job. Divine wisdom comes from above. Time and chance happen to us all. Satan is an adversary to all people and things made by God. God can use all things for good. Satan's goal is to destroy God's work and remedies in the minds of people as they live in the world. Satan distorts and twists the truth. And the list goes on. Did you notice Satan had to have permission from God to hurt Job? Think about it and let us learn from it!

Do not remove all pain from your or your children's paths. Instead, learn the God-directed lessons and show them to others through your responses to life's challenges. This response will benefit everyone around you. If used properly, even our pain can accomplish God's intended good.

How great is that! And how revealing it is of God's character. It shows how deserving of glory and honor God really is. It is almost too fantastic to grasp.

WEEK THIRTY-ONE

DAY 1

Spiritual Delicacies

When the debate is lost, slander becomes the tool of the loser. (Socrates)

So put away all malice and all deceit and hypocrisy and envy and all slander. Like newborn infants, long for the pure spiritual milk, that by it you may grow up into salvation—if indeed you have tasted that the Lord is good. (1 Pet 2.1–3)

Whom we have chosen to serve is made evident in our reactions when our heart's desires are not met. How someone responds to disappointment indicates whether they act from a heart influenced by God or a worldview devoid of spiritual things. Individuals who have matured in Christ are hungry for God's word and are thirsty for His righteousness. They have grown up and out of the world's view of things and into salvation.

A person's transformed behavior results from eating spiritual food. His heart understands things like trust, sacrifice, and steadfast love because he has been taught by God. Once someone tastes these delicacies, they know there is no nutritional value in a worldly meal served up by Satan. So, they simply leave it on the table, and not a bite goes into a God-directed heart.

For anyone who has not tasted God's Word, all that is available to them is tasteless speech devoid of any use or value to anyone. They just growl and attack like hungry dogs. But the God-directed heart has put it all away: deceit, hypocrisy, envy, and all slander. Continue to long for the spiritual milk, for we have indeed tasted that the Lord is good.

DAY 2

Not a Word

I stopped explaining myself when I realized people only understand from their level of perception. (Author Unknown)

When Herod saw Jesus, he was very glad, for he had long desired to see him, because he had heard about him, and he was hoping to see some sign done by him. So he questioned him at some length, but he made no answer. The chief priests and the scribes stood by, vehemently accusing him. And Herod with his soldiers treated him with contempt and mocked him. Then, arraying him in splendid clothing, he sent him back to Pilate. (Luke 23.8–11)

Jesus was unfairly maligned, accused, and reviled by a lying mob when the Jews put Him on trial and brought Him before the Romans. When Pilate sent Jesus to Herod to pass off the problem, Jesus chose not to answer him a word. Luke tells us Herod had a personal agenda in his desire to see Jesus because he hoped to see a sign. Still, Herod really had no interest in bringing fairness, justice, or resolution to the situation. So, Jesus did not give him additional ammunition to twist, misuse, or use to his advantage.

Sometimes today, we can find ourselves faced with the same kind of dilemma. We are surrounded by a mob that wishes to get its way at all costs. Their selfish agenda is paramount in their minds. Justice never enters into their thinking.

People ignore God's directions in many situations where the only motives at work are self-promotion, self-justification, retaliation, and vindictiveness. Remember, God used the wickedness of these very people Jesus was dealing with to save His righteous children for all time. And God still works in much the same way today.

When there is no justice sought or righteous motive at work, we will do well to remember there are times when we should answer "not one word," as our Lord modeled (Matt 27.14, NKJV). Let us be careful to be wise as serpents and gentle as doves as we navigate the evil all around us! Answering in a crowd that does not perceive or understand the whole situation can cause more harm than good.

DAY 3

When Luxuries Vanish (Part 1)

The minor prophets are as relevant as the morning newspaper. (John Coffman)

The LORD says,
The women of Zion are haughty,
    walking along with outstretched necks,
    flirting with their eyes,
strutting along with swaying hips,
    with ornaments jingling on their ankles.
Therefore the LORD will bring sores
    on the heads of the women of Zion;
    the LORD will make their scalps bald. (Isa 3.16–17)

Years ago, I had a preacher who said reading the ancient prophets was as relevant as reading the morning newspaper. I'm not sure how many people still read a morning paper, but I think it is an excellent way to describe their significance to us today. I understood what he meant back in the eighties, and the thought resonates even louder today.

As I watch what is happening in our country, I can see the nation drifting so far from the truth that it is moving entirely out of sight. The ancient prophets give us clues as to how faltering societies operate. They show us identifiers of decline that can be witnessed by a population experiencing a time of judgment from God. We can see the identifying conditions of Israel in the word of God spoken through the prophets, both major and minor, and they are still relevant today.

One identifier is that a nation's leadership is wanting because they rule as self-absorbed children and act without God's wisdom. In Isaiah, God says:

And I will make boys their princes, and infants shall rule over them. And the people will oppress one another, everyone his fellow and everyone his neighbor; the youth will be insolent to the elder, and the despised to the honorable. (Isa 3.4–5)

Further in the chapter, we see that morality vanishes, and the people celebrate immorality. God says:

For Jerusalem has stumbled, and Judah has fallen, because their speech and their deeds are against the LORD, defying his glorious presence. For the look on their faces bears witness against them; they proclaim their sin like Sodom; they do not hide it. Woe to them! For they have brought evil on themselves. (Isa 3.8–9)

We see that the people can no longer count on justice in the courts and may have to fear the government and its institutions. Amos 5.12–13 says:

For I know how many are your transgressions and how great are your sins—you who afflict the righteous, who take a bribe, and turn aside the needy in the gate. Therefore he who is prudent will keep silent in such a time, for it is an evil time.

Those participating in immorality and injustice deny their action and do not believe God will punish them. Micah 2.6 speaks to the identifier of opposing righteousness. He wrote,

"Do not preach"—thus they preach—"one should not preach of such things; disgrace will not overtake us." They are openly defiant and misuse scripture. They continue to despise discipline, which exposes their failings further. In turn, they cause their own demise over time.

In times like these, Isaiah tells us that the Lord will take His place to contend with the people as He stands to judge them. The Lord will hold the leaders accountable because they oppressed the common people for personal gain and neglected their responsibilities. Isaiah says:

The LORD will enter into judgment with the elders and princes of his people: It is you who have devoured the vineyard; the spoil of the poor is in your houses. What do you mean by crushing my people by grinding the face of the poor?" declares the LORD God of hosts. (Isa. 3.14–15)

A judgment in these kind of times will come to draw people back to God. So, the luxuries of the arrogant will also vanish (Isa 3.16–26). When judgment happens, the worshippers of God are few. The necessities of life become scarce and food is not readily available. Joel says:

Grain offerings and drink offerings are cut off from the house of the LORD. The priests are in mourning, those who minister before the LORD. The fields are ruined, the ground is dried up; the grain is destroyed, the new wine is dried up, the olive oil fails. (Joel 1.9–10)

Joel then gives God's direction for renewal:

Put on sackcloth, you priests, and mourn; wail, you who minister before the altar. Come, spend the night in sackcloth, you who minister before my God; for the grain offerings and drink offerings are withheld from the house of your God. Declare a holy fast; call a sacred assembly. Summon the elders and all who live in the land to the house of the LORD your God, and cry out to the LORD. (Joel 1.13–14)

Religious leaders and the people are all called upon to repent. They are to call out with one reverent sound to the LORD, pleading for forgiveness. And they are to dedicate themselves to holy service.

DAY 4

When Luxuries Vanish (Part 2)

In that day the LORD will snatch away their finery: the bangles and headbands and crescent necklaces, the earrings and bracelets and veils, the headdresses and anklets and sashes, the perfume bottles and charms, the signet rings and nose rings, the fine robes and the capes and cloaks, the purses and mirrors, and the linen garments and tiaras and shawls.

Instead of fragrance there will be a stench;
   instead of a sash, a rope;
instead of well-dressed hair, baldness;
   instead of fine clothing, sackcloth;
   instead of beauty, branding.
Your men will fall by the sword,
   your warriors in battle.
The gates of Zion will lament and mourn;
   destitute, she will sit on the ground. (Isa 3.18–26)

God's reactions to evil in any society begin when everyone starts to do what is right in their own eyes. The luxuries vanish followed by necessities like food, clothing, and protection. He tries His best to help people and societies turn and realize the origination of their blessings. He draws those to Him who wish to remain His people with discipline and judgment. Wise and loving parents will model this when their children are unruly. When they fail to do so, children grow up to be disrespectful and unprepared for life.

The delusional thinking and the lack of civility towards others in the public domain are staggering. The emotional immaturity is epic. Thanks be to God that He made it possible to recognize the times of correction. Even persecution strengthens those who are His children and highlights the truth for all to see. Each person can turn in faith to a God who can provide for all their needs, even in times of great trouble.

The heart of any Christian can respond just as the remnants did in the days of old. Habakkuk 3.17–19 explains:

> 'Though the fig tree does not bud and there are no grapes on the vines, though the olive crop fails and the fields produce no food, though there are no sheep in the pen and no cattle in the stalls, yet I will rejoice in the LORD, I will be joyful in God my Savior. The Sovereign LORD is my strength; he makes my feet like the feet of a deer, he enables me to tread on the heights.

No one can ever tell precisely when God is working or who or what God is working with, but we can read the times and respond accordingly. The prophets all speak of the fates of people in ancient times. We read about God's judgments on the faithless nations, not only on Israel and Judah, but also on others like Assyria, Babylon, Egypt, Edom, Philistia, and the list goes on.

These people did not believe God was working with them during their time either, but He is in control of nations whether anyone believes it or not. He has not stopped working with people as individuals or their respective nations. He has done so since the dawn of time. May all His people recognize the signs, repent, and save themselves from their wicked and perverse generation, when or wherever they live.

DAY 5

A Soul's Best Interest

Listen to no man who has not listened to God. (A.W. Tozer)

The secret of the LORD is with those who fear Him,
And He will show them His covenant.
My eyes are ever toward the LORD,
For He shall pluck my feet out of the net.
Turn Yourself to me, and have mercy on me,
For I am desolate and afflicted.
The troubles of my heart have enlarged;
Bring me out of my distresses!
Look on my affliction and my pain,
And forgive all my sins.
Consider my enemies, for they are many;
And they hate me with cruel hatred.
Keep my soul, and deliver me;
Let me not be ashamed, for I put my trust in You.
Let integrity and uprightness preserve me,
For I wait for You. (Psa 25.14–21)

Understanding that God gives us the correct information is so valuable. The constant onslaught of misinformation from various media sources helps us appreciate the value of knowing the truth and direction God supplies. We can rely upon His word as the only reliable standard of real and absolute truth.

God's revealed truth includes direction on how to save our souls, conduct our lives, deal with difficult people, raise our children, interact with the government, and learn how to accomplish all things pertaining to life and godliness. Having the right direction and applying the correct information to each problem keeps the godly from being caught up in webs of deceit that are intentionally woven to trap the righteous.

God's truth can keep believers safe and deliver their souls. It keeps us calm and teaches us how to trust and wait. It provides assurance and helps us trust that God is attending to our best interests, even when we do not completely understand how He works in our lives.

When the information you rely on causes confusion and doubt, always look to its originating source. When information comes from a source other than God and His revealed wisdom, it's originating from a starting point of unknown agendas and sometimes even deceit. Worldly sources usually have bias or self-promotion at work. It has very little value because it does not carry with it the veracity of a faithful source.

Always remember that only God has an eternal soul's interest at heart. Let all use God's wisdom as the filter when looking for truth because, my friend, it is the only way to find it. And failing to find the truth leads to utter ruin in this life and the next.

WEEK THIRTY-TWO

DAY 1

Fruits of His Promises

Why not go out on a limb? That's where all the fruit is. (Mark Twain)

And without faith it is impossible to please him, for whoever would draw near to God must believe that he exists and that he rewards those who seek him. (Heb 11.6)

To operate with godly direction takes what God calls faith. We must believe in the unseen things above to the degree that they affect our thinking and actions. As a child, I remember struggling with this concept. I could not even understand what Mark Twain was talking about, let alone grasp this godly principle.

Faith is one of those words that only God can define. It is the opposite of what He calls "sight." Sight is what you can see and discern with the evidence you perceive with your five senses. As Paul instructed the Corinthians, "We walk by faith, not by sight" (2 Cor 5.7).

But faith includes evidence that we see through eyes that can see into an unseen realm. And this kind of "seeing" is a choice. Mark Twain expresses "faith" in a way that anyone can see it—like we are moving out on a limb for some reward when we are not sure whether it will break or not. The mind of a Christian believes in the maker of the tree and trusts that the way to the fruit is to go out on the limp. In this case, the fruit is only seen through the eyes of faith.

Christians know the spiritual tree limb is not precarious. They see that the tree is strong and will hold them up. A Christian must remember that it is God's tree and God's fruit, and we must find His tree among all the deceptive ones that exist in a world under the sway of the wicked one.

People can only find it with open-minded thinking and a desire to know God from God.

Even to this day, we can learn from examples of faith. Abel teaches us that making the right choices for godly sacrifice is done by faith. Abraham teaches us to go where God directs even when we do not know where we are going and have no prior sensory knowledge that confirms our "worldly safety."

We may not always see where godly direction may lead us in our physical lives. But like Abraham, "we look forward to the city that has foundations, whose designer and builder is God" (Heb 11.10). May we all choose to walk by faith and not by sight in the areas that God has directed because that is where the fruits of the His promises reside.

DAY 2

Trained Discernment

The goal is to develop spiritual stamina so when a problem occurs, I don't react out of emotion but out of wisdom. (Author Unknown)

For though by this time you ought to be teachers, you need someone to teach you again the basic principles of the oracles of God. You need milk, not solid food, for everyone who lives on milk is unskilled in the word of righteousness, since he is a child. But solid food is for the mature, for those who have their powers of discernment trained by constant practice to distinguish good from evil. (Heb 5.12–14)

It is incumbent on Christians to be always learning and growing in spiritual discernment. This process requires constant "training." And it requires a sustained daily effort.

Remember that Satan can manipulate our emotions with deceit. We must all practice discerning the difference between God's desires and Satan's trickery to have enough stamina to respond correctly to difficulties in our lives. Our decisions should be based on godly wisdom when faced with difficult choices.

God expects His children to become as "wise as serpents and gentle as doves." Having these characteristics is all the more necessary in times when evil is running rampant. The devil is searching for the ignorant and unstable to devour them.

The group of Hebrew Christians the inspired author addresses above had allowed themselves to stop growing. They had become unaware of the most basic principles of righteousness from lack of use. In our present time, there is great danger in forgetting the meaning of things like holiness, responsibility, obedience, and self-sacrifice.

Let us all watch what we allow our minds to be saturated with because whatever we are repetitiously exposed to is what we are transformed by; will it be God, His word, and servanthood? Or will it be politics, self-help books, fear, television, news, hobbies, or the music of our time? Stay calm, wait, and carry on with God's work. And choose to be saturated with truth.

DAY 3

Steering Our Lives

Is prayer your steering wheel or your spare tire? (Corrie Ten Boom)

Many are the sorrows of the wicked,
   but steadfast love surrounds the one who trusts in the LORD. (Psa 32.10)

In whom are we trusting all the days of our lives? Prayer allows us to commune with God while understanding His strength and sovereignty compared to our weakness and lack of real purpose without Him. However, sometimes we do not use it unless we "need" it and so relegate our relationship with God to a *spare tire* status.

Are we seeking Him only in the times that we see trouble? Do we trust ourselves until we realize how little control we have and then approach Him for help? Do we seek direction from the instructional map in His word before making our life choices? Or do we think we already know the way, only to find ourselves lost and so off course that we look to God for deliverance?

A man trusting in himself has become the norm in this country. And then, something like a weather event, a pandemic, or a financial crisis happens. Some events occur without warning, and how little control we have over this life becomes readily apparent. Then, turning to God and trusting in Him becomes the only viable option for true deliverance.

People either give control over their lives to a higher authority or look for temporary pleasure and fall into traps of illusion and idolatry. The latter cannot seem to operate by faith in God. Fear reigns when faith is forsaken.

One of the things we can learn from these trials is to rely more on God to steer our daily lives. He is right there, ready and knocking on the door of our hearts, waiting to be allowed to enter or drive us where we need to go. Let us be people who continually give our lives over to Him. Let us remember the words of Isaiah:

> Seek the LORD while he may be found;
>   call upon him while he is near;
> let the wicked forsake his way,
>   and the unrighteous man his thoughts;
> let him return to the LORD, that he may have compassion on him,
>   and to our God, for he will abundantly pardon. (Isa 55.6–7)

DAY 4

A Present-Tense Life

Stop waiting for Friday, for summer, for someone to fall in love with you, for life. Happiness is achieved when you stop waiting for it and make the most of the moment you are in now! (Author Unknown)

Therefore do not be anxious about tomorrow, for tomorrow will be anxious for itself. Sufficient for the day is its own trouble. (Matt 6.34)

If there is one thought I wish to convey to young people today (and some older ones, too), it is the one illustrated in the quote above. So often, people are in "waiting mode" for things to get to where they have determined everything will be *better* in order to act. This illusion is just another one of Satan's tricks.

The sentiment seems to be an *if only* mindset. If only I could choose what I want to do instead of having to work. If only the weather were better.

If only I were in a satisfying relationship. If only things were easier. If only there was not a pandemic. If only things were normal. If only … well, we all can think of things to fill in the next blank. It seems so many people fail to use or enjoy the right now, today, the very moment they are in.

This mindset not only wastes time or leaves things undone, but it also has a very sinister component. It postpones an appreciation and thankfulness for what people are currently experiencing. They replace appreciation for what they perceive as a legitimate fear in their heart and mind. Our Lord died specifically so His children would no longer fear death. And this effort seems to be undermined and dismissed by even those who claim to be His children.

We all live a present-tense life. Let us use our time wisely! Enjoy it, see its blessings, and be thankful for what we have because that is all you can be assured that you will be allowed to experience.

Even if we do not realize it, we should all live with the expectation that circumstance can take away our physical life at any time. All that changes is the risk of death might be highlighted in our minds, and we become aware of it. Showing that life can be disrupted at any time may even be the purpose of plagues in the Old Testament. God wants us to realize He is in control, and we are not.

Always do what you need to do. Say what you need to say. Appreciate all your moments, and do not fret about what will happen tomorrow. If you feel compelled, be as careful as possible without leaving the command to worship undone. Without leaving undone the reaching out to those in need. Without neglecting the needs of your family. Without forfeiting efforts to teach or show love to a neighbor.

Today is the day of salvation. Make sure you are right with God because there is no guarantee of a tomorrow. Whether we face a judgment in time or await the judgment at the end of time, let us remember the words of Habakkuk:

> Though the fig tree should not blossom,
>   nor fruit be on the vines,
> the produce of the olive fail
>   and the fields yield no food,
> the flock be cut off from the fold
>   and there be no herd in the stalls,
> yet I will rejoice in the LORD;
> I will take joy in the God of my salvation.

GOD, the Lord, is my strength;
he makes my feet like the deer's;
he makes me tread on my high places. (Hab 3.17–19)

DAY 5

A Strong Attitudinal Response

[Jesus] produced mainly three effects—Hatred—Terror—Adoration. There was no trace of people expressing mild approval. (C.S. Lewis)

Who shall ascend the hill of the LORD?
And who shall stand in his holy place?
He who has clean hands and a pure heart,
who does not lift up his soul to what is false
and does not swear deceitfully.
He will receive blessing from the LORD
and righteousness from the God of his salvation. (Psa 24.3–5)

God's word and His teaching will not come back to Him void. There will always be some reaction from those who hear it. The response stems from whether a person has an open or closed mind. Our reactions to the truth will reveal either a pure and understanding heart or a hard, stubborn one.

Jesus was the manifestation of God on earth, and His teaching and actions impact people in differing ways. Some religious people of His day hated Him because they felt threatened, and their power was more important to them than the truth. The demons were fearful because they knew how much power and dominion Jesus had. Even the disciples experienced fear when He calmed the sea or raised the dead.

But some saw and comprehended His greatness when most were still looking on with wonder, confusion, or misunderstanding. This kind of insight was the case with the Gentile woman who said in Mark 7.28, "Yes, Lord; yet even the dogs under the table eat the children's crumbs." What great faith!

How do people react to God's word today? It is similar to what it was then. Most dismiss it altogether because they do not have a receptive heart.

Some may receive it until they realize discipleship's true personal impact and cost. But, oh, there are always some who receive the truth gladly.

And there always seems to be a strong response for or against Jesus by people confronted with His teachings. The reaction from each heart is either earth-shattering, mind-boggling, and life-altering, or rejection, dismissal, and mockery. The message itself solicits a strong attitudinal response from hearts that are either humble or combative.

The acceptance or rejection of the teachings of Christ further produces a pure or hardened heart in each person. And when disciples today teach what Jesus taught, these actions also solicit a strong response in others. Reactions never seem to be mild and timid. And a strong response is better than a lukewarm one because that typically leads to no hope at all.

I once heard a story of two people sitting on the same row, listening to the same gospel sermon, at the same time, by the same preacher. One repents, and the other leaves, never to return. Each person controls the heart they use to listen and individually respond to the truth. That is why it is such a good thing when someone responds positively and a sad thing when they do not.

Each person's choice is an intentional act of their own free will, granted to them by a loving God. And each person will be held responsible for that choice. May we all choose to respond wisely every day.

WEEK THIRTY-THREE

DAY 1

Christlike Coping Patterns

Until you heal your past, your life patterns and relationships will continue to be the same, it's just the faces that change. (B. Grace Jones)

All Scripture is breathed out by God and profitable for teaching, for reproof, for correction, and for training in righteousness, that the man of God may be complete, equipped for every good work. (2 Tim 3.16–17)

When people always get the same results from their life experiences and personal interactions, it has much to do with their adopted coping strategies. When we are young, we find ways to respond to conflict, disappointment, and failure. Everyone tries out and learns different strategies to navigate through difficulties, unfairness, and dealing with hurt. There are usually godly and ungodly coping strategies in everyone's life.

Only God's word provides the *good* and righteous strategies for coping with life's difficulties. Each person can choose to trust in God or to blame Him. Each can choose to serve himself or others. All can choose to confront their problems or to run away from them, to open themselves up or close themselves down, and to express their feelings or hide them.

Typically, all maintain the strategies they develop early in life and use them repeatedly. If they employ righteous ones, they avoid so many difficult issues. If they choose ones that are destructive to themselves or others, their results and story just repeat themselves. This cycle happens until righteous and effective strategies are learned and employed. Until then, the negative life patterns stay the same.

God has the answers to life's problems. But each person must search and find them. The Bible explains that all problems in life result from sin or acting in ways God has not ordained or authorized from the beginning of creation. The mutilation or skewing of His prescribed processes causes more problems, difficulties, and chaos.

In cultures where the plurality of people deny God, He still uses multiple ways to help the people that do seek Him to find Him. He uses the written word, His people, and eternal power and divine nature, which are evident within the creation itself (Rom 1.20).

God's prescribed processes and strategies for dealing with life's problems accomplish real change. Dare to make new, more Christlike coping patterns your norm. This humble approach is how real transformation and reconciliation with God is made. His processes make a person fit for divine association in a spiritual life after this one.

God helps those who choose to come out from the godless world to see physical death as less daunting. Those who have died to themselves reject the world's prescribed tricks and the lies of the evil one. Commencing at the point of conversion, they pass through this life in hope. As His children, we can move toward eternity with a loving Father, a righteous King, and a steadfast, loving God Almighty.

DAY 2

Overcoming Whatever Comes

A happy life consists not in the absence, but in the mastery of hardships. (Hellen Keller)

Now the Lord is the Spirit, and where the Spirit of the Lord is, there is freedom. And we all, with unveiled face, beholding the glory of the Lord, are being transformed into the same image from one degree of glory to another. For this comes from the Lord who is the Spirit. (2 Cor 3.17–18)

But we have this treasure in jars of clay, to show that the surpassing power belongs to God and not to us. We are afflicted in every way, but not crushed; perplexed, but not driven to despair; persecuted, but not forsaken; struck down, but not destroyed; always carrying in the body the death of Jesus, so that the life of Jesus may also be manifested in our bodies.

So we do not lose heart. Though our outer self is wasting away, our inner self is being renewed day by day. For this light momentary affliction is preparing for us an eternal weight of glory beyond all comparison, as we look not to the things that are seen but to the things that are unseen. For the things that are seen are transient, but the things that are unseen are eternal. (2 Cor 4.7–10, 16–18)

Paul had the grand work of communicating the Spirit of the Lord to the world. He explains to the Corinthian brethren how he and the other apostles were being personally transformed while confronting difficulties in the world. Like them, we can also have the experience of our inner self being renewed day by day.

Helen Keller learned how to trust God through suffering. She, like anyone transformed by God, embraced the unseen. Like the apostles, we must see this life as temporary. Difficulties do not crush His people because they can see what is beyond. Our Lord's suffering and death exemplified this kind of faith, and our suffering should lead us to Him. We look "to Jesus, the founder and perfecter of our faith, who for the joy that was set before Him endured the cross, despising the shame, and is seated at the right hand of the throne of God" (Heb 12.2).

We should not see hardships as negative but rather as learning experiences and teaching opportunities from God. Christians must never be complainers or view themselves as victims. These mindsets always lead to worldly attitudes of fear, bitterness, and accusations.

Paul also knew that some understand this process while others would not be able to see or comprehend it. Training our children to view hardships as instructive, even from their earliest years, is beneficial. So, parents should not overprotect their children from experiencing natural and uncontrollable hardships. Instead, we should explain that they are a tool for their spiritual growth.

With this attitude, children can learn to feel free and liberated because their external environment does not control them. They learn to overcome whatever comes with godly wisdom and with the help of unseen forces for good. There will always be deliverance from evil, even if you must wait for it until the next life.

When this concept is understood, the weight of things outside our control lessens, and the eternal forces surrounding us can be seen. The sea opening up before us does not seem impossible. Defeating giants with five small stones seems easy. And overcoming hardship is seen as achievable.

And even if we do not see a visible deliverance in this life, God's people know that God works in unseen ways and helps us trust in the outcomes. His people remain at peace and continue throughout life to master whatever hardship comes their way. And this will influence those around them to do the same.

DAY 3

Diligent in Study

If you have really handed yourself over to Him, it must follow that you are trying to obey Him… Not hoping to get to Heaven as a reward for your actions, but inevitably wanting to act in a certain way because a first faint gleam of Heaven is already inside you. (C.S. Lewis)

Jesus answered him, "Truly, truly, I say to you, unless one is born again he cannot see the kingdom of God." Nicodemus said to him, "How can a man be born when he is old? Can he enter a second time into his mother's womb and be born?" Jesus answered, "Truly, truly, I say to you, unless one is born of water and the Spirit, he cannot enter the kingdom of God. That which is born of the flesh is flesh, and that which is born of the Spirit is spirit. Do not marvel that I said to you, 'You must be born again.' The wind blows where it wishes, and you hear its sound, but you do not know where it comes from or where it goes. So it is with everyone who is born of the Spirit." Nicodemus said to him, "How can these things be?" Jesus answered him, "Are you the teacher of Israel and yet you do not understand these things? (John 3.3–10)

This exchange between Nicodemus and our Lord shows the vast disconnect on the part of Nicodemus. Notice that Jesus expected him to understand. Nicodemus should have been prepared to learn the truth as a teacher of the Law. However, people cannot comprehend Christ's teachings from a physically centered mindset.

When you choose rebirth, a new life, and a transformation in your spirit that is identifiable at baptism, this shows up in your choices from then on out. There is a force at work in your mind, unseen as the wind, that comprehends the truth from scripture, and it affects you just as the wind moves the trees. If it is present and working, people can see it too. C.S. Lewis takes the same idea a little farther. This new *you* is continuously learning and morphing into someone who operates more and more like the Lord.

Please do not allow the world's *flavor of the day* to blind you to our Lord's truth. Do not affirm the erroneous assumptions that are the foundation of the logical (and illogical) arguments of false teachings. Do not allow anything to dissuade you from understanding the plain teaching of the gospel message found in the scriptural text or the life of Jesus.

Christians believed and practiced baptism to be essential for salvation from the earliest of times. But as error came to be accepted in religious circles, the teaching went from true immersion baptism to a concept describing original sin, then infant baptism, sprinkling, and just asking Jesus to enter your heart. False teaching moves with the times, but God's truth does not.

All erroneous teachings trace back to accepting some man's misunderstanding of scripture or *twisting* the concepts found within. They were all teachers of God's Law in some way or another, but just like Nicodemus, they were also misguided in their thinking.

Let us not follow that way but, instead, follow the Lord's direction through our personal study of the inspired word. Allow your mind to be taught directly from the authoritative teaching itself. Be diligent in study and, after being born again, always grow up in your faith. Work out your own salvation with fear and trembling (Phil 2.12).

DAY 4

More Like Him

There is no excess of goodness. You cannot go too far in the right direction. (C. S. Lewis)

But the fruit of the Spirit is love, joy, peace, patience, kindness, goodness, faithfulness, gentleness, self-control; against such things there is no law. (Gal 5.22–23)

The attributes described as the fruit of the Spirit originate from God and are what God calls inherently good. There is no law against them. We also see the word *good* used every day of creation. When God saw what He had done, He declared it good. He deemed it *just right.*

The *fruits* listed in Galatians are how a Spirit-filled heart acts and expresses itself. These attitudes only come from God. There is no need for God to define their proper use for us. If anyone has them, they always come from and work for good.

When God details how to use something as it was originally intended, it has His approval. His commands and instructions define the proper use for which everything was designed. He defines adherence to His principles and practices as *good.*

God's word explains things like God's creation and mankind's history, how a family unit operates with its God-ordained roles, the purpose of the church, how people are to relate with each other, and conflict management and resolution skills. All of His people who study His laws can choose to align themselves with His purpose and intent.

But because of Adam and Eve's choice to defy God's law for them, sin entered our world. And everyone must differentiate between good and evil because, now, both exist. When people align themselves with God, He sees this as *good.* And the fruits of His Spirit are always appropriate and originate from a heart filled with His knowledge.

There is no need to explain their improper use. Against them, there is no law. They have no extremes or mutations that make them no longer *good.* When people exhibit them, others can identify their point of origin to be from God. They are God-produced from seeds that He plants in the soil of our hearts, which He prepares for these attributes to grow.

As someone learns about God, they become more like Him, and it shows up in their very being. They are transformed. This concept makes establishing divine authority and divine approval of extreme importance. A person needs to spend their lifetime learning the right direction and following it with all their heart, soul, and mind.

Each fruit of the Spirit comes in layers and grows in strength throughout a lifetime. If anyone ceases to learn or ignores the truth, even what they have can diminish or be lost entirely. So remember, we can never go too far in the right direction. And the right direction always originates with God. Anything else is the wrong way or a misguided one.

DAY 5

Writing in the Sand

The only One qualified to throw a stone didn't. (Author Unknown)

"Now in the Law, Moses commanded us to stone such women. So what do you say?" This they said to test him, that they might have some charge to bring against him. Jesus bent down and wrote with his finger on the ground. And as they continued to ask him, he stood up and said to them, "Let him who is without sin among you be the first to throw a stone at her." And once more he bent down and wrote on the ground. But when they heard it, they went away one by one, beginning with the older ones, and Jesus was left alone with the woman standing before him. Jesus stood up and said to her, "Woman, where are they? Has no one condemned you?" She said, "No one, Lord." And Jesus said, "Neither do I condemn you; go, and from now on sin no more." Again Jesus spoke to them, saying, "I am the light of the world. Whoever follows me will not walk in darkness, but will have the light of life." (John 8.5–12)

The entire scene in John 8 was orchestrated to trap Jesus. They knew he would not break the Law. They also knew He was teaching a gospel message threatening their power, so they wanted to kill Him. The good news of the coming kingdom is that it provides the savior, whereas the Old Law merely told of His eventual coming.

Jesus was not redefining sin with this New Law but rather demonstrating steadfast love. He was showing the world how to effect change in people's hearts and alter their actions. Both are required to keep people from sin. And He would eventually be the sacrifice for the sins of all men. Love touched the woman's accusers and allowed them to take advantage of His sacrifice after His death.

Now what about writing in the sand? Have you ever taken the time to think about what words Jesus may have written on the ground? We do not know what He wrote because it does not say. I wonder why?

Maybe he was writing the names of the prophets the Jewish leaders and the people had ignored. Maybe he was writing the names of the idols people worshipped during Old Testament times. Maybe he was writing about current events or people they excused in their society, who everyone knew were bad actors. Perhaps he wrote details showing insight into their scheme.

Whatever it was, He couples it with the statement, "Let him who is without sin among you be the first to throw a stone at her." We know His words convicted the people. When He offered them the opportunity to be the ones who passed judgment, they declined.

They all walked away from the scene, from the oldest to the youngest. As a people, they were guilty of the same type of sin: spiritual adultery. Throughout their history, they had joined themselves to idols. Whatever Jesus wrote helped them realize that they also needed mercy themselves.

But Jesus was innocent. He was under the Old Law and never broke it. As an innocent man and, ultimately, the lawgiver, He could have held the woman in His presence accountable. Instead, He extended to her the chance to stop her sin and the violence it caused. He helped all of these hearers understand elements of the gospel, which are grace, mercy, and forgiveness.

Jesus taught them to do justice, love mercy and walk humbly with their God. He taught them to look at the heart of Jesus and to emulate it in their lives. He taught them to leave the punishment for sin against law to the Lawgiver.

Do not fall into the trap of becoming guilty of the sin you abhor. Sometimes a person may need to calmly *write in the sand* to change the hearts around them or to motivate others to carry out justice in a godly way. We must use a method and attitude that carries the right message to be effective. Love and truth are the only remedies. So let us all be lights!

WEEK THIRTY-FOUR

DAY 1

Another's Highest Good

Love is unselfishly choosing for another's highest good. (C.S. Lewis)

We know that we have passed out of death into life, because we love the brothers. Whoever does not love abides in death. (1 John 3.14)

Sometimes it is hard to initially understand a passage because some word definitions in our head, which come from their meanings in our time, do not match God's intended definition. Only people familiar with God's word understand the definition of love that C.S. Lewis explains above. This kind of love identifies those whom God has taught to love as He loves. And Christ, with His sacrificial life, serves as their mentor, as well as their redeemer.

A person can choose the highest good for even their enemies because they understand love as seeking the well-being of others. They give preference to the spiritual needs of others as opposed to their physical needs. And when Christians express this steadfast, undeserving, unconditional love towards their enemies, those on the receiving end are completely confounded.

This dichotomy allows an honest heart to reflect and take a new look at things. Their eyes are open to a path forward that they were unaware existed. But when a person continually seeks their own interest rather than that of others, it identifies their mind as *of the flesh* and like the world. In the same scenario, a dishonest heart will typically misconstrue a loving heart's efforts and will eventually reveal itself for what it is.

I always think of Saul and David. Saul was confused and afflicted by the love David repeatedly showed to him. This type of interaction played out with Saul vacillating between appreciation and outright envy and jealousy. Saul's responses to David's love swung back and forth dramatically and for a long time. Saul did everything from throwing a spear at David to declaring his love for him.

But in the end, Saul's madness and defeat were evident, and God elevated David's love. The process was quite volatile, giving us insight into the same dynamic today. When God's love is employed, conflict can either escalate or bring peace, depending on the hearts of the people involved.

The story of David and Saul illustrates how God can work to accomplish His will among people over time, even if the responses to His love are negative. It is the task of a Christian to love as God loves. We must strive to acquire God's brand of love and express it in faithful obedience. And in doing so, let us be cautious to avoid the responses promoted by *the world*.

DAY 2

Learning like Hezekiah

Don't let what you see, make you forget what I said. (Author Unknown, a paraphrase of God's instruction to His people.)

[Hezekiah] trusted in the LORD, the God of Israel, so that there was none like him among all the kings of Judah after him, nor among those who were before him. For he held fast to the LORD. He did not depart from following him, but kept the commandments that the Lord commanded Moses. And the LORD was with him; wherever he went out, he prospered. He rebelled against the king of Assyria and would not serve him. He struck down the Philistines as far as Gaza and its territory, from watchtower to fortified city.

In the fourth year of King Hezekiah, which was the seventh year of Hoshea son of Elah, king of Israel, Shalmaneser king of Assyria came up against Samaria and besieged it, and at the end of three years he took it. In the sixth year of Hezekiah, which was the ninth year of Hoshea king of Israel, Samaria was taken. The king of Assyria carried the Israelites away to Assyria and put them in Halah, and on the Habor, the river of Gozan, and in the cities of the Medes, because they did not obey the voice of the LORD their God but transgressed his covenant, even all that Moses the servant of the LORD commanded. They neither listened nor obeyed.

In the fourteenth year of King Hezekiah, Sennacherib king of Assyria came up against all the fortified cities of Judah and took them. And Hezekiah king of Judah sent to the king of Assyria at Lachish, saying, "I have done wrong; withdraw from me. Whatever you impose on me I will bear." And the king of Assyria required of Hezekiah king of Judah three hundred talents of silver and thirty talents of gold. And Hezekiah gave him all the silver that was found in the house of the LORD and in the treasuries of the king's house. At that time Hezekiah stripped the gold from the doors of the temple of the LORD and from the doorposts that Hezekiah king of Judah had overlaid and gave it to the king of Assyria. (2 Kgs 18.5–16)

We usually remember Hezekiah as a good king. But his faith wavers as shown in these few short verses. Did you catch the reason? What happened in the years between the time God protected Hezekiah's and his kingdom against Assyria and the time Hezekiah chose to rob God's temple to pay tribute to Sennacherib?

Notice that between these two events, Assyria conquered Samaria in Northern Israel, exhibiting all their barbaric methods so that Hezekiah and all the people of Judah could see the devastation. The Assyrians were a brutal fighting force, and Hezekiah, at this point at least, did not have faith that God could defeat them. So, He robbed God's temple to glorify Assyria.

The greatest threat to a person's faith is when they face reality and a clear picture of the cost that God may require for their obedience. Fear is produced, and false faith is revealed. But these circumstances also provide extraordinary opportunities to show what genuine faith and trust in the Lord look like. When someone overcomes, especially under dire circumstances, it glorifies God in the hearts of honest men.

God wanted Saul to wait for Samuel to make sacrifices, even though the people pressured him to do it incorrectly. Saul gave in and disobeyed God. Instead, God wants His children to respond like the young boy David with the giant Goliath. When faced with the same overwhelming odds, the impulse of most would be to cut and run, but David trusted in God.

These stories show Saul's lack of faith and David's confidence in God as each faced difficult choices. At the same time, a choice like David's looks like a suicide mission to a worldly mind. It was not until David's victory in the battle with Goliath that God and His influence were revealed.

The greatest fear that Satan has is that godly people will respond with faith, even when they understand the hard realities that face them, and choose to obey God anyway. Think of Job. When Christians today face persecution, loss of income, abandonment, illness, or death, are you seeing them choose obedience to God like Job, or are they folding like Hezekiah?

Hezekiah's story reminds us to remember God's directions as we make our daily decisions. He wants us to remember to trust Him even in extreme circumstances. Assyria took Israel because they did not keep the Mosaic Law. They instead fell into step with those who served false gods. When they failed to respond with faith, the very fears that made them stumble came upon them.

God alone should be that which is feared. *Feared* in the sense of being reverenced because He is the one who is the most powerful. Satan always offers the easy way out. His tactic always involves lies, fear, rationalization, and compromise.

How are we all handling the fears and threats of our time? Do we stand like Joshua or cut, run, and hide like Saul? Do we depend on God or allow fear to make us cower, compromise, and lose faith? Hopefully, we are all learning, as Hezekiah did throughout his story, to grow more and more in trust and faithfulness toward God.

DAY 3

Going Barefoot Stories

Every summer, like the roses, childhood returns. (Marty Rubin)

As you do not know the way the spirit comes to the bones in the womb of a woman with child, so you do not know the work of God who makes everything.

In the morning sow your seed, and at evening withhold not your hand, for you do not know which will prosper, this or that, or whether both alike will be good.

Light is sweet, and it is pleasant for the eyes to see the sun.

So if a person lives many years, let him rejoice in them all; but let him remember that the days of darkness will be many. All that comes is vanity.

Rejoice, O young man, in your youth, and let your heart cheer you in the days of your youth. Walk in the ways of your heart and the sight of your eyes. But know that for all these things God will bring you into judgment. (Ecc 11.5–9)

My mother once told me of a memory my father had of his childhood birthday. His birthday was on May 2, and it would be warm enough by that time each year to run barefoot through the grass. So, this was the day his parents designated as the first day each year that he could go barefoot outside. He loved that!

Even as a grown man, my father's birthday held a grand significance because it highlighted a childhood memory that made him happy. Any memory, made in the countless moments of our lives, may turn out to be what we cling to and remember. It could be a place visited, a comment made, or even some thought that strikes us. I marvel at the particular things I remember, as well as how much I forget.

How we view life and see our days matters so much in the grand scheme of things. God wants us to know that all our time on earth is significant. We need to use it in ways that move us forward toward judgment with no regrets. We must find the good in life as it goes along, not perpetually waiting for the next milestone.

Children innately realize this. But as adults, we forget and waste our moments unless we approach them with the intent to see good and be thankful. As youths, we take emotional risks to form new relationships, say what we believe, and allow a vulnerability that can bring great joy or pain. So many things about our youth affect the rest of our lives. Each decision and each choice could have a life-altering consequence.

Let us try to remember our own *going barefoot* story but forget any pain that lies in our past days. God will take care of anything that remains. He will handle any outstanding injustice in the final judgment if need be.

Let us live each day as God directs, with purpose, always keeping in mind that God judges the thoughts and intents of the heart. We can only control ourselves and how we choose to be affected by life and everyone around us. Everyone is dealing with their own struggles. Let each of us be joyful, even amid the pain and uncertainty that will surely come to each person.

We all suffer the consequences of each other's decisions. You cannot live in a world dominated by sin and evil and not be touched by it. At the same time, we all can choose to be a light in the darkness. We can be the voice and character of God inserted into daily events. And we can point toward God's way and intended design for all things pertaining to life and godliness.

Help create the good and godly memories that keep coming around in your life and the lives of others. Just like summer and roses allow you to remember simpler times that were carefree and devoid of trouble, make a memory that can be recounted many years in the future for use and encouragement in an entirely new set of circumstances.

DAY 4

Focused Eyes

The more fascinated we become with the toys of this world, the more we forget that there's another world to come. (A. W. Tozer)

Then the angel showed me the river of the water of life, bright as crystal, flowing from the throne of God and of the Lamb through the middle of the street of the city; also, on either side of the river, the tree of life with its twelve kinds of fruit, yielding its fruit each month. The leaves of the tree were for the healing of the nations. No longer will there be anything accursed, but the throne of God and of the Lamb will be in it, and his servants will worship him. They will see his face, and his name will be on their foreheads. And night will be no more. They will need no light of lamp or sun, for the Lord God will be their light, and they will reign forever and ever. (Rev 22.1–5)

The primary obstacle in choosing to obey God over the world is that some get caught up in the trappings and toys of our time. Idols, you might say. These toys are put there by the Father of lies to purposely distract people from finding the righteousness of God.

In the book of Revelation, John uses apocalyptic language to remind the potential martyrs of his day of their intended final resting place. The tree of life God denied Adam and Eve after they sinned in the garden will be there. It will be multiplied and available to those with spiritual life and a union with the Heavenly Father. Those identified as kingdom subjects by being sanctified here on earth, by and through Christ the King, will enter the new heavens and earth.

God has accomplished His plan for redemption. He has provided light in the here and now for those with eyes that are willing to see. But a great day is still coming when the saints and the sinners will be parted right and left. We all need clear eyes, focused eyes, and eyes that do not have divided loyalties to overcome this world and find the way to ultimately enter the world to come. All who enter will see the face of their Heavenly Father.

Are you ready for that day to come? Have you passed from death to life by dying with Christ? May we all learn to see, focus, and avoid all belief-killing distractions. May we walk by faith until sight comes to us all.

DAY 5

Daily Choices

Good and evil both increase at compound interest. That is why the little decisions you and I make every day are of such infinite importance. (C.S. Lewis)

The LORD saw that the wickedness of man was great in the earth, and that every intention of the thoughts of his heart was only evil continually. (Gen 6.5)

From the first sin in the garden until the worldwide flood, we see that when people seek no direction or intervention from God, they will eventually destroy themselves or be destroyed by God. The illustration in Genesis applies to mankind in general, but we see the concept at work in individual people as well. Detrimental results will occur if people do not seek God, recognize their sins, and turn toward God in repentance.

People must seek God for His direction on how to promote and experience goodness in life on earth as He originally designed and intended. If they do not, they will deteriorate to the state of those on the earth during the time of Noah. Their thoughts will be on evil continually because His word cannot mold or transform them. Evil, by definition, is everything that is in opposition to God. Evil can only promote more evil. And without God's help, you cannot find what is good, because He is the very author of it.

From the story of Noah forward, we are all shown the scheme of redemption as God planned it through the family of Abraham. He shows us His care for the physical nation so we can understand His intent for spiritual Israel. God illustrates steadfast love and the concepts of trust, mercy, redemption, sacrifice, hope, faith, kingship, discipline, and truth, to name a few. He shows us all these principles throughout the scriptures in the context of their proper intent and purposes.

What is good is only understood by God's direction. It is chosen by those who look to His wisdom as the only standard of truth, one decision at a time. Each heart chooses to be grateful or selfish. Each chooses to live in harmony or conflict with those in its sphere. Each heart chooses God's direction for their lives or sees themselves as the gods who direct their own actions. Each heart chooses what to think about, what it allows in its mind, and what to do with its time. Each heart chooses the people they surround themselves with and the places they go.

Look at your choices. Consider your habits. Do they lead you to a life of godliness and good or to sin and separation from God through selfish and evil decisions?

Just as Joshua encouraged the people of Israel when he said, "Choose this day whom you will serve," each person must also choose today. It will make a difference. Good choices will make the next good choice easier, but this is also true for the evil ones. Will your choices be good or evil? Each will have consequences for yourself and others. Choose carefully with godly wisdom.

WEEK THIRTY-FIVE

DAY 1

The Spiritual Nation

Grace provides the foundation on which our assurance of salvation is based. Grace was so bloody and costly that God is willing to do anything, while protecting our free will, to bring us to the salvation we have accepted in Christ. (Ken Craig)

God is faithful, by whom you were called into the fellowship of his Son, Jesus Christ our Lord. (1 Cor 1.9)

If my people who are called by my name humble themselves, and pray and seek my face and turn from their wicked ways, then I will hear from heaven and will forgive their sin and heal their land. (2 Chron 7.14)

When all the people of Israel saw the fire come down and the glory of the LORD *on the temple, they bowed down with their faces to the ground on the pavement and worshiped and gave thanks to the* LORD, *saying, "For he is good, for his steadfast love endures forever."* (2 Chron 7.3)

I have seen 2 Chronicles 7.14 frequently used in yards and billboards to encourage people to pray for the Lord's help and provision. I believe many people in this country still understand how much we need God's help to exist. But sadly, I am not sure they truly appreciate the context of this verse or understand what it means.

Satan always systematically works to block people from understanding God's word by using his tactics of lies and seduction. God has always provided for His people in physical and spiritual ways. When we separate them, deny one or the other, or elevate one to negate the other, we start to believe the lies Satan wishes us to follow. We must all study to understand what God intends in the words He has preserved for us.

When Solomon finished the first temple, the Lord decided He would come and reside there among the people when He saw how they had humbled themselves. He promised to help the Israelites in times of famine and pestilence when they prayed for their land, along with providing for the forgiveness of sins as they looked forward to the coming Messiah. And He would continue to bless them in their humble state, but He would also curse them when they left it.

The physical nation of Israel serves as our illustration and teacher to help us see how God operates spiritually. God's interaction with His people in the Old Testament helps us understand His intents, purposes, and actions toward spiritual Israel. Of course, the spiritual nation is comprised of those who have chosen to be His children, while physical Israelites were physically born into it.

Today, God's people choose to have hearts that serve as a sanctuary into which He can reside or dwell. These have humbled themselves and died with Christ, deciding to sacrifice themselves for others and become a house and dwelling place for God. These are His temple individually (1 Cor. 3.16) and collectively. Peter says that we "like living stones are being built up as a spiritual house, to be a holy priesthood, to offer sacrifices acceptable to God through Jesus Christ" (1 Pet 2.5).

God can come to His people, regenerate their spirit, and make their lives valuable and productive. The realm in which God provides His assistance in these last days is more spiritual than in Old Testament times. But we cannot dismiss His role in our physical provision either. We pray for help to overcome the forces that come against us from the world, things like compromise, worldliness, and deception. But we can also pray for our daily bread and relief from sickness.

God was the sole provider of physical Israel and acted as their King until they decided they wanted to give themselves to the world. They intentionally chose a far inferior layer of protection when they asked for a physical king they could see with their eyes. Jesus is now the King of Kings and will hear and help those with a true heart, just as God helped physical Israel in the former days.

In these last days, let us all listen to the good news of the kingdom and allow God to wash us white as snow, to provide spiritual life and a lasting connection to Him. May He also provide us with spiritual understanding and increase our faith, so we do not fear and join ourselves to the idols of today for security. And let us pray that He will continue to heal us as His people whom He has called out of the world.

DAY 2

Humility in Learning

Every act of conscious learning requires the willingness to suffer an injury to one's self-esteem. That is why young children, before they are aware of their own self-importance, learn so easily; and why older persons, especially if vain or important, cannot learn at all. (Thomas S. Szasz)

The way of a fool is right in his own eyes,
  but a wise man listens to advice. (Prov 12.15)

Have you ever tried to teach somebody something and they say, *I already knew that?* You immediately sense that they don't want you to think there is something they do not already know. A person must first realize, and be willing to admit, that they are deficient in knowledge and need to pay close enough attention to new facts or instructions to learn more about anything.

This humility in learning is why, as we grow older (and wiser), we understand more and more about how much we do not know, and we become less and less opinionated. You can instantly tell if someone is willing to entertain the idea that they need to know something. You cannot force anyone to see or understand anything. And this fact is never more evident than in the passing of Biblical knowledge.

Remember, we only have control of our own hearts and growth. Let us ensure we are like the young children mentioned by Mr. Szasz so we can learn easily, especially in spiritual things. Let us be willing to let our self-esteem take a hit.

DAY 3

Revealing the Hidden Mystery

What we see often is only a fractional part of what it really is.
(Author Unknown)

To me, though I am the very least of all the saints, this grace was given, to preach to the Gentiles the unsearchable riches of Christ, and to bring to light for everyone what is the plan of the mystery hidden for ages in God, who created all things, so that through the church the manifold wisdom of God might now be made known to the rulers and authorities in the heavenly places. (Eph 3.8–10)

When writing to the Ephesians, Paul speaks of unseen things, "a mystery hidden for ages," which is now revealed through apostlic teaching. These hidden things are those that people must seek to learn and understand about the truth. But first, people need to realize that *they do not know* what *they do not know*. Until they do, the unseen things will remain a mystery, at least to them, because they do not know to look for them.

There will always be something that has yet to be comprehended by our minds. We must be careful in all situations, spiritual and otherwise, to realize there may be a wealth of truth underneath what we currently *see* and understand. We all have a relatively limited understanding of the *truth* or *reality* of almost every circumstance or subject. If a person fails to realize that they may not understand the entirety of a thing, they will cease to listen and learn.

We may only have partial knowledge of a subject by intent, deception, our own limitations, or lack of study. We can only clearly see the mystery God has revealed when He speaks through His word. God's word is truth and discerns the thoughts and intents of the heart of every man (Heb. 4.12).

So humbly do your best with what knowledge you have while keeping your mind and heart open for teaching and instruction. God will help you continue to see and learn if you have a desire and willingness to seek the truth. And we must seek it where God has chosen to communicate His will to mankind, which is in the written word found only in the Bible.

There is true power in the word. When writing to the Ephesians from prison, Paul describes it as a sword. He says:

In all circumstances take up the shield of faith, with which you can extinguish all the flaming darts of the evil one; and take the helmet of salvation, and the sword of the Spirit, which is the word of God, praying at all times in the Spirit, with all prayer and supplication. To that end, keep alert with all perseverance, making supplication for all the saints, and also for me, that words may be given to me in opening my mouth boldly to proclaim the mystery of the gospel, for which I am an ambassador in chains, that I may declare it boldly, as I ought to speak. (Eph 6.16–20)

God's word cuts through the world's argumentation so easily and completely when it is used properly, and when it lands on hearts that are prepared to listen. To a heart not ready to receive it, the word just sounds like rubbish. God designs it this way, and understanding this dynamic can forever change our perception of the Bible and its ability to work in people's hearts.

Like Paul, any teacher when using God's word properly can spread the gospel message to uncover the formerly hidden mystery to open hearts. These teachers are planting and watering seeds of truth. It is not their responsibility to accomplish what the word itself does. The written word is working with God and His hosts to help and reach hearing ears and honest hearts.

DAY 4

Beautify the Landscape

No rain, no flowers. (Author Unknown)

They do not say in their hearts,
  'Let us fear the Lord our God,
who gives the rain in its season,
  the autumn rain and the spring rain,
and keeps for us
  the weeks appointed for the harvest.'
Your iniquities have turned these away,
  and your sins have kept good from you.
For wicked men are found among my people;
  they lurk like fowlers lying in wait,

They set a trap;
  they catch men.
Like a cage full of birds,
  their houses are full of deceit;
therefore they have become great and rich;
  they have grown fat and sleek.
They know no bounds in deeds of evil;
  they judge not with justice
the cause of the fatherless, to make it prosper,
  and they do not defend the rights of the needy.
Shall I not punish them for these things?
declares the Lord,
  and shall I not avenge myself
  on a nation such as this?" (Jer 5.24–29)

God reveals Himself in the everyday processes of creation. An anonymous author once wrote, "We live on a blue planet that circles around a ball of fire next to a moon that moves the sea, and you don't believe in miracles?" People can see God in the daily *miracles* that take place. Through this and so very much more, everyone should be able to see an intelligent God as they look at the world He created.

Anyone can know there is a God. But we need His written word to know specifically what His will is for mankind and what He desires for our conduct and moral behavior. In Jeremiah, the children of Israel were rebellious. They did not realize that God gave the rain in Israel to feed them. Rain is a gift, and flowers and fruits are the glory it produces. They were not thankful and failed to acknowledge the creator. They went after their own idols while God was ever present to care for them as their sustainer.

The spiritual rain in our lives waters seeds in the *soil* that can bring forth flowers in the form of fruitful people who glorify God. Let all look up with awe at all the Lord has done for us. A true believer is not fearful but rather joyful and thankful through difficulties. They can find joy through hard times and calmly wait on the Lord, knowing He will rescue His children one way or another. They are thankful that He is always there. Through the difficulties, they listen to His voice and do His will.

Spiritual Israel must be careful not to make the same mistake as physical Israel in failing to acknowledge and fear God for His wondrous care and works. The physical nation began to look to themselves for deliverance from the consequences of their own faithlessness. They looked to themselves and nature's elements for gods while leaving the true God.

Their departure from God as the sustainer of life and the giver of their Law was their downfall. It precipitated the fall of their nation, and it can lead to the fall of any believer who follows the same path. When the people of a nation fall, the results are upheaval and chaos.

Any nation or system of government that refuses to have God in its knowledge will eventually disappear into obscurity and become irrelevant. It has been so throughout all of history. The process is God-directed because He always desires an intentional turning toward Him and away from wickedness. This true repentance can only be accomplished when a person sees the need to do so.

Thankfully, people can turn to God one person at a time. They are not dependent on their physical nation to accomplish growth and redemption for them. Any person can enter a kingdom not made with hands, eternal in the heavens. One that is ruled by the King of Kings and Lord of Lords, where the soul never dies, and your earthly location matters not.

So let each of us remember that where there is no rain, there will be no flowers to spring up and beautify the landscape. Choose to be a person that flowers. May we do as James directed, to "put away all filthiness and rampant wickedness and receive with meekness the implanted word, which is able to save your souls" (Jas 1.21).

DAY 5

Father Knows Best

He leads the humble in what is right,
    and teaches the humble his way. (Psa 25.9)

At that time the disciples came to Jesus, saying, "Who is the greatest in the kingdom of heaven?" And calling to him a child, he put him in the midst of them and said, "Truly, I say to you, unless you turn and become like children, you will never enter the kingdom of heaven. Whoever humbles himself like this child is the greatest in the kingdom of heaven. (Matt 18.1–4)

The question the disciples ask Jesus about *who is the greatest* indicates an improper understanding of what Jesus was trying to teach. They had hearts centered on self-promotion. Jesus was trying to get these listeners to *see* the underlying characteristic of reconciliation that He came to the world to demonstrate. Young children see themselves as subject to their father.

A good father sacrifices and provides for his children, and obedient children look up to faithful fathers. It is not hard to see that our present societal trends degrade the *man's role* in the family unit. The *man of the house* is frequently presented in books and television as some kind of absent-minded, bumbling, and uninformed idiot or a self-absorbed tyrant. Definitely, there are no more shows entitled *Father Knows Best*!

But the "gospel of the kingdom" necessitates having a heart that looks to God as a Father for His provision, guidance, and discipline, from a heart that is willingly subject to Him. Doing so requires an abiding trust in our heavenly Father's ability to keep His promises. God's word reveals His intents and purposes for our good and prompts a person to develop faith so that all may know that He is God.

Only when a person sees God and how they must humble themselves before Him will they willingly choose to bow their knees, follow Jesus, and become grateful, obedient servants who value the sacrifice of His Son. They will appreciate God's discipline. They will trust and obey His will. Until this kind of childlike heart is adopted, people will never turn from their own ways to embrace His Way. May all have humble and obedient hearts, allowing themselves to be *washed in the blood of the Lamb*.

WEEK THIRTY-SIX

DAY 1

Strength to Bless

Do small things with great love! (Mary Teresa)

Woe to you, when all people speak well of you, for so their fathers did to the false prophets. But I say to you who hear, love your enemies, do good to those who hate you, bless those who curse you, pray for those who abuse you. (Luke 6.26–28)

There is so much to discover in the first sermon Jesus preaches. And He structures it in a way that exposes the many differences between the erroneous thinking of the religious leaders of the day and those who will eventually accept the gospel of the kingdom. Those who accept and follow His teaching will be immediately recognizable from those who follow worldly thinking.

Jesus is speaking to primarily Jewish people who have, for generations, been taught the Mosaic Law in a way that God did not originally intend. He lines up their perceptions of it with its original purpose to expose the fallacy in the hearers' thinking. And He uncovers their misunderstandings regardless of whether they were Sadducees, Pharisees, scribes, priests, or the common person.

Our Lord addresses the proper concept of steadfast and enduring love. Love is a concept and commandment that permeates all truth. True love manifests a desire to put others before self, extending to even our enemies. In stark contrast, a worldly thought process only treats kindly those who speak well of them.

In the Old Testament, when Isaiah or Jeremiah or any other prophet told the people God's truth, they were typically persecuted, maligned, and targeted for extinction by those in power who felt threatened by their pronouncements. Jesus said, *Woe to you!* to those like them. A person with a self-promoting thought process, devoid of humility, will always be blind!

But a true God-influenced heart will do what God directs while loving even their enemies. They will adhere to truth while keeping a loving heart towards even those who hate and mistreat them. It is always easy to treat properly those that speak well of you, but the truly spiritually prosperous find the strength to bless even those that mistreat them. May all who profess knowledge and obedience to the kingdom glorify God by exposing His righteousness to a world in such need of it.

DAY 2

Do You Look Up?

Whatever type of blind spot you have—God will help you remove it. (Author Unknown)

Lord teach me what I cannot see. (Job 34.32)

The eye is the lamp of the body. So, if your eye is healthy, your whole body will be full of light, but if your eye is bad, your whole body will be full of darkness. If then the light in you is darkness, how great is the darkness! (Matt 6.22–23)

A prevalent Biblical theme God uses throughout the Bible has to do with sight. Light, life, understanding, blindness, and seeing are all relevant for understanding the concept of having spiritual eyes. Eyes that can see the wonders of creations and the scheme of redemption are derived from seeking God. Jesus says those with a pure heart can and will see God. And those with a self-determined and hardened heart will reject God and Christ because they believe in lies by choice.

When Jesus speaks about the eye being the lamp of the body, the concept includes what a person decides they want to see and focus on. Do you look up? Do you see Jesus? Do you ask for help to know the greatness, grandness, and glory of God? Or do you choose a more myopic view and blind yourself so that you can do what is right in your own eyes?

God is light and in Him is no darkness at all. And God has been made manifest to the world through His Son and through His word. These concepts cannot be separated. In Christ, light shines out of the darkness, which can lead a person to an eternal union with God and His goodness—a rekindling of a lost relationship with God. And without *the light*, a person is lost because they are dead in sin already and doomed to eternity without the ability to walk with God. They are separated from Him and need reconciliation.

May all pray to see the light so they can be reunited with God through Christ by taking advantage of, and participating in His death, making a life with God possible. Let all learn to trust and obey, showing God's saving light to others. True sight makes those in Christ shine. As a city set on a hill, they glorify the father because they are like Christ.

We must understand that worldly-focused people are blind by choice while others seek and see the light. God opens the eyes of men and works to help even the blind to see. Many choose the blinders and, in turn, choose fear and selfishness over light. Then some trust and become selfless, pointing others toward the only true way to hope.

God still spreads seeds in the hearts of men today that can expel any stones or weeds that reside in the soil. But first, there must be a desire to see and to learn. This yearning can clear space within a heart, allowing any planted seeds to take root. Seeds can exist dormant for years and then sprout and germinate. So let all servants of the Lord plant and water seeds of truth everywhere. God provides the increase!

Let Christians encourage, plead, and assist in spreading the seeds of truth in ways that can open hearts while praying for those who, as of now, have eyes that are willfully closed. Help others to see and know that if they cannot, they have chosen blindness. And to remove the scales from their eyes, they must allow God's word to enter and work in their hearts. Most of all, may each decide to choose sight in their own heart. May all take hold of God and His offering of eternal life in Christ.

DAY 3

Let Us Behold

The same sun which melts wax hardens clay. And the same gospel which melts some persons to repentance hardens others in their sins. (C.H. Spurgeon)

And David says,

> *"Let their table become a snare and a trap,*
> *a stumbling block and a retribution for them;*
> *let their eyes be darkened so that they cannot see,*
> *and bend their backs forever"*

So I ask, did they stumble in order that they might fall? By no means! Rather, through their trespass salvation has come to the Gentiles, so as to make Israel jealous. Now if their trespass means riches for the world, and if their failure means riches for the Gentiles, how much more will their full inclusion mean!

Now I am speaking to you Gentiles. Inasmuch then as I am an apostle to the Gentiles, I magnify my ministry in order somehow to make my fellow Jews jealous, and thus save some of them. For if their rejection means the reconciliation of the world, what will their acceptance mean but life from the dead? If the dough offered as first fruit is holy, so is the whole lump, and if the root is holy, so are the branches.

But if some of the branches were broken off, and you, although a wild olive shoot, were grafted in among the others and now share in the nourishing root of the olive tree, do not be arrogant toward the branches. If you are, remember it is not you who support the root, but the root that supports you. Then you will say, "Branches were broken off so that I might be grafted in." That is true. They were broken off because of their unbelief, but you stand fast through faith. So do not become proud, but fear. For if God did not spare the natural branches, neither will he spare you. Note then the kindness and the severity of God: severity toward those who have fallen, but God's kindness to you, provided you continue in his kindness. Otherwise you too will be cut off. And even they, if they do not continue in their unbelief, will be grafted in, for God has the power to graft them in again. (Rom 11.9–18)

There is a grove of olive trees at the base of Mt Carmel. These trees are grown all over Israel, and Paul uses them to explain how God was using the salvation of the Gentiles to discipline the Jewish nation. He was bringing about faith in the Jews by bringing the Gentiles, who wanted it, into salvation. Through their jealousy, the gospel might save some.

The whole concept of godly discipline seems to have gotten lost in our society. Satan attempts to elevate everyone's self-esteem and obliterates the idea of giving God the glory for all good. And this undermines the Christian's ability to trust Him in the hard times.

The world's attempts to vilify profitable discipline not only promote "self-esteem" but also selfishness. Carnal thinking cannot reason that trying times are used for God's good results, but a spiritual mind understands the process. And if we understand this reasoning, we can appreciate how discipline and difficulties can bring people to belief.

Paul explains the process of being grafted in and out of the "tree" to the Gentile Christians because they were developing proud attitudes towards the Jews who had rejected the Messiah. There was a problem with both Jews and Gentiles in these churches as they elevated their paths to salvation above the other. The Jews were elevating the Old Law out of its proper place. These misconceptions hindered the ability of both Jew and Gentile to fully comprehend all truth.

Today you can have Christians listening and learning the same gospel message from the same person simultaneously. One will accept it, and the other will not. The message is not the determining factor but rather the hardness or the softness of the listener's heart. And it may be that a hardship or emotional experience can cause a person to seek God.

Let us not make the mistake of being carnally minded, as the spiritual learners were tempted to be in the first century. Let us use times of difficulty or discipline as the learning opportunities they are designed to be. Let us elevate God and His wisdom, not the world's.

Let us understand how God used the Jewish nation and their Law to bring about the opportunity for salvation to all men. And let us not become prideful because of God's grace, lest we become grafted out of the tree ourselves. Let us behold the kindness and the severity of God.

DAY 4

We Can Live Knowing

Those who leave everything in God's hands will eventually see God's hand in everything. (Author Unknown)

The heart of man plans his way,
*   but the LORD establishes his steps.* (Prov 16.9)

God has given us the free will to choose our way, but He always remains in control. He can work His will even through a person's bad choices. And His plans will always be accomplished.

When Joseph revealed himself to his brothers, who were guilt stricken about what they had done, Joseph comforted them with this truth. He said, "As for you, you meant evil against me, but God meant it for good, to bring it about that many people should be kept alive, as they are today" (Gen 50.20). Even though Joseph had to suffer the consequences of his brothers' choices, God was with him and worked good things along the arduous journey. God saved many through his servant who became second in command in the land of Egypt.

It seems that most people in the Bible whom God used had come through difficult life circumstances. Abraham was constantly in dangerous scenarios. Moses went from the palace in Egypt through the land of Midian before God called him to lead the people out of Egypt. This pattern repeats throughout the Old and into the New Testaments. Paul is an excellent example of this with his story. The road through this life can be challenging. And it may be for a reason.

God may need a humble spirit produced from the learning that occurs when a person realizes God is God and we are not. They allow their faith in God and His comfort to hold them up. While we must bear the consequences of our decisions and the decisions of others, we can live knowing His purposes will always be achieved.

His children's work is to wait with faith and do God's will along life's way. In both positive and negative circumstances, God may use anyone to change someone else's world and bring them to Christ. And the person used may never even know it.

DAY 5

Fan into Flame

I survived because the fire inside me burned brighter than the fire around me.
(Joshua Graham)

For this reason I remind you to fan into flame the gift of God, which is in you through the laying on of my hands, for God gave us a spirit not of fear but of power and love and self-control. (2 Tim 1.7)

Paul exhorts Timothy to fan the fire within himself, taking advantage of the spirit of power, love, and self-control provided by God and shown by Christ's example. The answers to how to do this are shown in the life of Christ and through His word. He gives Christians the recipe to reproduce what Paul prescribes for having a heart *on fire* for the Lord.

Through His once-for-all sacrifice, Christ makes it possible for Christians to be made holy. And when they are made holy, their lifestyles and attitudes set them apart from the fearful. This knowledge changes a Christian's view of the world under any circumstances.

Christians need not fear physical death, evil, trials, tribulation, or even failure, for God is with them through all. What has been supplied to a servant in God's kingdom by the Almighty so outweighs all their earthly realities that they pale into insignificance. This spiritual understanding allows people to view their lives in light of what God, through Christ, provides without any fear or insecurity.

Christ has paid the price and provided the way, through His life, to deliver His people from eternal death. The Christian's work is to glorify Christ so others can see and take advantage of the gospel message. Proper actions and reactions to the stresses of everyday life reveal God's light to a spiritually dying world.

Let this light shine in your life today because you never know what tomorrow may bring. You never know who is watching now or who may be able to recall your efforts in the future. Let us fan into flame the fire in our hearts.

WEEK THIRTY-SEVEN

DAY 1

Living Peaceably

If you get down and you quarrel everyday, you're saying praises to the devil, I say. (Bob Marley)

It is an honor for a man to keep aloof from strife,
   but every fool will be quarreling. (Prov 20.3)

Bless those who persecute you; bless and do not curse them. Rejoice with those who rejoice, weep with those who weep. Live in harmony with one another. Do not be haughty, but associate with the lowly. Never be wise in your own sight. Repay no one evil for evil, but give thought to do what is honorable in the sight of all. If possible, so far as it depends on you, live peaceably with all. (Rom 12.14–18)

The distrust, sense of unfairness, and hatred in our time is epic. Amid such vile speech and blatant injustice, keeping the attitudes Paul describes in Romans is hard. But Christ did not retaliate under horrific mistreatment, even when He had the power to do so. And neither should His children. Instead, He saw the unrealized needs of those who treated Him with such contempt. Indeed, He lived in the worst of political times, similar to today.

Paul advised the Christians of his day, who had been baptized and put on Christ. They were expected to be among those with a mindset of God-directed, reasoned service to their heavenly king. Christians today follow Paul's direction as well and are those who can see past the noise of fear and hate. They are those who choose to turn away from retaliation, even when they are the target of mistreatment. They do not quarrel but still speak the truth in love, as the Lord directs. These show God's character and spirit in a dying world. When truth triggers a conflict, they refuse to respond hatefully. They can inject love into a quarrel and sometimes dismantle it.

When a person runs towards a fight, they act just like the unregenerate world. Sometimes a quarrel is targeted toward the undeserving or the godly simply because the opposition knows the person will not get down in the mud with them. They believe they can exploit a God-fearing person and that the foolish and simple-minded onlookers will believe their lies.

Jesus did not run toward a fight, but He also did not run away from conflict. He engaged His opponents with the truth and left these interactions for the onlookers to observe and for us to study today. This interaction is how Christians should do the Lord's work. Simply respond appropriately.

God always uses whatever means possible to protect the righteous, even when it comes in a form that they cannot immediately recognize. And He does not want His people to act or react in kind to the faithless. Paul writes, "Beloved, never avenge yourselves, but leave it to the wrath of God, for it is written, 'Vengeance is mine, I will repay, says the Lord'" (Rom 12.19–20). When God is working, He will ultimately get the glory.

This is not to say that a person should not stand for truth or battle injustice. But God's people should always do it with the correct attitude and a calmness that affirms a peaceful heart. Or perhaps sometimes with righteous anger that arises from a deep disdain for a blatant disrespect for God. The Lord's purpose wins out in the end even when, or perhaps especially when, it does not look like it at the time.

Even if you are confused by God's methods, you can, through faith, be assured that God will ultimately accomplish His purpose. This fact has always been the case in former times and is still true today. Just think what it may have been like to be one of God's people living in Judah in 722 BC when God raised the Assyrians to destroy Northern Israel. A barbaric people, they unknowingly did God's work. Then the Babylonians were raised up, again by God, to destroy the Assyrian's. Then 70 years later God gave Cyrus king of Persia the power to allow a faithful remnant to return to their land.

God does not need to tell us about His exact intentions for us to have faith that He is working. He has not changed. His people know how He has worked in the past and have faith that He is still working today. Satan still uses people, acting out of selfish desires, to deceive and draw people away from God. At the same time, God is working to protect His own.

What is different from those former days is that God's preordained plan to bring Christ into the world to provide as a sacrifice for sin has been accomplished. His word has been revealed in scripture and is available for learning. And God still exercises control of the nations of the earth, even if He does not give us a blow-by-blow account of His current activities. God's people still operate off faith in the unseen efforts of an omnipotent and Holy God.

So let none of His children be deceived, but rather let all be an acceptable living sacrifice in our own corrupt society and a faithless generation. Let us live peaceably with all so that those interested in finding the gospel truth may do so by seeing God in His people.

DAY 2

Always a Remnant

The real job of every moral teacher is to keep bringing us back, time after time, to the old simple principles which we are all so anxious not to see. (C. S. Lewis)

Behold, you trust in deceptive words to no avail. Will you steal, murder, commit adultery, swear falsely, make offerings to Baal, and go after other gods that you have not known, and then come and stand before me in this house, which is called by my name, and say, "We are delivered!"—only to go on doing all these abominations? Has this house, which is called by my name, become a den of robbers in your eyes? Behold, I myself have seen it, declares the LORD. ...

So you shall speak all these words to them, but they will not listen to you. You shall call to them, but they will not answer you. And you shall say to them, 'This is the nation that did not obey the voice of the LORD their God, and did not accept discipline; truth has perished; it is cut off from their lips." (Jer 7.8–11, 27–28)

Prophets were sent to the people of Israel over and over, explaining their errors and pleading with them to repent and turn back to the Lord. But, for the most part, it fell on deaf ears. All the while, they thought they were righteous. God destroyed Israel and Judah to show future generations the severe consequences of following their own path and doing it all their way.

Until the days when God sent Israel and Judah into captivity, most people were at ease. They felt comfortable in their idolatry, which included worshipping foreign gods with child sacrifices. Today, there is also a danger of trusting in our own thinking and failing to see or hear the truth in God's word.

But there was always a remnant. A small group of people did hear and see. God would make sure these knew the next step by promising and explaining that there was a coming Messiah. In our New Testament times, the Messiah has come, and God's completed scripture reveals the entire plan of redemption. So let all listen to the God of heaven, let all respond to His pleading to return, and let us trust and obey His word.

DAY 3

The Old Home Place

We never know how much we influence our grandchildren until the influences start showing up in their choices. (Author Unknown)

I thank God whom I serve, as did my ancestors, with a clear conscience, as I remember you constantly in my prayers night and day. As I remember your tears, I long to see you, that I may be filled with joy. I am reminded of your sincere faith, a faith that dwelt first in your grandmother Lois and your mother Eunice and now, I am sure, dwells in you as well. For this reason I remind you to fan into flame the gift of God, which is in you through the laying on of my hands, for God gave us a spirit not of fear but of power and love and self-control. (2 Tim 1.3–7)

A Christmas never passes when Mama Billie does not come to mind. She defined so much of how I experienced that time of year. Everyone in her extended family visited her house every Christmas Eve. Everyone knew they were invited, and everyone came. Somehow, she had a present for everyone. I still cannot comprehend how she accomplished that, never knowing who exactly was coming or when they would be there. She always had enough food, too.

It is fascinating how people and experiences shape our view of things and how family gives us a sense of belonging, even when our connections are short and infrequent. In the earlier times of the past century, extended families met at family reunions more frequently. These are rare today, as the practice has morphed into a more localized, nuclear family-oriented approach. It seems each family adopts the typical festivities that mirror the older get-togethers, with fewer people and bigger houses.

Hopefully, we can all realize how vital these connecting and truly life-altering attachments are to "the old home place." And hopefully, we can understand how much it impacts our mental stability. Let's ensure we are passing down the experiences and being the dependable people who will move the next generation forward with a sense of who they are and what is expected of them. The breakdown of the family unit is totally devastating to any culture, especially one that originated with principles centered on God and family.

Mama Billie touched everyone who ever knew her in a very positive way, and she still does. If we did not understand then just how precious she was, I would bet everyone who knew her understands now. I am sure almost everyone has their own *Mama Billie* or someone like her that means the same to you. Appreciate all your people in moments while they are here—they may soon be gone.

DAY 4

Careful Out There

The devil doesn't come to you with a red face and horns, he comes to you disguised as everything you've ever wanted. (Oscar Auliq-Ice)

Be sober-minded; be watchful. Your adversary the devil prowls around like a roaring lion, seeking someone to devour. (1 Pet 5.8)

In spring, my yard is like a wildlife preserve. Baby ducks and turkeys have just entered the world at that time of the year. Once, when a coyote showed up, I thought of this verse in 1 Peter. Animals are always so vigilant. There are predators out there, and every animal seems keenly aware of their specific threats.

Jesus uses nature to explain all kinds of things. He uses plant life, seeds, weeds, fruit, and gardens, as well as animals like sheep, wolves. And he uses shepherds. Because most live in cities and away from the land, people can miss the importance of these teachings. Concepts are more vivid when one takes the time to think and meditate on the imagery that the Holy Spirit uses in Scripture, especially when they are not always surrounded by it.

All animals have an instinct for danger. And their lives are full of strategies to protect them from harm. They are always watchful. Humans also need to be aware of their threats. And predators are stealthy, so Peter warns Christians of the prowling lion. God has made man above the animals by breathing an eternal existence into them, and sin and Satan are the things that threaten their spirit. Satan has made himself known, and his presence in the world should make us all cautious and wary.

Some people try very hard to deny Satan and God. That way, there is no threat of judgment in their minds because they do not believe in a God who has a law that they can break. If there is no law to transgress, then there is no sin to separate them from God or any other moral standard. To these people, Satan is just some mythical character who represents something to blame for all their missteps.

Do not be like people who deny ungodliness and turn Satan into a caricature. And do not fall for Satan's tricks that can make you believe you are realizing your *dreams*. God is the answer for all that you long for. Instead, beware of the dangers out there while at the same time being steadfast, immovable, and always abounding in loving kindness. Be very careful out there.

DAY 5

Leave Room for God

God, who foresaw your tribulation, has specially armed you to go through it, not without pain but without stain. (C.S. Lewis)

There is no way to peace along the way of safety. For peace must be dared. It is itself the great venture and can never be safe. Peace is the opposite of security. To demand guarantees is to want to protect oneself. Peace means giving oneself completely to God's commandment. Wanting no security, but in faith and obedience laying the destiny of the nations in the hand of almighty God. Not trying to direct it for selfish purposes. (Dietrich Bonhoeffer, A Nazi resister)

That is why it depends on faith, in order that the promise may rest on grace and be guaranteed to all his offspring—not only to the adherent of the law but also to the one who shares the faith of Abraham, who is the father of us all, as it is written, "I have made you the father of many nations"—in the presence of the God in whom he believed, who gives life to the dead and calls into existence the things that do not exist. In hope he believed against hope, that he should become the father of many nations, as he had been told, "So shall your offspring be." (Rom 4.16–18)

We cannot see some truths with our eyes and reason, so we must use scripture to direct our actions. By grace, we are saved through faith. God has provided for our peace by allowing a pathway back from sin to holiness. And if we do not understand that we are searching for godly peace, which He can only accomplish in us by steps of faith in His word, we may hold on too tightly to our life circumstances and attempt to control all the people and situations in our sphere of influence. We will not live trusting in God but rather in our own abilities.

To hold oneself together in difficult times can take two different mental strategies. You can try to control all facets of your life and situations so that external forces will not affect you. You want what *you* think is best. Sometimes this path also leads to self-preservation at the expense of others. People with this mindset are typically driven by a fear of suffering adverse consequences or by selfish ambitions.

Or you can have an attitude that you will choose the path to real mental peace, which does not focus on personal security but is more concerned with acting in faith and doing what God directs, even if it costs you. You unleash your mental restraints from controlling circumstances to choosing a path that allows God to work preemptively. Christians become faithfully patient, waiting to see what He will do. More difficulties may come with this path, but Christians prefer it, knowing God is in control and understanding He knows what is best.

This bold move of walking by faith and not sight changes our view of our role in all circumstances. We can help those whom God puts in our path. We can leave situations out of our control and allow God to act. We can walk through our lives in faith without fretting. Our only decisions involve whether or not we will do what God directs in our respective environments and circumstances.

This faith allows for the kind of inner peace that surpasses understanding. It cannot be comprehended by those who love themselves and the world. If you do not typically operate this way, try it in your life's situations. Let go and wait to see what God will do. Leave room for God to weigh in. It will literally rock your world.

WEEK THIRTY-EIGHT

DAY 1

Our New Heart

Judas had the best pastor, the best leader, the best advisor, and the best counsellor. Yet he failed.

The problem may not be the leadership or the church you go to. If your attitude or character doesn't change or your heart doesn't transform, you will always be the same. (Author Unknown)

"But behold, the hand of him who betrays me is with me on the table. For the Son of Man goes as it has been determined, but woe to that man by whom he is betrayed!" And they began to question one another, which of them it could be who was going to do this. (Luke 22.21–23)

I appeal to you therefore, brothers, by the mercies of God, to present your bodies as a living sacrifice, holy and acceptable to God, which is your spiritual worship. Do not be conformed to this world, but be transformed by the renewal of your mind, that by testing you may discern what is the will of God, what is good and acceptable and perfect. (Rom 12.1–2)

Notice that when Jesus revealed that the betrayer was one of the apostles sitting at the table, no one knew it was Judas. Judas must have looked the part of an apostle. This is scary when you think about it. He was in the presence of the best example, but it did not touch his heart because Judas loved the world. The text reveals that a thieving heart was the essence of his true character. At the same time, he appeared trustworthy enough to take care of the money for all the apostles.

We must be so careful to understand and remember that we are to become new creatures, leaving the world's lusts behind. They die in us, and we are reborn to a new purpose with an intense desire to spiritually develop so our works can bear the fruit of the Spirit. Our actions and our attitudes reflect our new heart. And as we watch and learn from Jesus, we become more like Him.

Remember when Judas reprimanded the woman for using the expensive oil to anoint Jesus?

> But Judas Iscariot, one of his disciples (he who was about to betray him), said, "Why was this ointment not sold for three hundred denarii and given to the poor?" He said this, not because he cared about the poor, but because he was a thief, and having charge of the moneybag he used to help himself to what was put into it. Jesus said, "Leave her alone, so that she may keep it for the day of my burial" (John 12.4–7).

Jesus knew his heart, but this exchange further reveals His attitude. If one allows God to direct them and to take on His nature, there will be a recognizable change in behavior as one learns to love as Jesus loves. When one learns to be kind and compassionate, showing consideration to others, you know this had to have been by some godly influence because the character originates from God Himself.

But realizing anyone, even ourselves, can be like Judas, we must continually examine our motivations. Anyone can put on the actions and behavior without transforming their heart and allow themselves to be used as instruments of unrighteousness while being concerned primarily with personal profit. People can be blind to the things of God even with all the best resources available to them.

When Jesus identified Judas as His betrayer, He was at the Passover table explaining how to partake of the Lord's Supper. He wanted His disciples to remember His sacrifice because He knew they would need it to keep their minds right. They, too, were to be living sacrifices. And they would continually need to examine their hearts to ensure they were not betrayers themselves.

DAY 2

Wisdom from God

Education without values, as useful as it is, seems rather to make man a more clever devil. (C.S. Lewis)

For the LORD gives wisdom;
from his mouth come knowledge and understanding. (Prov 2.6)

To be educated with what the *world* deems necessary, while neglecting the true wisdom from God, is valueless for those seeking righteousness, justice, and any kind of godly purpose. We must make sure we do not elevate one above the other. And we sure must learn to understand the difference.

Finding ways to elevate Biblical learning in our children's lives can be difficult. Just the daily and weekly exercise of helping our children learn their subjects in school and how to make friends, follow directions, interact with adults, and all the other things appropriate for the school environment takes a great deal of time and emotional energy. Nevertheless, it is imperative that spiritual teaching be a priority.

The best way to exemplify elevating God's purposes is to do it with your own decisions. There will be many conflicts between church and school, church and sports, and church and work. Let your children watch you make decisions about their school activities, and even your own activities, throughout their years of elementary education. Then allow them to make the hard choices themselves and endure the repercussions when it is time for them to make some of their own choices in secondary school.

Without godly wisdom, education can confuse, distract, or sharpen unbelief rather than lead to a true understanding of God's original intent for His people. Remember, what your child needs is truth and wisdom from God. These come from the creator of heaven and earth and can be seen in the things God has made. We just have to make sure Satan's lies and attempts to distort truth do not take hold in the eyes of our young ones. We must ensure our families, marriages, and study habits align with a strong desire to follow God's law if we want to have any chance in elevating the wisdom of God to our children.

DAY 3

Just a Taste

How little people know who think that holiness is dull. When one meets the real thing, it is irresistible. (C.S. Lewis)

Who shall separate us from the love of Christ? Shall tribulation, or distress, or persecution, or famine, or nakedness, or danger, or sword? ... No, in all these things we are more than conquerors through him who loved us. (Rom 8.35,37)

An old, popular song goes, *What the world needs now is love, sweet love.* And I would agree with the sentiment if we're talking about God's love. But that is not what the world typically means when they use the word *love*.

God's love draws Christians towards Him—His nature and holiness. When someone gets just a taste of it through understanding the gospel message, they will search diligently for more understanding until their dying day.

Have you ever been a part of a godly group of people doing the *right* things? Things that are service oriented without thought to oneself. Have you ever found peace from within that is indescribable to others? Have you ever been able to remain calm because you were trusting in something otherworldly?

Some people do not allow themselves to be touched by godliness. Their focus is always on the world's flavor of the moment. They consistently expose themselves to the flashy bobbles of this life. It is so sad.

When someone does taste His goodness, they cannot help but promote God's word and wisdom. It consumes them. They will sell all they have to attain it. The devil wants people to see holiness as dull as if they are missing something. That is Satan's lie, and he has been pedaling it from the beginning. The truth is that without God, we miss everything and can overcome nothing.

DAY 4

Daily Practice

I am practicing because I want to win every time. (Ella Parks)

Count it all joy, my brothers, when you meet trials of various kinds, for you know that the testing of your faith produces steadfastness. And let steadfastness have its full effect, that you may be perfect and complete, lacking in nothing. (Jas 1.2–4)

It strikes me how important the spirit of competition is for our motivation. One Christmas day, we noticed that my granddaughter Ella was playing alone on both ends of an air hockey table. When someone asked her what she was doing, she said, *I am practicing because I want to win every time!*

If we want to be good at anything, we must realize that practice is necessary and consciously decide to put in the time and effort required to improve. A competitive spirit often motivates our actions. Unfortunately, it seems that society is attempting to systematically drain this innate motivational tool from our children.

When people deemphasize individual accomplishment in sports and schools, they are ripping out the wiring for the growth process. It is all done under the guise of protecting the children's emotional stability when it really makes for a population that cannot withstand difficulties or even the most common trials. Let us all ensure we do not buy into this faulty thinking.

We must make sure we do not let the world use the abuses of the past or anything else to trick us into denying the proper use of anything, whether it be emotional attributes, family organization, gender roles, or the work of the Lord's church. They are under constant attack under the guise of unfairness, fairness, freedom or slavery, or diversity or sameness.

But God-influenced things all have their proper use. He uses trials of various kinds to enable us to be perfect and complete. He desires us to be immovable and steadfast so we may lack in nothing. But for trials to produce their God-intended result, we must *count it all joy* when our faith is tested. It is our daily practice! And as Paul told the Corinthians, we must run in such a way that we might win.

DAY 5

Crushed in Spirit

O dear friend, when thy grief presses thee to the very dust, worship there!
(Charles Spurgeon)

The LORD is near to the brokenhearted
and saves the crushed in spirit. (Psa 34.18)

The Lord is not slow to fulfill his promise as some count slowness, but is patient
toward you, not wishing that any should perish, but that all should reach re-
pentance. (2 Pet 3.9)

Peter says that God is patient with us so that each can *reach* or *come to* a state
of repentance. It is like we are all in a perpetual race to attain it. What precedes is a willingness to turn toward God. As the psalmist writes, He saves
those who are crushed in spirit.

We all need to see this as a crushing due to some sin. Of course, we can
be "crushed" by losing people or even pets or things with sentimental value.
All these things happen during the ordinary course of life in a fallen world.
But we need to be aware and so crushed by our sin that we realize our only
hope for redemption is to reach out for God. He is always close to those
with a receptive heart and can appreciate and fill their spiritual needs.

These crushed people are who God is close to. And He is attainable because they choose to have a contrite heart and plead for mercy. Jesus tells us
the same thing when he says, "Blessed are those who mourn, for they shall
be comforted" (Matt. 5.4). God comforts those who mourn because of their
own sin. May we all *reach* to find God, understanding His great desire to
move us to a blessed position of adopted children. He is a loving Father who
protects those who are His.

WEEK THIRTY-NINE

DAY 1

Profitable Teaching

The single biggest problem in communication is the illusion that it has taken place. (George Bernard Shaw)

And he said to them, "When I sent you out with no moneybag or knapsack or sandals, did you lack anything?" They said, "Nothing." He said to them, "But now let the one who has a moneybag take it, and likewise a knapsack. And let the one who has no sword sell his cloak and buy one. For I tell you that this Scripture must be fulfilled in me: 'And he was numbered with the transgressors.' For what is written about me has its fulfillment." And they said, "Look, Lord, here are two swords." And he said to them, "It is enough." (Luke 22.35–38)

Before His death, Jesus talked to His disciples about how they were received on their previous evangelistic effort. All had been provided for because the people wanted to hear their message, but this next time it would be challenging because the people would not want to hear. The apostles missed the point, and when Jesus says, *It is enough,* I believe it indicates His frustration at not being understood. Communication is a complicated subject. It can be a problem when the mindset of the listener is on a different plane than the speaker.

Sometimes we have that same problem when teaching our children but do not realize it. It is a marvelous thing to be involved in the lives of children. But it is also a huge responsibility. We constantly look for learning opportunities and teachable moments as we attempt to teach. But even when you believe your message is well received, you may be mistaken.

My two oldest grandchildren both have gotten interested in photography. One finds the location for pictures and stages them, and the other takes the pictures. All my grandchildren are showing signs of genuine interest in many things. I have no idea which things will stick with them in the long term, or how it might ultimately affect their spiritual outlook. They may misinterpret my encouragement and approval.

When my children were grown, I realized I had failed to understand many facets of child-rearing. The way my attempts at teaching were interpreted and applied in their actions never entered my mind. All things have a proper use and can be misused or overused.

In 1 Corinthians 6.12, the Bible says, "All things are lawful for me, but not all things are helpful. All things are lawful for me, but I will not be dominated by anything."

There is nothing good or bad about photography. I see natural talent blooming in the efforts of my grandchildren. Their skills far exceed my own. But now they will take what I introduced and approve and choose how to use it. I should have taken this concept into account when raising my children. I did not realize they could take the lawful things I introduced to them and misuse them.

Once a person is taught information or a skill from any source—from a parent, grandparent, school, church, or even God through His word—a learner can choose how their heart will interpret and use it. Remember this in your teaching. Your influence may not always be understood how you intended it. And anyone learning from you can improve your skill, take it to another level, or use it in ways you never intended.

Children and grandchildren eventually come of age and realize that they will need to make life choices and prioritize the things that are spiritually profitable over those that are not. If their teachers help them feel the weight and importance of their decisions, and if they believe your intentions in teaching them are for their benefit, there can be progress. They may be more careful and deliberate in making their choices.

Pray for everyone in your realm to make choices that put the Lord first. Pray that what you are teaching and what they are learning will be what God approves. And always be aware of the possibility that you may be misunderstood.

DAY 2

Rites of Passage

We cannot always build a future for our youth, but we can always build our youth for the future. (Franklin D Roosevelt)

Fathers, do not provoke your children, lest they become discouraged. (Col 3.21)

When one of my grandsons turned twelve, his father took him on a forty-two-mile hike on the Appalachian Trail. When his next son turned the same age, he took him on a nearly thirty-mile trek to the bottom of the Grand Canyon. I am sure my grandchildren will never forget those memories. There are advantages to purposely orchestrating these kinds of one-on-one trips when the children are young.

A preacher of ours who was also a psychologist first suggested this teaching method in a sermon I heard when my children were young. He said that the period from twelve to eighteen in a child's life is filled with opportunities to make a lasting impact. Most cultures have specified ages or times to indicate when a child enters adulthood. But in our American culture, this span of years is a kind of limbo for teens—they are not considered children or adults. America does not have a precisely-defined *rite of passage* into adulthood. So, these trips can help change the status of children, both in the eyes of the child and those around them.

This preacher suggested creating a rite of passage in each child's mind because leaving their status undefined can cause issues and turmoil. The recommendation was that in the twelfth year before the teen years start, fathers and mothers should take their boys and girls on a trip alone to talk to them about the upcoming years. These discussions include the upcoming choices the child will make, the difficulties they may face, changes in their bodies, etc. My husband and I tried this. My daughter and son-in-law eventually decided to do it as well.

This period in a child's life falls right before many significant changes that all adolescents experience. It is also before peer pressure becomes almost overwhelmingly intense. Age twelve is significant because what a parent says at this age is still seen by a child as extremely important. There can be frank discussions that open lines of communication for later questions a child may have about sensitive topics.

In tandem with the trip, our preacher also suggested that parents should start trading off privileges for responsibilities. At age twelve, we had our children take over their laundry duty in exchange for their ability to set their bedtime. Then we repeated these trade-offs throughout the next few years, allowing the children to bear more and more responsibility as they gained privileges.

You move responsibility over to them in stages so that by the time they are in *full teenage mode, they understand that privilege and responsibility are entirely interconnected.* They tend to make more responsible decisions if they understand and feel responsible. It helps to facilitate their learning to take control of themselves.

Remember, God gives everyone the choice to follow Him. And He teaches His children how to discipline. If parenting is done correctly, it will not lead to discouragement. Genuine trust and respect are freely given and not mandated.

When children are young, we typically control behaviors to help a child understand what we expect of them and to help them develop good habits. But if you desire to turn the reigns over to your children at the appropriate time, parents need to let go of their children slowly, bit by bit. Otherwise, they must throw a child into the metaphorically deep end of the pool, forcing them to sink or swim while making critical life choices.

That method does not always turn out too well. Growing up is hard to do folks. It is hard on children and parents. Having good strategies to facilitate the process is always a good thing.

The child should help plan and decide where to go on the *rite of passage* trips. It will have to fit into your family's budget, but within reason, it should reflect something the child desires to do. And the child should have time enough beforehand to get excited about it and see it as a milestone.

After my daughter and I took our trip, I had a memento of the occasion done in the form of a drawing of my daughter at that age. It still hangs on my wall today. It reminded me of my need to start the process of letting go. And this may be the most challenging part for the parents. But it is one of the primary responsibilities and purposes of discipline and parenting.

We are helping to create the future lives of our children. They will choose to learn and allow God to direct their steps resulting in emotionally peaceful lives, or they will reject Him and experience chaos. Ultimately, it has no value if there is no conscious choice in their minds to serve the Lord. At the same time, we must do our very best to guide them and prepare them to make the only right choice.

DAY 3

Showing Appreciation

You see, I believe that appreciation is a holy thing, that when we look for what's best in the person we happen to be with at the moment, we're doing what God does. So, in loving and appreciating our neighbor, we're participating in something truly sacred. (Fred Rogers)

You, however, are not in the flesh but in the Spirit, if in fact the Spirit of God dwells in you. Anyone who does not have the Spirit of Christ does not belong to him...

Likewise the Spirit helps us in our weakness. For we do not know what to pray for as we ought, but the Spirit himself intercedes for us with groanings too deep for words. And he who searches hearts knows what is the mind of the Spirit, because the Spirit intercedes for the saints according to the will of God. (Rom 8.9, 26–27)

The subject of the Holy Spirit and the concept of being holy are so lost in today's fleshly narratives. In the quote above, Mr. Rogers inserts the word "holy" into the conversation in a way that helps us understand it better. The mindset and attitudes of a Spirit-influence person become set apart and recognizable as a reflection of God Himself.

According to Paul, God's Spirit works in those that belong to Him. It helps each Christian die to self-seeking, carnal-thought processes and moves them closer to the mind of God as they expose themselves to His teaching in scripture. His Spirit helps us to be holy. His people change their thought patterns and actions to reflect the thinking that comes from the mind of God.

This mindset takes the form of compassion that moves us to help others. Assistance can take the form of anything, from a small smile to a concerned look, or directly helping the person in need. But the reciprocal gesture of showing appreciation is a holy work because it is others-centered as well.

When anyone receives help under challenging conditions, appreciation is the godly response from the one shown compassion. Let us embrace the attitude of the one Samaritan leper who returned to thank Jesus.

The work of God's Spirit is alive and well, even in these times when self-motivated actions bombard us every day. His Spirit enables us to reflect Him to the world and helps us talk to Him when we cannot even find the words. It allows God's people to reflect His mindset, which makes them all the more recognizable to those with eyes that are looking for Him.

DAY 4

More Than Conquerors

You will want to stop. Don't. (Author Unknown)

We are afflicted in every way, but not crushed; perplexed, but not driven to despair; persecuted, but not forsaken; struck down, but not destroyed; always carrying in the body the death of Jesus, so that the life of Jesus may also be manifested in our bodies. For we who live are always being given over to death for Jesus' sake, so that the life of Jesus also may be manifested in our mortal flesh. (2 Cor 4.8–11)

During a very difficult time in my life, when I felt I was spinning out of control, I asked a preacher, *How do you get off this fast-moving train?* His response was, *You don't.* Life can be hard. Sometimes, the combined weight of combating evil and our responsibilities seems too much for us.

Some do give up. They fall out of step. They run with difficulty. They try to find an easier and more comfortable way. However, the Christian view of difficulty must differ from those advocated by a fleshly mindset. Our role, responsibility, place, and purpose are different. The way we confront hardship is different. The Christian life inherently contains multiple pressures. God planned it like that for when sin entered the picture.

Peace comes to us as we experience difficulties and the consequences of evil. In His wisdom, God uses the pressures of life and mistreatment from others to demonstrate His ability to strengthen, calm, and comfort us. And it validates our own faith to ourselves. When we give up, shift blame, refuse to confront problems, or generally act like those in the world, we fail to show others Christ and His principles.

So, let's all keep going. We are not alone. Our difficulties allow us to reflect Jesus and His teachings to a lost and dying world! Those who endure and overcome the *world* manifest Christ and His sacrificial life. God through Christ is our strength and our redeemer. In Him, we are more than conquerors!

DAY 5

As You Speak

Surely what a man does when he is taken off his guard is the best evidence for what sort of man he is. (C. S. Lewis)

The good person out of his good treasure brings forth good, and the evil person out of his evil treasure brings forth evil. I tell you, on the day of judgment people will give account for every careless word they speak, for by your words you will be justified, and by your words you will be condemned. (Matt 12.35–37)

In teaching the gospel of the kingdom, Jesus reveals how the inner mind, heart, and spirit work. The words and actions of a man reveal the thoughts and intentions of his heart in so many ways. The admonition in these passages focuses on our ability to be mindful and watchful of what we think and speak.

When we are idle, careless, or lack God-directed purpose, we will reveal the sad state of our hearts. You may not even be aware of the built-up anger or bitterness you have developed over time. Only a relationship with God and a decision to be transformed to have a spirit like His Spirit will produce a heart with an outpouring of righteous fruit.

And our words are the fruit of our heart. I once heard someone say that as you speak, you leave the door open, and people can see how you really are inside. It will become apparent if you are working in opposition to God's Spirit. And when any of us do this, we have taken the side of evil.

Let us feed our minds with what is good to produce hearts that are good. Without God's input and wisdom, doing His will for the right reasons is impossible. We will be judged and exposed by each careless word because it reveals who we really are inside.

WEEK FORTY

DAY 1

Useful Grain

During times of universal deceit, telling the truth becomes a revolutionary act.
(George Orwell)

Hear this, you heads of the house of Jacob
    and rulers of the house of Israel,
who detest justice
    and make crooked all that is straight,
who build Zion with blood
    and Jerusalem with iniquity.
Its heads give judgment for a bribe;
    its priests teach for a price;
    its prophets practice divination for money;
yet they lean on the Lord *and say,*
    "Is not the Lord *in the midst of us?*
    No disaster shall come upon us."
Therefore because of you
    Zion shall be plowed as a field;
Jerusalem shall become a heap of ruins,
    and the mountain of the house a wooded height.

But they do not know
    the thoughts of the Lord;
they do not understand his plan,
    that he has gathered them as sheaves to the threshing floor.
Arise and thresh,
    O daughter of Zion,
for I will make your horn iron,
    and I will make your hoofs bronze;

you shall beat in pieces many peoples;
   and shall devote their gain to the LORD,
   their wealth to the LORD *of the whole earth.* (Mic 3.9–12, 4.12–13)

Truth is the new hate speech. But there is nothing new under the sun. Just as in ancient times, God is working His plan even when evil seems to reign, and real and absolute truth is always available. It may be veiled somewhat as in the time of Micah, but even then, a remnant could rejoice for the spiritual strength provided by God in times of great evil.

Those with hardened hearts are oblivious to the truth even when they hear it. Good is called evil and evil is called good. There are always pockets of this in the world. And it is always possible we are living through a judgment in time, about to experience a period of devastation or renewal.

Yet God provides for His remnant. His Son makes it possible for anyone to overcome from a spiritual standpoint, even if their physical lives are in danger. It takes a gentle, loving heart and a wise and sharp mind to succeed in such times. It also takes standing up for truth and abiding trust in God. His people and their responses do not mirror those of the world.

How are we handling the judgments in our time? Are we standing strong or scattering? Are we following the crowd or speaking the truth? Are we trusting in God or ourselves for deliverance? What is our view of what is happening and our role in it?

Jesus intended to separate the wheat from the chaff. John said, "His winnowing fork is in his hand, to clear his threshing floor and to gather the wheat into his barn, but the chaff he will burn with unquenchable fire" (Luke 3.17). When the wheat sheaves were gathered and shaken, the useful grain fell to the ground, and the light chaff was carried away. Are we fit for God's use in our present difficulties or are we just flying away with the wind?

DAY 2

Indescribable Peace

Human history is the long terrible story of man trying to find something other than God which will make him happy. (C.S. Lewis)

For this reason I bow my knees before the Father, from whom every family in heaven and on earth is named, that according to the riches of his glory he may grant you to be strengthened with power through his Spirit in your inner being, so that Christ may dwell in your hearts through faith—that you, being rooted and grounded in love, may have strength to comprehend with all the saints what is the breadth and length and height and depth, and to know the love of Christ that surpasses knowledge, that you may be filled with all the fullness of God. (Eph 3.16–14)

God provides Himself as a refuge from the anxieties and difficulties of this life. We live in a corrupted world, but God's children are part of a heavenly kingdom where there is refuge from the storms of life. God is the wall around the city, a rock of foundation, and provides its light and power. He gives it safety as those within shine as lights to a dying world.

The heavenly kingdom transcends this world and goes into the next. It has no night because God is always there, and He is light. Yet all generations can choose to serve the God of Heaven or themselves. His light can only dim or darken in our world by the self-determined blindness of those who refuse to see and hear.

Why not give your story a happy ending with Christ as the Lord of your life today and all the days that follow? Enter His place of salvation and refuge. The choices made by degenerate society do not have to be our choices. God made it possible for us to come out from among them and be set apart in a kingdom of His own making. It cannot be shaken or destroyed.

God's kingdom brings all glory and honor to Him for providing salvation and refuge. It brings a peace that is indescribable to someone who has never experienced it. It enables God's people not to fear evil because He is with them. They see this world as a moment in eternity, making all life's difficulties seem insignificant compared to the glory that awaits. And it keeps a child of God calm in times of great turmoil.

DAY 3

Firmly Planted

Choose your habits carefully, they decide your future. (Author Unknown)

Take care, lest you forget the covenant of the Lord your God, which he made with you, and make a carved image, the form of anything that the Lord your God has forbidden you. For the Lord your God is a consuming fire, a jealous God. (Deut 4.23–24)

The desire to change our lives is the key to choosing our habits. And having an idea of what a transformed life looks like goes a long way in changing from idolatry to godliness. When we decide to change things, new habits must be established and practiced.

God gave the children of Israel the Ten Commandments so they could understand the underlying character He wanted them to exhibit. He explained what to do and what not to do to serve Him and to remain free of sin and idolatry. God desired a change in heart and behaviors that differed from the nations around. These teachings would then pass from them to their children, their children's children, and so on through the generations. Their behaviors, and even their mindset, needed to be habitually centered toward godliness.

Whether spending quality time with children, increasing Bible study and meditation time, attending services more regularly, or developing productive habits works to achieve our spiritual goals. If you have the desire, you will find ways to accomplish change. People will sacrifice things they enjoy to build the habits they recognize are important.

And when hard times come, you will stay with the habits you believe are most important. Sometimes, we must push through to eliminate bad habits. This resistance can be just as important as developing good ones. You will become a tree firmly planted and stable so that others can use you for shade and shelter during the storms in their lives.

Your good habits will yield rewards in the days and years to come. They pay dividends. When you get to your later years, all the time spent in Bible study, church attendance, learning, maintaining friendships, preserving your health, and taking care of your responsibilities make for a better life. But if you squander your time on earth, there will be consequences.

Most of us will make good decisions and bad ones. We will create some good habits and some not-so-good ones. The consequences in our lives will stem from both. But if we have invested in learning God's wisdom, we will deal more effectively with both. You will not miss anything that was sacrificed to attain a real and abiding relationship with God. He has a way of working all things for good to those who love Him.

DAY 4

Persecution Opportunities

Be patient with yourself. Nothing in nature blooms all year.
(Author Unknown)

Then he said to them, "Nation will rise against Nation, and kingdom against kingdom. There will be great earthquakes, and in various places famines and pestilences. And there will be terrors and great signs from heaven. But before all this they will lay their hands on you and persecute you, delivering you up to the synagogues and prisons, and you will be brought before kings and governors for my name's sake. This will be your opportunity to bear witness. Settle it therefore in your minds not to meditate beforehand how to answer, for I will give you a mouth and wisdom, which none of your adversaries will be able to withstand or contradict. You will be delivered up even by parents and brothers and relatives and friends, and some of you they will put to death. You will be hated by all for my name's sake. But not a hair of your head will perish. By your endurance you will gain your lives." (Luke 21.10–19)

When Jesus explained the forthcoming judgment to come to Jerusalem with His disciples, He said there would be great persecution in the immediate future for those who had accepted His teaching. But He says that persecution is an opportunity to teach and bear witness of Him. This concept is not what typically comes to mind when some Christians think of persecution. But God's people should view it as an opportunity.

In the early stages of preaching the gospel message, there was opposition from every side. The Jewish leaders were thwarted in their efforts to squash Christ and were angry and scared of losing the people's support. The

Romans were wary of the teachings of a different king. The silversmiths were losing their idol-making business. The demon-possessed were being dispossessed and could no longer be used for profit. There were uproars in commerce, the political realms, and among the Jewish nation. The disciples were turning the world upside down.

Jesus indicates that people must decide how to react to persecution before the hard times come. That way, one will remain strong. God's teaching will facilitate a Christian's understanding of what to say and how to respond. Jesus' apostles were miraculously assisted when they taught those in the first century. And help is there for us as well if we study what the apostles taught.

Each one should be patient with themselves and others when we suffer hardship and persecution. Our lives are a testing ground, and trials produce stability in those that are righteous. Even present-day Christians may be accosted by family, friends, brethren, or government officials, but one can withstand persecution with God's wisdom, patient endurance, and long suffering. Yet, today's persecutions are not nearly as extreme as in those early New Testament days. Evil eventually produces such, so more intense persecution will soon manifest in our society.

I wonder sometimes how the faithful will hold up. None of us in the United States have been tested to the degree that we worry about being thrown to the lions, crucified on a cross, or lit on fire for lamps like the Christians in Rome. No one can be certain of the depth of their faith until they are tested. We can only hope we will stand under so great a persecution.

Each person today has trials resulting in success and failure. We sometimes stand and sometimes fall. We strive to learn and grow so we will be able to glorify the Lord in our testing. It's like the way the stock market works. We go up and down, in small or large degrees, but in the long term, we always go up even if there are some crashes along the way.

Christians always remain children of a heavenly king and members of the household of God in all the seasons of their lives. Growth may be frozen or dormant for a time, but springtime and summer do come. And God protects His own from spiritual death even if the corrupt world can still hurt the physical body. Be faithful even to the point of death. That is what overcoming Satan is all about.

DAY 5

Every Person Now

The good old days are now. (Tom Clancy)

For he says,

"In a favorable time I listened to you,
and in a day of salvation I have helped you.

Behold, now is the favorable time; behold, now is the day of salvation." ... We
have spoken freely to you, Corinthians; our heart is wide open. You are not
restricted by us, but you are restricted in your own affections. In return (I speak
as to children) widen your hearts also. (2 Cor 6.2, 11–13)

We all continually live in a little bubble of *right now*. We must do our best to align with God's desires in each expression of *now* that we are in today. But sometimes, we look backward to the good old days or forward to a brighter day rather than deal with where we are in the present.

We must evaluate our spiritual condition not on what we have done before or will do tomorrow but on our relationship with God in the present. We must find Him *right now*. In his letter to Corinth, Paul tells the saints that their problem is not with what God has supplied or with the effectiveness of the apostle's example but rather with their own desires to be like the world.

Paul's admonishment was to come out of worldly thinking and be separate. We must not participate in those things God has prohibited. If we want a life using God's help and we want to walk with Him, we need make decisions that reflect that choice. That is how God is found in every person's *now*.

The same instruction that Paul provides the Corinthians resonates with each of us today, in our time, in every moment and decision we make. Let us all operate like Paul, forgetting what is behind and looking forward, always making sure we are holy in the present. Then we can wholeheartedly say, "This is the day that the LORD has made; let us rejoice and be glad in it" (Psa 118.24).

WEEK FORTY-ONE

DAY 1

Smelling the Roses

Life is a series of thousands of tiny miracles. Notice them. (Roald Dahl)

For his invisible attributes, namely, his eternal power and divine nature, have been clearly perceived, ever since the creation of the world, in the things that have been made. So they are without excuse. (Rom 1.20)

We are all familiar with the phrase, *stop and smell the roses*. We must pay close attention to the tiny everyday miracles, the order clearly seen in nature, and the wisdom around us in all God has made. The world tries hard to say that what we see in nature has somehow come from nothing. And that chaos attached to nothing has made all that we see. I marvel that those who perceive a designer are the ones who are considered misguided in society.

God will give any person that wants to learn of God eyes that can and do see. Honest hearts can discern that a creator must orchestrate the creation. God's little miracles scream of His existence. A blooming flower in spring, the quiet peacefulness of falling snow, and a newborn baby's tiny hands and feet all teach us there is a God. They point to the creator. And the Bible reveals He wants a relationship with each of us.

We find the way to Him and life's answers in His word. Do we stop and listen? Or are we too busy? The very existence of scripture to reveal God's purpose is a miracle. The Bible is a collection of sixty-six books written by forty writers over sixteen-hundred years. They don't conflict when properly understood. They all combine to tell one story with one theme of God's sacrifice and man's redemption.

Oh, how marvelous and wonderful it is that God provides us with a pathway to hope and righteousness. Look up! Humble yourself and take advantage of this extraordinary gift. Take time to smell the proverbial roses of God's creation and His revealed word. Take the time to learn about God and be holy as He is holy.

DAY 2

Confidence in Him

Tomorrow, is the first blank page of a 365 page book. Write a good one. (Brad Paisley)

Say not, "Why were the former days better than these?"
*   For it is not from wisdom that you ask this.*
Wisdom is good with an inheritance,
*   an advantage to those who see the sun.*
For the protection of wisdom is like the protection of money,
*   and the advantage of knowledge is that wisdom preserves the life of him*
*   who has it.*
Consider the work of God:
*   who can make straight what he has made crooked?*

In the day of prosperity be joyful, and in the day of adversity consider: God has made the one as well as the other, so that man may not find out anything that will be after him. (Ecc 7.10–14)

When a people see God in everything, their perspective changes. Those God directed alter their thinking about all their life experiences. And when dealing with others they use wisdom learned from God. Their altered view of life under the sun allows them to decide to use whatever circumstances they encounter to their spiritual advantage. They do not mourn the loss of the former days as better than the here and now. Instead, they use any day and all situations for good purposes.

The wise person sees God as in control and searches for how He wants them to use each day. They have allowed wisdom to teach them God's view on things. It leads them. They are not trying to control their circumstances but rather understand how best to use them. The foundational truth around which they build their actions is the underlying realization that God will always bring about His purpose.

We all must live in the here and now. God intends it so. He desires our trust because faith is necessary for our salvation. Attach your heart and your actions to His word and His wisdom. Plan to prioritize good. Do not see adversity as your adversary. Appreciate the joys and use any adversity to grow.

We get to start over new every day. In the moment, God does not make it possible for us to see how He plans to use things in the future. He desires our trust and our faith. This confidence in Him will free us from the harmful effects of feeling like we must control everything. We see life as an adventure, a learning event, a teaching moment, and a practicing exercise.

We never see our lives as something we must align with our personal desires. We rather see each day as a God-directed opportunity for faithful instruction. God designed us to live in whatever circumstance we find ourselves in. God, with the help of wisdom in our thinking, will bring His children safely home through any travails this life presents.

DAY 3

As to the Lord

Do what is right, not what is easy nor what is popular. (Roy T. Bennett)

And whatever you do, in word or deed, do everything in the name of the Lord Jesus, giving thanks to God the Father through him. Wives, submit to your husbands, as is fitting in the Lord. Husbands, love your wives, and do not be harsh with them. Children, obey your parents in everything, for this pleases the Lord. Fathers, do not provoke your children, lest they become discouraged. Bondservants, obey in everything those who are your earthly masters, not by way of eye-service, as people-pleasers, but with sincerity of heart, fearing the Lord. Whatever you do, work heartily, as for the Lord and not for men, knowing that from the Lord you will receive the inheritance as your reward. You are serving the Lord Christ. (Col 3.17–24)

When my grandkids were recently at my house, one of them, age seven, had made himself a bow out of wood. His father helped him make it and then taught him how to shoot it. And then, my husband instructed the youngest, at age four, how to build a fire in the wood stove. It warms my heart to watch the kids grow and learn new things. And to see their fathers and grandfathers taking the time to teach them.

Parents, remember, all your hard work adds up and pays off. It promotes the joy of learning to teach the young and help while they still have a healthy desire for it. The proper interaction between fathers and their children should represent how God interacts with His children. A loving father teaches, and he also disciplines.

The character of the Lord shines through His followers. Godly thinking is from above and exposes worldly thought processes for what they are. An out-of-this-world Sovereign has generated it. If one has it, it has been implanted through His word. We need to understand that. It will help a Christian see oneself in a proper, humble light and see God as holy and worthy to be praised.

Hopefully, we all remember that as we maintain our God-ordained roles as husbands, wives, children, servants, fathers, and mothers and exhibit the servant-centered traits of our Master. Christians must always adhere to the teaching of our Lord, and so we teach with words and through our conduct and interactions with others. Christians should all *do everything as to the Lord.*

DAY 4

The Right Things

Be brave enough to always, always, always do the right thing when others don't. (Author Unknown)

As he passed by, he saw a man blind from birth. And his disciples asked him, "Rabbi, who sinned, this man or his parents, that he was born blind?" Jesus answered, "It was not that this man sinned, or his parents, but that the works of God might be displayed in him. We must work the works of him who sent me while it is day; night is coming, when no one can work. As long as I am in the world, I am the light of the world." Having said these things, he spit on the ground and made mud with the saliva. Then he anointed the man's eyes with the mud and said to him, "Go, wash in the pool of Siloam" (which means Sent). So he went and washed and came back seeing...

They said to him, "What did he do to you? How did he open your eyes?"
He answered them, "I have told you already, and you would not listen. Why
do you want to hear it again? Do you also want to become his disciples?" And
they reviled him, saying, "You are his disciple, but we are disciples of Moses.
We know that God has spoken to Moses, but as for this man, we do not know
where he comes from." The man answered, "Why, this is an amazing thing!
You do not know where he comes from, and yet he opened my eyes. We know
that God does not listen to sinners, but if anyone is a worshiper of God and
does his will, God listens to him. Never since the world began has it been heard
that anyone opened the eyes of a man born blind. If this man were not from
God, he could do nothing." They answered him, "You were born in utter sin,
and would you teach us?" And they cast him out.
Jesus heard that they had cast him out, and having found him he said,
"Do you believe in the Son of Man?" He answered, "And who is he, sir, that I
may believe in him?" Jesus said to him, "You have seen him, and it is he who is
speaking to you." He said, "Lord, I believe," and he worshiped him. Jesus said,
"For judgment I came into this world, that those who do not see may see, and
those who see may become blind." (John 9.2–7, 26–38)

Jesus' disciples had fanciful ideas about why the man in this text was born blind. Jesus explains to them that their assumptions about who sinned were wrong. The man was born that way because God had always intended him to be a teaching tool. God is always working and using people as instruments for righteousness to bring sight to anyone who wants to see.

The blind man's parents, the Jews, the Pharisees, and the disciples were all involved in this dynamic by showing varying responses to the miracle and teaching. The blind man himself comes away seeing. His parents succumbed to fear and failed to learn. The Jews revealed their dishonesty, and the Pharisees showed their motives and hatred, while the disciples took it all in.

All day long we observe God's truth and Satan's lies. We must choose what we see, what we focus on, and how we respond to the events and the people around us. Sometimes, it isn't easy to understand why things happen the way they do. It must have been hard in the days of Jesus as well.

We have opportunities every day to insert God's truth into the realms in which we operate. Our actions and responses will have an impact as well. We must act and react in life with so much care and with good and honest hearts, realizing that God uses truth and/or the faithfulness of His children to illicit responses in the hearts of those hearing or looking on. The responses from the people around us will be varied, just as in this instance with Jesus. God teaches with the biblical text and the actions of those following His will.

If something is presented to an honest heart in the right way, at the proper time, then God will be glorified by the responses. This is not to say all will take advantage of the truth, but all will be able to respond to it. People may see the light, resulting in learning and growth, or blindness and immaturity may be manifested. Let us all always be brave enough to do the right things in the way God defines as *right*.

DAY 5

Let it Shine

We are mirrors whose brightness, if we are bright, is wholly derived from the sun that shines upon us. (C.S. Lewis)

We aren't to shine our own light; we are called to reflect His. (Author Unknown)

And whatever you do, in word or deed, do everything in the name of the Lord Jesus, giving thanks to God the Father through him. (Col 3.17)

In the same way, let your light shine before others, so that they may see your good works and give glory to your Father who is in heaven. (Matt 5.16)

Any light that shines forth from a person comes from the father of all light. When we respond to life with actions using God's wisdom and direction, it reflects Him to the world. We are to reflect His goodness, His hope, His love, His mercy, His grace, and His righteousness. These things originate with Him and are His light in the darkness.

When we act, make decisions, and plan our days, we must always consider this concept. Paul directed the Colossians to always operate *in the name of* Jesus, with His authority and character. He is our teacher, our example, and our only hope. His life and words were given to us for direction, like an instruction manual for successful living in this life.

Without light, no one can see. Darkness always operates under the sway of the evil one. When light is absent, neglected, misunderstood, or forsaken, there is all manner of confusion and chaos. But when one chooses to work for God and others, God's work is accomplished and seen through His followers.

As Paul wrote to the Philippians, "For it is God who works in you, both to will and to work for his good pleasure" (Phil 2.13). Through obedience, you obtain all that is required to reflect His light. God's power is shown and seen in a changed life. Let Him work in all of us to reflect Himself. Let's remember the old children's song: *This little light of mine, I'm going to let it shine! Let it shine all the time, let it shine.*

WEEK FORTY-TWO

DAY 1

Strong Shoes

If God sends us on strong paths, we are provided strong shoes.
(Corrie Ten Boom)

And of Asher he said,

"Most blessed of sons be Asher;
let him be the favorite of his brothers,
and let him dip his foot in oil.
Your bars shall be iron and bronze,
and as your days, so shall your strength be.

There is none like God, O Jeshurun,
who rides through the heavens to your help,
through the skies in his majesty.
The eternal God is your dwelling place,
and underneath are the everlasting arms.
And he thrust out the enemy before you
and said, 'Destroy.'
So Israel lived in safety,
Jacob lived alone,
in a land of grain and wine,
whose heavens drop down dew.
Happy are you, O Israel! Who is like you,
a people saved by the LORD,
the shield of your help,
and the sword of your triumph!
Your enemies shall come fawning to you,
and you shall tread upon their backs." (Deut 33.24–29)

Throughout the Biblical text, there is an emphasis on foot coverings. God's people removed their sandals on holy ground. Shoes did not wear out in the wilderness. We walk in the light. Our feet are shod with the gospel of peace. Shoes are removed to show reverence and indicate strength and protection from God.

God provides stability and direction to those who walk in His ways. Corrie ten Boom makes the connection as she applies the concept to her own experience. She dealt with the horrors of living in a Jewish concentration camp with her sister, yet she could keep the Lord at the forefront of her mind. After it was over, she told how God helped them walk the *strong path*. He provided strong shoes. What a difference it makes to have strength, stability, and protection from God!

Are we aware of God's help in our lives? Do we credit God with the attribute of being able to turn horror into blessings? Are we poor, barefoot, and without help because we lack an abiding faith in the ability of God to operate in a fallen world? Let us shod our feet with sound, well-made, and comfortable *shoes* provided by a loving, faithful, and capable God.

DAY 2

What Is Good

A clever arrangement of bad eggs will never make a good omelet.
(C.S. Lewis)

For as the heavens are higher than the earth,
  so are my ways higher than your ways
  and my thoughts than your thoughts.
For as the rain and the snow come down from heaven
  and do not return there but water the earth,
making it bring forth and sprout,
  giving seed to the sower and bread to the eater,
so shall my word be that goes out from my mouth;
  it shall not return to me empty,
but it shall accomplish that which I purpose,
  and shall succeed in the thing for which I sent it.

For you shall go out in joy
and be led forth in peace;
the mountains and the hills before you
shall break forth into singing,
and all the trees of the field shall clap their hands.
Instead of the thorn shall come up the cypress;
instead of the brier shall come up the myrtle;
and it shall make a name for the LORD,
an everlasting sign that shall not be cut off. (Isa 55.9–13)

God is working when acts of goodness emanate from minds directed and influenced by our Heavenly Father above. They produce fruits of the Spirit and reveal the influence of God's Spirit working in the affected person. These spiritual fruits are one way the Holy Spirit works in this fallen world.

We can only identify direct operations of the Holy Spirit with God-breathed revelation, but we all can witness the effects of the Spirit's working at any time. Scripture has made them known to us: "love, joy, peace, patience, kindness, goodness, faithfulness, gentleness, self-control; against such things there is no law" (Gal 5.22–23). They can be born in someone who knows the scriptures or seen when mimicking someone who knows scripture. These spiritual fruits are how God operates through his people. When fully comprehended, it helps us understand more fully the role of Christians in working for God.

When considering that *good* comes from a mind influenced or directed by the mind of God, it also alters our view of evil. Evil things are done without the direction and acceptance of the Lord. And in most cases, the results will have no valuable return. The works of the flesh are evident: "sexual immorality, impurity, sensuality, idolatry, sorcery, enmity, strife, jealousy, fits of anger, rivalries, dissensions, divisions, envy, drunkenness, orgies, and things like these" (Gal 5.19–21).

Evil does not work the will of God. Evil does not glorify God. Evil works in opposition to God's will. When people use carnal thinking, they remain blind and double-minded, always focused on selfishness and self-promotion. It becomes evident to a trained eye.

We know God's revelation does not come back void. It yields perfect results if executed properly. Even creation itself recognizes His effort and claps. But when God's efforts are misused and abused, only those with truth can decipher falsehood. A primary purpose for Jesus coming to earth was to provide a visual representation of what is *Good*.

We must remember James 1.17, "Every good thing given and every perfect gift is from above, coming down from the Father of lights, with whom there is no variation or shifting shadow." What is truly *good* cannot result when we leave God out of our thinking. And when that happens, we know evil is present. This is true whether it be in ourselves, our friends, institutions, or our churches. Look for the disconnects and apply godly wisdom to them to magnify His truth.

Give God the glory the next time you witness an act of unselfishness, mercy, or grace. They cannot be brought to bear by anyone without the influence of God's word. Remember, these are all alien concepts to a fleshly mind. The world thinks them foolish. Let us prepare our minds to work what is *good* to the glory of God with no expectation of reward for ourselves.

DAY 3

Spiritual Seeds

We cannot force someone to hear a message they are not ready to receive. But we must never underestimate the power of planting a seed. (Author Unknown)

For the ministry of this service is not only supplying the needs of the saints but is also overflowing in many thanksgivings to God. By their approval of this service, they will glorify God because of your submission that comes from your confession of the gospel of Christ, and the generosity of your contribution for them and for all others, while they long for you and pray for you, because of the surpassing grace of God upon you. (2 Cor 9.12–14)

So neither he who plants nor he who waters is anything, but only God who gives the growth. He who plants and he who waters are one, and each will receive his wages according to his labor. (1 Cor 3.7–8)

In 2 Corinthians, Paul explains to the saints how their monetary contribution will impact other Christians. It is a good work that glorifies God, results in overflowing thanksgiving, and further spreads the gospel message. All expressions of Biblical teaching in our attitude and behavior constitute spiritual *seeds* that can increase the faith of another.

With God's help, our service can produce growth in ourselves and others, either in that moment or at some later time of reflection. We must never underestimate the impact of truth and righteousness upon the hearts of others. There should never be an attempt to control someone's actions or reactions. The goal of a Christian is merely to seize opportunities to leave behind seeds of truth scattered along life's journey.

Christians should see their work for the Lord as planters, waterers, tillers, and gardeners in a vast field ready for harvest. A Christian works where they reside, wherever that may be. They never wait for an ideal time and place to begin. They just always work in whatever situation they find themselves in. If we wait for perfect opportunities, we may never start.

Opportunities are not always formal and planned in Bible classes or home studies with others. They happen along the way. Maybe with the teller at the bank. Perhaps with someone standing alongside you in a long line. Or when you are in the presence of a child who asks you for advice. It is any time you can communicate some facet of gospel truth to someone else.

Anytime you encourage or teach another in the ways God directs, you spread seeds. It occurs in short responses and or in more extensive explanations. Some show by their actions that they understand and practice the truth. For others, it may be in their silence when attacked.

DAY 4

Near to Him

If you want to get warm you must stand near the fire: if you want to be wet you must get into the water. If you want joy, power, peace, eternal life, you must get close to, or even into, the thing that has them. (C.S. Lewis)

There is a place of quiet rest,
near to the heart of God,
a place where sin cannot molest,
near to the heart of God.

Refrain:
O Jesus, blest Redeemer,
sent from the heart of God,

hold us, who wait before thee,
near to the heart of God.

There is a place of comfort sweet,
near to the heart of God,
a place where we our Savior meet,
near to the heart of God.

There is a place of full release,
near to the heart of God,
a place where all is joy and peace,
near to the heart of God.
(Cleland Boyd McAfee, "Near to the Heart of God," 1903)

Therefore, brothers, since we have confidence to enter the holy places by the
blood of Jesus, by the new and living way that he opened for us through the
curtain, that is, through his flesh, and since we have a great priest over the
house of God, let us draw near with a true heart in full assurance of faith, with
our hearts sprinkled clean from an evil conscience and our bodies washed with
pure water. (Heb 10.19–22)

The world searches for joy and peace in all sorts of places, like earthly relationships, wealth, or materialistic desires, and sometimes even in their abilities and accomplishments. We sometimes forget we can only find a place of quiet rest and joy in the heart of God. There are whispers of these attributes everywhere to help us understand their value. But we can only find true rest by having a heart transformed by God's love.

While the elements in a good marriage carry real insights and feelings that we find in a spiritual relationship with God, these only point one to the real source of contentment. He is the one who created the marriage relationship and joined the two together. Some marriages would flourish more if the participants did not expect their mate to supply what is outside their companion's ability to provide.

Likewise, society has put unrealistic expectations of *happily ever after* in all the wrong places. It is a flawed belief that earthly relationships or accomplishments carry any form of long-lasting contentment. I sometimes worry that even Christians try to find the things that only exist in a relationship with God without first drawing close to Him.

Anytime someone believes that they can find joy and peace in places where they do not exist, it makes for unrealistic (and unrealized) expectations of others. These misinformed people can only find what they are looking for once their understanding is corrected. It is a tragedy for all involved when humans expect others to provide things only our supernatural sovereign can provide.

Let us all stay close to godly wisdom and truth and ensure we are in Christ where we find all spiritual blessings. Let us not be perpetrators of notions of happiness or peace that are not biblically based. If we fail to see where hope, power, and joy reside, we will never find peace, even though it is never really very far from anyone who wants it. God has made it readily available, but a person must first seek to be near to Him where He can supply it.

DAY 5

To Choose Good

Why do bad things happen to good people? That only happened once, and He volunteered. (R. C. Sproul, Jr.)

And a ruler asked him, "Good Teacher, what must I do to inherit eternal life?" And Jesus said to him, "Why do you call me good? No one is good except God alone." (Luke 18.18–19)

When we grasp that only God is good, we strive to learn how He has directed us to live so we can do the good He instructs. Those with no knowledge of God still use the terms *good* and *bad* without having a clear understanding of how to distinguish between the two. We innately know some bad things we shouldn't do, but God's word further elucidates the difference. And we can only learn the specific instruction God has for His people from divine revelation.

No one is good but God alone. We should be quick enough in our responses to point people to this vital concept. When a person truly tries to understand right and wrong, it leads them to the core principle that God is ultimately the source of all truth, and He determines what is right. God and everything that comes from Him is good. Everything else comes from the father of lies and is bad.

Once we understand God, His goodness, and His wisdom, we will learn how to deal with all that is not good. God provided Christ as a one-time sacrifice for mankind. To choose good is not only a choice, but it is the primary choice each person makes in determining their eternal destiny. Because to choose *good* is to choose God.

The answer to the question, *why do you call me good?* should have been because people realized that Jesus was God in the flesh. And Jesus the Christ wants people to come to that knowledge today and recognize Him as the lawgiver. His resurrected self has been given all dominion and power here on earth and in all the heavenly places. His name is above every name.

When we consider the true meaning of goodness, the question, *why do bad things happen to good people?* is misstated. People should rather ask why the innocent suffer bad consequences when others choose to sin and follow the father of lies. This reality is a consequence of God allowing mankind the free will to decide whether or not they will follow Him.

Things are happening in this fallen world of sin that God did not initially direct or intend for man. The fact is that every person eventually chooses not to obey God. When anyone acts on principles that do not correspond with God's original purpose for things, people around them usually suffer unintended consequences.

Let's say a drunk driver crashes into a school bus full of young children. The injustice of this will have ramifications for multiple families. The pain will be so severe that some will ask why God let this happen. Some good or bad choices can be far-reaching and have generational ramifications. And all choices can have eternal consequences.

The Bible also tells us in Ecclesiastes that "time and chance happen to all" (Ecc 9.11). Sometimes, a person is in the wrong place at the wrong time. No one's sin prompted the injustice. It is simply a consequence of nature or some other heavenly work, as man lives in a fallen world where death can happen because sin is in it.

Choose this day to make the free-will choice to serve God. He can negate the effects of this fallen world that has been under the sway of the evil one since Adam and Eve first fell to temptation. It is the way forward for those seeking reconciliation with a Holy God after they have sinned and separated themselves from Him. And He provides the hope of a better home once our lives in the fallen world have passed.

WEEK FORTY-THREE

DAY 1

Bringing Them Up

It is crucial that when our children look into our eyes, regardless of the circumstances bearing down on them, what they see is somebody who believes in them. (Author Unknown)

Fathers, do not provoke your children to anger, but bring them up in the discipline and instruction of the Lord. (Eph 6.4)

The role of parents is to emulate the kind of attitude God has towards His children. When parents are rearing their children correctly, children see a parent as someone who always has their best interest at heart no matter the circumstance. They see someone who makes sure they know the Lord's will on matters. And they see parents who emotionally plead with them to make Him the Lord of their life, too.

At the same time, parents should always help a child realize that serving God is their choice. When children are young, parents must help them develop habits that will move them toward their personal choice of obedience. They should encourage things like Bible study and church attendance, but not without exemplifying godly principles like helping others and making personal sacrifices to do what is right.

Discipline should be measured and appropriate for the offense, just as the Lord's is. God chooses not to manipulate or control His children but is faithful, caring, and merciful so His children will willingly follow and serve Him. In showing forgiveness and unconditional love, the parent must sacrifice for their children even when they do not deserve it. The point is that the child sees God in the parent's actions.

If a parent controls and manipulates rather than allows their children to experience the consequences of free will choices, there can be no learning or sense of accomplishment. Nor will a child know that their good decisions led them to righteousness and peace. Parents must teach children to own their choices as they reap the consequences of decisions, both good and bad.

But to have the luxury of owning good choices, they must accept the consequences of poor choices as well. Parents need not remove the consequences of bad decisions. This temporary suffering will enable them to appreciate the good choices all the more.

Parents must enable their children to make choices so they can learn these essential lessons. When they are grown, the desire is for them to choose God as their heavenly Father. All the while, parents are admonishing their children, disciplining them as necessary, and always showing love. In doing so, they bring them up in the nurture and admonition of the Lord.

DAY 2

Repurposed

Oh, darling, it's true. Beautiful things have dents and scratches too.
(Author Unknown)

For God has consigned all to disobedience, that he may have mercy on all. Oh, the depth of the riches and wisdom and knowledge of God! How unsearchable are his judgments and how inscrutable his ways! (Rom 11.32–33)

Do not be conformed to this world, but be transformed by the renewal of your mind, that by testing you may discern what is the will of God, what is good and acceptable and perfect. (Rom 12.2)

Here in Romans, Paul explains to Jews and Gentiles how God takes their broken, disobedient hearts and provides a way back to obedience and newness. His mercy is the root source of stability with Christ. And this illustrates to us how we, too, are *repurposed* by the renewal of our minds.

After people have used themselves up with the wrong heart, Christ offers salvation through grace, mercy, and faith. He then directs His followers to use that same path to draw others to Him. God's mercy facilitates our transformation back to renewal, and this is our map to help others as well. Ultimately, their redemption is tied to personal, obedient faith, but we must be willing to show everyone mercy because we understand and admit our undeserved forgiveness.

Christians are to show the same brand of mercy to the people in this broken world that Jesus has been shown to them. Christ offers mercy to people while they are still in sin. He gave Himself as a sacrifice on our behalf, looking to the potential of our revitalized souls rather than basing deliverance on any deserved action.

That is one reason why I believe people are so attached to the *repurposing* of old treasures. They love recrafting something to serve a new purpose. When you look at people, try to see their potential instead of magnifying the brokenness. And let us remember we are all still broken in some ways, continually seeking repair.

Christians can't make others new, but they can point them toward the One who can. With a savior, we can find a way back to usefulness. Now, there is hope that extends into eternity. No one needs to fear what men can do to hurt them because He protects them from total loss.

Christians can help others see what a working faith in God looks like. We can help them come to recognize a need to experience reconciliation. This understanding can help others choose a will and desire to seek the truth so God can facilitate their learning in the entire saving process. Then, they can experience mercy and saving grace through obedient faith.

DAY 3

The Spiritual End

If all you did was just look for things to appreciate, you would live a joyously spectacular life. (Author Unknown)

Woe to them! For they walked in the way of Cain and abandoned themselves for the sake of gain to Balaam's error and perished in Korah's rebellion...
 ...These are grumblers, malcontents, following their own sinful desires; they are loud-mouthed boasters, showing favoritism to gain advantage.

But you must remember, beloved, the predictions of the apostles of our Lord Jesus Christ. They said to you, "In the last time there will be scoffers, following their own ungodly passions." It is these who cause divisions, worldly people, devoid of the Spirit. But you, beloved, building yourselves up in your most holy faith and praying in the Holy Spirit, keep yourselves in the love of God, waiting for the mercy of our Lord Jesus Christ that leads to eternal life. And have mercy on those who doubt; save others by snatching them out of the fire; to others show mercy with fear, hating even the garment stained by the flesh. Now to him who is able to keep you from stumbling and to present you blameless before the presence of his glory with great joy, to the only God, our Savior, through Jesus Christ our Lord, be glory, majesty, dominion, and authority, before all time and now and forever. Amen. (Jude 1.11, 16–25)

Sometimes, we need to view both ends of the physical/spiritual spectrum to see the truth in anything. We all choose our approach to life—our view of pain, our response to unfairness, and how we choose to deal with the consequences of our choices and those of others. Our underlying spiritual view matters as to whether we see ourselves as victims or victors.

The text in Jude reveals both views of the spectrum. One originates from a fleshly, self-centered mindset. These views spur the choices made from envy like Cain, compromise like Balaam, or jealousy and rebellion like Korah. They all lead to complaints and chaos.

But at the other end of the spectrum is a view that is Holy Spirit-centered and learns to wait on the Lord. It learns to trust God and appreciate all things good while helping others who may also be trying to learn. And it even helps and bears with those who have become confused along the way.

Those living at the spiritual end of the spectrum make choices with an understanding of their dependence on God, a dedication to service, and a constant appreciation for their blessings. They are always trying their very best to pass along the mercy and grace they have experienced to others. At the same time, they never fail to recognize we still live in a world where there are always those who make choices from a fleshly mindset.

If you find yourself grumbling and unhappy, realize that your view of your circumstances needs to change. God gives you the ability to have a spiritual mindset that allows you to act with the mind of Christ. Appreciate this! And spread joy and strength rather than fear and cowardice.

DAY 4

Tested People

The circumstances we ask God to change are often the circumstances God is using to change us. (Max Lucado)

Now is my soul troubled. And what shall I say? "Father, save me from this hour?" But for this purpose I have come to this hour. (John 12.27)

Jesus changed so much for everyone when He went to the cross. The excruciating death fulfilled His purpose in the world. Christ finished God's plan from the beginning. His death made it possible for His mystery to be revealed. It changed the Law. It made being saved by grace through faith in Christ entirely possible. The horrific event accomplished good. And before it all happened, His willing obedience was stated in the words, *Thy will be done.*

Don't you think God still uses difficulty to accomplish obedience in us and fulfill His will? James says to count it all joy when we encounter various trials because the testing of our faith produces endurance. God makes us complete when we overcome trials using His wisdom that He supplies to anyone who asks.

This sure is different from what we hear all around us. Let us be very careful to do God's will in whatever circumstance we find ourselves. God is always helping His children grow. And you never know if you may be in a situation *for such a time as this.*

Throughout the Bible, you see God using difficulties to teach and mold His people. Joseph was sold as a slave before becoming a high-ranking government official. Moses was exiled to Midian before leading God's people out of Egypt. Saul oppressed David on his way to the throne of Israel. Esther was an orphan before she was chosen to be queen of Persia. And all the original apostles left all their earthly possessions behind to follow Jesus.

Most Biblical figures were humbled through extreme difficulties before being lifted and used by God. Ensure you are not clearing your path of challenges and stunting your spiritual growth. Don't allow the world to beguile you into taking a fast and easy course to some earthly goal on an inappropriate path. God uses tested people. Trials turn us into those who can help others.

DAY 5

Like Nehemiah's Day

God calls sin lawlessness. The devil calls it freedom. You have to decide who is telling the truth. (Edwin Crozier)

For they all wanted to frighten us, thinking, "Their hands will drop from the work, and it will not be done." But now, O God, strengthen my hands. (Neh 6.9)

Nehemiah had enemies who used a tactic of fear to hinder rebuilding the wall around Jerusalem. Nevertheless, it was finished in just fifty-two days despite the opposition (Neh 6.15). Even the enemies of Nehemiah had to acknowledge that God was working with him.

Our enemy, Satan, works in similar ways today. All the false narratives we encounter are recounted by people under his sway who know nothing of God. Anytime evil gets a stronghold, it is because of a lack of knowledge of God and His teaching.

We see a denial of God as our Creator in the teachings of evolution and the arrogance of some who believe men can implement ways to circumvent climate change. Believing there is no God makes soiled, faithless men think themselves in charge of things they do not understand. These show themselves as foolish when they ridicule those who believe His word.

We see a denial of God's plan for marriage and the family unit in attempts to eliminate all discipline in the home. They want to destroy gender markers and do away with the nuclear family. Without them, people cannot see how God works with His children or how the church should deport itself as the bride of Christ.

We even see a denial of God's word in religious practices that are more like rock concerts than sacred assemblies. They view the Bible as a set of guidelines rather than the inspired, God-breathed truth that it is. They deceive people into thinking they can choose how to worship God rather than making God holy and adopting His direction.

Our leaders devalue life itself by screaming for abortion access and legalizing the murder of babies even after birth. If the babies are deemed inconvenient, there are governmental laws in place that give the parents the right to extinguish it. They merely redefine life. And some harbor the same attitude toward the elderly.

There is pride and arrogance all around by those who think they control everything from the weather to the political powers at work. These distractors come from a society that has refused to acknowledge God. He is no longer allowed to be part of any narrative in public life in our country. But their ignorance is in full view of the minds that are trained by His word.

God's people need not fear, for God is with them. Even death itself cannot separate one from God and His love. The work of His people today is still the work of building up. They don't labor in the former physical temple that lost its glory, but rather the spiritual one where God now comes to dwell.

We come to Him as living stones that are holy and precious in His sight. We are being built up as a spiritual house to be a holy priesthood that offers spiritual sacrifices (1 Pet 2.4–5). When His followers operate with a common purpose as one local church, they show God's love to a dying world. Ask for strength from God to continue His work, even in the face of the evil that surrounds us. Like in Nehemiah's day, some may see God through the results. So, stop worrying and start praying. God will change everything!

WEEK FORTY-FOUR

DAY 1

This Changing Process

Don't worry that you're not strong enough before you begin. It is in the journey that God makes you strong. (Author Unknown)

No one born of God makes a practice of sinning, for God's seed abides in him; and he cannot keep on sinning, because he has been born of God. (1 John 3.9)

When I was younger, I remember being afraid that I would not be able to be a *perfect person* after being baptized. But my picture of the process was all wrong. Some think, like I did, that their obedience must be complete from the standpoint of perpetual sinlessness based on man's ability to keep all the rules. Although man is made whole and sinless through obedience to the gospel, God provides it through the sacrifice of Jesus, not our perfection.

Another extreme view is that Jesus' sacrifice covers everything for everyone under all circumstances, even without obedience. Of course, His sacrifice potentially covers everyone, but they must repent, deny self, and die with Christ in baptism to take advantage of it. And the ongoing forgiveness of sins depends on each saint's enduring, obedient faith.

A person's obedient faith puts them in contact with the gift that removes sin by the slain Lamb of God. God knew from the beginning that none of us are perpetually without sin, so, he provided a way to redeem an imperfect people using the sacrificial system.

God's light, mind, will, and character take a lifetime to learn. God knew none of us could keep His will perfectly living in a world where Satan has any degree of influence or power. God's scheme of redemption provides mankind with a method by which He can forgive them as they learn. God's Spirit works with our spirit over time to transform us into instruments of light.

Jesus died to pay the judicial price for our sins, allowing us to also die with Him to our sinful selves and be raised to a state of righteousness that God bestows on us. In the book of 1 John, the apostle explains that God's true children always repent, recognize their wrongs, and return to the righteous path He has provided. As soon as God's children see any discrepancies between their attitudes or behaviors and God's word, they repent and change it.

Do we see this changing process in the lives of Christians today? Is it something we do ourselves if we profess to be God's children? As we understand more perfectly, we should be more willing to sacrifice ourselves and wait on the Lord.

Christians see themselves as disciples seeking instruction and greatly desire to make corrections in their hearts and actions. They are vigilant about their personal growth. So be calm, take courage, and trust the process. Christ, our Redeemer lives!

DAY 2

Undeserved Blessings

Trade your expectations for appreciation and the world changes instantly.
(Tony Robbins)

And whatever you do, in word or deed, do everything in the name of the Lord Jesus, giving thanks to God the Father through him. (Col 3.17)

We typically learn our strategies for dealing with disappointment early in childhood. When parents do not meet our expectations, we learn to moderate and be grateful for what we have and to trust God first and foremost, or we continue to have unrealistic expectations from our relationships and be shocked when things do not work out to our advantage. The latter attitude can lead one to see the world with bitter eyes and a broken, blaming heart.

But when a person learns to look and see the undeserved blessings showered on them every day, it changes everything. That is why people who grow up in turmoil learn these hard lessons early. And those who live in prosperity sometimes never learn them at all. This concept is true no matter one's socioeconomic status.

People can still be grateful for whatever they have, even when they have little. And those high on the monetary scale may still not believe they have enough. What anyone has should be sufficient no matter what, at least in their perception. They will not feel entitled or victimized. This attitude allows us to look outward and consider how we can help others *see* and cope.

We will always be disappointed if we focus our expectations on our inward, fleshly desires. But when we open our spiritual eyes to understanding appreciation and gratefulness, the world and all its antics and bobbles become less attractive. The significance we place on them diminishes. Love, grace, and mercy become real and identifiable, and one is far more willing to share.

DAY 3

Who You Really Are

We cannot give our hearts to God and keep our bodies for ourselves. (Elizabeth Elliot)

Oh, Lord, prepare me,
To be a sanctuary,
Pure and holy,
Tried and true.
I'll be a living
Sanctuary for You. (J. W. Thompson and Randy Scrugges, "Sanctuary")

If anyone destroys God's temple, God will destroy him. For God's temple is holy, and you are that temple. (1 Cor 3.17)

God and His wisdom reside in His people individually and collectively. His Holy Spirit transforms us into salt for the earth. Our bodies house spirits with the wisdom and revelation provided by God's Spirit found in the written word. Without godly instruction, no one can independently generate holy thoughts or produce properly motivated service, actions, speech, and attitudes.

When people try to serve themselves and God simultaneously, they end up living a dual life. Some wear different hats, so to speak, depending on whom they are with. They may even become very good at the ruse and be able to fool people for short periods. But it never works in the long term without leaving pain and destruction in its wake.

There is no way to hide who you really are on the inside. If God is not the true author of your efforts, people will see that your will does not align with His. Even if you are trying as hard as you can to control your behavior in the presence of others, your true motives show up in words and actions in unguarded moments. People are not fooled indefinitely, and the internal conflict can destroy someone.

God prefers our lives to be hot or cold. People destroy themselves and God's message with lukewarm hearts. Our inner person is directed either by the Holy Spirit or the father of lies. We all must continually change and choose one over the other, over and over again, throughout our lives. It is a continual process as we learn to be like Christ in all manners of life. Let us examine our hearts daily and live boldly for Him.

DAY 4

Growing in Faith

Refuse to be swamped by "the cares of this world." (Oswald Chambers)

Therefore I tell you, do not be anxious about your life, what you will eat or what you will drink, nor about your body, what you will put on. Is not life more than food, and the body more than clothing? Look at the birds of the air: they neither sow nor reap nor gather into barns, and yet your heavenly Father feeds them. Are you not of more value than they? (Matt 6.25–26)

Jesus teaches His disciples about God's role as a provider for His children. Understanding this concept is vital to living a faithful Christian life. How we respond to the daily cares of life in our attitudes and behaviors indicates the level of our faith in Him.

Faith comes by hearing and hearing through the word of Christ (Rom 10.17). One should desire to learn who God is and how He operates in the world. God speaks to mankind through His Son, who speaks to us today using the apostles' teaching and all the other inspired writers throughout the Bible. People must study the Bible on their own to grow in faith.

There is no real substitute for reading and rereading the Biblical text. And each reader can fall in love with the writer. We must understand and trust that God provides for all our daily and spiritual needs so we can focus on Him! God takes our needs out of competition with His needs so we can calmly leave the cares of this world to Him. We can dedicate our time to help with His work to manifest truth to the world.

Christians are not expected to divide their allegiance but wholeheartedly attend to all things God directs without worry. His will should always be the goal in our lives, in just the same way Jesus lived His life on earth. So, let us learn from His word, grow in faith, and always trust Him to provide.

DAY 5

Strength of Courage

Do not pray for an easy life, pray for the strength to endure a difficult one. (Bruce Lee)

And now, Lord, look upon their threats and grant to your servants to continue to speak your word with all boldness, while you stretch out your hand to heal, and signs and wonders are performed through the name of your holy servant Jesus. (Acts 4.29–30)

The Jewish leaders made life difficult for the apostles and first-century Christians. After they arrested Peter and John for healing the lame man in Acts 4, they did not ask for the threats to go away but for the strength to stand and boldly speak the message of redemption. Their focus was on God's glory and His plan.

Strength and courage come when a person overcomes trials. When they realize they can do so, they become more willing and able to stand firm when the next trial comes. The more trials one overcomes, the more a person grows in strength of courage. Boldness to teach others is the goal.

And if life is always easy, then a person will never know how well they may act or react under pressure.

Do our attitudes and actions show our focus to be on God's glory? Or do we act upon what we think will make everything easier for ourselves? As we deal with life's choices and its persecutions, we should not necessarily take the path that shows that our self-ease and preservation are the first and foremost priority. Let us remember our primary responsibility is to glorify God.

WEEK FORTY-FIVE

DAY 1

Remnant Status

As Christians we are not here for our own purpose at all—we are here for the purpose of God, and the two are not the same. (Oswald Chambers)

For those who live according to the flesh set their minds on the things of the flesh, but those who live according to the Spirit set their minds on the things of the Spirit. For to set the mind on the flesh is death, but to set the mind on the Spirit is life and peace. For the mind that is set on the flesh is hostile to God, for it does not submit to God's law; indeed, it cannot. Those who are in the flesh cannot please God.

You, however, are not in the flesh but in the Spirit, if in fact the Spirit of God dwells in you. Anyone who does not have the Spirit of Christ does not belong to him. But if Christ is in you, although the body is dead because of sin, the Spirit is life because of righteousness. If the Spirit of him who raised Jesus from the dead dwells in you, he who raised Christ Jesus from the dead will also give life to your mortal bodies through his Spirit who dwells in you.

So then, brothers, we are debtors, not to the flesh, to live according to the flesh. For if you live according to the flesh you will die, but if by the Spirit you put to death the deeds of the body, you will live. For all who are led by the Spirit of God are sons of God. (Rom 8.5–14)

In His prayers in the Garden of Gethsemane on the night before His crucifixion, Jesus said, "Not my will, but yours, be done." In doing so, He demonstrates the mindset it takes to be a child of God. His children choose to change their character, hopes, purpose, and direction to match those of their heavenly father.

And if it requires suffering, all His children decide to endure it. This *heart change* moves God's people from a mindset of accomplishing their own will and desires to accomplishing His. This essential motivational change plays out in our actions and is recognizable to others.

Does the church today make a conscious effort to identify the difference between these spiritual and fleshly mindsets? Do those in our churches change plans and schedules from their desired itinerary to do what the Spirit (through the word) directs, just as Paul did? Do we see choosing God's will as the right path when it involves suffering in the same manner as our Savior?

Our daily choices have far-reaching consequences in so many ways. Some reach all the way into eternity. Will God's people choose to be His directed children to whom belong the kingdom of heaven? Or will they decide to be self-directed idolaters, worshipping themselves, others, or the things made by men's hands? Can this generation even see the difference?

If we are living through a judgment in time, who is the judgment directed at? Is there enough of a remnant of God's children in our country to preserve it, or is it already too late? Or maybe a remnant is being prepared to take God's will into a more challenging set of circumstances.

No one can know for sure. But anyone who wants the protection that comes from being a child of the Heavenly Father must make sure they are in a remnant status and *not of this world*. Remember, but not for God's love and His Son's sacrifice, all would be without hope in this faithless generation. Let us all be careful about what we choose and whom we serve.

DAY 2

His Kind of Love

Sometimes we are just the collateral damage in someone else's war against themselves. (Lauren Eden)

Beloved, let us love one another, for love is from God, and whoever loves has been born of God and knows God. (1 John 4.7)

Difficulties in life are sure to come if you love and serve others. Just look at our Lord. He loved, served, and taught and was hated by those with minds set on fleshly things. But the very concept of love is the remedy for the ills of the world.

Everyone is in a fight with themselves. Love and service comprise the winning position, and they originate with God. When those around us are losing their personal battles, we can express God's unfailing love at a time when it can resonate. All Christians are touched by love in this way and instinctively understand its source on some level.

God's love is not natural. Some hearts do not know His kind of love, either because they have not seen it expressed by their parents, they have never heard the good news, they choose to hate instead, or because they are losing their personal battles. And they tend to lash out at those who help them.

When Christians are in their sphere, we may suffer with them. But our priority should be to show them the love of Christ. This is our chance. But do not be surprised when you try to show love and experience suffering. A person may respond negatively for any number of reasons.

Maybe they feel they have let you down and resent themselves but turn the resentment towards you. They may be envious or jealous because they do not understand that any success you have is not of yourself but rather God working in you. They may attack your motives. They may attack you.

Jesus saved us through this kind of suffering. A Christian's love or service has that same potential because people can see God's love through our expression of it. It is really God they are attacking. The Christian involved is simply the target. The war of the ages is at work. It is good versus evil—God versus Satan. And God wins. If we can endure the suffering, it has the potential for others involved to be redeemed as well.

DAY 3

Valuable Suffering

Strength does not come from winning. Your struggles develop your strengths. When you go through hardships and decide not to surrender, that is strength.
(Mahatma Gandhi)

Although he was a son, he learned obedience through what he suffered. And being made perfect, he became the source of eternal salvation to all who obey him, being designated by God a high priest after the order of Melchizedek. (Heb 5.8–10)

We understand that when the Hebrew writer says Jesus was *made perfect,* he refers to completeness rather than sinlessness. The verse references Jesus suffering in the process of God defeating Satan through His death. Suffering helped our Lord understand and experience the strength it takes to overcome evil. And it enabled Him to be perfectly qualified to be a high priest who can sympathize with us in every way.

It can be sobering to experience or watch others suffer the consequences of disobedience. But suffer we will. God imposed enmity between good and evil. And God, in His infinite wisdom, uses this conflict for good.

Through His suffering, Jesus shows us what overcoming true evil looks like. He did not suffer because of His own disobedience but due to the very existence of evil. He died for us and was killed by some of the same people whom His sacrifice would save. Believers must learn to understand this dynamic regarding our spiritual discipline.

Winning can be the by-product of learning through your struggles and hardships, but it is not necessarily the overriding goal. Overcoming difficulties, unfairness, worldliness, political oppression, false teaching, abandonment, and loss produces strength and spiritual endurance. So why do some try to mitigate or even eliminate suffering from the inevitable conflict between obedient and disobedient actions?

The world so undermines the process that we have a generation that has grown up with very little strength of character because they were coddled rather than tested or restrained. Children have not been held accountable but bailed out repeatedly when violations occurred. There is no incentive to endure punishment or strive toward excellence.

In general, our world glosses over failure. People do not use competition to teach children how to win gracefully or lose with good sportsmanship. Everyone wins, no matter what they do. No value is attached to effort or hard work, so people do not learn to recognize it. It may be one of the saddest societal changes over the years.

But we should value godly discipline rather than avoid it. Likewise, we must learn to use suffering in how we discipline our children in the loving way God models it through Christ. If we desire to promote strength and obedience through disciplinary actions, they should encourage self-control and patience. And it all needs to be directly tied to the principle that has been violated.

Let us all be very careful how we teach children. Additional chances should be available for those who realize the mistakes that lead to suffering because of their transgression. Without that, there is no appreciation for the ultimate Redeemer nor a strengthening of the heart or mind of those who are redeemed.

It takes overcoming suffering and trials if any person is to attain the goal of self-control and patience. And if the Lord needed to suffer to complete Him to fit His God-directed role, what makes us think we or anyone else will avoid it? Our reactions to the sufferings in this life help us see what we are made of as they manifest our strengths and weaknesses. And we are to count it all joy, knowing that testing our faith produces patient endurance.

Suffering from our transgressions can be easily understood and communicated. But suffering for the transgression of others is what the Lord had to do to accomplish His task. And all His children will suffer like that to some degree or another. A servant is not greater than His master. If Jesus suffered at the hands of ungodly people, His followers will also.

Those who do not realize the concept of valuable suffering will always avoid it and follow the path of least resistance. In essence, they will surrender to peer pressure or mob rule. Then, they will go along with the safest path forward and choose the most prevalent worldview they believe will get them there.

But God's people *swear to their own hurt* (Psa. 15.4), meaning they tell the truth and do what is right no matter the personal cost. Let us all be careful how we view our trials. Do not be deceived, life can be hard and can still be overcome. Like Christ, we can complete the journey and allow it to strengthen us for an everlasting life of peace with a loving God.

DAY 4

Saturated with Truth

The New Testament brings us right down to this one issue—if sin rules in me, God's life in me will be killed; if God rules in me, sin in me will be killed. There is nothing more fundamental than that. (Oswald Chambers)

Do you not know that if you present yourselves to anyone as obedient slaves, you are slaves of the one whom you obey, either of sin, which leads to death, or of obedience, which leads to righteousness? But thanks be to God, that you who were once slaves of sin have become obedient from the heart to the standard of teaching to which you were committed, and, having been set free from sin, have become slaves of righteousness. I am speaking in human terms, because of your natural limitations. For just as you once presented your members as slaves to impurity and to lawlessness leading to more lawlessness, so now present your members as slaves to righteousness leading to sanctification.

For when you were slaves of sin, you were free in regard to righteousness. But what fruit were you getting at that time from the things of which you are now ashamed? For the end of those things is death. But now that you have been set free from sin and have become slaves of God, the fruit you get leads to sanctification and its end, eternal life. For the wages of sin is death, but the free gift of God is eternal life in Christ Jesus our Lord. (Rom 6.16–23)

Every person who lives serves either good or evil. We all work for God or Satan. Some serve Satan as a cognitive and willing participant in evil because they are self-serving. Others are deceived and led astray by a lack of knowledge with no prior motive. On the other hand, those who serve God do so when they study to know what God desires of them. His word describes how He intends mankind to operate in this world. One cannot serve God unless they know Him and come to understand His will.

Those who learn, understand, and choose the way of righteousness make a conscious effort to turn away from sin toward God's will and embrace His instruction. The more a Christian is saturated with truth, the more their character is replaced with the same mind that Christ models. The desires of the flesh decrease and become more recognizable as their desires for righteousness increase. These people are more aware of sin and less susceptible to the trickery used by Satan and the people he controls.

When Paul asks the Romans, "But what fruit were you getting at that time from the things of which you are now ashamed?" he wants them to think about their personal conversions. He wants them to look back and see they have changed. They act and respond to life differently since turning towards God's teaching. And they can now see the difference between being set free from sin and the death it used to produce. They now reap sanctification and spiritual life.

Let us look at our lives and consider the same question. Understanding the contrast should make it much easier not to let sin reign in our mortal bodies to obey its passions. Instead, we present ourselves to God as those who have been brought by Him from death to life. And we offer our members to Him as instruments for righteousness (Rom 6.12–13).

DAY 5

Inwardly Joyful

Happiness cannot be traveled to, owned, earned, worn or consumed. Happiness is the spiritual experience of living every minute with love, grace, and gratitude. (Denis Waitley)

For David says concerning him,

"I saw the Lord always before me,
 for he is at my right hand that I may not be shaken;
therefore my heart was glad, and my tongue rejoiced;
 my flesh also will dwell in hope.
For you will not abandon my soul to Hades,
 or let your Holy One see corruption.
You have made known to me the paths of life;
 you will make me full of gladness with your presence." (Acts 2.25–28)

The concept of "spiritual joy and gladness" is foreign to many people. Today's generation often uses the word *happy*, and they apply it to all manner of things. What people mean when they say they want to be happy usually involves a momentary feeling of elation that is difficult to sustain because it depends on external circumstances.

But spiritual joy is explained by Peter when he quotes King David in Acts. He tells us gladness and joy come from knowing God sent Christ into the world to provide hope in this life. It comes in a life lived with God in the here and now and then in the next life, too, if one follows the path to righteousness He so lovingly provides.

Peter says David was a prophet who foresaw and spoke about the resurrection of Christ. However, David talks about himself, too. David has God at his right hand. He is right there, helping him in his daily life and in helping him make his decisions. David doesn't have to vacillate in what he decides to do if he listens to God and follows His direction. He is convinced in his life choices, not shaken. He feels the Lord's presence all day, and it calms him. He is inwardly joyful.

The world thinks of what influences their happiness in terms of finding it in their accomplishments or earthly relationships. Some even think they can find it in material possessions. But the godly experience real joy when they live lives full of grace, gratitude, and hope. This joy comes from God-influenced action, not self-directed choices and activities.

God's children realize this world is not their home, and they must not depend on the emptiness of a fleshly mind, short-lived satisfaction, or earthly bobbles to sustain them. We must know God, love Him, and serve others wholeheartedly. And we live confidently, knowing he will not abandon us in this life or the next. This mindset manifests itself internally as true peace and joy in the hearts of those who cultivate it.

WEEK FORTY-SIX

DAY 1

Suffering Servants

I am impressed and have been for many years that there are no shortcuts to achieve what God wants to accomplish. I cannot look for some easy way to get it done.... I believe one of the weaknesses of the church today is trying to achieve without sacrifice ... always looking for some shortcut. (Homer Hailey)

Share in suffering as a good soldier of Christ Jesus. No soldier gets entangled in civilian pursuits, since his aim is to please the one who enlisted him.

...Remember Jesus Christ, risen from the dead, the offspring of David, as preached in my gospel, for which I am suffering, bound with chains as a criminal. But the word of God is not bound! Therefore I endure everything for the sake of the elect, that they also may obtain the salvation that is in Christ Jesus with eternal glory. The saying is trustworthy, for:

> *If we have died with him, we will also live with him;*
> *if we endure, we will also reign with him;*
> *if we deny him, he also will deny us;*
> *if we are faithless, he remains faithful—*

for he cannot deny himself. Remind them of these things, and charge them before God not to quarrel about words, which does no good, but only ruins the hearers. (2 Tim 2.3–4, 8–14)

Paul encouraged Timothy to suffer as any soldier would. Soldiers recognize a higher authority and consider suffering as part of the sacrifice for their cause. Even when mistreated, they do not complain. Jesus suffered all, and Paul suffered for Christ, leaving us excellent examples. Christians are to be soldiers for Christ using the armor given to them by God. They are to be suffering servants.

Are the churches nowadays presenting this as the reality? Or is the congregation where you attend looking *for shortcuts*? Does it highlight suffering and hardship as part of the gospel message? Is comfort and an easy way to salvation elevated above cost and sacrifice? Are the members warned about quarreling about words? Is there a willingness by most Christians today to suffer anything at all?

In a 1985 lecture series on Humanism, Homer Hailey predicted that we may be headed for a time of judgment and tribulation. Perhaps we are now living within one. It is becoming increasingly apparent that the same *judgment identifi*ers spoken by the Old Testament prophets are present with us in the 2020s. Things such as a lack of justice in the courts, unprepared leaders abusing their control, people calling evil good and good evil, and those putting darkness for light and light for darkness.

Only those who are properly trained, exercised, and have their armor in place will be ready to endure the trials and persecution of their time. Oppression has a way of making the strong stronger and the weak fall away. Suffering is what makes love shine. And shining love provides a beacon of light to those with no hope. Without it, people will be lost.

DAY 2

Daily Bread

Talking about our problems is our greatest addiction. Break the habit. Talk about your joys. (Rita Schiano)

Then the LORD said to Moses, "Behold, I am about to rain bread from heaven for you, and the people shall go out and gather a day's portion every day, that I may test them, whether they will walk in my law or not." (Exod 16.4)

When the children of Israel started grumbling in the wilderness, God reacted with a test of faith. He responds to their request by providing food. But it is a measured response. God will provide their daily bread because He desires their trust to be ongoing. Some failed this test and gathered more than they should, and then the bread from heaven spoiled. Some gorged themselves. Some trusted and followed His directions.

When God provides spiritual bread from heaven by measure, are we patient enough to take one day at a time and trust Him to provide? He is the same God who showed His great power to the Israelites in Egypt. Certainly, he can manifest His great power to provide for us.

Remember, the ten plagues and the exodus from Egypt preceded the wilderness wanderings. These Israelites passed through the Red Sea but still adopted the mindset of petulant children who did not get their way. Do we do the same? When you know and trust your providers, then you follow them. Did they not learn the lessons of the plagues? God protected them while at the same time punishing some of them.

People with unrealistic desires and expectations usually believe they will not be satisfied, so they tend to complain. But complaining shows a lack of trust in whomever one complains about. Are we doing any better than the Israelites?

God is faithful and can be trusted. He has proven it over and over again. Are we trusting in the physical and spiritual blessings given to us today? Remember, we show how much faith we have by our words and actions. He will provide our daily bread. Let us trust in the care and deliverance God promises us.

DAY 3

Always Becoming

You become. It takes a long time.
(Margery Williams Bianco, *The Velveteen Rabbit*)

[S]o that we may no longer be children, tossed to and fro by the waves and carried about by every wind of doctrine, by human cunning, by craftiness in deceitful schemes. Rather, speaking the truth in love, we are to grow up in every way into him who is the head, into Christ.... (Eph 4.14)

The Velveteen Rabbit is about the love a little boy has for his velveteen rabbit, which transforms the stuffed animal from a nonliving thing to a real, live rabbit. This children's story, written by Margery Williams in 1922, has such depth. Adults need to take note. The love that Jesus shows mankind can also regenerate a person who is dead in sin back to a life with God that then stretches into eternity.

One day in the story, in the room where all the old toys are kept, the Skin Horse has a conversation with the Velveteen Rabbit. Here is how the exchange reads in Margery's words.

> "What is REAL?" asked the Rabbit one day, when they were lying side by side near the nursery fender, before Nana came to tidy the room. "Does it mean having things that buzz inside you and a stick-out handle?"
>
> "Real isn't how you are made," said the Skin Horse. "It's a thing that happens to you. When a child loves you for a long, long time, not just to play with, but REALLY loves you, then you become Real."
>
> "Does it hurt?' asked the Rabbit.
>
> "Sometimes," said the Skin Horse, for he was always truthful. "When you are Real you don't mind being hurt."
>
> "Does it happen all at once, like being wound up," he asked, "or bit by bit?"
>
> "It doesn't happen all at once," said the Skin Horse. "You become. It takes a long time. That's why it doesn't happen often to people who break easily, or have sharp edges, or who have to be carefully kept. Generally, by the time you are Real, most of your hair has been loved off, and your eyes drop out and you get loose in the joints and very shabby. But these things don't matter at all, because once you are Real you can't be ugly, except to people who don't understand."
>
> "I suppose you are real?" said the Rabbit. And then he wished he had not said it, for he thought the Skin Horse might be sensitive. But the Skin Horse only smiled.
>
> "The Boy's Uncle made me Real," he said. "That was a great many years ago; but once you are Real you can't become unreal again. It lasts for always."

Just like the nursery magic makes the loved toys *real* in the story, God's love initiates each Christian's transformation. Everyone must put on Christ to *grow up* in Christ. We become more mature in understanding and overcoming the disappointment of others to become a new creature.

The process is slow. Our minds have to overcome trials, withstand unfairness, and flee evil. It takes an attitude of understanding, a heart that cares for others, and a love learned from God, which was freely given and then freely accepted to become alive. And then we are always becoming more like Him.

If one is focused on self, too sensitive to be taught, too prickly to learn, or too scattered in mind and heart to focus on the essential things, they will not ever grow up in Christ. Let each one speak the truth in love to each other and love others as our Lord loves us. These things will take a lifetime to learn.

Be patient with yourself and others, and wait on the Lord to work in you. Love God and love your neighbor. Be a servant and let harmless offenses pass. Let us all be aware and mentally, emotionally, and spiritually stable enough to become His kind of *real*.

DAY 4

Fearing Not

Your perception of the world around you is not necessarily the same as what is actually occurring. (Peter Ralston)

And I said:

"Hear, you heads of Jacob
*   and rulers of the house of Israel!*
Is it not for you to know justice?—
*   you who hate the good and love the evil,*
who tear the skin from off my people
*   and their flesh from off their bones,*
who eat the flesh of my people,
*   and flay their skin from off them,*
and break their bones in pieces
*   and chop them up like meat in a pot,*
*   like flesh in a cauldron.*

Then they will cry to the LORD,
*   but he will not answer them;*
he will hide his face from them at that time,
*   because they have made their deeds evil.*

Thus says the LORD *concerning the prophets*
*   who lead my people astray,*
who cry 'Peace'
*   when they have something to eat,*
but declare war against him
*   who puts nothing into their mouths.*

Therefore it shall be night to you, without vision,
  and darkness to you, without divination.
The sun shall go down on the prophets,
  and the day shall be black over them;
the seers shall be disgraced,
  and the diviners put to shame;
they shall all cover their lips,
  for there is no answer from God.
But as for me, I am filled with power,
  with the Spirit of the LORD,
  and with justice and might,
to declare to Jacob his transgression
  and to Israel his sin.

Hear this, you heads of the house of Jacob
  and rulers of the house of Israel,
who detest justice
  and make crooked all that is straight,
who build Zion with blood
  and Jerusalem with iniquity.
Its heads give judgment for a bribe;
  its priests teach for a price;
  its prophets practice divination for money;
yet they lean on the LORD and say,
  'Is not the LORD in the midst of us?
  No disaster shall come upon us.'
Therefore because of you
  Zion shall be plowed as a field;
Jerusalem shall become a heap of ruins,
  and the mountain of the house a wooded height." (Mic 3.1–12)

The false prophets in ancient Israel attempted to deceive people by reconstructing truth to manipulate the general perception of reality. The same kind of people today choose a *lens* and exaggerate the focus to show people what they want them to see in the world. They think that if they can change the underlying tenets of reality in your mind, they can control outcomes.

Manipulators exaggerate small actions and minimize significant ones. They make what is evil seem good and what is good seem evil. Power-hungry individuals understand they must deceive others into seeing a perversion of reality to be in control. Although it may only now seem prevalent in society, this has happened everywhere since ancient times.

Micah describes the same process used by the religious leaders of his day. When dishonest, powerful people feel threatened, they resort to manipulating perception. They abuse their power. They accuse others of their own nefarious activities.

But God repeatedly tells his people to *fear not*. He is in control of the nations and always has been. Anyone can review history or even their own lives to see it. Eventually, God will thwart all kinds of manipulative efforts or turn them into blessings for His people. All the while, His people faithfully trust in the depth of the riches of His wisdom and knowledge. "How unsearchable are his judgments and how inscrutable his ways" (Rom 11.33).

We all must suffer the consequences of this evil in our daily lives, but truth always shines forth in the minds of those who know that things are not always what they seem. The curtain is eventually drawn back, exposing the lies and deceivers for what they are. Those who search for truth amid lies can *see and hear* with the spiritual wisdom God supplies in His word.

God's people will not be deceived when they come to know His word. The Lord designed it so. Let us all be as wise as serpents and gentle as doves. Let us trust His word and promises. Let us fear not!

WEEK FORTY-SEVEN

DAY 1

Season Every Choice

Never look for justice in this world, but never cease to give it. If we look for justice, we will only begin to complain and to indulge ourselves in the discontent of self-pity, as if to say, "Why should I be treated like this?" (Oswald Chambers)

Live in harmony with one another. Do not be haughty, but associate with the lowly. Never be wise in your own sight. Repay no one evil for evil, but give thought to do what is honorable in the sight of all. If possible, so far as it depends on you, live peaceably with all. Beloved, never avenge yourselves, but leave it to the wrath of God, for it is written, "Vengeance is mine, I will repay, says the Lord." (Rom 12.16–19)

When we expect fairness from anything or anyone other than the Lord or someone discipled by Him, we will always be disappointed. Realizing we live in a fallen world can free us from the *sting*, which is our natural human reaction to injustice. Even when we cannot escape the consequences of unfairness, looking to God for comfort and relief is always possible.

Learning that true justice resides in God is the key. He is the only one with enough information and enough power to exact it, and knowing this helps to manage our expectations when others execute it imperfectly. It can keep us from adopting a complaining attitude that comes from an entitlement mentality.

Unfairness reigns in this fallen world. If anything is *good*, God has produced it. But if we find ourselves in an environment where God is not respected or appealed to, injustice and chaos will result. But even amid all the chaos, anyone can attain a grateful heart and peaceful mindset. It all comes from an understanding of God's truth. And with it comes redemption and a willingness to spread it around.

The Spirit-filled heart does not complain when encountering unfairness. It has no self-pity or bitterness and rejects a victim mentality. These individuals have a knowledge and understanding of its origin. It is a direct result of sin that originates with the father of lies.

Those with a God-directed heart have already fought it and won, choosing to emulate the example of Christ's overcoming of this world. These Christians adopt a worldview that leads to a humble heart and gratefulness of spirit that comes to season every choice, thought, and motive in their life. There is no thought of complaining or irritation because they do not expect justice from that which is evil.

The good news is that God exacts justice for our sins in the death of Christ. It is in Him that we find restoration and the peace of God that surpasses all understanding. And it only comes when a person puts on Christ, follows His example, and lives a transformed, servant-centered, sacrificial life.

DAY 2

Wish Them Well

Know this: Some people will not hear you regardless of how much, how loud, how truthful, how loving, or how profound you speak. Wish them well and let them go. (Author Unknown)

But when Pharaoh saw that there was a respite, he hardened his heart and would not listen to them, as the LORD had said.

… Then the magicians said to Pharaoh, "This is the finger of God." But Pharaoh's heart was hardened, and he would not listen to them, as the LORD had said.

… But Pharaoh hardened his heart this time also, and did not let the people go.

… And Pharaoh sent, and behold, not one of the livestock of Israel was dead. But the heart of Pharaoh was hardened, and he did not let the people go.

… But the LORD hardened the heart of Pharaoh, and he did not listen to them, as the LORD had spoken to Moses.

... But when Pharaoh saw that the rain and the hail and the thunder had ceased, he sinned yet again and hardened his heart, he and his servants.

(Exod 8.15, 19, 32; 9.7, 12, 34, Pharoah's resposnes to the plagues)

Then the LORD said to Moses, "Go in to Pharaoh, for I have hardened his heart and the heart of his servants, that I may show these signs of mine among them, and that you may tell in the hearing of your son and of your grandson how I have dealt harshly with the Egyptians and what signs I have done among them, that you may know that I am the LORD."

So Moses and Aaron went in to Pharaoh and said to him, "Thus says the LORD, the God of the Hebrews, 'How long will you refuse to humble yourself before me? Let my people go, that they may serve me.'" (Exod 10.1–3)

The plague story gives us a sense of how God uses even the stubborn hearts of people to work His will in the world. As Christians, we understand that no amount of evidence, no matter how strong, can affect someone with a mind made up not to believe His word. And there really is no incontrovertible evidence because other factors in the equation are faith and the condition of a person's heart. Their inherent free will allows them to choose to believe the evidence or not. Some do not want to believe such things.

Pharaoh saw himself as a god and did not want to believe there was only one true and living God. This human dynamic plays out for all to see every day. It can be raining hard outside, and someone who does not want to believe it is raining will deny it. When we encounter these hearts we must wish them well and let it go. You will not change that mind.

Whether a person rejects the truth due to a refusal or denial of unwanted information, or they are hardened by hate, they will choose to disbelieve no matter the weight of the evidence. In those cases, we need to retreat. We may try again if we love them or see a situation that would greatly benefit them from God's word. But your efforts will not be successful if their heart is hard and the truth is something they do not want to hear or believe.

If you stay calm and react properly, the natural consequences of sin may have an impact that can hopefully penetrate the bitterness, the bias, or the rage of a hardened heart. Even Pharoah briefly repented when he saw the severity of God's judgment. And although none of us can control the hearts of others, we do have control of our hearts.

Let us all be open-minded enough to see the truth. Let us be willing to listen to the arguments from God's word without rancor or stubbornness. Let us confront our issues head-on without being stiff-necked and uncircumcised in heart. If we must change, let us do so with humble hearts and steadfast love.

DAY 3

Never Alone

One of the best lessons you can learn in life is to master how to remain calm. Calm is a super power. (Bruce Lee)

And leaving the crowd, they took him with them in the boat, just as he was. And other boats were with him. And a great windstorm arose, and the waves were breaking into the boat, so that the boat was already filling. But he was in the stern, asleep on the cushion. And they woke him and said to him, "Teacher, do you not care that we are perishing?" And he awoke and rebuked the wind and said to the sea, "Peace! Be still!" And the wind ceased, and there was a great calm. He said to them, "Why are you so afraid? Have you still no faith?" (Mark 3.36–40)

When I was younger, I remember being so concerned with the outcomes of things that I was fearful. Truth be told, I still must remind myself to stay calm. But as time and spiritual maturity take hold, the outcomes of things matter less because you know that God will use all that happens, both good and evil, to work for what is profitable to those who love Him.

In the boat with His disciples, the Lord was astonished that these men had not yet begun to understand that they need not worry when He is near. They were with Him daily. They watched Him make wine from water, multiply food from bread and fish, and cast out demons, yet they were not making the connections. Eventually, they did learn, and, with the direction of God and His Spirit, many came to use their experience with the Lord to teach us.

How well have we all learned to stay calm in the storms of life? Do those around us see faith or fear in our reactions to circumstances outside our control? Are we asking for help from the One who can control such things, or are we trying to fix it all ourselves, using our wisdom? Do we believe Jesus can calm the wind and the sea?

Christians are never alone in the boat. The one who can calm the physical wind and our personal fears is so close we can just ask for help. Christians can live through the storms of this life because Jesus is there to calm them. Then, those who trust in the Lord can simply be active in loving God and keeping His commandments. Let us connect to the one who rebukes the wind and calms the sea. He can hush the storms of our lives!

DAY 4

Heart-First Change

Christianity isn't about behavior modification. It's about heart transformation. (Author Unknown)

I appeal to you therefore, brothers, by the mercies of God, to present your bodies as a living sacrifice, holy and acceptable to God, which is your spiritual worship. Do not be conformed to this world, but be transformed by the renewal of your mind, that by testing you may discern what is the will of God, what is good and acceptable and perfect.

For by the grace given to me I say to everyone among you not to think of himself more highly than he ought to think, but to think with sober judgment, each according to the measure of faith that God has assigned. (Rom 12.1–3)

In these two pieces of advice Paul gives to the Romans, he describes the mindset by which a Christian can be set apart to God and be holy. The first is to be transformed by the renewing of our minds, and the second is not to think more highly of ourselves than we ought to. These attributes are in direct opposition to worldly wisdom.

So often, we work on outward behavior rather than an inward transformation of our thinking. I remember as a child how my Bible class teachers tried to make this distinction for us in the kindergarten classroom with the "Be Kind" and "Be Patient" posters. The emphasis was on *being* kind and patient, not just acting the part. We must reinforce these concepts through our lives with the true teachings of Christ.

You cannot do it for anyone else. We can only do it for ourselves. And we must allow enough space, free will, and personal responsibility for each person to decide on their own to change. You can only dictate behavior so far. There comes a time when we must let go and trust them to trust God. Otherwise, you can have seemingly good behavior without a proper heart.

The way to change a bad attitude is to change the heart first, and the proper behaviors will naturally follow. However, people often overlook this method, and controlling behavior seems the go-to response for keeping people out of trouble. But when we decide to do what Paul prescribes, it allows us to find the proper road to the *mind of Christ*. Internalizing the concept of a heart-first change is life-altering!

DAY 5

Seeing Things Clearly

Too many are willing to sit at God's table, but not work in his field. (Vance Havner)

For whoever is ashamed of me and of my words in this adulterous and sinful generation, of him will the Son of Man also be ashamed when he comes in the glory of his Father with the holy angels. (Mark 8.38)

At certain points in His ministry, neither the disciples nor the Pharisees seem to understand what Jesus is saying. Mark 8 starts with Jesus feeding four thousand people. Shortly after, the Pharisees ask Him for a sign from heaven. Jesus cautions the disciples to beware of their *leaven*, and then they become upset because they think it is because they forgot to bring bread.

On the boat to Bethsaida, Jesus reminds them that He fed five thousand people and then four thousand. He asks them how many baskets were taken up after each event. They answers were *twelve* and *seven*. They had not forgotten. But then Jesus asked, *Do you not yet understand?*

He seems somewhat frustrated but continues using signs to communicate His message. While in Bethsaida, He heals a blind man in two stages. In the first, Jesus spits on the man's eyes, and he sees men walking around looking like trees. Jesus then lays hands on his eyes again, and the man sees everything clearly.

Next, Peter identifies Jesus as Christ but then rebukes Him for talking about His role as a sufferer. Christ responds with a strong rebuke for Peter, saying *Get behind me, Satan!* Peter was setting his mind on the things of man rather than those of God.

There is a progression from seeing, hearing, and understanding to seeing things more clearly. Jesus wants His followers to understand something profound. His mission and purpose are to be the Lamb of God and a suffering servant. All this must be understood by His disciples and become their mission and purpose, too.

He tells them, "If anyone would come after me, let him deny himself and take up his cross and follow me" (Mark 8.34). If we have not become servants ourselves, our hearts are still hard, and we are still blind. If we are ashamed to suffer with Him, He will be ashamed of us.

His children will always be seen as foolish by the world while simultaneously having a lasting impact on honest hearts. That is just the way it works. We must understand all this to perceive something more than men as trees walking around. The cost of true discipleship is not burdensome to those who see things clearly—it is the gift of life.

WEEK FORTY-EIGHT

DAY 1

Injustice

Many books can inform you but only one can transform you!
(Author Unknown)

A worthless person, a wicked man,
  goes about with crooked speech,
winks with his eyes, signals with his feet,
  points with his finger,
with perverted heart devises evil,
  continually sowing discord;
therefore calamity will come upon him suddenly;
  in a moment he will be broken beyond healing.

There are six things that the LORD hates,
  seven that are an abomination to him:
haughty eyes, a lying tongue,
  and hands that shed innocent blood,
a heart that devises wicked plans,
  feet that make haste to run to evil,
a false witness who breathes out lies,
  and one who sows discord among brothers. (Prov 6.12–19)

Everyone hates injustice. God has put that in man. But to truly understand injustice, you must see, recognize, and be trained by God's just standard. Unfortunately, our society considers justice relative, so it never seems to apply equally. At any time, regardless of circumstance, one side believes that an injustice reigns in the other.

God defines injustice in His word. Worldly wisdom and injustice breed conflict, confusion, and every vile thing (Jas. 3.16). God is where real power and hope reside. We must be led by the Lord and trust in His will. And learning from God changes a person's character. His followers are identified by their fairness amid unfairness, while we recognize the unjust by the mess they leave behind.

The Bible outlines our entrance into His heavenly kingdom, which is the only way to absolute safety. We cannot put our trust in leadership from any other source. Let us not look for deliverance in the wrong places or expect to see righteousness from those educated solely in the *world*. God is in control as He works and judges in the affairs of men, even while allowing free will.

God's people can always be at peace knowing that He is the final judge. They are at rest because they know that, whether by God acting now or on judgment day, all will be made right. His determination on anything is all that matters in the end. So even during a social or political upheaval, the transformed Christian can (as the motto goes) *Keep Calm and Carry on.*

DAY 2

Elijah's Chariot

Wear your tragedies as armor, not shackles. (Author Unknown)

And when Elijah heard it, he wrapped his face in his cloak and went out and stood at the entrance of the cave. And behold, there came a voice to him and said, "What are you doing here, Elijah?" He said, "I have been very jealous for the LORD, the God of hosts. For the people of Israel have forsaken your covenant, thrown down your altars, and killed your prophets with the sword, and I, even I only, am left, and they seek my life, to take it away." And the LORD said to him, "Go, return on your way to the wilderness of Damascus. And when you arrive, you shall anoint Hazael to be king over Syria. And Jehu the son of Nimshi you shall anoint to be king over Israel, and Elisha the son of Shaphat of Abel-meholah you shall anoint to be prophet in your place. And the one who escapes from the sword of Hazael shall Jehu put to death, and the one who escapes from the sword of Jehu shall Elisha put to death. Yet I will leave seven thousand in Israel, all the knees that have not bowed to Baal, and every mouth that has not kissed him." (1 Kgs 19.13–18)

We can learn so much from the story of Elijah. Following the defeat of the Baal prophets at Mount Carmel, we see Elijah transition from an incredible act of faith to a condition of complete despair while fleeing from Queen Jezebel. God's reaction is so gentle. He directs Elijah to finish performing the necessary work for God's plan to be accomplished. God also reveals to Elijah that there is a remnant in Israel that He is still protecting and that it will remain. Then Elijah is miraculously taken up in a whirlwind.

The story proceeds in the book of Kings to recount how God's directions play out. He is in complete control and is working His plan to save all those who have not followed the foreign gods but chose to surrender themselves to the one true God. This discussion allows people an inside look at the purpose and workings of God in physical Israel, and it helps us to comprehend the unseen workings of God in spiritual Israel today.

From Elijah, we learn that faith sometimes ebbs and flows. It is constantly growing, and people act on it differently depending on their circumstances and energy levels. Of course, God spoke to Elijah directly, while He speaks to Christians today in scripture where His word directs us to do all things with the character of our Lord. God has a plan, and we need to focus on His plans for us, not our own.

Christians also learn that we are not alone. There was tremendous religious upheaval and evil political antics at work during the time of Arab and Jezebel. The effects of Jezebel's abuses of power surrounded Elijah, making him weary. Like Elijah, God's people must understand that we have God's protection and that there are other faithful workers out there. Other souls in our extended family have the same heart because the same spiritual direction produced it. They are also working for the Lord's cause.

Let none be distracted by the clamor of worldliness all around us. Instead, let us calmly be about the Lord's work. God is working in our day to help people find His rest who are willing to learn and be faithful. A personal chariot waits for those who are mouthpieces for the Lord like Elijah. He focused on following the direction God supplied. So should those today in God's spiritual kingdom, where service is not based on mere rule-keeping but rather God-seeking.

As he speaks of Jesus as the risen Lord, John says, "When I saw him, I fell at his feet as though dead. But he laid His right hand on me, saying, "Fear not, I am the first and the last, and the living one. I died, and behold I am alive forevermore, and I have the keys of Death and Hades" (Rev

1.17–18). Everyone can respond to John's vision. Jesus is the way out of this hectic, dying world even as one lives physically.

Christians can use this mindset to go to the place of rest even amid difficulties, pain, exhaustion, and confusion. God's people do not have to leave this physical world to find rest. They merely need to step into where God dwells, then follow His directed scheme of redemption.

All people have the choice to be faithful servants like Elijah and John. His people live here on earth, but once they have separated from it through physical death, they will pass spiritually alive into an eternal union with God. If you have chosen to be faithful, keep this in mind— your chariot awaits!

DAY 3

Absolute Truth

If there is no absolute moral standard, then one cannot say in a final sense that anything is right or wrong. By absolute we mean that which always applies, that which provides a final or ultimate standard. There must be an absolute if there are to be morals, and there must be an absolute if there are to be real values. If there is no absolute beyond man's ideas, then there is no final appeal to judge between individuals and groups whose moral judgments conflict. We are merely left with conflicting opinions. (Francis Schaeffer)

Why does the wicked renounce God
    and say in his heart, "You will not call to account"?
But you do see, for you note mischief and vexation,
    that you may take it into your hands;
to you the helpless commits himself;
    you have been the helper of the fatherless.
Break the arm of the wicked and evildoer;
    call his wickedness to account till you find none.
The LORD is king forever and ever;
    the nations perish from his land. (Psa 10.13–16)

Almighty Jehovah created man and provides for all mankind, and Christ is King to all in His kingdom. God has given us the truth, but we watch daily as the wicked oppose Him, deny Him, and mock Him. Christians dwell in

God's spiritually free land. They have metaphorically come out of *Egypt* and *Babylon* into the unseen realm of His everlasting kingdom.

The stories in the Bible convey God's absolute truth. He provides a way out of our polluted world to be made clean through the death, burial, and resurrection of His Son. Christians choose to "die" in baptism when they are buried and resurrected with Christ to a new life and a restored spiritual relationship with God. Christ becomes their king, and His people are not of this world. They cease to act like the world acts.

By their actions, Christians make God's absolute truth known to others. When they correct their behaviors or entreat others to correct theirs, they proclaim that God directs our conduct. Our culture denies this and focuses on self-elevation rather than the elevation of a loving Father and God. Eventually, everyone who rejects God's direction will pay dearly for that oversight.

The gospel is for all, but no one will ever find it until they see God as their real provider and learn His redemption process found in the gospel message. Let us look to God for truth and live accordingly so others can see Satan's lies. Let us pray that those who are deceived will see and take advantage of His truth. And let us pray that evil in the world will come to nothing in whatever physical nation we reside.

Abraham Lincoln once said, "I have been driven many times upon my knees by the overwhelming conviction that I had nowhere else to go. My own wisdom and that of all about me seemed insufficient for that day."

God directs Christians to pray for their enemies who deny His truth. Christians want all to come to repentance. They endure suffering and grow in faith in times of adversity, all while processing the peace of God that surpasses understanding.

Stephen, while being stoned by an angry mob, saw the Son of Man standing at the right hand of God while the rocks were flying. He cried, "Lord, do not hold this sin against them." Look up and see the unseen! Exit the chaos, even if it costs you your physical life. We must try to teach the truth to those who want their own way and cause anger, deceit, and violence. At the same time, we harbor a deep desire for God to forgive those who finally come to repentance.

It is possible, and even desirable, for Christians to live a peaceful and quiet life amid upheaval so that the world is made aware of a more profitable and stable path available to them. May God use Christians as His examples so all may see the Light. This is the day the Lord has made. Let us glorify His name through our character as we navigate the trials of this life.

DAY 4

Up Those Mountains

These mountains that you are carrying, you were only supposed to climb. (Najwa Zebian)

"Ah, stubborn children," declares the LORD,
  "who carry out a plan, but not mine,
and who make an alliance, but not of my Spirit,
  that they may add sin to sin;
who set out to go down to Egypt,
  without asking for my direction,
to take refuge in the protection of Pharaoh
  and to seek shelter in the shadow of Egypt!"

And though the LORD give you the bread of adversity and the water of affliction, yet your Teacher will not hide himself anymore, but your eyes shall see your Teacher. And your ears shall hear a word behind you, saying, "This is the way, walk in it," when you turn to the right or when you turn to the left. Then you will defile your carved idols overlaid with silver and your gold-plated metal images. You will scatter them as unclean things. You will say to them, "Be gone!" (Isa 30.1–2, 20–22)

Through Isaiah, God rebukes His people for putting their trust in their judgment as they go to Egypt to seek the protection of Pharaoh. He pleads with them to trust the Holy One of Israel. People will either follow and trust God, listening to His direction and climbing the necessary mountains in trusting faith, or carry them as if their own abilities can *work it out.*

Some ascribe success in this world to riches, relationships, fame, or positions of governmental authority. They work towards these improper goals to become healthy, wealthy, powerful, and wise. But true satisfaction is only found in God's will, His power, and His provisions of grace and the forgiveness of sin.

The *idols* of our day are not of silver and gold as in Isaiah's time. Today, people trust in worthless pursuits, temporal relationships, the strength of youth, the wisdom of age, the economy, or some fleeting ability that takes their focus off God. As such, we people will take on responsibilities that are not ours to carry and, by doing so, deny God's promises of care and protection to work in our lives. When someone looks at the life of a Christian, they should readily see that they could not be where they are without some help from heaven.

May we all start "walking" up those mountains with God's protection and care instead of trying to carry them ourselves. Let us say to our idols, *Be gone!* Then, others will know that we are blessed, not because of our efforts but because God works in our lives.

DAY 5

Hearts Set on Him

Expect nothing and appreciate everything. (Author Unknown)

[P]ut on the new self, created after the likeness of God in true righteousness and holiness. (Eph 4.24)

All that we need as Christians is made manifest in Christ. He models a God-directed character for those who choose to see it. He shows His own how to serve by serving them. He demonstrates how to teach, how to love, and how to show mercy.

A transformed heart and spirit come from an altered view of ourselves in our relationship with God and others. A person with a worldly mindset feels entitled and lives with an expectation that they *deserve* to be served and appreciated. This self-centered mindset is attracted to a victim mentality when their desires are not met. Anger, resentment, and bitterness often result in them and those they interact with.

But a person with a godly mindset sees themselves as an unworthy servant. This God-centered perspective knows they deserve nothing, so they appreciate everything. They see gifts and blessings when given and even see them in places where others see none. They are humbled by all acts of kindness, words of wisdom, and a God that shows love and mercy through sacrifice and suffering. The result is a quiet spirit, a forgiving mind, and a humble heart.

They typically stand out as oddities and are misunderstood because they are so unlike the self-serving. They choose to dedicate themselves to God for His use. Consequently, their choices are quite different and are noticed by an eye trained to see such things. Those in the world think them foolish and often mock or ridicule them.

That is how Satan works. But Jesus always recognizes those with a heart set on him. He typically comments on them in scripture. Remember the widow and her mites? Or the Gentile women who asked for the crumbs from the children's table? How about the women with the discharge of blood? Or when Jesus let the children come to him? And what about eager Zacchaeus?

Jesus also points out those with improper motives, especially those who present themselves as righteous, when they are not thinking or behaving rightly. The Pharisees, the Scribes, and the Jewish leaders fall into this group. Jesus even harshly chastised Peter and his other disciples when they failed to have a servant mindset but rather exhibited a proud and self-serving spirit. Jesus' discipline, when he calls them hypocrites or servants of Satan may sound a bit harsh to us as we read them in light of our current culture.

But we know Jesus was always working from a loving Spirit. He also had the right to direct others and pronounce judgment. May we all see these differences and choose for ourselves to put on Christ. And when we do, let us truly reflect His God-directed heart and mindset.

WEEK FORTY-NINE

DAY 1

To the Work

Courage isn't having the strength to go on—it is going on when you don't have strength. (Napoleon Bonaparte)

I hear, and my body trembles;
*   my lips quiver at the sound;*
rottenness enters into my bones;
*   my legs tremble beneath me.*
Yet I will quietly wait for the day of trouble
*   to come upon people who invade us.* (Hab 3.16)

My blueberries are about to ripen, and I will use them to make jam. So today's fruit will continue its use for some time to come. Likewise, the spiritual fruit God produces in His children becomes helpful to others and glorifies Him, and He will preserve His glory into eternity. This is a marvelous thing! We must allow God to produce His spiritual fruit in us.

Habakkuk writes his words in anticipation of Babylon coming to destroy Israel. Only those who would eventually become the remnant could comprehend the violence to come. The glory of God is seen from a spiritual mindset. And those who hear and understand quietly wait for the day of judgment to come upon a disobedient people who seek to destroy the godly. They maintain courage as they go forward because they see into eternity.

Times are coming when we may require this strength. The fruit of the Spirit we display today will serve us in our day of trouble tomorrow. So, as Fanny Crosby wrote in her well-known hymn, "To the Work" with us all!

To the work! to the work! We are servants of God,
Let us follow the path that our Master has trod;

With the balm of His counsel our strength to renew,
Let us do with our might what our hands find to do.

DAY 2

Persistent Transformation

If you are persistent you will get it. If you are consistent you will keep it.
(Harvey MacKay)

And he told them a parable to the effect that they ought always to pray and not lose heart. He said, "In a certain city there was a judge who neither feared God nor respected man. And there was a widow in that city who kept coming to him and saying, 'Give me justice against my adversary.' For a while he refused, but afterward he said to himself, 'Though I neither fear God nor respect man, yet because this widow keeps bothering me, I will give her justice, so that she will not beat me down by her continual coming.' And the Lord said, 'Hear what the unrighteous judge says. And will not God give justice to his elect, who cry to him day and night? Will he delay long over them? I tell you, he will give justice to them speedily.'" (Luke 18.1–8)

Persistence and consistency are essential tools anyone can use to help them accomplish important things. This is no truer than in the realm of learning the mind and will of God for mankind. If you persist in your desire to gain spiritual knowledge and wisdom, they will be given to you. God will answer your requests if you consistently seek and pray for the appropriate things. If you obey and value God, you will strive to become like Him, and He will transform you.

People tend to act on what they think about and value. So, God asks Christians to pray without ceasing. This act keeps our mind on spiritual things and on God as creator and provider. When Christians have faith and trust in God, He is faithful to hear and respond. Persistence and consistency are vital parts of what God desires for His people as they pertain to their thoughts and actions.

People have short memories and get all wound up in the inconsequential things of life. So, God instituted consistency into His plan for us by requiring Christians to remember the sacrifice of Christ every *Lord's Day*. This simple, collective act recenters our thoughts on the most critical event in the history of the world every first day of the week.

When people focus solely on things that are of the world, they transform into weeds that grow among the wheat. But even then, unrighteous judges may respond to persistence in ways that are helpful to the righteous. Persistence is a valuable tool anyone can use to progress on almost every important task. And it always reveals where a person's heart and mind are.

Let us consistently follow the godly command, "Whatever is true, whatever is honorable, whatever is just, whatever is pure, whatever is lovely, whatever is commendable, if there is any excellence, if there is anything worthy of praise, think about these things" (Phil 4.8). Always remember that when one focuses on the things of God, they will be transformed by the renewing of their mind into an image like His. And these lights will shine in the darkness to glorify God and His purposes.

DAY 3

Increase Our Faith

What may seem like a disappointment could be God setting you up for a rescue. Trust His plan even when you don't understand the path. (Author Unknown)

And to this people you shall say: "Thus says the LORD: Behold, I set before you the way of life and the way of death. He who stays in this city shall die by the sword, by famine, and by pestilence, but he who goes out and surrenders to the Chaldeans who are besieging you shall live and shall have his life as a prize of war. For I have set my face against this city for harm and not for good, declares the LORD: it shall be given into the hand of the king of Babylon, and he shall burn it with fire." (Jer 21.8–10)

The book of 1 Chronicles tells us, "Jehozadak went into exile when the Lord sent Judah and Jerusalem into exile by the hand of Nebuchadnezzar" (1 Chron. 6.15). Apparently, this priest from the tribe of Levi decided to follow the instructions the Lord gave through Jeremiah. He chose to surrender when the Chaldeans were allowed to take God's people captive as a consequence of their disobedience.

Even under this judgment, God made a pathway to fulfill His promises to Abraham. These directions, of which those in the remnant were obedient, must have been difficult. Jeremiah told them to surrender to the enemy, while some of their *leaders* were telling them otherwise.

I am sure not all the family members agreed with those who chose to obey. Some may have chosen not to obey because they felt the instructions must be wrong. Some may have disobeyed because they loved something or someone so much that leaving would mean suffering a significant loss. Or just like Eve in the garden, some believed *they surely would not die*, a lie likely coming from multiple sources.

The faithful would have had great courage to obey this command under this extreme circumstance. And so many other directives God gave throughout the Old Testament would have called for a level of heroic faith when people faced testing under horrific circumstances. God required obedience in those times and still does today. Such is needed to grow a faith that can squelch any fear as it rises in the heart of each person when faithful obedience is required.

People must choose to have this level of trust in the Lord. That is why the Bible has so many examples of the faithful and faithless. They are there for people to ponder. Each can choose to emulate the heroes of old because they see the ruin of the faithless or the advantages of the faithful. Having gone through the directive to surrender to the Chaldeans, Daniel grew his faith over time and could enter a den of lions without fear.

There are many times in a Christian's life when the directions from the Lord toward the pathway of righteousness seem to be just as difficult. I am not talking about decisions where there may be some uncertainty or when the choice is not perfectly clear. I am referring to the clearly stated instructions found in the Biblical text.

Sometimes a Christian knows what God says to do, but for some of the same reasons that the people of old faltered, they follow the same reasoning and choose to disobey. And some suffer the consequences of disobedience that last a lifetime. On the other hand, when people decide to obey, their faith increases, and these choices also have ramifications that last a lifetime.

Each day Christians live, they can make better decisions, garnering godly results and better consequences. Look forward, not back. Over time, the Lord can even use people's poor choices for good. The Jewish leaders chose to crucify our Lord, which God used to justify all those who obey the gospel.

Always remember that it may not be easy to do God's will in your life, especially at first. What God asks of you may be very difficult. But each time obedience is done and done with the right heart, your mind will be less troubled by the cost attached. And compared to the rewards, any affliction seems momentary and light.

Anyone can have the faith it took Abraham to be willing to offer his son Issac, the faith it took Joseph to forgive his brothers their faithlessness, or the faith it took David to suffer the consequences of his sin with Bathsheba gracefully. When we encounter those hard commands, let us ask God, like the early disciples, *to increase our faith*. And let us remember that the testing of that faith produces endurance.

DAY 4

A Reasoned Service

Six Important Guidelines in Life:

1. When you are Alone, mind your Thoughts.
2. When you are with Friends, mind your Tongue.
3. When you are Angry, mind your Temper.
4. When you are with a Group, mind your Behavior.
5. When you are in Trouble, mind your Emotion.
6. When God starts blessing you, mind your EGO.

(Author Unknown)

I appeal to you therefore, brothers, by the mercies of God, to present your bodies as a living sacrifice, holy and acceptable to God, which is your spiritual worship. Do not be conformed to this world, but be transformed by the renewal of your mind, that by testing you may discern what is the will of God, what is good and acceptable and perfect. (Rom 12.1–2)

Christians are to offer God a continual sacrifice by properly using their intellect, thoughts, and actions. They control their minds and spirit, which alters their actions if they truly take on the mind of Christ. If a person is not truly transformed by the renewing of their minds, they are merely actors playing the part of what they perceive a Christian to be.

This renewal of the mind is a foreign concept in today's culture of rights, where people run from difficulties to self-indulgence. Self-sacrifice and self-control get lost in all the hype. These verses explain the concept of a mind-changing, life-altering renewal, but their significance does not always shine through in our modern-day translations.

In the English Standard Version, the words at the end of Romans 12.1 are: "which is your *spiritual worship.*" In the New International Version, "spiritual worship" is translated as "true and proper worship." Neither seems to express the real meaning of the original Greek. The New King James Version uses "reasonable service," which comes the closest, but it still seems to miss the point given our current understanding of these terms today.

The Greek term is the same word from which we derive the word "logical," and it conveys the idea of using our minds in this way. Maybe "reasoned" or "logical thinking" would work best here. Christians must use their intellect, change their thinking, change their heart, and change their motives by intentionally altering their mind as they align them with scripture. They are transformed with this effort and made to be new creatures with their use of reasoned, spiritual thinking.

God, through His inspired word, provides the way to transformation. This spiritual mindset does not always coincide with a person's feelings or desires at a given time. But they choose to override the emotions that oppose God's teaching, knowing He works through a person's reasonable thinking abilities to change their feelings too.

Satan works by perverting the proper use of our God-provided feelings and emotions. And he uses fleshly desires to deceive people into using them in ways God never intended in their design. Remember James 1.14, "But each person is tempted when he is lured and enticed by his own desire." In contrast, God works inside man by educating the spirit of each of His children on the proper use of all created things through scripture.

Christians today seem to be falling for some of the emotional arguments for all sorts of things—things that a reasonable mind using God's word should know to reject. All Christians must make a conscious effort to obey God's word. That is how God enables His people to find the most value in this life. They must use their mind, spirit, and heart, directed by godly teaching, to sacrifice themselves. They are not to use their emotions, feelings, or works from a mind devoid of godly influence to serve themselves. A God-directed mindset can alter a person's emotions to coincide with the proper use of things.

When Christians operate in God-intended ways, they become more and more like Christ over time. But the entire concept is getting lost with the constant bombardment of worldliness we are exposed to every day. James goes on to say:

> Do not be deceived, my beloved brothers. Every good gift and every perfect gift is from above, coming down from the Father of lights, with whom there is no variation or shadow due to change... Therefore put away all filthiness and rampant wickedness and receive with meekness the implanted word, which is able to save your souls. But be doers of the word, and not hearers only, deceiving yourselves (Jas. 1.16–17, 21–22).

Service to God is a reasoned action. It rejects any worldview that differs from that which is God-ordained, directed, and originates in His word. Each man has the ability to control himself and the free will to choose to learn from God. This freedom is why each person will be held accountable for their choices. May we all choose wisely.

DAY 5

Spiritual Habits

People don't behave badly because they lack information about their short-comings. They behave badly because they've fallen into patterns of destructive behavior from which they're unable to escape. (David Brooks)

Look carefully then how you walk, not as unwise but as wise, making the best use of the time, because the days are evil. Therefore do not be foolish, but understand what the will of the Lord is. And do not get drunk with wine, for that is debauchery, but be filled with the Spirit, addressing one another in psalms and hymns and spiritual songs, singing and making melody to the Lord with your heart, giving thanks always and for everything to God the Father in the name of our Lord Jesus Christ, submitting to one another out of reverence for Christ. (Eph 5.15–21)

It is sad to watch people who want to make substantial changes in their lives but fail to do so. They never take advantage of growth opportunities because they are so ingrained in negative mental habits that always lead them into a continuous, destructive cycle. Some have not yet grasped how God directs them to change. Others need more faith to make the hard choice to modify their behaviors long enough to develop new and constructive habits.

We can only help someone else through example, teaching, and encouragement. Everyone must recognize the need for personal improvement. We must all do this hard work with the Lord's help to transition from destructive habits and mindsets to righteous ones.

We will only succeed if we plan to transform ourselves inside and out. Spending a great deal of time with a conscious effort to change our habits and behavioral patterns is always required. We must choose to saturate ourselves with the truth. We must make every effort to transform our thinking or our actions will never change. And we must train our children to develop good and righteous habits while they are young. They will choose to continue them or not. But this effort will go a long way in helping them throughout their lives.

Let us not pass along our destructive thought processes. Working on ourselves is always the first order of business. Everyone is watching and taking their cues from somewhere and someone. We need to ensure our actions are spiritually motivated and helpful to others in our realm of influence.

WEEK FIFTY

DAY 1

Be a David

David was Saul's enemy, but Saul was not David's. David didn't allow Saul's hate problem to become his. The world is full of Saul's, be a David. (Author Unknown)

And Saul hurled the spear, for he thought, "I will pin David to the wall." But David evaded him twice. Saul was afraid of David because the LORD was with him but had departed from Saul. (1 Sam 18.11–12)

There is an ongoing deterioration of the relationship between Saul and David in the book of 1 Samuel. It is a fascinating study. After David kills Goliath, David and Saul become very close. Saul brings him into his family, and David calms him with his harp playing. Then Saul realizes David is revered among the people in Israel and sees God is with him. Once he realizes that God will eventually make him king, all Saul's goodwill towards David sours.

Jealously takes over and turns into envy, which turns into rage. Eventually, Saul becomes mentally unbalanced. While Saul persecutes him, David still shows great love for Saul as his king, former friend, and family member. David does not retaliate in kind. And oddly enough, this response actually seems to hasten the deterioration of Saul's mental state.

There are several tactics David uses to deal with the situation. He tries to evade Saul, shows his allegiance to Saul, serves Saul, and spares Saul when given the opportunity to kill him. Nothing works! David loves Saul while Saul hates him. You never know in any given circumstance how Saul will respond. It is so sad, really. When division, chaos, persecution, and unfairness are prevalent, let us try our best to be a David, or we could end up like Saul.

DAY 2

Ingredients for Growth

Those speak foolishly who ascribe their anger or their impatience to such as offend them or to tribulation. Tribulation does not make people impatient, but proves that they are impatient. So everyone may learn from tribulation how his heart is constituted. (Martin Luther)

Blessed is the man who remains steadfast under trial, for when he has stood the test he will receive the crown of life, which God has promised to those who love him. (Jas 1.12)

Everyone is being tested and trained by trials and tribulations in their journey through life. As people age, they should find themselves more and more able to remain steadfast, forward-looking, and calm during times of extreme stress. Each difficulty strengthens a man's mind and spirit when handled in a God-directed way.

Using His ways, a person can grow and prosper spiritually with each trial. They find themselves to be more and more patient and mentally stronger under pressure. And the only measure that helps a person see how they are doing is to compare their actions and attitude to God's standards.

Everyone must realize that trials or tests reveal the weak places in a person's character. These are opportunities for correction, growth, and glory to God. So, when impatience, fear, or anger present themselves, a wise person can see and correct them. If a person has not truly become patient but merely acts the part, it typically shows up when they are under pressure. And when someone blames circumstances and others for their weaknesses rather than themselves, they do not own up to their accountability in such matters.

Martin Luther's point is so relevant to everyone today. Blaming others or circumstances does not promote growth. And James tells us to count trials as joy and consider tribulation a valuable tool, knowing that the testing of our faith produces endurance. Our attitude in this kind of learning shows a Christian's love for God.

A godly man always allows God to transform his inner self by following Christ's teaching with trust and obedience. A man's journey toward righteousness is ongoing. It never ends. Progress should show in our actions and reactions as we become more and more steadfast as time goes by. Following our Lord's commands will renew our minds and strengthen us to practice godliness. The Christian should view learning, trials, and discipline as good. These should always be admired and appreciated. They are the ingredients that cause all kinds of growth in each man.

Those who hate instruction and fail to take advantage of difficulties always reveal a foolish heart. Let all God's children avoid the foolish mistakes of those who do not know God or His teaching. Let us all journey together and appreciate the progress each has made rather than focusing on the weaknesses of others.

A flaw that has not been made manifest and acknowledged cannot be corrected. These dynamics are ultimately God-directed and facilitate a man's transformation towards godliness. Let all take advantage of these God-provided blessings.

DAY 3

Heart Communication

It is easier to build strong children than to repair broken men.
(Frederick Douglass)

And they came again to Jerusalem. And as he was walking in the temple, the chief priests and the scribes and the elders came to him, and they said to him, "By what authority are you doing these things, or who gave you this authority to do them?" Jesus said to them, "I will ask you one question; answer me, and I will tell you by what authority I do these things. Was the baptism of John from heaven or from man? Answer me." And they discussed it with one another, saying, "If we say, 'From heaven,' he will say, 'Why then did you not believe him?' But shall we say, 'From man'?"—they were afraid of the people, for they all held that John really was a prophet. So they answered Jesus, "We do not know." And Jesus said to them, "Neither will I tell you by what authority I do these things." (Mark 11.27–33)

Words can be hammers! was a phrase used by a corporate consultant I knew. They can be very painful to hearts that have been abused. Emotional damage may result even when we think we have the best intentions in what we say and do. Misunderstandings in general are a frequent and prevalent problem, especially when the words said or heard are not measured properly. And self-focused speech almost always leads to the hurt or ruin of a relationship or someone else.

In the passage above, our Lord asks a question of these chief priests and scribes to check the level of sincerity in their hearts as they question Him. Their dishonest responses made Him decide that their inquiry did not warrant a word or response. The answer was not in their favor, so they said they did not know. They would have been just as dishonest with any answer He gave as they had with the previous response. It would not have done anyone any good.

In any relationship or word interaction, we must consider the condition of the heart that is speaking and listening. Whether we choose to discipline, decide whether to elevate the truth or even to respond, or choose to be hurt or offended, we should consider many factors, but most importantly, the person's heart. We should determine if we are entering an arena where our efforts can positively impact the other person and ourselves. This consideration is true whether we decide to speak or internalize someone else's words.

When you speak or listen, remember the age, background, level of knowledge, and understanding the person you are conversing with. Always check your motives before speaking and the condition of the heart you are listening with. The intent of any receptive heart should always be for the promotion, benefit, and improvement of another rather than self-promotion, self-elevation, or even self-defense.

Remember that speaking (and hearing) positive or negative words can have lasting and unintended consequences. Hurtful words can say, *I have no need of you.* Disinterested responses can say, *I have no time for you.* Belittling words can say, *You have no worth to me,* and on and on.

Be even more careful when communicating with young children. They may not mean their words the way you hear them. And your parental discipline must always have the proper motives. It needs to be verbalized clearly and executed in a calm and caring manner for a child to understand them properly and for any God-driven results to occur.

And all of us should be extremely careful when dealing with the children of God in any capacity to make sure we cause them no harm. We never want to allow words or actions that come from a broken heart to cause damage to others. But rather, with contrite hearts, we must actively build others up using God's directions.

And lastly, be trustworthy and fair in all your communication. Use the best connotation you can. Always tie your speech or response to a biblical truth or wisdom from God and ensure it is revealed in the words or actions of His Son. Any one of us can be an adult who has been impacted negatively by the careless actions or words of others. We need to allow God to fix us through His word and use His word to mend others.

When any hearer realizes and believes there is some higher authority behind the words and that the messenger has their best interest at heart, the ability to touch the heart of anyone increases by leaps and bounds. And when the speaker and the listener both have the proper heart, well folks, that glorifies God and impacts the world all around.

DAY 4

Trust and Obey

As you do not know what is the way of the wind,
Or how the bones grow in the womb of her who is with child,
So you do not know the works of God who makes everything.
(Ecclesiastes 11.5, NKJV)

For while we are still in this tent, we groan, being burdened—not that we would be unclothed, but that we would be further clothed, so that what is mortal may be swallowed up by life. He who has prepared us for this very thing is God, who has given us the Spirit as a guarantee.

So we are always of good courage. We know that while we are at home in the body we are away from the Lord, for we walk by faith, not by sight. Yes, we are of good courage, and we would rather be away from the body and at home with the Lord. So whether we are at home or away, we make it our aim to please him. (2 Cor 5.4–9)

By faith, we know that God works in the lives of men, but sometimes we are too willing to identify by *sight* what we think He is doing in our lives and in the world. God works more like the wind blows. You can observe the effects of its presence, but you cannot see the wind itself.

Even God's children, those entrenched in the work of the heavenly kingdom, cannot clearly see His particular work in their own lives. Even

Paul walked by faith. And the Bible tells us that even angels seek to discover God's plans (1 Pet 1.12).

Even when we obey by faith, with proper knowledge of His word and the intent to follow His will, we may only be able to recognize some of the effects of His work while looking at our lives in hindsight. But attributing specific results or events to Him as we see them unfold in the world can be dangerous. If we always had full knowledge of how God works, then our obedience would no longer be a result of faith but be based on our sight and intellect.

Knowing that God does not control our free will or that of others, we realize that the consequences of our decisions and those of others are always in play and factored into God's work. But we cannot distinguish between His work and the natural consequences of our actions or those of others. What is astonishing and faith-building is that God, through His Spirit and wisdom, can work His will no matter what choices are made by any of us lowly humans. Oh, how marvelous and wonderful is that! This blessing provides us with hope and helps us find peace even in chaos.

God wants our service and our motives to be led by an abiding hope and trust in Him based on who He is and what He has done for us, not on circumstances that we may deem ideal. We trust Him whether times are good or bad. And when we shed this physical tent, our service will be from sight because we will then see the Lord.

Even the weather cannot always be predicted very far in advance. Some meteorologists are better at it than others because they are better trained or more experienced. But even the best ones understand that no one knows how it will all play out until it actually happens.

God does not want us to take control and manipulate circumstances to derive what we think He is trying to accomplish. He wants us to look at His word, see what He directs, and follow Him. When God's children operate with faith, they walk calmly even in a storm. They are constantly seeking direction from their father above. They are not trying to understand where the winds originate or how the weather patterns form. They simply trust and obey.

DAY 5

The Narrow Way

If it was easy, everyone would do it. (Susie Clark; to me from an Atlanta Colt Football Mom)

[T]he blind receive their sight and the lame walk, lepers are cleansed and the deaf hear, and the dead are raised up, and the poor have good news preached to them. (Matt 11.5)

The quote above by Susie Clark was once said to me when I served as a volunteer at our local ballpark when my children were young and in sports. I thought there would be a list of step-by-step instructions provided as to how to perform the role of an athletic director. But the ballpark was looking for someone who wanted to serve, had an eye for the needs, and was willing to lead people who were under no compulsion to follow.

In the Matthew passage, Jesus answers a question as to whether He is the *one sent* to redeem the Jews. He uses evidence of His divine power and the good news being preached as the answer that the disciples would deliver to John the Baptist. Jesus knew that John would understand the response and that it would encourage him.

John initiated the teachings of the coming-kingdom message. He came into the world to introduce Jesus as the Messiah. When he baptized Him, God identified Jesus to John the Baptist and those around him when the voice from heaven pronounced, "This is my beloved Son, with whom I am well pleased" (Matt 3.17). The process is explained in John 1.32–33 and then in verse 36 John introduces Jesus to Israel as "The Lamb of God."

The time had come for Jesus to fulfill His purpose. His entire ministry and all His miracles were meant to identify Him as the Son of God to any with honest hearts. And by believing, one could see the character and nature of God through His life.

Jesus went to the Jews first. The Old Law should have prepared them for His coming. Some believed and seemed to be anticipating His arrival. And some, like the Pharisees, likely recognized scriptural connections but were more concerned about losing their prominent positions than seeing the truth.

Jesus is looking for people willing to repent, see, serve, act, and lead. Some say that repentance is the first and hardest command to obey. The vast majority of people Jesus taught, especially those who should have recognized Him, were unwilling to see and learn, much less serve. Repentance cannot come from this type of heart.

It takes a sacrifice of self to submit and serve. That is why obedience has so much value. It expresses your level of commitment. Jesus was the Lamb of God. He is the sacrifice that the God of heaven and earth provided for all people from before the foundation of the world (1 Pet 1.18–20; Rev 13.8). His children are to offer themselves as sacrifices too.

The same evidence that allowed John to know his work was not in vain is what encourages people today. And all the same kinds of healing happens, but in a spiritual sense. The blind see and His people walk in the light. Sinners are cleansed and ears are opened. The spiritually dead are raised to life in baptism and spend their lives spreading the gospel message by being faithful servants.

Seeing people who put the needs of others first identifies them as those whom God has taught. Jesus said, "The gate is narrow and the way is hard that leads to life, and those who find it are few" (Matt 7.14). If it was easy, everyone would do it.

WEEK FIFTY-ONE

DAY 1

Working Together for Good

God is using all your experiences, good and bad, to match your character with your calling. You never know how God will use you unless you let Him. (Author Unknown)

And we know that for those who love God all things work together for good, for those who are called according to his purpose. (Rom 8.28)

In His mercy, God provides for all those who put Him first and accept His pleading to come to Him for rest. God uses all that they are, all they know, all they have learned, and all their experiences to lead, draw, and redeem them to Himself and use them in His service. He provides the sacrifice for those who desire it. With it comes the hope of accomplishment, knowing our efforts will work together for good, according to His will.

And He keeps on providing opportunities no matter the circumstances. By this, all can know that He is the Almighty God. He works for good, and all can understand that He deserves our trust because He alone keeps all His promises.

It is such a comfort to comprehend this truth. It helps a person to know that God can use all people with all their choices, no matter their circumstance or ability, and no matter their age or physical stability, to work His will. This knowledge can take a considerable weight off those who feel it is their responsibility to fix and control everything.

Let God work and wait to see what He will do. He works things for good using the free will choices of those who are called according to His purpose. Come all ye that labor and are heavy laden and Jesus will give you rest.

DAY 2

Seeing Lessons

Every teacher can be a natural teacher! (Author Unknown)

Look at the birds of the air: they neither sow nor reap nor gather into barns, and yet your heavenly Father feeds them. Are you not of more value than they? (Matt 6.26)

Some classrooms nowadays go outside for nature walks so kids can interact with the natural environment. All the children in the class react differently to what they see. Some children may be totally absorbed while others want to nap. The point is that nature itself is the real teacher. The classroom teacher just points to it for the lessons. Each child can choose what to think of what they observe.

God provides nature for our learning and gives us the wisdom to apply its lessons through His word. We can choose to worship it, be philosophical about it, be fascinated with it, be bored with it, or ignore it while we scroll on our phones. God's word is a *natural teacher* in many ways. His creation provides learning opportunities, but it takes His wisdom and revelation to explain its spiritual implication.

Trees can be firmly planted, scared, and still grow, or strong winds can completely uproot them. Our faith is like that. And seeds produce life and grow when properly planted and watered, as does God's word when it enters people's hearts. His word takes root and increases when a heart accepts it and is properly watered and nourished.

Tides come in and go out. Storms come, but then the sun comes back out. Seasons change. Life and its circumstances fluctuate over time. Conditions for planting and sowing seeds change with the seasons. The birds are cared for by a loving God and He adorns the flowers of the field. And He does so for us when we trust Him through all the change.

Nature can be calm and soothing or rough and unyielding. We can apply its teaching within our hearts if we choose to. We can see its power in God's interpretation or decide not to see or learn anything about what it all means. Let us seek to see nature through the eyes of its creator. And once we see, let's become *natural teachers* who point others to God.

DAY 3

Kitchen Table Studies

Unless someone like you cares a whole awful lot,
Nothing is going to get better. It's not. (Dr Seuss)

Do your little bit of good where you are; it's those little bits of good put together
that overwhelm the world. (Desmond Tutu)

And after some days Paul said to Barnabas, "Let us return and visit the broth-
ers in every city where we proclaimed the word of the Lord, and see how they
are." (Acts 15.36)

One of the most prevailing principles throughout the Bible is that God uses a few people to take the truth to many. In the Patriarchal Age, God worked through the heads of families. We see Him using Abraham, Isaac, Jacob, and Joseph to gather His people to bring Christ into the world. He used Moses and Aaron to bring His people out of Egypt and used Joshua to bring them into the Promised Land. Then God gave them judges. Some kings, priests, and prophets also served God as leaders all throughout the Old Testament.

When Christ came, He chose twelve men to go into all the world to spread His word. Men blessed with the Holy Spirit also helped, and we still learn the truth of Christ from those men today. Autonomous congregations were directed to choose a few righteous elders to lead them. Fathers are to lead their families, and older women are to train the younger ones. Bible studies around a kitchen table are still the most effective way to transfer knowledge.

You did not frequently see Paul speaking in large arenas, even though all cities had one. Instead, he visited towns and local churches to work with smaller numbers. Paul occasionally responded to sovereigns and even taught Caesar's household, but he spent much of his time writing letters to church-es and individual Christians. However, the methods used by some today have taken on a more concert-style, stadium arena-type approach. That's not the way our brethren did it back then.

I still believe God wants us to change the world, one person, one child, one family member, and one coworker at a time. You may never be elevated for your service, and what you do may never be recognized by anyone except the Lord. But you can produce spiritual fruit in your personal sphere by serving Him. And when you get old and look back on your life, you will see the results of this type of labor. There will be smiling and appreciative people that help you realize just how effective a God-centered life can be.

We must challenge ourselves to do our best, helping others where we can. It will make a difference. You can bring wisdom and calm to those in your little area of operation. Our churches, homes, and even businesses and schools will stand out as lights. Don't wait for others to direct you. Let God do that.

DAY 4

Also Freely Give

Hate the sin, Love the sinner. (Mahatma Gandhi)

Now that I come to think of it, I remember Christian teachers telling me long ago that I must hate a bad man's actions, but not hate the bad man: or, as they would say, hate the sin but not the sinner. For a long time I used to think this a silly, straw-splitting distinction: how could you hate what a man did and not hate the man? But years later it occurred to me that there was one man to whom I had been doing this all my life—namely myself. However much I might dislike my own cowardice or conceit or greed, I went on loving myself. There had never been the slightest difficulty about it. In fact the very reason why I hated the things was that I loved the man. Just because I loved myself, I was sorry to find that I was the sort of man who did those things. (C. S. Lewis)

Freely you have received, freely give. (Matt 10.8, NKJV)

When the woman caught in adultery was before Jesus, He said, "Let him who is without sin among you be the first to throw a stone at her" (John 8.7). The Jewish nation was no different than this woman caught in adultery. Although God redeemed a remnant, the Jews had gone after foreign gods and committed spiritual adultery. It could be that when everyone left without throwing a stone, from the older to the younger, they recognized the spiritual parallel. Regardless, everyone eventually understood they were all likewise guilty of sin.

The story illustrates the difference between the limitations of the Old Law and the completed gospel message. The Old Law was waiting to be completed with the New Testament. And Jesus, knowing what it is like to be human, can help us with our weakness and offer the way to obtain forgiveness of sin. By His sacrifice, He provides a path of obedient faith that we should first emulate through baptism in our own death, burial, and resurrection with Him. And by grace, we are saved through faith in the very author of our salvation. We can forgive others more easily once we see our personal weaknesses and sin.

We show our faithfulness in passing on the blessing of forgiveness by showing it to others. Jesus freely gave it to us, and we must also freely give it to others in our interactions. Stephen, when being stoned, said, "Lord, do not charge them with this sin" (Acts 7.39). He forgave them. And while God will be their eternal judge, Stephen made it clear that he had the mind of Christ.

So, let us forgive others as we have been forgiven. We are all unworthy sinners for whom our Savior has shown grace. And as our Lord said to the woman caught in adultery, let us *go, and from now on sin no more*.

DAY 5

A Clear Choice

You may not know that Jesus is all you need, until Jesus is all you have. (Corrie ten Boom)

Declare his glory among the nations,
    his marvelous works among all the peoples!
For great is the LORD, and greatly to be praised;
    he is to be feared above all gods.
For all the gods of the peoples are worthless idols,
    but the LORD made the heavens.
Splendor and majesty are before him;
    strength and beauty are in his sanctuary.

Ascribe to the LORD, O families of the peoples,
    ascribe to the LORD glory and strength!
Ascribe to the LORD the glory due his name;
    bring an offering, and come into his courts!

Worship the LORD in the splendor of holiness;
tremble before him, all the earth!

Say among the nations, "The LORD reigns!
Yes, the world is established; it shall never be moved;
he will judge the peoples with equity. "

Let the heavens be glad, and let the earth rejoice;
let the sea roar, and all that fills it;
let the field exult, and everything in it!
Then shall all the trees of the forest sing for joy
before the LORD, for he comes,
for he comes to judge the earth.
He will judge the world in righteousness,
and the peoples in his faithfulness. (Psa 96.3–13)

Corrie ten Boom was among those who faced persecution for her beliefs during World War II. She and her family helped to hide Jews during the war, and as a result, she gained a perspective on faith in Christ that many would have a tough time understanding today. Even a cursory attempt to reflect on the horrors of those days and the trials Corrie endured should give us pause.

Most of our difficulties will never compare to hers, at least not yet. However, there are times and circumstances when all of life's trappings are stripped away, and our primary choice to believe or disbelieve in God becomes clear. This can happen when a person is in imminent danger from circumstances outside their control or when they have been abandoned by those they trusted. In the worst times, we can truly see the one who is our only faithful rock and savior.

When Jesus comes into full view, a person understands what it truly means to praise Him. Only He can fill their needs and desires, and then an abiding faith can take root in a person when they realize just how deserving God truly is in all His glory. And passages like the one in Psalms 96 begin to resonate fully.

Jesus, tempted as all men and yet without sin, sacrificed Himself and was elevated as the only one truly worthy of praise. He is illuminated as our best choice, being the exact imprint of God Himself and the radiance of His glory. A wise person learns to hold fast to the only trustworthy thing. When we do, our obedience and transformation to God's nature, as found in Jesus and through the written word, begins and never really ends.

The opposing choice is a self-consuming fear, bitterness, and hate that take grip on a heart. The negative emotions do so in such a way that people run away from the pain, blames others for their plight, becomes bitter and angry, or just denies the creator altogether. They turn to themself as their god, trusting their abilities as they serve their own desires.

Corrie chose God in the worst of times. She had a favorite quote that she often used: *There is no pit so deep, that God's love is not deeper still.* Sometimes the purpose of difficult or evil times is to bring people to a place where they desire to repent. The godly should not bemoan times like these.

We must not love this life, even up until the point of physical death. Those who are the Lord's have everlasting life. This earthly life is but a vapor that soon fades away. We cannot compare it to the wonders of an eternity with God. The things we see with our physical eyes are temporary, but the unseen spiritual things are eternal.

Faith, hope, love, and mercy come from God. Accusations, fear, bitterness, railing, lies, and hate come from Satan. Learn to distinguish between the two and choose God over and over again. If anyone really looks for God, they will find Him. God is still accomplishing this promise even in our time. He will be found by everyone who seeks Him.

When the choice becomes clear, let us pray that each one will repent and change to a course that God directs through Christ and the truth. When people become like Jesus, they will be willing to sacrifice for those all around them, even when others are undeserving. Only then will there be a real improvement in any corner of this world.

WEEK FIFTY-TWO

DAY 1

An Accurate Perception

The reason we struggle with insecurity is because we compare our behind-the-scenes with everyone else's highlight reel. (Steven Furtick)

Not that we dare to classify or compare ourselves with some of those who are commending themselves. But when they measure themselves by one another and compare themselves with one another, they are without understanding. … For it is not the one who commends himself who is approved, but the one whom the Lord commends. (2 Cor 10.12, 18)

When trying to assess our worth or gain approval, we sometimes choose the wrong measuring stick. Using the wrong standard is a real issue with people today. We all get to decide how we see ourselves, but we can make several mistakes while doing so. It is crucial to remember that our relationship with God determines our worth, not human standards.

We look at snapshots of others' best times and allow this to lessen our appreciation for our own situation. We allow it to steal our gratefulness. We degrade ourselves because we think that is what it takes to be humble. We elevate ourselves when making improper comparisons and measure ourselves by the standard of others. Like Paul tells the Corinthians, it is all without understanding. But we can find an accurate perception of ourselves when we look to God for His approval.

God loves us and has proven it through the sacrifice of His Son. He directs us through His written word. We may sometimes be confused about what God would have us do in every situation, but we must never forget that whatever God prescribes is what we should measure ourselves by. It defines whether we will be deemed *profitable* in how we think, act, or respond to others. We all should be seeking God and His validation because, in the end, it will be all that matters.

DAY 2

One Heart at a Time

Most people do not listen with the intent to understand; they listen with the intent to reply. (Stephen Covey)

Let your reasonableness be known to everyone. The Lord is at hand; do not be anxious about anything, but in everything by prayer and supplication with thanksgiving let your requests be made known to God. And the peace of God, which surpasses all understanding, will guard your hearts and your minds in Christ Jesus. (Phil 4.5–7)

The word for "reasonableness" in Philippians 4.5 is more like patience, mildness, or gentleness when translated to English from the original Greek. And when Paul writes that the Lord is "at hand," it means He is near or attainable to us as a resource. So, the verse instructs Christians to be seen as thoughtful, patient, and looking to the Lord for guidance while trying to understand His will as we love and serve others.

True Christians should always try to communicate effectively and see all sides of any issue or argument. If our country has "woken" to anything, it is evil and godlessness, and many have embraced it. Individual Christians must not follow suit. God directs His people to look for and to find ways to solve problems using His wisdom, not their own. It takes great focus and effort to remember to look and listen carefully for the relevant issues at hand in any matter.

I visited the Capital in Washington a few years back. I learned that in the room where Congress meets to pass our laws, there is a bust of Moses, indicating the value our nation once placed on incorporating godly principles in the law-making process. At times in our nation's history, some people approached God for answers. In my lifetime, though, I have not noticed godly wisdom considered very much in the halls of Congress. Today, many godless leaders merely give lip service to honoring God's values.

As a nation, we view it as normal and acceptable that our lawmakers need not even try to understand or help the people they serve, let alone keep their word. We are used to those in power who are intent on getting their way, exploiting others to gain their agenda, or want control so badly that there is no love, care, or civility in their motives as they work to operate this country. This demoralization is compounded by the fact that it has become favorable for people who believe in God and His principles to remove themselves from the governmental arena of lawmakers. As such, there is little influence from people with godly wisdom and "out-of-this-world" thinking as our nation makes the laws of the land. God's moral standards are left out of all collective reasoning as a country.

I do not intend to elevate our political affiliations or involvement over living the Christian life. Rather, the opposite. Christians must live in this world while trying not to reflect it, but this does not mean a total dereliction of the duties allowed to us in a democratic society. The more power the self-serving mob achieves, the more persecution will result. The enmity and conflicts between good and evil will naturally become more and more pronounced. Without a restoration of Biblical principles, hate will win the day because, without God, there is no true love.

As a young person, people would tell me that the most effective way you can help with the problems in our country is by sitting down at your kitchen table and teaching someone the gospel. I did not fully understand it then, but this is clear now. Conversion happens one heart at a time. Anyone can only control themselves and influence their immediate contacts. God's people do have a way, and they have a savior. We must all seek Him, find Him, and represent Him where we are. It is the only way to find real peace during such obvious judgments in our time.

Christians who actively stand up for godly values, practice good works, and pray for this country are participating in the work of the Lord. And when the masses do this, it shows up in all our institutions. We can all be like Joseph in Egypt, Daniel in Babylon, or Esther in Persia. God has put all His people where they are at this time in our history. We are all here *for such a time as this!*

What the world needs now are God's love and truth. Do not fear or be dismayed. Do not let the world manipulate you with lies and propaganda representing godlessness. Let your godly *reasonableness* be known to all men. There is great courage in this brand of gentleness. Faithfulness may cost us in our present situations, but it will most definitely keep you from the evil one for the rest of eternity.

DAY 3

The End of Ourselves

The reason why many are still troubled, still seeking, still making little forward progress is because they haven't yet come to the end of themselves. We're still trying to give orders and interfering with God's work within us. (A.W. Tozer)

And you show that you are a letter from Christ delivered by us, written not with ink but with the Spirit of the living God, not on tablets of stone but on tablets of human hearts. (2 Cor 3.3)

When addressing the Corinthians, Paul describes saints as easily recognizable by their behaviors and attitudes. Their demeanor exhibits faith and total dependence on God. They have received and obeyed the gospel and are being transformed by God and clothed with Christ as they continually take His wisdom into their hearts. This transformation is so apparent that it can be seen by others and used as testimony to the veracity of the teaching they have received from the apostles. Their examples are so strong they serve as metaphorical letters from the apostles themselves.

Faithful saints leave their old selves behind in the *watery grave* of baptism, are reborn, and remade into new creatures born of God. They are concerned with answering these questions: Do I reflect the values of this *world* or the love of God? Who am I turning to and trusting to fight my battles? Do I trust in myself, someone else, or God? Does wisdom shine out through my behaviors and attitudes while dealing with everything in this life, or do I hide behind veiled self-reliance? Or, as put by A.W. Tozer, have I reached the end of myself?

This transformation is a lifelong process. Even after each saint makes Christ Lord of their life there is still work to do. Everyone knows they still fall short in their daily walk compared to God's will for them. It takes some time even to learn what His will is. There is much misunderstanding in the religious world regarding this concept today. It is hard for the human mind to understand how a saint is protected by God's grace while at the same time learning to get it all right.

In one sense, it is a conscious effort for saints to maintain their faith. Their inner man is aware of the conflicts of life and is consciously in the fight for their hearts and minds. But they should be able to see the work being done in their hearts and minds by God's Spirit as he works with their spirits. The unseen Spirit of God works in each saint to assist and move him or her toward righteous choices, to be sensitive to their impact on others, to be loving in their service, and to proceed with faith even when it is hard and they do not understand it all.

Believing saints are being cleansed by the Holy Spirit making them whole when they miss the mark of complete holiness because they are striving to walk in God's light. This activity seals the saint that is under construction by God. They are identifiable to others by their obedience to the written word and identifiable to themselves when they realize God is in total control. Faith overcomes their fear, and a grateful heart overcomes ideas of self-entitlement.

God knows each person and their heart. He can count the hairs on their head as easily as the grains of sand in the sea. God knows his or her background and access to whatever truth was available to him or her in their own time. He is aware of each person's experiences, resources, and intellect. And God knows the choices made by each person when confronted with the gospel message.

Before the world began, God planned to work with those who would consciously choose faith in Him in this life (Rev 13.8). But ultimately, it is His Spirit working in us that cleanses our imperfect efforts and makes us holy through the death of one willing and perfect propitiatory sacrifice. This gift is why those who are sanctified are saved by grace through faith.

> For by grace you have been saved through faith. And this is not your own doing; it is the gift of God, not a result of works, so that no one may boast. (Eph 2.8)

This message is God's good news and understanding; it can lead any heart to a right relationship with the creator of the universe. So let each of us choose this day to serve the Great I AM and, in doing so, decide to reach the end of ourselves.

DAY 4

Keeping His Promises

God is using your present circumstances to make you more useful for later roles in His unfolding story. (Louie Giglio)

When Joseph's brothers saw that their father was dead, they said, "It may be that Joseph will hate us and pay us back for all the evil that we did to him…"
His brothers also came and fell down before him and said, "Behold, we are your servants." But Joseph said to them, "Do not fear, for am I in the place of God? As for you, you meant evil against me, but God meant it for good, to bring it about that many people should be kept alive, as they are today." (Gen 50.15,18–20)

God gives us hints as to how He works His providential care for us in His word. Over and over, He uses the circumstances created through the freewill choice of people to prepare and sharpen those who are faithful and those He chooses to use for His plans. Whether our circumstances are good or bad, we never know what He is doing to mold people or shape future events. But we do know it works that way.

There are many illustrations of this principle throughout the Bible, but Joseph states it most directly, "You meant evil against me, but God meant it for good." He had been sold into slavery, unfairly convicted, and sent to prison before helping the Israelite nation. Only God knew He was preparing Joseph to save many people. And we later see the process repeated, as Moses spent 40 years in Midian before leading God's people out of Egypt.

The Bible is filled with evidence of God using people to accomplish His will. God is training His people to be ready and capable of service. As events unfold, He works through people, their decisions, and their circumstances.

We should view our circumstances with the same question that Mordecai posed to Esther, "And who knows whether you have not come to the kingdom for such a time as this?" Understanding how God accomplishes His purpose can give one courage, hope, and peace in times of great difficulty. God has the power to work today in the same ways He has from the beginning.

God is keeping His promises. He wants us to trust Him even when things look bleak, and we may never know exactly how He is doing it. But we know that if we are in line with His will and purposes, He answers us. So be calm in the storm, understanding that God is in control and can use even our missteps to work His purposes.

DAY 5

The Raised Imperishable

For a seed to achieve its greatest expression, it must come completely undone. The shell cracks, its insides come out and everything changes. To someone who doesn't understand growth, it would look like complete destruction. (Cynthia Occelli)

But someone will ask, "How are the dead raised? With what kind of body do they come?" You foolish person! What you sow does not come to life unless it dies. And what you sow is not the body that is to be, but a bare kernel, perhaps of wheat or of some other grain. But God gives it a body as he has chosen, and to each kind of seed its own body...

So is it with the resurrection of the dead. What is sown is perishable; what is raised is imperishable. It is sown in dishonor; it is raised in glory. It is sown in weakness; it is raised in power. It is sown a natural body; it is raised a spiritual body. If there is a natural body, there is also a spiritual body... Just as we have borne the image of the man of dust, we shall also bear the image of the man of heaven. (1 Cor 15.35–38, 42–44, 49)

As a child, I remember the second I understood that I would never cease to exist. I was young, maybe 8 or 9, and standing on the floor in the back-seat of our car coming home from church (this was before mandatory seat belt laws). I even remember the exact place on the road we were traveling on when my mind grasped the thought that my spirit would never die. I realized there was a life after this one. It was like I had just woken up. It scared me then, but it also opened my eyes to the spiritual realm and the reason for living.

God often uses what we understand to teach us about things we could otherwise not understand. And from there on illustrations, discernment and understanding are required to produce any abiding faith. We will all change in the twinkling of an eye at the resurrection. In 1 Corinthians 15, Paul uses the illustration of seed, germination, and growth to help us comprehend what the process will look like. The fear I first experienced with my first glimpse of an afterlife started a journey on my road of faith that casts out fear rather than causes it. And now, that faith gives meaning to my life here and the one hereafter. I see physical death as a passage to a new spiritual life where there is no more physical or emotional pain.

So many people I love have now moved on to the next realm. They wait with us all for the resurrection to life eternal that will come without warning. When Christ comes, there will be some faithful who are still living in our world filled with conflict and pain. Others will have already gone over to the eternal abode. The view we hold of death and the life hereafter can help us all understand who we are and what we should be, and it can dispel the fear of physical death.

May God, bless those who mourn the passing of those who have departed this life. Bless those who still feel the void of a loved one who has moved on. We all praise you for allowing us to have no fear of death. Instead, you supply comfort and hope that has been made possible for all who avail themselves of the sacrificial offering you provided through your Son. Please give us all a spirit of wisdom and revelation in the knowledge of our Lord Jesus Christ as we travel through life in this fallen world.

INDEX

OTHER DAILY DEVOTIONALS

Flight Paths
A Devotional Guide for Your Journey

When encroaching blindness took her music teaching career away, Dene Ward turned her attention to writing. What began as e-mail devotions to some friends grew into a list of hundreds of subscribers. Three hundred sixty-six of those devotions have been assembled to form this daily devotional. Follow her through a year of camping, bird-watching, medical procedures, piano lessons, memories, and more as she uses daily life as a springboard to thought-provoking and character-challenging messages of endurance and faith.

Word for Word
A Daily Lexicon for Your Spiritual Journey

Word for Word is a book about who we are—every one us. It's about our feelings—our ins and outs, our joys and sorrows, our times of weakness and failings. Hal takes us on visits to special places—like family fun, and bad drivers, and thoughts about how foolish we all are sometimes. He takes us down a melancholy street by suggesting some pensive moments—moments of love, heartache, and down right, belly-laughable humor—special feelings, all. Ultimately, every little snippet of information is intended for only one purpose: to take you to the Bible. Hal Hammons shows in every sketch an undying, indefatigable faith in God's message. Foreword by Dee Bowman.

For a full listing of DeWard Publishing
Company books, visit our website:

www.deward.com

Printed in the USA
CPSIA information can be obtained
at www.ICGtesting.com
LVHW050457131124
796385LV00006B/353